DATE DUE

NOV 2 4 1994	
DEC 0 6 1994	
APR 1 2 1995	
SEP 1 5 1996	
SEP 1 9 1996	
OCT 0 8 1996	
OCT 1 7 1996	
OCT 1 0 1996	
OCT 2 1 1996	
NOV 0 5 1996	
NOV 1 9 1996	
APR 1 7 1997	
MAY 1 9 1998	
JUN 1 6 2003	

BRODART   Cat. No. 23-221

HUMAN ECOLOGY
AS HUMAN BEHAVIOR

HUMAN ECOLOGY AS HUMAN BEHAVIOR

Essays in Environmental and Development Anthropology

John W. Bennett

Transaction Publishers
New Brunswick (U.S.A.) and London (U.K.)

Library of Congress Catalog Number: 92–12088
ISBN: 1–56000–068–6
Printed in the United States of America

Library of Congress Cataloging-in-Publication Data

Bennett, John W., 1915–
Human ecology as human behavior : essays in environmental and development anthropology / John W. Bennett.
    p.   cm.
Includes index.
  ISBN 1–56000–068–6
  1. Human ecology. 2. Conservation of natural resources. 3. Applied
anthropology. I. Title.
GF40.B46   1992
304.2—dc20

92–12088
CIP

To
K.G.B.

Contents

Preface

This book is based on research and writings produced over the past thirty years dealing with aspects of human relationships with the physical environment. The original essays have been carefully edited but not extensively revised; some have been assembled from previously published papers; and two were written especially for this volume.

Chapter 1 will begin the book with comments on the principal underlying ideas that shaped the essays. While change occurred in these ideas through the years, it is my feeling (subject to critical correction) that there is a good deal of consistency. My basic intellectual conviction is that of disciplinary eclecticism, a bias I acquired at the University of Chicago in the late 1930s and early 1940s, when graduate students in anthropology were encouraged to take substantial course work in such fields as history, sociology, philosophy, and statistics. This exposure to horizons somewhat broader than anthropology alone, plus the fact that my first significant cultural fieldwork research concerned contemporary American communities, led me toward a multidisciplinary outlook that I never relinquished. This was hardly a popular stance during the period of intense intellectual involution experienced by anthropology during the 1950s and 1960s, and I am gratified to see a greater tolerance of eclectic approaches emerging again in the 1980s and 1990s. It is my belief that despite many attempts to "freeze" anthropology, the field remains a remarkably tolerant, eclectic inquiry into the nature of human affairs. This is, in fact, its strength, although others may count it a weakness.

My interest in the general topic of human-environmental relationships appeared first in an archaeological context. While a graduate student, I spent two summers (1940 and 1941) as a member of the University of Chicago team excavating portions of the great Kincaid site in southern Illinois, along the Ohio River. The sequence of prehistoric settlements in the vicinity of that site exhibited significant changes in ecological patterns—something that awakened my interest in ecological problems. During the second season, I was a member of another team, working under Professor Lloyd Warner, studying the agricultural and social basis of food habits among the rural residents of the area. Comparison of their ways of dealing with the environment with those of the prehistoric groups was a natural consequence of the two-edged fieldwork; the results were published in a paper,[1] which, due to its rather juvenile formulations, I have decided not to republish here, though it does represent my initial attempt at ecological analysis of human groups at varying levels of technical and institutional development, a theme which resurfaced later in my work, as illustrated by chapter 10. Although my interests strayed into other fields through the years, I returned at intervals to the ecological theme, and in the 1980s this interest fused with my work in the social dimensions of economic development.

In 1976 Pergamon Press published my *Ecological Transition: Human Adaptation and Cultural Anthropology*, an attempt to bring together the insights and ideas of the 1970s ecological movement with the research interests of anthropological ecologists. In the subsequent years I reworked some of the ideas in this book in the form of separate articles and chapters for books edited by others, and some of these are published in the present volume. They represent, to some extent, elaboration of certain themes in the *Transition* book. I am very grateful to Irving Louis Horowitz, an old friend and former colleague, for giving me the opportunity to republish these post-*Transition* essays. Gratitude is also extended to my editorial assistant, Rose Passalacqua, for helping to prepare these materials for publication.

Note

1. John W. Bennett. 1944. "The Interaction of Culture and Environment in the Smaller Societies," *American Anthropologist* 40: 461–78.

PART I

Theory and Concepts

1

Underlying Ideas: Ecological Transitions, Socionatural Systems, and Adaptive Behavior

The theoretical background of most of the chapters in this book is informed by three concepts: "ecological transition," "socionatural system," and "adaptation." The first pertains to changes in relations of *Homo sapiens* and the physical environment, as *sapiens* entered into his full capacity to shape the environment to his own ends. The second concept emphasizes an enduring reciprocity between humans and the environment, regardless of the level of technological complexity or the particular "transition" under consideration. The third concept concerns the distinctive features of human behavior that underlie the human relationship to the environment—in particular, the remarkable plasticity of response and the ability to solve problems arising from such responses.

Ecological Transition

The phrase was used as the title of a book (Bennett 1976), but the term was mainly rhetorical, used to convey a sense of ever-changing adaptations to the earthly environment (including other humans). That is, human adaptive behavior is responsible for these changing and expanding ways of utilizing the environment—a process that has a dual character: on the one hand, by making use of increasing quantities of natural substances and other living species and enhancing their productivity by transforming them into "natural resources," humans might be said to have freed themselves from the constraints of Nature; on the other hand, this increased freedom created exponential functions, especially population increase and an increasing *dependence* on Nature. These are broad generalizations, and the many dimensions of the process give rise to many exceptions. Some resource transformations protect sustainability

3

better than others; some resources, if exhausted, can be replaced by others; population may be controllable in certain places and under certain conditions; and destructive feedbacks from any exploitative process can help to control or scale down such processes and their dangers.

In fact there were several "transitions" in *Homo sapiens* history. V. Gordon Childe's presentation (1942) of the panorama of human prehistory and its technical achievements was a pioneer statement, the categories of which remain influential. He distinguished the "food-producing revolution," or Neolithic, as it was known in nineteenth- and early twentieth-century literature, the "urban revolution," or the Bronze-Iron Ages, and the Industrial Revolution of our own era (and if he were still alive perhaps Childe would find still another Industrial Revolution taking place in East Asia and even an "information revolution" occurring everywhere). Other, earlier ones may be added: the increase in hunting skills associated with the late Paleolithic development of superior projectile weapons like the spear-thrower or, in North America in later times, the rapid-fire small arrowhead projectile; the first attempts at partially sedentary settlement prior to food production, based on intensive exploitation of particular wild foods (so-called "Mesolithic"). Each of these and other more localized technical achievements was associated with increases in human population, distinctive settlement patterns, and quantity of food intake. The relatively recent history of *Homo sapiens sapiens* (roughly, the past 50,000 years) thus seems to proceed in a series of leaps or steps, each representing a "transition" in the human capacity to utilize natural substances. Or, as Charles Deevey (1960) pointed out some time ago in graphing the increase in human population, the logarithmic curve becomes a series of step-functions, each more or less associated with some major technological achievement and often combined with major changes in the physical environment. On the other hand, if the demographic data for the same period of time are viewed arithmetically, they display a steep exponential rise. This same exponential function appears to characterize various technological data, like increases in utilized energy and efficiency of tools.

In traditional scholarship the triggering artifact or process in the important transitions was viewed as material or technological. The issue excites anthropologists, who continue to search for primary causes or origins, even though they are far more sophisticated about the systemic relationships of mentality, social organization, and technology than they were in the nineteenth century. The attitude is reinforced by the nature of the data: since earlier transitions must be recovered archaeologically, little other than material objects remain. But through observation of contemporary tribal peoples living mainly by subsistence pursuits, it is possible to show that social organization and symbolic culture play equally important roles. The issue arises again in contemporary history because of the increasing importance of instrumental concerns—technology, economics—in shaping the world system. So the ideology of materialism undergoes recurrent revivals, as in the case of anthropologist Marvin Harris, who proposed that "cultural materialism" represented the only relevant or profitable scientific position (1960). The anthropologist Julian Steward was more cautious: while he considered the econotechnological system of a society to be its "core," around which other social and cultural phenomena were molded, he recognized that this was prone to overgeneralization (Steward 1955). The real issue is one of constantly shifting parameters of technology and culture: a new tool can encourage new behavior, but a new value can restrict use of the tool, and so on. Thus the transitions are complex interactive matrices of human behavior, its social manifestations, and the objects and processes created by humans to deal with the physical world.

The behavioral significance of such observations concern the way human adaptive capacities, while natively superior to those of any other large mammal, are nevertheless dependent on communication and interactive learning in order to manifest their full potential. The anthropological exegesis is based on both archaeological and ethnological evidence: from archaeology we obtain data on long periods of virtually static technical and aesthetic social culture, punctuated by sudden intrusions of superior tools and evidence of sophisticated social organization—one of the most dramatic of the latter being the apparent replacement, in a relatively few centuries, of the *Homo sapiens neanderthalensis* populations and their relatively simple culture by the more dynamic culture of the *Homo sapiens sapiens* types like Cro Magnon. This particular classic case is a bit difficult to handle, since it involves a series of unanswerable questions about the relationship of cultural expressions to different biological varieties of *sapiens*. More familiarly, the archaeological record of every continent contains dozens of examples of how relatively isolated populations of *sapiens* with long-persisting, conservative styles of life changed rapidly under the stimulus of in-migrants bearing new artifacts and ways of organizing themselves. The increase in cultural complexity and skills was not due solely to the imported ideas, but also to the inter-stimulation of two groups with simply different ways of conceiving the world and the tasks of survival. In addition, there is the factor of generational locus of social and technical leadership: in long-isolated groups leadership tends to devolve on older generations, who have a special interest in maintaining the status quo. In other cases, where leadership can shift downward in the age pyramid, younger and more innovative members tend to speed up change and development.

From ethnology comes abundant data to show how recent and living tribal populations relatively isolated from each other remained in a state of cultural stasis for generations. The condition was especially marked in specialized environments: rainforests, savannahs, deserts, the Arctic. Each of these environments contained human populations that had achieved a highly specialized, low-energy adaptation to resources and that built their symbolic culture around these specializations. The Eskimo and their predecessors, the Australian Aborigines, Indians of the North American Great Basin, the Pueblo Indians of the desert Southwest, the pygmy hunting tribes of the African equatorial forest (see chapter 3), the migratory herdsmen of the Middle East (see chapter 10), and the Indians of the Great Plains (see chapter 9) are all classic examples of such specialized adaptations. Each of these groups figured in the development of ethnological theory since they showed the potential of human populations to achieve an intricate but ingrown adjustment to distinctive habitats. Populations with distinctive cultures always existed on the fringes of civilizations, and only when substantial contact with complex cultures occurred did the tribal groups change significantly. The acceleration of worldwide cultural development in the past several centuries was associated with the opening up of refuge areas and the exposure of indigenous peoples to exogenous ideas, a process ocurring repeatedly through human history but never on the impressive scale of the recent past. "Economic development" in the Third World is the most recent expression of this process.

An ecological transition, then, is also a cultural transition. The changed adaptation is not isolated from human activities and ideas; it is an expression of decisive change in the life-styles and world views—new paradigms—that also imply a change in the level of expectations and in the age of the leaders. The progressive transitions each display a heightened anticipation of rewards, or at least an awareness of the need for increased resource utilization due to rising population. The twin process—increase in demand and increase in the number of demanders—interrelate and reinforce each other to yield alterations in the way of life, a rise in the level of self-confidence, and a sense of mastery over habitat. The evolution of the *sapiens* relationship to Nature is thus different from that for any other species: the distinctive forms of *sapiens* behavior are an engine, driving species adaptation through behavioral and mental change, which may have ultimate genetic consequences but which are not caused by genes. Humanity thus continually widens the gap between its own behavioral approaches to the environment and those of all other animal species.

One theme of these chapters is whether this process can be directed into channels less abusive of Earth's resources. On the whole, the position implied in this book is pessimistic, although this is subject to qualification since the very dynamism of human behavior and its derivative, culture, proscribes easy certainty or prediction. Rational thought may not be the sole or dominant characteristic of human behavior, but its potentiality or availability means that corrective controls or changes are always possible. If we take a generally pessimistic view, it is because institutional complexity is an independent variable affecting the ability to achieve correction: the more complex the social system and the larger number of vested interests, the more difficult it is to initiate corrective measures (hence human ecology is also political ecology).

But an ecological transition is not simply triggered by a cultural transition. Equally important is the incorporation of natural or earthly phenomena into Culture. The classic instance is that of water flowing over a dam: prior to the construction of the dam the water ran free, it was part of Nature. But once it flows over the dam under the guidance of human beings and drives turbines or irrigates fields it becomes a cultural object, a part of human endeavor incorporated into human institutions: the water is assigned value and its value can then be expressed or compared to other values and phenomena either natural or manufactured. This typically engenders a trade-off process: if the water over the dam endangers the population of a valued species of fish it may be counted as a debit. But if the flow of the water over the dam is defined as beautiful it may acquire greater value regardless of what it does to the fish.

As Nature is appropriated by Culture, the process creates philosophical tension. We spoke of the anthropocentrism of civilization, an increasing trend. But by the same token Culture and Nature are dichotomized:
Culture is a thing of Man; Nature is outside, free, unspoiled, raw,
undeveloped. Depending on the attitude toward the Nature-into-Culture
process, the meaning or value assigned to the two halves of the dichotomy
will vary. If Culture—that is, Man—is seen as the despoiler, the destroyer, Nature is revered as pristine, and the preservationist position
emerges. If Man is seen as the measure and master of all things, then the
incorporational process is seen as "progress," and Nature is viewed as a
"resource." These attitudes have arisen repeatedly through human history, but only since the recent Industrial Transition has the mastery
outlook taken on global proportions. This means, in effect, that the Earth
and its natural species are at Man's mercy. This also means, of course,
that the environmental situation is at root a moral dilemma. Morality in
this context implies two principal issues: one is the question of human
wants, which morally becomes the problem of human greed. The second
is the question of posterity, that is, the effects of current resource practices
on future populations.

The first issue means that any inquiry into ecological and environmental matters that has normative aims must be concerned with the problems
of limits to human endeavor and aspiration, the control of blue-sky
gratification, a critique of the tendency to make promises before the
resource base or fertility rate is assessed, and the consequences of further
technological intervention. To question human wants is always politically difficult and in many contemporary cases is defined as an offense
against cultural or national self-determination. If we are to safeguard the
Earth and its resources, such human-centeredness needs modification.

Let us examine the problem of the causes of human greed (I use the
word advisedly and mean by it wanting more than one needs, or wanting
more than available resources can bear). There are two principal arguments:

1. Greed is a *constant*, built into human behavior, and inescapable; it
has no finite limits, and it is conferred on humans by their genetic makeup
and by their need to realize themselves in a social milieu; it is consequently inevitable both biologically and socially.

2. Greed is a *variable*; it is ultimately punished or checked, or can be
so checked, and it is stimulated or diminished by the social environment

or created by cultural values, particularly when Culture refers to satis-factions stimulated by detachment from or ignorance of Nature. The first argument is pessimistic if one assumes inevitability of overweening aspiration; the second is optimistic if one assumes that control is possible through exhortation, discipline, and reason. However, the dichotomy is largely false. Both positions collapse into one: greed *is* an innate mani-festation of human behavior, but human behavior *is* always capable of modification by Culture. If Culture can encourage greed, it can also restrain it. Greed must be known both in its psychobiological and its cultural aspects; wants are basic to the organism, but wants can also be formed or controlled by experience. So, from an anthropological stand-point, the problem becomes a matter of the social mechanisms that encourage excess in the human spirit. At the most general level, *greed is accentuated in human behavior by civilizations that permit large num-bers of people to exist in apparent "freedom" from environmental constraints.*

The most recent demonstration of the principle is seen in developing nations since the end of World War II. The energy behind economic development was the promises made to the populations of these countries by their governments and by Western nations extending development assistance, enouraging the belief that resources were infinite and either there for the taking or obtainable at reasonable prices elsewhere. The promises did encourage aspirations: an attempted breakout from ages of acceptance of poverty and hardship. The ancient persisting lifeways were redefined as "poverty" and rapidly took political form. Demands esca-lated and continue to do so, creating all sorts of secondary effects, including massive environmental destruction.

In the 1950s the problem of development was visualized by social scientists of all fields as simply a matter of finding ways to awaken the spirit of innovation and change in peasant societies (e.g., Hoselitz 1952). Peasants were viewed as innately conservative—whether this was con-sidered to be biologically or culturally caused. However, by the 1970s this was no longer a crucial problem: the awakening had indeed begun, and the problem became one of political control and direction of the energies thereby released. But the need to adjust these attitudes to the realities of physical resources (as well as the consequences of locating oneself in the political-economic realities of a market-oriented world economy) was beyond the capabilities of political leaders. Consequently, almost everywhere expectations have exceeded the possibilities of realization, or at least have failed to conform to practical limits. Anthropological research on development continues, but on the margins of the discipline and not in mainline theory (Bennett 1986). Moreover, the discipline is reluctant to award academic prestige for development-oriented research, even though the underlying cultural issue of development is the morality of human intentions and their environmental consequences. Whatever the academicians think, it will be *the* problem of the coming century.

The second issue—the effects on posterity—becomes, in the context of morality, a problem of *responsibility*. Organized social life, and the continuity of that life in both social and biological senses, rests on the carrying out of tasks and duties that arise within the social order, in interaction with the conditions of biological survival in the physical environment. Thus, ecology is incorporated into social systems through this parcelling out of functions and tasks and the consent of members of the society to take responsibility for their wants and actions. Another meaning of the term is didactic: humans are "responsible" for what they do to Nature, especially when their actions jeopardize the survival of future generations. That is, the meaning here is that the actors will be "called into account" for their actions. (Chapter 11 contains further discussion of these problems of what Roderick Nash (1989) summarizes as "environmental ethics.")

Now, the most significant "anthropological" issue is that such a normative approach to human *ecology* has the same problems we find to be associated with the theory of *society*. Humans approach Nature as they approach Society: they do unto the natural world what they do unto themselves. The final morality would thus become the Golden Rule. From one point of view there is really no such thing as an "environmental ethic," if by this term we mean a separate and distinct ethical principle outside of the context of social morality. To construct such a principle is to preserve the dualism: Culture vs. Nature. If Culture is believed to be superordinate over Nature, then humans must create a separate ethic to deal with the environment. But rarely do effective ethical-moral restraints emerge from positions of moral superiority. Of course, in the flux of contemporary ecological crises some positive results will come of such views. But in the long run this will not serve to clean up the mess or to promote reasonable conformity to conservationist practices. We once considered the "environmental crisis" of our time solely as matter of humans doing bad things to the environment, but in recent years the other side of the coin has emerged: humans injuring the environment in order to injure other humans. The examples are multiplying: the deliberate firing of the Kuwaiti oil wells, the systematic and illegal dumping of toxic wastes on Amerind reservations, the deliberately set forest fires in the United States.

Thus the sources of modern evil—greed, slavish dedication to the "market" as the measure of all things, nationalistic impulses, institutionalized aggression and war, excessive permissiveness toward destructive technology, sexual abuse, unrestricted fertility, and so on through the litany of horrors which our technological barbarism has created or facilitated—are all behind and beneath our mistreatment of the Earth. Resources we must have, but it is how we obtain them and what we do with them to serve social ends that is the problem.

Socionatural System

This term was introduced in the *Ecological Transition* book (1976) in the context of the persistent dualism in environmental thinking that in one form or another has characterized all societies that have moved toward large-scale resource development to meet the increasing demands for consumption. In our own era of the Industrial Revolution the Nature-Culture dichotomy emerged in the nineteenth century out of anthropogeography, a field that generally regarded humans as the masters of the Earth, acting outside Nature and on Nature in order to build Civilization. Evolutionary philosophy acknowledged that Man was part of the universe and evolved as a physical and biological phenomenon, but human evolution was believed to be special, ordained, or driven by different forces. The background of this thought in Christian doctrine has been pointed out often enough: the Bible requires that man, as a steward, control and manage Nature, but the implications for genuine conservation are unclear and undeveloped (Black 1970). Most students of the Bible have taken the gist to be mastery or domination.

The Culture-Nature dichotomy was both fostered and refuted in the early twentieth-century anthropology often associated with Franz Boas and his students. One group of anthropogeographers considered that Culture was largely determined by physical environmental constraints, but the ethnologists correctly showed that this was not true because different "cultures" could use the same natural phenomena quite differently. On the other hand, by insisting that Culture was its own reality, *sui generis*, a separate order, anthropologists fostered the conceptual separation of Nature and Culture. This helped to create the cultural-causation view, or "cultural determinism," and delayed an analytic approach to the actual relationships between humans and the physical world for several decades, until Julian Steward and others rephrased the whole question in at least partially interactive terms.

As suggested above, for a brief period the "emergent evolutionary" ideas of Jan Christian Smuts influenced several anthropologists, particularly Alfred Kroeber (1917). This scheme conceived of several "levels" or domains of reality, each with its own laws of being and change. Kroeber's "superorganic" notion was the most familiar anthropological version of this idea, implying that Culture was "above" the organic and inorganic levels of reality and therefore had to be studied per se. The writings of Leslie White (1948) revived the idea. The concept was never widely accepted because of its dogmatic reification. Since the superorganic was fired by neural and physical forces emanating from organisms and the environment, it was impossible to explain the significance of these if one adhered to a notion of separate and autonomous cultural reality.

Essentially anthropology has been in the process of working its way out of a series of monistic and simplistic attempts to explain human reality. This is why this writer, and most contemporary anthropologists, consider that *Homo sapiens sapiens* is a multipotential organism, who not only manifests an enormous variety of response patterns to the changing world but is also capable of engineering the change itself, thereby creating new response patterns, and so on. This process is the ultimate basis of the concept of "adaptation." Subscription to the concept means that one must accept the fact that generalizations about human affairs are extremely difficult to come by and that most meaningful research must be informed by issues arising in the human mind and behavior of people in real-life situations. The world of "empirical generalizations" is thus the most useful and profitable world for anthropologists to explore—as it is for most other social and behavioral scholarly fields.

As with other social disciplines, a kind of cultural determinism characterized the theoretical stance of American anthropologists during the earlier part of the century. The term has also been used to describe ecological perspectives like the writer's, when adaptation, resource management, and kindred behavioral concepts are used to denote the human relationship to the environment. It seems to me that this position illustrates the tendency among anthropologists to fail to distinguish between Culture, as a descriptive-historical-heuristic tag, and the domain of ethical concern and responsibility for Nature. Thus "human ecology" is simply the human proclivity to expand the use of physical substances and to convert these substances into resources—to transform Nature into Culture, for better or worse. This position is confused by some anthropologists with the notion of causation, that is, that human relationships to the environment are "caused by Culture," thus excluding causal factors emanating from environmental constraints. This is a misunderstanding of the environmentalist position, which views humans as responsible for their own fate but also dependent on Nature and therefore subject to destructive feedbacks from the degraded environment. Humans exploit and degrade, but they also conserve and protect. Their "stewardship" refers to constructive management of Nature, not cultural determinism.

The term "socionatural system" is an empirical generalization that attempts to combine both Nature and Culture. Empirically, socionatural systems can consist of any ongoing relationship between human activities and environmental phenomena in which the humans provide the goals and means and the environment the wherewithal. These can be very large affairs, like a major system of agriculture adjusted to a particular climate; or they can be specific, localized land-use or extractive systems (like a large plantation) involving a degree of reciprocity. When coal is removed from the land surface and the land contours and fertility restored, a socionatural system with a conservationist dimension is in operation. Socionatural systems can be of very long duration, if environmental abuse or extraction is not excessive and regeneration possible (as in traditional fisheries), or they can be short-term operations, as in the case of a forest clear-cutting operation and subsequent replanting, which delays reuse for several decades until tree growth has been completed (see chapter 5).

A conscious or objective analysis of a socionatural system tends to be made when a problem is seen to exist: in the previous paragraph we emphasized issues of abuse, regeneration, and, of course, sustainability. In tribal societies based on subsistence pursuits, the system was itself coterminous with the conduct of life and the food quest, and the role of Nature was explicitly recognized with ceremony and symbol. Such people displayed a consciousness that they were part of Nature, and its bounty was something to be at least used carefully, if not actually conserved. In the Industrial Transition this attitude has given way to a confidence in the human ability to solve all problems and to use technology for the purpose of dominating resources regardless of consequences (called "technological neutrality" in Bennett and Dahlberg 1990). Consequently, the inherent rightness of human wants and their means of satisfaction is assumed, and research on the dimensions of the system is likely to occur only when something goes wrong.

In actuality, *all* intersections of human activities and the physical environment can be analyzed as "socionatural systems" of greater or lesser complexity, since any interaction between two or more phenomena possesses systemic properties. "System" is simply a recognition of ongoing relations between phenomena that influence one another over a period of time. There are systems of greater or lesser complexity and duration—generally the longer the duration the greater the complexity (a process that runs counter to the larger universe-wide process of entropy, in which relationships are supposed to become simpler in the sense of reaching a steady, low-output state). However, we must not make too much of these scientific paradoxes, since they may be largely the products of scientific rhetoric. What *is* important is that in the past several thousand years of human history the overall tendency has been to increase human involvements with Nature and that this tendency is also found for particular populations, in particular regions, and with respect to particular resources. No two cases are identical, and each requires empirical analysis; so there is always doubtful predictability or transferability from case to case.

If socionatural systems contain a high quotient of situational specificity, then two things follow. First, to change or reform them requires a considerable amount of indigenous participation. But in an expanding world system, with power becoming increasingly centralized in large organizations, and with resources everywhere falling into the hands of organizations extraneous to the localities that possess them, it becomes increasingly difficult to permit local determination of resource use and conservation. The local system is no longer the exclusive property of its former owners and developers; they must now conform to the values and practices of the larger market, company, or state. But the process cuts both ways: frequently the outside interests, when benign and genuinely concerned about sustainability, must take control of resource practices or endeavor to persuade local people to change their use patterns. And in the late 1980s most of the large international development agencies began cutting back financial and technological assistance for national projects that were judged to be environmentally unsound. Local people are certainly the victims of the larger world system, but they are also culprits in the sense that their own aspirations can lead to environmental abuse (although they may be driven toward such behavior as a result of their increasing need to sell their resources in order to survive in a cash economy).

Second, if socionatural systems are specific to particular places, people, and resources, then considerable effort must be expended in their analysis. Distinctive human needs, cultural values, and social relations are embedded in the system, along with distinctive physical processes: varying combinations of temperature, air movements, soil types, water loci and movement, biochemical processes, and so on. All of these social and physical elements must be ferreted out prior to any serious attempt at understanding the system. This strong multidimensional empirical character of ecological situations and systems makes their study one of the most difficult of all scientific endeavors. To understand just one system—for example, weather and climate—is an unfinished task of major proportions. Thus, while a minority of climatologists knew that the Greenhouse was going to show itself one of these years, decades, centuries, no one could have predicted what was heralded as its sudden onset in the summer of 1988—that is, *if* the heat, droughts, storms, and other climatic disturbances of that year were indeed due to the discharge of CO_2 and other insults to the atmosphere. The ambiguity will persist, since we tend to apply extraordinary canons of proof to phenomena that threaten major interests and institutions.

The socionatural system concept is also concerned with theoretical matters. The underlying idea is that social and natural scientists are on parallel tracks since both view reality similarly: the human actions that influence the environment are subject to the same logic of analysis as natural phenomena. Both human actions and the physical environment change and at varying rates, and hence their interactions also change or evolve. In taking this philosophical position the Culture vs. Nature dichotomy is avoided. Well and good, but this cannot dispose of the differences between them. Nature functions on the basis of emergent physical feedback; Culture functions on the basis of cognitive and emotional feedback. Consequently, one cannot easily predict cultural changes on the basis of change in physical factors, but, conversely, when Culture, defined for the moment as human behavior, acts upon the environment a causal relationship can easily be seen. That is, while the social component of interactive systems clearly dominates natural phenomena, the converse may be true only when and if humans allow it to happen. Yet when human actions create conditions that threaten survival it may be said that Nature dominates Culture. What usually happens, however, is that the socionatural system functions so as to cause degradation in both domains.

In contemporary thinking the cultural side is viewed as an influence upon the environment: humans "impact" Nature. Nature "strikes back," as the jargon has it, when its benign resources no longer function so as to maximize or benefit human needs and wants. Thus it is extremely difficult to escape the Culture-Nature dichotomy, not only because the motive forces are different, but also because our civilization encourages active-passive, dominance-submission thinking.

Socionatural systems exist in time and are always in the process of emergence and change. Some are complete, functioning; others are tentative, unformed, or partial. An example of the more firmly established would be agricultural systems of long duration and complexity: rice culture in monsoon East Asia, migratory pastoralism in Africa and the Middle East, and livestock-grain systems in North America—systems that stress subsistence and those that emphasize production for the market. However well formed these agricultural systems may be, and however intricately interwoven may be traditional practices and concepts, the systems regularly undergo change and cyclical alteration. In the commercial agricultural systems economic factors induce fluctuation; in the partly commercial, partly subsistence systems cultural values or social relational elements may be more influential in inducing change. The conventional approach to agriculture emphasizes economics, but the system is driven by complex political, symbolic, and other cultural factors as well. The broader approach must be used if we are to see agriculture as a socionatural system (for discussions see Dahlberg 1986; Dahlberg and Bennett 1986, especially Bennett's Chapter 13 on interdisciplinary conceptions of resource ecology).

As socionatural systems become more complex and as they spread through Nature, they also begin to intersect. An example would be the Greenhouse Effect and its impact on agriculture. That is, human interaction with the atmosphere through the use of fossil fuels can result in a rise in mean temperature and many associated effects; this temperature change influences the conditions of crop growth and may force changes in cultivation practices. If fossil fuel use declines, this will influence the human labor component in agriculture, which may have to increase due to the diminution of mechanical power. If this occurs the causal balance tips toward Nature, but this will certainly result in an increased human effort to modify or control climate, creating new social involvements. Similar cyclical movements may be seen in species decline and rebuilding: the loss or diminution of species due to human appropriation of habitats results in stepped-up activities of biological conservationists to breed, train, and release the threatened animals into the environment—a process now well under way for wolves, some species of birds, primates, and others. However, it is doubtful if such efforts will result in a major replacement of threatened animals. What may be happening is that a new kind of managerial socionatural system is emerging, featuring the human responsibility to maintain biological diversity on the planet.

One relevant theoretical issue in socionatural systems is the relationship of the socionatural concept to the ideas of *ecosystem* and *social system*. Socionatural systems are not simple conbinations of the two, since they function differently. Ecosystem is a concept developed to analyze the interchange of food and energy among living species in a defined habitat or environment; its most cogent idea is that of the "niche," or particular position in an energy network occupied by one species. The analysis of such phenomena by bioecologists originally aimed at showing the order and regularity, hence predictability—or the relationships among various organisms giving rise to concepts like homeostasis or trophic systems. Ecosystems display regularity and cyclicality, however, only when they are undisturbed over relatively long periods of time. The initial aim of ecological research was to find such systems and reconstruct their operations in order to create ideal models. Later research took a more dynamic perspective, observing that ecosystems were frequently subject to intervention and change due to natural as well as human causes.

The social system, on the other hand, is usually defined as a highly dynamic affair, changing in accordance with human intervention and behavioral principles conferring novelty and unpredictability (although there was a brief period in the 1950s and 1960s when concepts like homeostasis were borrowed from biological and mechanical systems, giving an artificially static definition of social phenomena). The forces driving social systems include large measures of emotion, cognition, and adaptive anticipation (see Buckley 1967 for the classic analysis). Social system is a heuristic concept, applicable to human activities and institutions if one wishes to conduct an analysis of interaction among the components. Social systems thus can be modelled on a variety of principles: social role interaction, energy exchange, decision making, power, and economic bargaining. When this is understood, it becomes clear that "social system" is simply a concept for grouping familiar aspects of social existence in order to show their relationships. Concepts like feedback and other terms developed in the study of biological and mechanical systems can be used analogically, but at the risk of conveying imagery that may be misleading.

If we accept the concept, social systems may be said to be more dynamic than natural systems, since they are governed by human behavior rather than by food supply, available energy, breeding habits, or predation. All these factors are present in human systems as well, but they are managed by anticipatory objectives and controls that arise within the social system itself. But the social system is a projection of human behavior and its derivatives, and this makes all the difference. Social systems can remain in a relatively unchanged state for indefinite periods, so long as exogenous influences are prevented from entering. However, due to the impressive symbolic capacities of humans and the communication devices this capacity makes possible, few systems remain shielded from external inputs. Anthropologists have carried on a debate for years as to the principal source of change in culture: from stimuli that originate inside the system or those that enter from the outside, from "other cultures." Both sources are available, but there obviously is a tilt toward exogenous stimulation in relatively isolated "traditional" societies studied by ethnologists.

The crucial issue in the study of socionatural systems is the fact that different disciplines are expected to supply the data and the analyses. That is, there are no sociologists who can study biological systems *qua* biology—although there are a few anthropologists who can, or least who participate intimately with biologists in such research. The ambitious Turkana Project of the State University of New York at Binghamton was an example, where biologists, anthropologists, range specialists, and others cooperated during the 1980s on a series of studies of tribal pastoralist adaptation to the northern Kenya desert. This project yielded some unexpected findings: for example, the corrals of the Turkana tribesmen over the years contributed to an increase in vegetation on certain grazing lands and the campsites. This finding suggests that humans, in traditional regimes where commercial interests do not result in excessive exploitation of a physical resource, are capable of becoming part of ecosystems—but these become socionatural systems with strong ecosystemic properties, called "sustaining" in the development-project jargon of the late 1980s (for discussions see chapters 4 and 7). Thus, it could be argued that such sustaining systems are really ecosystems; the "socionatural" system then becomes that in which human goals dominate without due consideration of resource conservation.

While natural and social scientists can collaborate on specific research topics, the two inevitably view the situation differently. As Brian Spooner points out, "However objective his research design, the ecologist is led by his assumptions to discriminate in favor of the survival of the system" (1982, 4–8). Since humans are now involved in all natural systems, this view contributes to confusion: humans *use* the natural phenomena which means they contribute to change in the system, for better or for worse. Moreover, the very survival of a "pure" natural system includes non-beneficial results for some members of the process, for example, prey. When humans replace a natural grazing species like bison with domestic livestock the substitution per se might preserve the energetic relationships between animals and vegetation, but the problem is not the substitution of a domestic for a wild organism but the commercial pressures that result in an inordinate increase in the grazing species. Consequently, the ecologist tends to blame the human factor for change or deterioration of the natural components of the system.

Most socionatural systems do not simply *exist* like biological systems: they are, or must be, consciously managed by the users. Since this is the essence of their social dimension, the problem has emerged on a political level in the controversy over U.S. national parks. In the past decade or so the orientation of management has shifted away from preservation of the parks as natural habitats, as close to their original, pre-park status as possible; instead, the policy has increasingly emphasized public use and recreation, as commercial interests and politicians responsive to these interests achieved control at the national level. This policy also happened to coincide in Yellowstone National Park with an unprecedented pile-up of dead vegetation resulting from years of preventing forest fires that would have consumed the material. Increased public use and increased fuel meant that fires were certain to be extensive, and so they proved in the summer of 1988, triggered by an unusually hot, dry summer. This is an example of a socionatural system out of balance: human mismanagement and Nature's response resulted in a situation with political consequences for government and discomfort and irritation for the public. The park will regenerate, but on its own time scale, not the human. There is, of course, no inherent reason why humans could not have managed the parks more intelligently, but in a public democracy management is subject to cultural values, and one of the most prominent in the past century was that fire was bad and not to be tolerated.

Similar out-of-balance cyclicality is visible in populations of wild animals managed by humans. Rapid population increase and sudden "crashes" when the food supply diminishes relative to the population are common in Nature. But when this happens in managed socionatural systems like national parks, with their deer, elk, bear, and other ubiquitous populations, they become subject to vigorous but usually misinformed public action. It is "wrong" to kill animals, hence the natural predators had to go. In the absence of predatory wolves the deer multiply until they run out of food, and then humans must step in and decimate the herds with guns or poison, which arouses public outrage; then the practice is stopped, permitting the cycle to begin again.

The problem in human management of socionatural systems is to keep misinformation out of procedure, especially when it partakes of ideology. The extent of distortion of vital issues this can cause is no better illustrated than in Third World economic development and its relationship to population growth. With birth rates averaging over 2 percent in a majority of countries during the 1980s, economic investment or production could not keep up with the natural increase, let alone accumulate enough surplus to pay off debts. Yet any effort to promote population control measures was curtailed or suppressed by ideological groups. Every responsible international authority from the World Bank on down recognized the futility of meeting expectations and increasing well-being so long as any small advance was immediately consumed by additional mouths. By the late 1980s, on several fronts, the world environmental and human social-biological situation had really come to a series of impasses: unrestricted economic growth, unrestricted technological applications, and unrestricted population growth were all challenged by persuasive arguments and scientific data, but, at the same time, all these trends were fostered by vested interests and diehard ideologists.

The ultimate question, then, is whether it is possible to create socionatural systems that are truly sustaining, that is, to avoid the features of contemporary systems in which the human factor dominates to the detriment of the environment. This question cannot be answered with any degree of assurance so long as the concepts of growth, technological neutrality, and unlimited gratification tend to prevail. Social policies shaped by these concepts, in a world of population growth, offer little hope for sustained-resource regimes. Balances may be achieved in particular countries, but these will most likely be places where cultural traditions and styles offer the possibility of ethical control and consumption restraint. Eventually, of course, resource shortages will requires changes, and since after the oil scare of the 1970s energy consumption levels did in fact fall, there is room for hope. In the long run, shortages and severe constraints and dangers based on resource deterioration may be a more powerful force for reform than conservationist values or rational arguments.

Literature Cited and Consulted

Bennett, John W. 1976. *The Ecological Transition: Cultural Anthropology and Human Adaptation.* New York: Pergamon.

_____ . 1982. *Of Time and the Enterprise: North American Family Farm Management in a Context of Resource Marginality.* Minneapolis: University of Minnesota Press.

_____ . 1986. "Research on Farmer Behavior and Social Organization." In *New Directions for Agriculture and Agricultural Research*, ed. Kenneth A. Dahlberg. Totowa, NJ: Rowman and Allanheld.

_____ . 1986. "Anthropology and Development: The Ambiguous Engagement." In John W. Bennett and John R. Bowen, *Production and Autonomy: Anthropological Critiques and Research on Development.* Boulder, CO: Westview Press.

Bennett, John W. and Kenneth A. Dahlberg. 1990. "Institutions, Social Organization, and Cultural Values." In *The Earth as Transformed by Human Action*. Cambridge: Cambridge University Press.

Black, John. 1970. *The Dominion of Man*. Edinburgh: The University Press.

Buckley, Walter. 1967. *Sociology and Modern Systems Theory*. Englewood Cliffs, NJ: Prentice-Hall.

Burling, Robbins. 1962. "Maximization Theories and the Study of Economic Anthropology." *American Anthropologist* 64: 802–10.

Childe, V. Gordon. 1942. *What Happened in History*. London: Penguin Books.

Dahlberg, Kenneth A., ed. 1986. *New Directions for Agriculture and Agricultural Research: Neglected Dimensions and Emerging Alternatives*. Totawa, NJ: Rowman & Allanheld.

Dahlberg, Kenneth A. and John W. Bennett, eds. 1986. *Natural Resources and People: Conceptual Issues in Interdisciplinary Research*. Boulder, CO: Westview Press.

Dalton, George. 1963. "Economic Theory and Primitive Society" *American Anthropologist* 63: 1–25.

Deevey, Edward S. 1960. "The Human Population." *Scientific American* 203: 194–205.

Firth, Raymond. 1955. "Some Principles of Social Organization." *Journal of the Royal Anthropological Institute* 84: 1–20.

Harris, Marvin. 1960. "Adaptation in Biological and Cultural Science," *Transactions of the New York Academy of Sciences*, series II, 23: 59–65.

Henry, Jules. 1963. *Culture Against Man*. New York: Random House.

Hoselitz, Bert F. 1952. *The Progress of Underdeveloped Areas*. Chicago: University of Chicago Press.

Kroeber, Alfred L. 1917. "The Superorganic." *American Anthropologist* 19: 447–49.

Malinowski, Bronislaw. 1929. *The Sexual Life of Savages in Northwestern Melanesia*. London: Routledge.

Martin, Paul S. and Richard G. Klein, eds. 1984. *Quaternary Extinctions: A Prehistoric Revolution*. Tucson: University of Arizona Press.

Nash, Roderick F. 1989. *The Rights of Nature: A History of Environmental Ethics*. Madison: University of Wisconsin Press.

Redfield, Robert. 1939. "The Folk Society and Culture" *American Journal of Sociology* 45: 731–42.

Spooner, Brian. 1982. *Desertification and Development: Dryland Ecology in Social Perspective*. New York: Academic Press.

Steward, Julian. 1955. "The Concept and Method of Cultural Ecology." In Julian Steward, *Culture Change*. Urbana: University of Illinois Press.

Tylor, Edward B. 1881. *Anthropology: An Introduction to the Study of Man and Civilization*. New York: D. Appleton.

White, Leslie A. 1948. "Man's Control over Civilization: An Anthropocentric Illusion." *Scientific Monthly* 66: 235–47.

2

Anticipation, Adaptation, and the Concept of Culture in Anthropology

Anthropology, a field of study dealing with both physical and behavioral aspects of the human species, is not an integrated discipline like biology, but rather a congeries of topics held together by descriptive interests. Since most of these topics concern prehistoric or living humans outside the confines of European civilization, a scholarly discipline formed around them. Although anthropologists have repeatedly claimed that their field is the only one to seek a universal science of humanity, this objective has been slow to mature. This failure has been attributed to various characteristics of anthropology that stem from the diversity of its subject matter.[1]

This diversity and the lack of a clear theoretical aim were matters of concern to anthropologists from the beginnings of the academic field in the 1880s. After the decline of evolutionary theory, American anthropologists in the early twentieth century seized on the descriptive humanistic notion of "culture" and converted it into a "scientific" discovery—a new order of reality. Although the concept immediately spread through the social and behavioral sciences, only cultural anthropology continued to

Originally published in *Science* 192 (28 May 1976: 847-53), this essay is reproduced with minor editorial changes. The emphasis on "adaptation" reflects a preoccupation among members of the American Association for the Advancement of Science current in the early 1970s, and the gist of the essay is to establish the process as philosophically basic to thought and behavior. Adaptational studies in cultural anthropology have been to some extent superseded by studies of symbolism and meaning—what I call in the essay "interpretive anthropology"—and adaptation has been taken up as an empirical topic in applied anthropology, especially in studies of the changes and experiences associated with economic development, resource use, and the "sustainability" issue. But anthropology, as a preparadigmatic science or scholarship, is prone to fluctuation and faddism—empirical, not theoretical, interests govern the field and its central tendencies. From a view that values academic consistency, this can be deplored; from a perspective that values the dynamism of human behavior and culture, it can be applauded.

use it as a central explanatory concept. In the early 1950s, Kroeber and Kluckhohn (1952) acknowledged the descriptive or "substantive" basis of the concept but insisted that it retained an "explanatory dimension." Even so, they found it necessary to qualify the explanatory function—"anthropologists do not claim that culture does provide a complete explanation of human behavior, merely that there is a cultural element in most human behavior." While Kroeber and Kluckhohn were attempting to retain a degree of explanatory power for the concept, other anthropologists were looking elsewhere—into ecology, in Julian Steward's case (1955)—for explanations of human affairs. One consequence of having a descriptive core concept for a field that aims at generalizing or explanatory (scientific) status is the difficulty of distinguishing cultural anthropology from history or literature.[2] At the other extreme, the increasing tendency to adopt sociological concepts like "social exchange" makes it difficult to distinguish cultural anthropology from sociology or economics.

I believe this situation has generated a continuing intellectual crisis that is compounded by the gradual disappearance of the focal subject matter of ethnology—the isolated tribal society. As such societies are transformed into self-conscious nations, ethnic groups, or classes, the pull towards social science becomes even stronger. Some anthropologists begin to play roles comparable to those of sociologists or economists—people who are responsible for changing or assisting formerly isolated populations in coping with the pervasive institutions of contemporary society. This change in roles generates countervailing forces in cultural anthropology that seek to return to "culture," that is, to use semantical and phenomenological approaches in order to avoid social scientism. This has led to a diversification of subject matter to the point where there now exist separate "anthropologies" for economics, politics, society, education, symbolism, ecology, and so on.

If the task is to find a theoretical approach that will avoid both mechanistic social science and evocative humanism and, at the same time, provide for a degree of synthesis of the many subdivisions of the discipline, then a likely possibility is found in the concept of adaptation. This concept appears to introduce a new level of generalization. Instead of abstractions from behavior, like culture, or the reductive formulas of psychology or genetics, it focuses on human actors who try to realize objectives, satisfy needs, or find peace while coping with present conditions. In their coping, humans create the social future in the sense of generating new problems or perpetuating old ones and may even modify the biological constitution of the population in the process (as in the case of the sickle cell gene).[3] By analyzing the factors that guide the choices of strategies, one gains knowledge of the possibility and direction of change and the relation of human behavior to the milieus.

Anticipation: The Basis of Adaptation

On the basis of a careful study of A. N. Whitehead, Burgers (1975) proposed that the classic problem of teleology has not really been solved, despite the fact that it was discarded by modern science in favor of material and linear causality. The difficulty with linear causality is that it cannot determine causes of events that occur, in part, because of precedents built into the structure of the phenomena. For example, the formation of a crystal is caused by the molecular anticipation of crystallization, which is triggered by an assortment of external factors. But how can one predict exactly when a crystal will form if it is not possible, except in laboratory situations where human will and purpose intervene, to specify when these triggering factors will appear or become effective? More cogently, how can one speak of material causality of human actions when the unpredictable and creative powers of the human mind are at work in nearly every situation?

Anticipation in the human realm may appear in the form of purpose, needs, desire, foresight, will, or simply consciousness of continued existence. The process of anticipation is recognized in anthropological theory when we speak of cognition and symbolism as conferring a "time-binding" capacity on human behavior, but instead of being used as the core of anthropological intellectual effort the concept has been presented as a psychological fact that lies behind culture. The traditional view conceptualized culture as a cause of human behavior. Furthermore, if anticipation is characteristic of all life and even the inanimate realm, then the idea that culture—the human version of anticipation—is exclusive to the human species is at least partly false or, at best, ambiguous (a position apparent in the work of animal behaviorists and ethologists; e.g., Kummer 1971, chap. 1).

However, if the cognitive form of anticipation is an especially important characteristic of humans, then much human behavior is devoted to reordering phenomena to avoid a random or entropic state. This proposition counterbalances the recurrent tendency (as in sociological functionalism) to make stability or, at least, homeostasis the normative basis of theory in human phenomena or to apply concepts appropriate mainly to nonhuman realms to the much more dynamic human realm. The persistent developmental or exponential tendency in human behavior, visible whenever the time span observed is long enough, should be evidence that the regularity and return to preexisting states characteristic of homeostatic movement are temporary phenomena that are useful in analyzing limited sequences but not for understanding the basis of species behavior.[4]

A few anthropologists used the model of a game as an analogy for the coping behavior of humans in instrumental (technical, economic, political) situations (e.g., Davenport 1960). The specialized and limited game analogy might perhaps be generalized to include the major pattern of human existence or even of all life. That is, in adapting the organism plays a game with the environment, endeavoring to learn, manipulate, or change the rules in order to realize goals, satisfy needs, or maintain a degree of freedom of choice and action. This process presupposes what Whitehead calls anticipation: the future is structured by what the organism does in the present, which in turn has been conditioned by what happened in the past.[5] Thus, regardless of what the actual outcome may be or precisely how much "freedom" the organism may have or acquire, there is an attempt to move through time and space as though freedom or autonomy were attainable and, by so doing, constantly to restructure the conditioning factors. This is one definition of the evolutionary process; the possibility that human thought and action can be fitted into a general evolutionary scheme has existed since Irving Hallowell's classic paper of 1960. It is now generally assumed that "mind" was a factor in the evolution of hominids.

For Whitehead, the universe was a problem of constant evolution, not empirical existence, since, while each event grew out of prior events, it was also shaped by present circumstances. Whitehead also believed that the emergence of one event out of another induced conceptualization; that is, a change in phenomena necessarily creates awareness or understanding of the old and the new. This, in turn, creates a sense of the future. Whitehead believed this process extended beyond human intelligence into the whole universe; that is, the evolution of material substance has similar characteristics insofar as future events are constrained or made probable by built-in mechanisms that have emerged as a consequence of prior events and processes. Simple or linear causation is not ruled out as a concept of explanation, but it is redefined as a descriptive or short-term version of a temporal process featuring complex systemic reciprocities. An analogy in anthropology is the distinction made by Sahlins and Service (1960) between specific and general evolution in culture—the specific historical sequences of change or evolution often can be understood fairly adequately by simple causation, but the long-term movements and the frequent unpredictable shifts of direction and focus can be grasped only by an understanding of the systemic character of general evolution. An example is the exponential curve of energy utilization by all humans, which is superimposed over many specific curves with flat or cyclical shapes (Bennett 1976, chaps. 3 and 4).

The phenomenological element in Whitehead's position is found in the implication that, in living organisms and perhaps humans in particular, the factor of mind, intention, will, purpose, or whatever must be considered as distinct, for purposes of analysis, from strictly material elements of a process. That is, one cannot explain mind, or "minding," as Leslie White (1958) would have called it, by atoms, even though atoms are involved in the process. More exactly, for a particular problem involving anticipatory functioning, human behavior has to be considered as an independent phenomenon. White (1959) and Kroeber (1917) called this phenomenon "culture," but my position is that this terminological habit has obscured the underlying issue. Culture is a linguistic convention used to describe the empirical consequences of minding; therefore, minding is what we should be concerned with. And a more descriptive label for it is adaptation.

The perceptive reader might object that, since I have suggested that the anticipatory function of reality is most easily visible in complex, reciprocal events in long time sequences where linear causal explanations do not work, it is contradictory to apply the theory to individual human action. First, simple causation frequently does work at the individual level and in society over short periods. Second, there will be an interplay between anticipation and causation. For example, we can say about the study of human social kinship that its persisting structure (a mental thing) is created by role expectations that are conditioned by past precedents. However, the behavior of an individual in kinship contexts is only *somewhat* explainable by this anticipatory function, since an individual can choose to follow the structure or not. If the topic shifts from the kinship system to the coping behavior of individuals, we find that the styles of both conforming and nonconforming behavior also create patterned or anticipated structures within, or outside of, the kinship structure. Third, long and short time are relative concepts; the emergence of "patterned deviations" may be perceived as taking place over a long period of time from the standpoint of the lifetime of an individual. From the standpoint of the kinship system, which may not change over many generations, it may be a minor squiggle on a long-term curve. Thus the use of an anticipatory-adaptational frame clarifies the relativity of time and levels of generality.

The Concept of Adaptation

In biology the term adaptation has two meanings. The first has to do with genetic evolution, which concerns feedbacks into the gene pool in response to the environment leading to the persistence or development of traits favorable to the survival of a population. The second concept pertains to behavior during the life span of an organism which enables it to cope with the environment. Such behavior operates by cognitive and perceptual processes. Although adaptations selected through the genetic-evolutionary process may provide the basis for the capacity, in most organisms adaptive selection is sufficiently general to provide excess capacity ("generalization") and thus the organism maintains a degree of adaptive autonomy.

The basic meaning of adaptation in the sciences of human behavior[6] is derived from the second of the two biological concepts, that is, coping mechanisms utilized by organisms during their lives. However, among humans this behavior is subject to interpretation by values, thus introducing a judgmental dimension in addition to the survival or need-satisfying function. This requires a series of elaborations of the concept; of these, the most fundamental is that what may be adaptive (reducing tension, satisfying needs) for the individual may be maladaptive for the group (threatening survival and integrity). Warfare is, of course, the obvious example; an individual may gain satisfaction and social honor from participation, but the activity can be judged as destructive for society. Thus the influence of value judgments must be weighed in analyses of coping adaptations in humans—failure to do so leads to misleading and incomplete analyses. This multidimensional process of behavioral adaptation shapes the rhetoric of politics and social change and reform and is also fundamental in what we consider to be normal and abnormal individual behavior.

Since adaptation with regard to human behavior is the positive half of a paired concept (the negative half is maladaptation), the neglect of the value dimension leads to neglect of the anticipatory aspect of behavior. While the element of freedom contributes a flow of novel or creative responses, the majority of coping mechanisms is based on precedents. Likewise, the values used to assess the consequences of adaptation are almost always derived from the mind-sets established before the particular adaptive event. The difference between human and nonhuman adaptive behavior seems to lie in the greater frequency of both the creative and the precedental forms among humans, whose adaptive behavior is characterized not merely by symbol generation (that is, culture), but also by memory storage (learning) and the preservation of outmoded (perceptually maladaptive) solutions that generate conflict. Similar patterns are apparently found in all organisms and, analogically, nonliving things, but the precise loci and magnitudes of the functions obviously vary from realm to realm. However, since there is continuity between the living and the nonliving, to call culture a "superorganic" is to exaggerate the differences between humans and all other phenomena.

The statement "culture is man's way of adapting to the environment" is characteristic of the effort to shift to an adaptational frame of reference while retaining culture as the central referent. Presumably the intention of such a definition is to exclude nonhumans, who adapt mainly by programmed mechanisms built into the genes. Such a proposition has to be qualified in light of work by animal experimentalists and field observers who have observed, in various species, plasticity and innovativeness that transcend programming and clearly belong in the cultural—learning—domain. However, if we define culture as, for example, "the distinctive human cognitive interplay between constraint and freedom of action," that proposition is not false; at least, it is a typical heuristic statement that can be neither entirely supported nor entirely refuted.

More serious objections to the idea of culture as an adaptive mechanism stem from the levels of generalization implicit in the statement. If culture is a descriptive concept, an epiphenomenal construct, or a generalization of a complex natural process, then it cannot be a *method* of adapting. If Whitehead's doctrine of the basic continuity of anticipation and freedom is correct, then the human differs from the nonhuman only in degree and in emphasis on particular features. Cognition is present in humans and not in crystals, but cognition, in varying degrees, is present in mammals.

The term "preadaptation" is used in evolutionary biology to refer to an opportune coincidence between an existing trait and some new environmental factor. There is a question as to whether this properly refers to the anticipatory function. If we understand preadaptation in its most general sense, then it can be included. However, when we are concerned with human coping behavior, anticipation becomes coterminous, in large part, with foresight or cognitive understandings of future contingencies. These certainly exist in humans but are not by any means universally operative. That they are not has been a perennial problem in human thought, as evidenced by attempts to forecast the future. Such forecasting or planning represents an attempt to subject the anticipatory function to a degree of conscious control. The frequent failure of planning, persistence of maladaptive precedents, or emergence of unanticipated consequences testifies to the incompleteness of cognitive anticipation. Thus the human species has both directional movement (teleology) and uncontrolled drift or stagnation, although hominid evolution perhaps has featured a reduction of the latter. Obviously, interplay between directional movement and randomness is required in order to retain the freedom or flexibility component of adaptation.

The principal problem of the concept of adaptation in a broadened science of human ecology concerns the relation between adaptation in a biological sense and adaptation defined as a social and behavioral process. In the biological sciences, adaptation tends to refer to entropy functions; the behavior of organisms results in steady states or homeostatic rhythms. However, in social behavior the organism may do just the opposite—disturb or overturn existing conditions in order to satisfy needs. In general, the biological conceptions of adaptation have had a strong element of mechanistic teleology—as, for example, in research that seeks to demonstrate that predator and prey interaction tends to stabilize species populations, or in the investigation of trophic cycling of nutrition in a relatively closed environment, like a pond. There is nothing wrong with these interpretations, since they seek to define the structure of anticipatory phenomena in a domain devoid of cognition.[7] However, in the human case, teleology tends to become equivalent to conscious causation or history; that is, it assumes a cognitive role and anticipation becomes a conscious focus of policy. This means that projection of mechanistic teleological assumptions onto the human social organ is a dubious enterprise at best, although there is no doubt that directional movements out of awareness of the human actors do seem to occur in society and in relations between man and Nature. Such directional movements—vectors—must be treated as empirical possibilities, not as natural laws. Anthropology has periodically, for example, in both past and present cultural evolutionary theory, fallen into a mechanistic teleological mood, which makes it extremely difficult to handle short-term adaptive behavioral sequences and outcomes. One result is the tendency for cultural anthropology to oscillate between particularistic, microsocial depiction and grand evolutionary generalization.

However, the union of biological and social adaptational phenomena may be defined on a different level, that is, in terms of tension reduction in the organism. In Alland's definitions, tension reduction is equivalent to what he calls "internal adaptation," or the resolution of various processes within the individual in the course of behavior (Alland 1973). Alland contrasts this concept to "external adaptation," or, presumably, what I call coping. There is no doubt that tension or stress reduction figures in human coping behavior. Perhaps neurosis may be defined broadly as a state of perpetual conflict between functional coping styles and inner needs for satisfaction. If so, then neurosis is nothing more than hypertypical human behavior. This observation may provide an opportunity to orient culture and personality studies in anthropology towards adaptation, bringing them into conjunction with other subdivisions of anthropology.

Adaptive and maladaptive behavior in humans is based on the capacity for "self-objectification" and the "normative orientation" (Hallowell 1960). Humans, with their impressive symbolic capacity (that is, capacity to become relatively free of arbitrary or one-to-one determining stimuli), also have the capacity to perceive the self in relation to the environment, which is of course the basis of human ecology. The self-objectification capacity is also quantitative. Tribal societies apparently possess this capacity to a lesser degree; that is, they perceive the self, or human beings in general, as largely in synthesis with the environment whereas industrial societies appear to develop the most pronounced sense of self detached from the environment. This is, of course, a facet of the more general subject-and-object conceptualization that is strongly developed in these want-dominated societies and that surfaces in the persistent dualisms, Man-Nature and Culture-Environment.

If we consider adaptation in terms of human relationships with the physical environment, the significant behavioral process is probably the ability to create an image of the physical world that is only partially congruent with empirical reality. The degree of congruence is variable; there exist no known generalized psychological or inborn controls over this symbolizing capacity, which varies only by individuals or within particular groups by experiential vectors controlled by degree of exposure to alternatives. However, it is this variance in experience and exposure that also lies at the root of the ethnological concept of discrete cultures. Since the human capacity for symbolic constructions of milieus is theoretically indefinite, different cultures are simply products of temporal and spatial positions that affect experiences. A particular culture is a time-slice description of experiential constructs, subject to change as experience and environment change—granting some lags in individuals and in particular segments of the symbolic constructions.

The principal consequence of the disharmony between empirical nature and symbolic views of nature is, of course, the projection of human rhythms and purposes onto the physical universe. These human intentionalities can be defined as "natural" at a high level of generality, and theory must take this into account even though attempts to deal with it border on philosophy and religion. (For example, are human actions, destructive or problematic for nature in the short run, part of some larger design which contains cyclical patterning or homeostatic controls?)

In any case, the short-term consequences of human intentionality and anticipatory behavior have a more massive potential impact on the physical environment than the behavior of any other species. It is this impact that is currently conceived as problematic, since there appears to be no reliable means of control. The utilization of resources for the satisfaction of human purposes is subject to conceptions that are generated within the social organ and that have no reliable controlling relation to rational considerations such as sustained resource yield. Thus the distinctive characteristic of anticipatory behavior in the economic sphere is that it generates a form of adaptive behavior in which anticipation is keyed to satisfaction of present felt wants or consummation rather than to future consequences (or, following Whitehead, the freedom component tends to dominate over prudent anticipation). This has been an overall evolutionary tendency in the human species; particular societies over limited spans of time may demonstrate otherwise, but the general vector has been towards increasing use of resources to satisfy wants and desires. Hardin's "tragedy of the commons" (1968) is an ever-present possibility, not the exceptional case.

One argument for eventual control relies on the concept of ultimate naturalness. This can be expressed as a process of slow self-correction feedback or as faith in the human ability to appraise dangers. These doctrines tend to neglect the way human intentions are bound by the communication systems called institutions or vested interests and reciprocities. Planning is expected to mitigate pressures, but its recent trend is to seek compromise with vested interests, which ameliorates conditions or assuages conscience but does not affect fundamental direction.

Adaptation and Cultural Anthropology

In cultural anthropology the first statement of the behavioral background of resource utilization or energy generation was presented by Barnett (1953), who was concerned with innovation as the basis of cultural change. Using Gestalt psychology, he defined innovation as the ability to synthesize components of perceptual and experiential fields in order to create new combinations or images of reality. The process as defined is not unique to humans, so its properties alone cannot wholly explain superior human capacities; we must consider, among other factors, the sheer quantitative differences in capacity between humans and other species. For adaptational theory, the key is the cognitive capacity to visualize changes in contemporary phenomena, that is, to conceive of new things and thereby establish new anticipations. When existing phenomena need to be altered in order to achieve these anticipated ends, we can speak of coping. This appears, for all practical purposes, to be included in the concept of innovation. I believe that the adaptational rhetoric is superior to the cultural since it focuses attention on the human actor and his behavior rather than on abstractions from his behavior. Generalization is achieved when we speak of group styles or modes of coping, that is, social adaptation. These are not really equivalent to culture as classically defined, since we remain at the level of behavior and human purposes.

Implicit in the above is the proposition that the important phenomena for an adaptational or "environmental" anthropology are dynamic human purposes, needs, and wants. Most of the earlier ethnological work on tribal cultures assumed or described static patterns of purpose and want. Hence, ethnological theory, or cultural anthropology generally, has been poorly equipped to handle situations with rapidly changing purpose and want vectors. Anthropology has generally neglected the fact that tribal societies represent sidelines but not the main thrust in behavioral evolution. If cultural anthropology is to focus on contemporary society, it must make this shift to a theory with factors of reality, not abstract models, as its central component.

The first anthropological attempt to conceptualize coping behavior and to contrast it to the cultural level of description was Firth's distinction (1955) between structure and organization. He defined "structure" as the relatively slow-to-change anticipations that are called values, norms, or expectations of the behavior of others. "Organization" refers to the more quickly changing behaviors designed to attain immediate ends or to cope with shifting temporal circumstances. The distinction is therefore basically a temporal, not a substantive one, and Firth's essays can be read as an attempt to keep an explanatory role for culture for while giving recognition to the need and purposive dimension of behavior which is of paramount importance in the everyday movements of human existence.

Firth's distinction helped to liberate cultural anthropology from its preoccupation with reified, fixed systems and began the transition to an adaptational framework. Any consideration of everyday reality alters the generalizing, timeless modes of classic ethnological description; it requires the anthropologist to become concerned with purpose and accomplishment, that is, to deal with instrumental activities as significant in their own right. Ethnology's frame of reference has shifted since the introduction of Firthian concepts—from essentially archaeological description of self-contained tribal societies to studies of human behavior in tribal contexts under varying degrees and conditions of involvement with larger systems.

I conclude from the emphasis of published reports that the trend in recent years is towards a three-way classification of the data of cultural anthropology. This classification, which can handle both tribal and nontribal materials, is as follows.

1. *Thought*. Description of symbols, ideas, values, goals, and purposes as articulated by the members of the group under study. These need not, of course, be unique to that group. The collection of thought patterns should be made without prejudice as to their permanence or changeability, since the depth or rootedness of particular mental constructs cannot be known in advance. Societies differ in the extent to which mental concepts actually define the ends of living and the degree of adaptive flexibility. To an increasing extent in the contemporary world, people learn differing and often compartmentalized systems.

2. *Interhuman activity*. In the social dimension, relations between people are expressed by structural diagrams and reciprocities of behavior. Mental constructs from (1) may or may not define the parameters of these interhuman relationships, since, to an increasing extent, situational coping tends to set style of response. However, every society retains a corpus of relationships that may be described by such terms as consensus, conflict, compromise, affiliation, individualism, or role playing.

3. *Adaptive behavior*. Obviously the distinction between this category of data and the others is purely analytical, because both thought patterns and interhuman relationships are involved in adaptation. However, in the adaptational mode, the emphasis shifts towards strategic coping, that is, the attempt to realize individual and social objectives through the mobilization of social and material resources. This category of behavior has become dominant in the contemporary world with its interdependence and growing constraints on free action.

The empirical question for the cultural anthropologist concerns the extent to which these three categories of data are integrated in any concrete social situation. When congruence can be demonstrated—for example, when the observed social behavior and thought articulations are mutually consistent and coping is handled mostly by precedent—one might well speak of the existence of a culture. This usage of the term is reminiscent of Redfield's distinction (1953a) between culture and civilization which implies that in the latter inconsistency between the sectors of experience is typical and thus requires rational action for resolution or suppression of the resultant conflict—a process largely unknown in the "folk society." This distinction is, of course, relative and idealized, since all human societies display inconsistencies.

However, a conception of culture as the precedents that people use to construct patterns of coping is more appropriate for an adaptational approach. Precedents may be derived from either the thought or the interhuman activity data categories and therefore can be called by a variety of names: norms, values, role expectations, prestige, and the like. However, precedents, made increasingly available by advanced communication in the human species, do not determine coping behavior at all times. The degree to which precedents are operative, and their quantity, is an empirical, not a theoretical question. Since few human actions occur without precedents, either manifest or latent, these precedental factors (culture) become part of the milieu to which humans respond. To simplify the argument, the *adaptive nexus* of human action can be defined as the relation of present goals to past precedents—a nexus in which causation is absorbed into the context of reciprocal functioning as a temporal process. This does not, of course, eliminate cause-and-effect sequences that are a result of factors, like a natural catastrophe, that compel a sudden redirection of action along new lines—although in such cases the adaptive nexus soon comes into operation.

In an adaptational approach it is also essential to distinguish the microsocial and macrosocial levels of behavior and function, since in human societies (and to a real but unknown extent in nonhuman societies) these characteristically differ in their consequences. The microsocial description concerns behavior of individuals in defined group situations and pertains mainly to their instrumental actions, that is, satisfaction of purpose, need, and want. This mode also has both manifest and latent meanings that depend on the particular precedental components and their quantity. The macrosocial level pertains to the consequences of these individual actions for other and larger groups and society in general. Here judgments must be based on both neutral, scientific assessments and on values and purposes believed to be representative of a general trend. It cannot be assumed (contrary, incidentally, to traditional democratic ideology) that microsocial actions are always consistent with macrosocial aims and standards. In the tribal society such consistency was probably of high order; in modern pluralistic societies of all levels of development the consistency is much less visible. The satisfaction of individual needs characteristically may violate (that is, be maladaptive for) social well-being.

The details of the anthropological synthesis suggested by the use of adaptation as a paradigm can be summarized. Among the topical fields of anthropology, political, economic, ecological, and social-transactional studies appear to constitute a core that is increasingly concerned with human coping with real events.[8] I shall call this *instrumental anthropology*. If this constitutes one wing of cultural anthropology, then the other consists of *interpretive anthropology*, including the study of thought, that is, of symbolism, meaning, the combination of symbolism and semantics known as structuralism, hermeneutics, and other "literary" anthropologies. Methods of research in this wing may also feature especially intimate interaction with human subjects. In general, this interpretive wing of anthropology exploits the descriptive mode of the culture concept— Geertz's term, "thick description," is apt. The instrumental wing moves towards "science," that is, towards generalizations and explanations of human behavior with the use of a variety of more or less formal models. An adaptational approach would appear to be more securely based in the instrumental wing, but since values, symbols, and precedents are part of the adaptive nexus they cannot be ignored. Psychocultural anthropology stands between these wings.[9]

The current feasible limits of synthesis in cultural anthropology are thus suggested. For instrumental anthropology culture is the qualitative and quantitative precedents for decision or opportunities for and constraints on free choice; interpretive anthropology sees culture as the qualitative corpus of symbols characteristic of the era. While the two are mutually dependent, the multidimensionality of human behavior requires differing conceptual foundations; the culture concept is, at best, a heuristic device.

Summary: Adaptation and Policy Science

The central issue in human affairs is dual. It includes the search for autonomy in the midst of constraint and the countervailing search for control in the face of license. Humans, like all organisms, and metaphorically like all physical phenomena, seek satisfaction of anticipations; while this search is governed in part by built-in controls and possibilities, there is a large domain of freedom and novelty. Humans have greater freedom ("will") than other species and phenomena, but at the same time it is apparent that this capacity can be abused and survival or peace of mind threatened by disregard of prudent restraint. As Boas observed in a neglected essay (1940), humans exist in a milieu of their own making that is always a mixture of freedom and conformity. I believe that this should be the central issue in the concept of culture if the concept is to be salvaged.

My proposal for this salvage (or replacement) operation is to focus on adaptation as the central topic of cultural and perhaps of all anthropology. Adaptation, a word for the human capacity for coping with milieu in order to establish protocols of both freedom and constraint, is a field that is worthy of attention by researchers since anthropology has already developed many of the necessary concepts, however disguised these may be by the abstract language of patterns, values, and the like.

A cultural anthropology conceived in terms of social adaptation will almost automatically become a science oriented towards policy (Belshaw 1976). Its findings will pertain to the basic question of what humans need and want, how they go about acquiring these, and what consequences for society and the environment will result. While the program outlined here can apply to tribal and peasant society, it is perhaps more cogently represented in the study of modern life, wherever this may be found—in the industrial societies or in the new, formerly tribal nations. Within the discipline the approach, at the least, prefigures a synthesis between the subdivisions now labeled social, economic, political, and ecological anthropology, and possibly psychological anthropology as well. In addition, the importance of valuational phenomena for the study of adaptational processes means that anthropological studies of symbolism, art, religion, and values may eventually become part of a joint effort. Whether he considers himself humanist or scientist, the anthropologist will acknowledge that man lives by both bread and dollars, art and the spade, belief and pragmatic accommodation. It is the union of these modes that constitutes the distinctive human version of Whitehead's anticipation and his homogeneous, but also varied, universe.

Afterword: 1992

While preparing this essay for publication, two issues struck me as deserving of critical comment. The first of these concerns the ambiguity of my position concerning differences and similarities between the behavior of *Homo sapiens* and other species. I seem to imply in some passages that the difference is fundamental, qualitative, and in others that it is simply quantitative. I suppose that the issue is really spurious, insofar as major quantitative differences—for example, the speed and complexity of basic thought patterns—add up, phenotypically, to qualitative differences. The issue is one of rhetoric rather than ontology. In addition, the quantitative differences in, say, anticipatory functioning has major consequences: it creates for *Homo sapiens* the corpus of precedents and coping behaviors called "culture" and also provides human behavior with a unique temporal process: the ability to live simultaneously in the "past" and the "present."

The second issue concerns the definition of anticipation as a fundamental human capability that can be seen to lie at the root of human culture and accomplishment. As a theoretical statement of the behavioral process, it stands as written. However, the fact that anticipation can encourage erroneous and biased constructions and the tendency to ignore likely consequences, although mentioned in the text, is not given sufficient attention. From the standpoint of environmental problems and resource conservation, however, this becomes a crucial issue.

Indeed, if anticipation is a fundamental habit of the human mind, so is the unwillingness or inability to anticipate correctly or to act upon anticipated consequences because the prevailing ethos or power structure prevents it (i.e., makes it too risky to do so for purely social reasons having nothing to do with the particular procedure or process). When this occurs, we confront another human proclivity: the tendency to do things we know will create problems or dangers in the future or things we know are "wrong" but that cannot be stopped. This aspect of human behavior and its environmental consequences will be given more attention in the next chapter.

Notes

1. Relevant here is Thomas Kuhn's (1962) distinction between scientific fields with a central theory or paradigm and those without. The concept was adopted by George Stocking (1968), who called anthropology a "preparadigmatic" science (the ambiguity of the term—later acknowledged by Kuhn—obscures the meaning of its application to anthropology). Anthropology is a congeries of topics which can be viewed either as the advantage of diversity or as the cause of its disunity. The inherent variety of subject matter, the multidimensionality or multipotentiality of human phenomena, and the close empirical contact with the subject matter characterize anthropology and distinguish it from fields with more unified topical coverage.

2. Controversy over the scientific as opposed to the humanistic identities of cultural anthropology persists. For a classic review of the issues see Redfield 1953b. Clifford Geertz, in his collection of essays on culture, appeared to have abandoned scientific postures and accepted the humanistic; he considered cultural anthropology's objective to be the preparation of "thick description" (Geertz 1973, chap. 1). A similar methodological concept, "depictive integration," was popularized by A.L. Kroeber and others. Both of the above authors really describe an approach identical to historical writing. I hesitate to choose sides; although I wish to introduce more generalizing capacity into cultural anthropology, the choice of a Whiteheadian source for the approach provides a link to phenomenological and humanistic orientations. I believe there are many relationships between science and humanistic study, but there appears to be continuing difficulties in combining the two.

3. I refer here to the interrelation of tribal agricultural methods, population and migration, and malarial disease on the one hand and the build-up of the sickle cell gene in West African populations on the other. This is a clear case of how human activities influence human biology and the reverse. While a great deal of information on sickle celling has appeared in recent years, the classic statement remains Frank Livingstone's article (1958).

4. In my opinion, the most cogent discussion of potential applications of general systems theory to human society is that of Walter Buckley (1967). The most intensive attempt by an anthropologist to apply ecosystem theory (which is quite different from general systems theory) to a cultural situation is Rappaport's study of swine management in a New Guinea tribal society (1967). My paper, however, is primarily concerned with adaptation as a concept useful for the analysis of human behavior in modern or historical populations. When adaptation is applied to archaeological populations or ethnological populations of a residual character, the concept takes on more generalized and often more biologically oriented meaning. In such studies, the central issue of human purpose and the means devised to fulfill it are present but are generalized over longer historical periods or large demographic or geographic units. To some extent, however, the use by archaeologists and ethnohistorians of adaptation as a central concept has produced findings of greater significance for resource management and human engineering than has cultural anthropological research. For an example of the combined ethnographic, archaeological, and ecological approach to human adaptation (in this case the Aleut people), see Laughlin 1975.

5. The basic ideas were presented by Whitehead (1929), but the most accessible phraseology appears in his *Adventures of Ideas* of 1933: "'to be something' is to be discoverable as a factor in the analysis of some actuality. . . . Any set of actual occasions are united by the mutual immanence of occasions, each in the other. To the extent that they are united they mutually constrain each other . . . one occasion will be in the future of the other. Thus the earlier will be immanent in the later according to the mode of efficient causality, and the later according to the mode of anticipation" (Whitehead 1955, 199). However, "the antecedent environment is not wholly efficacious in determining the initial phase of the occasion which springs from it" (Whitehead 1955, 200). (See also G.H. Mead 1932.)

6. For some discussions of the concept of adaptation in anthropology see Montagu, ed. 1968, Holling 1969, and the following: Harris 1960, Sahlins 1964, and Rappaport 1971.

7. Although data is accumulating from plant and animal ecology to demonstrate that the stability bias in bioecology has been excessive (Holling 1969).

8. A random selection of articles on instrumental cultural anthropology follows: Barth 1967, Sahlins 1964, Bennett 1968, Rhoades and Thompson 1975, Westermeyer 1973, Netting 1974,
   Hay 1973, Britan and Denich 1976, Despres 1975, Whitten and Whitten 1972.
9. "Instrumental anthropology," with its concerns for rational and purposive behavior, would appear to be concerned with phenomena similar to those contained in Daniel Bell's (1976) "techno-economic" domain; and my "interpretive anthropology" appears similar to that in Bell's "culture" or "expressive symbolic" domain of contemporary society. Bell's third domain, "polity," or the field of social control, is echoed in my emphasis on "policy" as a consequence of applying adaptational analysis to social behavior. However, I read Bell's book after completing this article, and there has been no effort to bring concepts in line with his thesis.

Literature Cited and Consulted

Alland, Alexander. 1973. *Evolution and Human Behavior*. Garden City, N.J.: Doubleday.

Barnett, H. G. 1953. *Innovation: The Basis of Culture Change*. New York: McGraw-Hill.

Barth, Fredrik. 1967. "On the Study of Social Change" *American Anthropologist* 69: 661–69.

Bell, Daniel. 1976. *The Cultural Contradictions of Capitalism*. New York: Basic Books.

Belshaw, Cyril S. 1976. *The Sorcerer's Apprentice: An Anthropology of Public Policy*. New York: Pergamon.

Bennett, John W. 1968. "The Significance of the Concept of Adaptation for Contemporary Sociocultural Anthropology." In *Proceedings, Eighth International Congress of Anthropological and Ethnological Sciences*. Tokyo: Science Council of Japan, vol. 3, 237.

_____.1968. "Reciprocal Economic Exchanges Among North American Agricultural Operators" *Southwest Journal of Anthropology* 24: 276–309.

_____.1976. *The Ecological Transition: Cultural Anthropology and Human Adaptation*. New York: Pergamon.

Boas, Franz. 1940. "Liberty Among Primitive Peoples." In *Freedom: Its Meaning*, ed. R.N. Anshen. New York: Harcourt Brace.

Britan, Gerald and Bette S. Denich. 1976. "Environment and Choice in Rapid Social Change" *American Ethnologist* 3: 55–72.

Buckley, Walter. 1967. *Sociology and Modern Systems Theory*. Englewood Cliffs, NJ: Prentice-Hall.

Burgers, J. M. 1975. "Causality and Anticipation" *Science* 189: 194–98.

Davenport, William. 1960. *Jamaican Fishing: A Game Theory Analysis*. New Haven, CT: Yale University Press.

Despres, Leo A. 1975. "Ethnicity and Group Relations in Guyana." In *The New Ethnicity: Perspectives from Ethnology*, ed. John W. Bennett. St. Paul: American Ethnological Society and West Publishing.

Firth, Raymond. 1955. "Some Principles of Social Organization." *Journal of the Royal Anthropological Institute* 85: 1–7.

Geertz, Clifford. 1973. *The Interpretation of Cultures*. New York: Basic Books.

Hallowell, A. Irving. 1960. "Self, Society and Culture in Phylogenetic Perspective." In *The Evolution of Man*, ed. Sol Tax. Chicago: University of Chicago Press.

Hardin, Garrett. 1968. "The Tragedy of the Commons." *Science* 162: 1243–48.

Harris, Marvin. 1960. "Adaptation in Biological and Cultural Science" *Transactions of the New York Academy of Sciences* Series II, 23(1): 59–65.

Hay, Thomas H. 1973. "A Technique of Formalizing and Testing Models of Behavior: Two Models of Ojibwa Restraint" *American Anthropologist* 75: 708–30.

Holling, Crawford S. 1969. "Stability in Ecological and Social Systems." In *Diversity and Stability in Ecological Systems* (report and symposium held 26–28 May 1969 at Brookhaven National Laboratory, Upton, New York).

Kroeber, Alfred L. 1917. "The Superorganic." *American Anthropologist* 19: 163–213.

Kroeber, Alfred L. and Clyde Kluckhohn. 1952. "Culture: A Critical Review of Concepts and Theories." *Papers of the Peabody Museum of American Archaeology and Ethnology* 47(1).

Kuhn, Thomas. 1962. *The Structure of Scientific Revolutions*. Chicago: University of Chicago Press.

Kummer, Hans. 1971. *Primate Societies: Group Techniques of Ecological Adaptation*. Chicago: Aldine.

Laughlin, W. S. 1975. "Aleuts: Ecosystem, Holocene History and Siberian Origin." *Science* 189: 507–15.

Livingstone, Frank. 1958. "Anthropological Implications of Sickle Cell Gene Distribution in West Africa." *American Anthropologist* 60: 533–59.

Mead, George Herbert. 1932. *Philosophy of the Present*. Chicago: Open Court, 1932.

Montagu, M. F. Ashley, ed. 1968. *Culture: Man's Adaptive Dimension*. New York: Oxford University Press.

Netting, Robert M. 1974. "Agrarian Ecology." In *Annual Review of Anthropology*, ed. B. Siegel. Palo Alto, CA: Annual Reviews.

Rappaport, Roy A. 1967. *Pigs for the Ancestors: Ritual in the Ecology of a New Guinea People*. New Haven, CT: Yale University Press.

_____.1971. "Ritual, Sanctity and Cybernetics." *American Anthropologist* 73: 73–76.

Redfield, Robert. 1953a. *The Primitive World and Its Transformations*. Ithaca, NY: Cornell University Press.

_____.1953b. "Relations of Anthropology to the Humanities and Social Sciences." In *Anthropology Today*, ed. Alfred L. Kroeber. Chicago: University of Chicago Press.

Rhoades, Robert E. and Stephen I. Thompson. 1975. "Adaptive Strategies in Alpine Environments: Beyond Ecological Particularism." *American Ethnologist* 2: 535–52.

Sahlins, Marshall D. 1964. "Exchange Value and the Diplomacy of Primitive Trade." In *Essays in Economic Anthropology*, ed. J. Helm. Seattle: American Ethnological Society and the University of Washington Press.

_____.1964. "Culture and Environment: The Study of Cultural Ecology." In *Horizons of Anthropology*, ed. Sol Tax. Chicago: Aldine.

Sahlins, Marshall D. and Elman R. Service. 1960. *Evolution and Culture*. Ann Arbor: University of Michigan Press.

Steward, Julian. 1955. "The Concept and Method of Cultural Ecology." In *Theory of Culture Change*, ed. Julian Steward. Urbana: University of Illinois Press.

Stocking, George. 1968. *Race, Culture, and Evolution: Essays in the History of Anthropology*. New York: Free Press.

Westermeyer, Joseph. 1973. "Assassination and Conflict Resolution in Laos" *American Anthropologist* 75: 123–31.

White, Leslie A. 1958. "Science is Sciencing." In *The Science of Culture*, ed. Leslie A. White. New York: Grove.

_____ . 1959. "Man and Culture." In *The Evolution of Culture*, ed. Leslie A. White. New York: McGraw Hill.

Whitehead, Alfred North. 1929. *Process and Reality*. New York: Macmillan.

_____ . 1955. *Adventures of Ideas*. New York: Mentor Books.

Whitten, Norman and Dorothea Whitten. 1972. "Social Strategies and Social Relationships." In *Annual Review of Anthropology*, ed. B. Siegel. Palo Alto, CA: Annual Reviews.

3

Human Ecology as Human Behavior:
A Normative Anthropology of Resource Use
and Abuse

The Problem

The concept of culture was defined in chapter 2 as a set of descriptive generalizations made from observing behavior. It therefore follows that culture cannot be a cause of that same behavior. However, some of the empirical phenomena included in the traditional catchall conception of culture are undeniably influential in shaping concepts and practices related to the physical environment. These phenomena have differing roles to play in this complex process and therefore must be researched separately. For example, while ideology may influence, say, conceptions of the conservation of resources for the benefit of posterity, consumer desires may exert pressure in the opposite direction. To say that "culture" shapes or determines our use of the environment therefore has no precise meaning. It is necessary to specify what components of culture, in what circumstances, at what times. Moreover, it is necessary to translate these cultural elements into active behavioral tendencies: responses and adap-

This chapter is a rewritten version of a paper originally published as a chapter in the book *Human Behavior and Environment* (ed. I. Altman, A. Rapoport, and J.F. Wohlwill; vol. 4, *Environment and Culture*; New York: Plenum, 1980), supplemented by material from chap. 3 of Bennett's *Of Time and the Enterprise* (Minneapolis: University of Minnesota Press, 1982). The purpose of the paper was to suggest how anthropologists might view human behavior in an environmental context. I attempted to set such an analysis for contemporary industrial societies against interpretations of behavior in isolated tribal societies made by ecological anthropologists. Perhaps the burden of the argument is that modification of our present destructive environmental practices requires more than government regulation or humanistic exhortation but a basic change in culture and a realization that so long as we exploit and brutalize other human beings we will continue to treat Nature the same way.

tations made by real people in real-life contexts. That is, although human behavior is multipotential, at any point in the life cycle of individuals the number of possible responses to a given situation is in fact constrained by previous learning, standardized responses, and conventional values. Still, it is never possible to rule out completely novel and unforeseen responses.

Anthropologists also use the term "culture" to refer to distinctive life-styles associated with particular groups of people. In this usage, each "culture" might be considered to have its own pattern of adaptation to the physical environment. These could in turn be classified into types or stages of adaptation based on major subsistence patterns: hunting and gathering, pastoralism, settled agriculture, and so on.

Research on ecological adaptations to environments associated with culture types and stages contributed important information, but such typologies were not capable of dealing with adaptation as a behavioral process. Lacking the capacity to view human adaptation and use of the physical environment as a dynamic process, it was not possible for cultural ecologists to provide answers to the question of why humans do what they do to the environment (and to each other). Reasons and cures for particular forms of abuse are not easily found without a behavioral theory of use of the environment emphasizing distinctive characteristics of human behavior.

Since human engagement with the physical environment is multidimensional, it has been difficult to evolve a coherent unified theory of "human ecology."[1] Only philosophical approaches are available for synthesis, and generally these take an environmentalist form: the question of why humans abuse Nature when they know it is wrong or self-destructive, the importance of restraint in order to provide for posterity, the need to conceive of Nature as possessing "rights" and values, and the necessity for moral controls over excess and greed. Within the social sciences, at least, three important dimensions need study: the cultural, the institutional, and the behavioral. The first of these defines values and expectations concerning resources and the environment evolving in any population with relative social unity; the second, the means and ends of key activities; and the third, the distinctive patterns of individual need-satisfaction and coping mechanisms.

Social groups vary in the extent to which individual behavior is under the control of institutional rules. In societies with weak institutional controls, one also finds disjunction between the various social dimensions. A society with a well-publicized ideological respect for Nature can nevertheless exploit and degrade its resources if there are social elements which can safely ignore the ideology. Japan is a case: in the post-World War II period the government and the economic oligarchy considered economic growth to be more important than nature-respecting values in the aesthetic culture. But tribal cultures have similar problems: in the Sahel, for example, pastoralists who had achieved a stable balance between their population, herds, and vegetation for centuries began abusing their pasturage under the influence of economic development programs and the drawing of political boundaries which prevented normal transhumant movement. In this case, the forces accelerating degradational use of the habitat came from the outside; in the Japanese case the source of the impetus was both external and internal: Japan's need to contend with Western industrialism and the stimuli this brought to the economy and consumer wants.[2]

A normative psychology of environmental use[3] should carry the assumption that humans are multipotential organisms, whose varying capacities emerge and change as they deal with wants and survival necessities. This is a temporal process since it requires various degrees of anticipation, desire, foresight, and planning. As humans deal with the various contexts of existence (which include social and mental milieus) they create new problems, so that living becomes a matter of solutions to a chain of problems, each solution involving a combination of past precedents and present innovations.

From this it follows that to understand behavior one must view it both as a set of psychological processes that are probably universal, or nearly so, and as a set of novel behavioral responses adapted to particular times and situations. One must, therefore, know about institutions and precedents in order to determine why people do what they do in particular times and places. But this knowledge can never answer all questions. One must always allow for some emergent novelty in the situation, or simply a certain basic unpredictability as to which of the many possible or logical responses are likely to make their appearance. There are some generalizations at the cultural and institutional levels about the causes of the human abuse of the physical environment, but they do not work for all societies at all times. While resource abuse is a psychological problem, it is also a problem of how behavior is shaped by cultural values and social institutions.

A basic psychological aspect of behavior can be called the *tilt toward gratification* or, in terms of evolutionary processes, a tendency for people to engage in activities that result in exponential growth of gratification-oriented technology and economy. This process suggests that human behavior lacks a set of physiological or neural controls over gratification or goal accomplishment. The most salient example is the process of *relative deprivation*. Deprivation is, by and large, a subjective category, at both the individual and cultural levels. Deprivation is defined by the individual or the group on the basis of idiosyncratic and/or learned responses to a perceived loss of some kind or degree. In other words, it is difficult to establish a direct one-to-one relationship between the responses and any measurable quantitative change in the situation. The process operates at a psychological level, and thus deprivation can be felt with respect to material resources, commodities, privileges, and so on.

If humans are to control their wants or needs, they must do so by particularized responses to situations; or they must be constrained by available technology at given levels of development, by scarcity that is either natural or induced by humans, or, finally, by moral or legal controls. However one classifies these control measures, the point to be emphasized is that none of them can be assumed to operate automatically. Humans are not extensively or reliably subject (as are animals) to automatically operating controlling processes based on systemic rela-tionships and feedbacks, since humans can manipulate and change the systemic processes. However, the fact that human systems can be subject to governing forces *to a degree*—as, for example, in the case of tribal groups who lived by hunting and the gathering of vegetable foods—does not modify the fact that humans eventually overcome such forces and bend the physical environment in desired directions to serve gratification. In other words, no useful public purpose or policy objective can be served by treating the existence of homeostatic processes in human ecology as though they were the ultimate answer to environmental abuse. They are too easily overridden, as the exponential curves of population growth and energy use indicate.

Another important issue is the distinction between the control function at individual and at group or societal levels. An individual who has learned to control his wants is not necessarily the prototype of the group that uses fewer resources or abuses them least. That is, individual want-control can be irrelevant for group resource use-control, since, in the quest for control over the use of some resources, the group may abuse other resources (adaptive behavior in one context may be maladaptive in another). Moreover, low individual use can add up to high aggregate use by the group. Aside from the case of population increase, there are instances like some of the cultural dropout or hippie communities that appeared in wilderness areas during the 1960s and attempted to live in tune with natural processes but eventually became abusive of the environment. At a more imposing level, the quest for less abusive mass energy sources may simply introduce alternatives that have even more serious impacts. Moreover, the finding of alternatives to abusive practices, while satisfying behaviorally or cognitively, may not alter the basic institutional fact of abuse in a larger sense.

The Process of Adaptation

The concept of adaptation is central to the human use of the physical environment. In everyday usage, "adaptation" is a term that refers to change in modes of behavior designed to manage or improve the lot of the individual and the group. However, by applying the concept to both individuals and groups one obscures the obvious differences in the actual processes. Individuals "adapt" by a variety of behavioral modalities, with a variety of needs, objectives, and strategies. Group adaptation is simply the state of management of physical resources at any given time; it is described with terms of a second order of generalization, for example, "culture pattern," "subsistence system," "institutions," and so on. Individuals can be said to "cope"—innovate, improve, enhance, do better, bide time, and so on—but coping does not necessarily mean changed behavior if the individual assesses the situation and determines that maintenance of a given behavior will satisfy the circumstances. But the cognitive process involved in this decision recognizes the possibility of change. Any change in adaptive patterns in the group usually involves a collective decision, or at least a degree of discussion and often a considerable element of leadership, the exercise of power, or concession by leaders for the purpose of satisfying popular needs or demands. That is, adaptation at the group level is coincident with social action, interaction, and the dynamics of social organization and change. The use of the environment is taken inside society and the physical substances are transformed into "resources," that is, into aspects of culture. Modern economics is perhaps the most familiar example: the values assigned to the environment do not come from nature but from culture.

This means that the process of adaptation at any level in human behavior possesses an element of uncertainty and contradiction—just as any form of action behavior in a social system does equally. Thus:

1. What may be adaptive—that is, good—for the individual may be maladaptive—bad—for the group, and vice versa. The individual's gratifications may be at the expense of group welfare or continuity, or the group's solidarity may require individual sacrifice.

2. What may be adaptive for the individual or group may be maladaptive for the environment and vice versa. This is one basic problem in the contemporary environmental situation: in order to protect our resources or to shield ourselves and the environment against pollution, we must suffer deprivation or even endanger the survival of part of the human population.

Thus, while for scientific purposes it is possible to study the adaptive process objectively and without reference to values, for long-range solutions it is necessary to see it as a *normative*—really, moral—process. On a practical level, it means that we solve problems of environmental use and abuse by juggling contradictions that emerge out of the normative intersections described above and making trade-offs and compromises. As the conceptual and physical transformation of natural substances into cultural resources proceeds, these contradictions become more numerous: hence, adaptation becomes, in fact, identical to the interplay between them—as population increases, we adapt more to each other in order to resolve human-made contradictions than to the physical environment.

As described in the previous chapter, behavioral adaptation is based on the psychological factor of anticipation: foresight, memory, timebinding, and so on. There is an ability to envisage complex sequences of behavior over indefinite spans of time, even though the capacity of humans to institutionalize this as "planning" is severely limited and subject to power constraints, unforeseen consequences, and changes in attitudes and values. The importance of anticipation means that *time* is an inherent factor in adaptive processes, and temporal aspects of adaptation must always be studied if the movements of the behavioral systems are to be thoroughly understood. Adaptive behavior or "strategies" alone cannot determine the overall adaptive consequences of a particular sequence of events and processes. This is so because the time when the observation is made may be merely one point or phase of a complex process. Too many generalizations about human affairs, including the ecological, are made on the basis of incomplete understanding of the importance of temporal unfolding in adaptive processes.

The ability to envisage outcomes and anticipate gratification obviously facilitates the process of exponential accumulation. The establishment of *precedents* (anthropologists generally use the word "tradition") means that there is always a stimulus available in past accomplishment which can feed present desire. As already noted, the only reliable way this stimulus to accumulative action can be overcome is deliberately to limit its function by moral, social, or physical constraints. The problem with precedents is that they become embodied in institutions, where they become interrelated with other elements of the system and therefore extremely resistant to change. That is, the dynamic qualities of human existence are only one side of a complex system, the other being conservatism and resistance to change. This creates a classic paradox: one way to guarantee change is to preserve or conserve the precedents since by resisting changing them they might not be available at some future time to stimulate change. Thus, the behavioral and institutional levels of human action interrelate and create paradoxes for the scholar who works within only one dimension.

There is another paradox: adaptation by individuals involves both tolerance and also satisfaction of present conditions. Thus the term connotes both active and passive change in the individual. However, at the group level and over the course of history, altered milieus have generally provided a stimulus to change—Toynbee's "challenge and response"—rather than the opposite. In any case, tolerance of conditions has never formed an absolute limit or stopping point to aspiration: sooner or later a movement towards bettering or changing conditions begins. *Adaptive tolerance* merges with exploitation when vested interests utilize the ability of populations to "suffer in silence" in order to enhance their own wealth and power.

Embedded in adaptive tolerance is the process of comparative or relative choice: X may be bad, but one can tolerate it in order to obtain Y. In the environmental context, this frequently results in the tolerance of pollution if employment or income is related to the conditions producing the pollution. The process leads towards the search for means of avoidance or retreat before the polluted conditions or resource rather than elimination of the condition. An example is the mechanical filtering of impure air or water, instead of removing the industrial effluents that cause the impurity.

There is a high value placed on adaptation in the sense of coping or adjusting in all societies; it is, perhaps, one of the few "universal patterns" that older anthropologists spent so much effort searching for. Sometimes the concept of mastery over nature is linked to the normative process of coping, an especially common pattern in Western civilization since the Industrial Revolution and its increasingly adept transformation of physical substances into resources. In fact, the concept of "resource" is a recent one and a product of the linkage between superior coping skills and the superordination of human among the natural species. Once the concept of resource appears, then the way is clear to using resources without limit, restraint being produced only by the social means already noted.

The problem of the human relationship to nature is thus in one sense simply the quantitative accumulation of coping solutions—not solely to survival needs but to the needs or wants that emerge in the process of social living, with or without relationship to the state of physical phenomena. This detachment or alienation of humans from the physical processes and feedback that control the behavior of other species, and maintain balanced (though changing) systems for those species is perhaps the most general cause of our mounting ecological problems and has given rise to a literature that has attempted to formulate a behavioral ethic more closely integrated with natural processes (e.g., Dubos 1969, Hardin 1972, Leopold 1949). This is an essential preliminary step towards reasserting control, but it cannot do the job alone. Values constitute only one of the several necessary modes of control over behavior and the institutions that stimulate this behavior.

The Process of Rational Choice

One guiding principle of human behavior in the context of use and abuse of resources is the choice of alternative goals and the strategies to achieve them.[4] This process of choice is rooted in human psychology, stimulated and reinforced by industrial society, and elaborated by economic theorists. Rational choice becomes meaningful only in relation to real issues and purposes, not vaguely defined or artificial categories. One must be concerned with *what* humans strive to accomplish; there must be sensitivity to the intrinsic nature of the goals that shape the direction and intensity of behavior. This material or empirical significance of choice is one reason why it appeared as a theory initially in consumption economics: humans want things; this was seen as the, or a, guiding force in society, a force that has become more significant as control over the transformation of material substance into resources has progressed (the materialistic element has, of course, been overgeneralized to apply to sectors where it is inappropriate).

The basis of rational choice is a form of thought involving the comparison of two or more goals in order to choose among them or to effect a compromise. Usually an intervening third factor will influence the choice or trade-off. Undoubtedly animals make such choices, although the mental processes may not involve cognition in the full human sense. Humans make rational choices on an anticipatory basis: the choice between two or more possible goals and wants is made partly on the basis of expected differences in future gains or losses. The classical paradigm of rational choice is represented as a right-angled diagram with desired phenomena on the two axes; for more than two choices, one must construct more complex diagrams or break the paradigm into two or more two-valued sequences (e.g., if x, y, and z are wanted, then paradigmatically the chooser must decide between x and y, x and z, and y and z). The advantage of this paradigm is that the diagrammatic logic apparently often approximates the actual sequences and patterns of thought. There is probably no other abstract model in the social sciences that comes so close to actual mental processes. While the process is limited in scope, since it cannot easily handle aesthetic and egocentric values and choices, it remains an important tool for the analysis of the behavioral components of resource use and abuse.

To begin, it is necessary to consider that rational choice takes place in a social field, not in a vacuum (or, in Herbert Simon's terms, "bounded rationality"). The resource user receives signals from many sources: his associates, neighbors, competitors, government, the economic marketplace, and the media. The rationality of the choices and decisions made is thus always "substantive," which means that allowance has been made for contrasting or conflicting demands, and therefore the choices are

vectorial compromises. This means that pure quantitative rationality—
for example, maximization of profits, or the most at the least cost—is an
ideal type and rarely found in real life. Its ideal typicality is useful in
creating models and criteria for analysis, but there is always a danger that
people will confuse the real with the ideal, as has been done repeatedly
with the "economic man" concept. The fact that choice is made in a
substantive and constraining social milieu does not compromise the
degree of rationality involved: the thought process of comparative choice
is the same, whether the choice is made in a theoretically pure uninflu-
enced self-interested vacuum, or whether it is made in a complex milieu,
with winds blowing from every direction.

The element of time is represented in the process by the anticipation
of future gains. That is, the choice between the phenomena in the
two-valued model is made on the basis of which of the two will produce
the most satisfaction in the future ("expected utility"). In the more
elementary applications in economics this element of time is not really
measured but is rather taken as a given. In more sophisticated sociological versions either or both of the axes may represent not only quantities
to be gained by choices but also the *change* in these quantities over time.
This will become clearer in a moment. The process of decision or choice
culminates in a *trade-off* in the type case: a gain along one value or choice
axis usually implies a loss along some other, and the ideal solution is, of
course, a choice point where exactly the same amount of satisfaction can
be gained for both, in relationship to third factors (this process creates
the so-called "indifference curve"). In such a case no trade-off is involved. Whether a trade-off must occur or an equalization or gain can be
achieved depends on the phenomena themselves.

In any case, it is important to underline the fact that outcomes depend
on situational factors, including behavior patterns and cultural definitions. In real situations of choice this can become extremely complex,
since each phenomenon is accompanied by many other factors. In some
situations the choice will be governed by powerful elements which
themselves may represent needs; for example, a choice between two
phenomena, say profit and social influence, may be resolved by another
valued phenomenon, say the adherence to some ritual behavior pattern
which confers prestige. Thus the chooser may decide to take less profit
in order to gain influence over others by behaving in prescribed ways.

The choice of a particular line of action or goal can be influenced by factors emanating from the social milieu or process and not only by the condition of the resource itself. As social systems become more complex, the likelihood of a decision on environmental matters being made on purely pro-Nature, conservationist grounds is lessened, and the risk of abuse accordingly increases. Thus humans can abuse their resources even though they know they are doing so since other values have emerged that dictate abusive exploitation, and these values cannot be resisted. This is not an abnormal situation, but it is the rule because it is a reflection of the institutions emerging out of behavior that then feed back to channel subsequent behavior.

An Example: Agricultural Resource Use and Decision-Making

To exemplify one application of these ideas we shall present a simplified paradigm of agricultural resource use, based on the diagrams, figures 3.1 and 3.2.[5] Figure 3.1 shows the rate of resource depletion varying in accordance with particular strategies used; and figure 3.2 a particular variable strategy, which includes the three idealized possibilities in figure 3.1 represented as alternative choices made over a period of time. Taking figure 3.1 first:

Resource depletion is deliberately simplified here as a function of desired yield. The higher the yield, the more rapid the rate of depletion. Obviously, many factors affect depletion other than desired yield alone. However, "desired yield" is used here as a kind of central or summary factor to suggest that in the long run the human use of resources—the demand placed upon them—will result in their change or depletion. All use curves thus should be convex to the point of origin of the diagram: over time, use of any physical resource will serve to deplete it. What is called "sustained-yield use" is simply a time function: ultimately, the use will change the resource beyond recovery. However, there are degrees of this; time is a variable; alternative resources can be found; and so on through a number of qualifying possibilities.

In any case, figure 3.1 shows three idealized possibilities: A, B, and C. A is the high-yield, rapid-depletion case; C is the low-yield, low-depletion case; and B is the moderate-yield, moderate-depletion case. Relating these to existing strategies in North American agriculture, A represents the "hit hard and get out" or "get rich quick" strategy, in which no thought is given to the condition of the resource in the future. C is the classic low-population, low-energy utilization strategy characteristic of tribal environmental use. In modern terms, however, it might describe the careful underutilization strategies followed by conservative ranchers, whose grazing acreage is large enough to permit income satisfaction from the beef produced with minimal use of pasture. One of the key problems of human resource ecology is to determine just which factors of economic scale, population size, and income demand may influence the choice of a strategy of resource use. One suspects that this cuts through the classic culturally defined levels of socioeconomic complexity (herders, farmers, and so on). If this is true, it is clear that these older typologies could impede construction of an adequate theory of resource ecology in human societies since it perpetuates disciplinary boundaries that make it difficult for students of, say, tribal-peasant society to communicate effectively with economists and other specialists concerned with contemporary societies.

Depletion curve B is a medium-use or medium-yield curve, which like A will eventually deplete the resource, but at a moderate rate. To know if the rate is moderate implies the existence of specific information on the quick degradational effect of a higher yield; and the extreme caution, or ignorance, implied by curve C. That is, B represents in some respects a more sophisticated type of strategy than either of the others, perhaps behaviorally a very different approach, not just a midpoint of some kind. This, if true, suggests that while yield and resource depletion are continuous quantitative functions, the behavioral strategies expressing them are qualitatively different. This denotes the importance of understanding the behavioral and institutional bases of particular resource use strategies and the reason for not reducing them to quantitative least common denominators. The crux of the issue is the nature of the knowledge and the attitudes which permit the exact location of curve B with respect to a particular resource use pattern. Since knowledge is relative to the general cognitive milieu, there is always a degree of uncertainty because of incomplete information. However, if incentive exists to locate such a strategy curve B may become easier to locate.

Now let us turn to figure 3.2. This figure defines a typical pattern of variable resource use as it might be found in an agricultural producer's environment like the Great Plains, where there are known risks of serious abuse of resources but, at the same time, variable pressures emanating

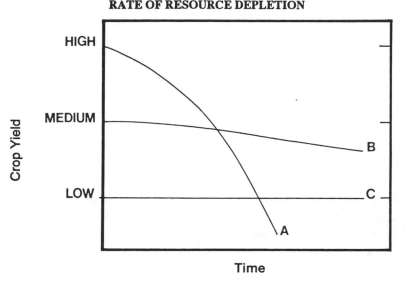

Figure 3.1
RATE OF RESOURCE DEPLETION

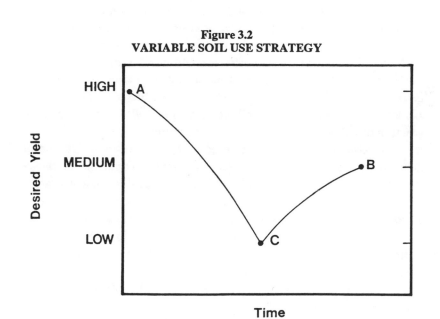

Figure 3.2
VARIABLE SOIL USE STRATEGY

from the market and consumer culture for income. The V-shaped curve shown in figure 3.2 is that of a producer who varies his strategies, moving from A to C, then to B; that is, he risks resource abuse one year by choosing a high yield (going for broke), then compensates (overcompensates?) by moving down to a very safe choice, C; then attempts to regain a balanced strategy by proceeding to B. While this type of mixed strategy is typical for agriculturalists in high-risk and and marginal-resource environments, something like it is characteristic of most resource regimes, and the problem it presents is the necessity to take account of strategy choices over extended periods of time in order to be certain just which average or vector is being followed. For example, if the producers whose choices for three time points follow the pattern in figure 3.2 and if the amount of abuse is proportionate to the concepts of high, medium, and low, then the descent to C and the return to B at regular intervals compensates for the abuse displayed by the recurrent choice at A. However, once again the complexities of the situation make this logic doubtful of application in all cases. Nature may "bounce back" only in particular types of resources. As already suggested, the resource situation in Nature is a kind of zero-sum game: once used, never returned, or only partly returned. This finite function is, of course, qualified by stretch-out of the depletion rate in more conservationist strategies, which, as previously suggested, may allow sufficient time for finding substitutes or accumulating better information about strategies. However, where the mixed strategy course illustrated in figure 3.2 does work, we may consider it an optimal one, since both *reasonable* yield and *reasonable* protection of the resource are achieved over time.

Another common phenomenon in contemporary resource utilization systems is the location of curve B at some higher level than the one shown on the diagrams as medium. That is, a high or physically abusive strategy may be *culturally defined* as "medium." This contingency has been analyzed as a function of defective information, but it also commonly occurs deliberately, even in the face of available knowledge to the contrary. Such strategies are then "sold" or urged upon producers for various reasons, and they may become established as a kind of illusion of conservation. We saw examples in the 1970s and 1980s in the form of attractive advertisements produced by extractive industries like oil and timber, designed to give the impression that they are following sustained-yield practices whereas in fact they may not be doing so.

Embedded in this situation are the basic ethical and moral questions of contemporary ecological relations. Why do people abuse resources, thereby jeopardizing posterity, when they know, or at least suspect, that they are doing so? How can people value present gain over future losses or disaster? The answers to these questions do not lie wholly within the domain of psychology but perhaps more importantly in institutions that free the individual from group responsibilities, since present gratification is considered a right rather than a privilege. Perhaps the gratification orientation, which is fundamental in human behavior, will give rise to these hedonistic institutions eventually in all cases, but this does not necessarily mean we are powerless to control them.

Examples of the applicability of this elementary model can be taken from livestock production (recalling that Garret Hardin's 1968 classic "tragedy of the commons" behavioral paradigm was also based on cattle and their pasturage). Such an example serves to remind us that the strategy choices and their effects on yield depletion or sustainment will vary depending on the particular set of opportunities and constraints peculiar to the resource itself—in this example, pasture. In livestock production the basic ratio of constraint to opportunity is expressed as "carrying capacity," the maximum number of animals that can be supported at a given level of nutrition by the forage produced with a particular technique. If the present carrying capacity of a pasture is five animals to the acre for a grazing year and there are ten acres available, then a yield of fifty animals can be achieved with, presumably, a resource sustained-yield condition, i.e., the choice of technique represented by curve B. Let us also say that this sustained-yield (year after year) condition can be obtained by ten acres *only* if the land is grazed in yearly rotation on several adjoining ten-acre plots, so that overuse of any one plot is avoided. Thus the particular technique chosen becomes a crucial factor.

Now, if this defines the conservationist strategy at the existing curve B, the resource user can also visualize several other possible alternatives. He can, first, move up to A in years when rainfall is exceptional, so that he can produce more animals at relatively little risk of abuse of his grass. But if he increases his herd *without* a corresponding increase in resource capacity, he endangers his grass. However, this may be possible if he falls back on the third year to C, thereby allowing his pasturage to recover. This alternating type of strategy is called, in this example, the rotational grazing system. In other words, the optimal movement between strategies is assisted by the particular resource use technique. Obviously, not all resource use situations have this feature. In fact, each one is unique. An entirely different strategy pattern must be followed, for example, if the user decides to supplement his grass by irrigated forage production.

Let us consider this case, because it could involve the "illusion" mentioned earlier. That is, it suggests that, under human manipulation, B is not fixed but can move, depending on technology and knowledge. Such movement is extremely common and is a capsulized definition of the overall grand strategy of North American and other resource economies that have been influenced by the North American (or, generally, market-capitalist) model. The question that arises, however, is whether the move to higher production levels is really yield- or resource-sustaining. Fertilizer use is a case in point: it has been assumed that by putting fertilizer on the soil one achieves higher yield without harming the soil. However, it is now known that many artificial fertilization techniques are harmful in various ways and may gradually reduce the capacity of the soil to sustain plant growth.

One additional dimension needs discussion. This is the problem of *uncertainty* and *risk*.[6] The definitions used here view risk as the assessment of the degree of uncertainty. How much risk is perceived or measured will certainly influence the choice of technique or strategy, but it would appear that there is no simple relationship. That is, the relationship between the state of the resources, the goals sought, and the techniques chosen depends on combinations of these factors and on others not mentioned, particularly those related to conditions in the marketplace that will help set the intensity of the goals. If the goal of financial gain is strong and the pressures from the market such as to make satisfaction of that goal advisable or urgent, then risks will be minimized and resource abuse becomes highly probable. If the risk is still great, resource practices are still likely to tend towards the abusive because the goal system is powerful; hence, the user is in a mood to "take risks."

When goals are moderate to weak—that is, not particularly pressing— and risk perception high, then resource use is likely to be conservationist. There is little doubt that economic depressions have generally resulted in a letup in abusive practices, and prosperity and growth in an increase. However, there are exceptions, particularly in resource contexts where poverty or the small scale of operations result in practices that are abusive because the capital available to make them less so, through technological means, is not available. In other words, technology is another variable that has its effects on the equations; as it evolves the relationship between risk and resource use also varies. But, in general, and over a period of time, a fall in economic values or a rise in prices (the same thing) tends to result in overall lessening of resource abuse.

There are related considerations pertaining to economic scale. In some production regimes large scale may result in resource protection. Examples can be found in some of the large ranches in the North American West, where land and water supplies are large enough to permit income satisfaction at lower levels of livestock yield, or in the case of large timber companies where capital is sufficient to finance reforestation and other conservationist practices. On the other hand, large-scale production can lead to severe resource abuse where the economic goals are rapacious or where production is controlled by external ownership that is concerned only with "making a quick buck and getting out."

The preceding discussion is based on agricultural resource practices, and since the conduct of agriculture in modern nations is based on capitalist concepts of productive efficiency and yield, the rational-choice model is relevant for the analysis. For resource practices guided by subsistence considerations or where supernatural considerations influence the measurement and value of human effort, the rational-choice and maximization models would be of lesser significance. In addition, if our problem shifted from food production resources to such activities as the preservation of threatened species, natural landscapes, or wilderness areas, the application of these economistic models is difficult and often wildly inappropriate—for the reason that it is extremely difficult to assign monetary or "market" values to such commodities: their values are cultural, not financial—although, as noted, it may be necessary to find some economic value if they are to be preserved (consequently, the hocus-pocus of benefit-cost analysis).

In general, conservation aims are ill served by the pure concept of economic interest. As Aldo Leopold pointed out a long time ago, ultimately an economic model of the value of Nature devolves upon the individual because the models themselves are based upon the individual as the unit of decision and choice. And since economic values are not inherent in Nature but must be assigned to it by Society or by individuals who care, there is no guarantee of a general conservationist ethic. Such an ethic might emerge, but not *via* economic values.

In these considerations, as in all others, it is important to remember that the configurations of resource use vary greatly from resource to resource and from situation to situation: there are few across-the-board generalizations other than the basic behavioral processes we have been describing. The overall quotient of resource abuse must be determined from empirical studies of many significant contexts; it cannot be determined on theoretical grounds or limited-factor observations. The system of resource use is governed by an unfolding and changing matrix of comparative choices that vary sensitively by changing circumstances; and while we know in general the process that guides these choices, we cannot determine their precise vectors or the dynamics of the relationships between all the contributing factors without empirical study.

Adaptive Styles and the Problem of Control

In the preceding sections, we mentioned the case of tribal societies that appear to maintain, for relatively long periods at any rate, styles of adaptation which underuse or preserve resources (point C on figure 3.1). This section will examine this problem with the help of some research by anthropological ecologists. The underlying premise is that the scale of resource use and abuse is influenced by situation, levels of economic-technological development, and various cultural elements. The interrelationship of these factors is so complex that it has been only recently that we have begun to understand how adaptive styles are established and maintained. The policy issue here is whether the fact that some human societies have been able to avoid progressive or exponential resource exploitation might give us some hope that the present situation can be brought under control.

The story begins with the ecologically simplest societies known: the nomadic bands of hunters and gatherers that have populated refuge areas like deserts and rainforests in recent times but were much more widespread before food producing began.[7] In fact, the longest span of *Homo sapiens* history—roughly from about 100,000 years ago to about 4,000 years ago, when food-producing spread rapidly—was lived out in the context of the nomadic food-collecting style. Given the intelligence and behavior of *Homo sapiens*, there has always been a question as to why this period lasted so long. Various answers have been given. One is biological—that the prevailing hominid varieties were less evolved intellectually and the thrust towards a more sophisticated style required the presence of *Homo sapiens*. Then, there is the challenge-and-response theory: archaeological evidence that suggests that the onset of the last glacial period, with its climatic change, reduction in available game, and migrations provided the necessary stimulus for more intensive adaptations. Other approaches emphasize fortuitous factors: accidental dropping of plants that could grow in human loci or the gradual association of animal species with human groups—both of these processes leading eventually to selective change and the emergence of tame varieties of plants and animals.

The precise sequence of events will never be known in full, and perhaps the problem of origins is mainly an academic or scholarly one. Historically, progressively more intensive uses of resources *did* appear; this has encouraged or reinforced the thought and behavioral patterns already described, and it is the cumulative results of this process that create our present problems. So we can turn to the living remnants of the earlier, simpler styles to see how the controls were exercised—or, whether the concept of control over resource use really applies to such cases.

The first issue to be dealt with is that of the relatively static populations of these bands of hunters and gatherers. Obviously, their populations did increase slowly, since eventually this style of adaptation covered the earth. However, when these people retreated into refuge areas their populations appear to have become more stable, so that natural increase seems to have maintained only that population that could subsist on the resources made available by simple subsistence techniques. However, in other cases hunting and gathering peoples were capable of dynamic and expansionist styles: the Plains Indians, once they incorporated Spanish horses into their cultures, are a good example; and the evidence from the cave art in the case of the postglacial European *Homo sapiens sapiens* population suggests another vigorous episode. Hunter-gatherer populations of this type can exert considerable pressure on resources: the effect of Indian firing of grass on the Great Plains in the course of bison herding and hunting is a case in point. And there is a theory which suggests that the extinction of some of the great Pleistocene mammals may have been due to human hunting pressure (Martin and Klein 1984).

So we are really examining a particular case of hunting and gathering populations: those who were restricted to bounded territories and who therefore had to work out some kind of control system that restrained resource use and population growth. Most of the research available in the early 1980s came from two sources: the !Kung Bushmen of the Kalahari Desert in Africa, studied by Richard Lee (1972a) and an East Africa forest group, the Hadza, studied by James Woodburn (1972). Additional, but less complete, data for Central African pygmy bands had been contributed by Colin Turnbull (1972). In these studies an effort was made to locate unspoiled or aboriginal populations; but these are becoming rare or nonexistent in the modern world, and questions have been raised as to the validity of some of the findings as referring to truly aboriginal groups. Moreover, as I have suggested, the refuge character of these populations probably is mainly responsible for their extraordinary stability; that is, this static character is itself an adaptation to circumstances that created a need for low-risk strategies.

As for slow population growth, Lee (1972b) proposed that the nomadic way of life is disadvantageous for childbirth. Women must carry infants on their backs, and this would tend to lengthen birth intervals, since they cannot carry more than one—although the older children are usually pressed into service on this, so that the argument does not carry conviction. But there are other factors: the need for women to perform much work connected with plant food gathering and the general physical stresses of the way of life. Lee feels that all these factors combined to reduce birth rates, and his findings seem to be reinforced by his studies of Bushman groups which have become sedentary and are supported by wage labor and agriculture. These groups have shortened birth intervals and higher fertility rates.

Woodburn's data on the Hadza featured a different set of factors: the interrelationship of various social components to produce restraint in fertility and also resource use and development (1972). The key factor is what he calls the threat of conflict, which increases when group size becomes larger. This tends to reinforce small band size, which in turn creates a distinctive social world into which people are socialized, a world of extreme intimacy with a very small number of people, all relatives. Once this exists, the adult individual finds it extremely difficult to adjust or adapt to a more heterogeneous and larger social situation.

A third major factor, cited by both Lee and Woodburn and by several other anthropologists, is the influence of nomadic life on work output and the related factor of subsistence intake. There are several facets here, some of them partially contradictory. One is the fact that the hunter-gatherer adaptation can, when resources are abundant, be a remarkably easy life, since only a short time is needed to collect enough food to satisfy basic needs. This case of subsistence can be attractive in comparison with tribal agriculture, which presumably requires more labor; hence, hunter-gatherer groups on the margins of agricultural populations would tend to preserve their less arduous means of subsistence. Another factor is the lack of food storage facilities and the corresponding emphasis on short-term accumulations—a pattern called by Marshall Sahlins (1972) an orientation towards survival rather than towards wealth or property accumulation. This orientation in turn produces an emphasis on cooperative sharing of food or personal acquisition of anything tends to be negatively valued. Again, once this orientation is established, the argument goes, it tends to be self-reinforcing, and conscious administration or regulations need not be used.

Well, this might be. There is, of course, an element of tautology in all such explanations, but they do shed some light on the issue of stability: the conditions that permit or direct human populations to live in a static or homeostatic relationship to nature. "Homeostatic" is in fact the more appropriate term, since it allows for fluctuation around various points; for example, it should be assumed that population probably fluctuated with resource availabilities, droughts, and so on, rather than remained absolutely static. Such conditions were, quite simply, extraordinary. Rather than supply us with models we might copy today, these cases tell us that control over resource use can become automatic or systemic—that is, built into the social system—only under special and remote circumstances. The key factors are low-energy technology, geographic isolation, spatial boundedness, and small populations. Humans under such conditions sooner or later learn to control population growth and also their own wants.

Nomadic food collection is not the only adaptational mode that possesses control over use of resources. Another is the sectarian agricultural societies associated with various cultural traditions. Most of them are found in the Western world, where they represent an alternative interpretation of Christian principles. There are somewhat similar groups, principally monastic, in Asia. All these groups have perhaps four major features: an emphasis on humility before God and/or Nature; a conscious taboo on personal wealth and excessive consumption generally (that is, an austerity ethic); economic institutions based on the idea that most property and wealth belongs to the group, not to the individual; and decision-making procedures requiring maximum participation of the group membership. The groups vary with respect to their attitude towards population growth, their use of technology, and their degree of contact with the outside world and the institutions of growth economics.[8]

In this mixture of characteristics there exist the seeds of care in dealing with resources and the environment in general: humility tends to reinforce the idea that humans must respect Nature because she is the powerful source of sustenance; communal property means that the group has a collective responsibility for resources, which tends to guarantee care and conservation; the austerity ethic means that consumption pressures tend to be low, removing one major stimulus to resource abuse; and, since these groups believe they have a special mission in the world (as true of the secular versions as for the religious), they tend to believe they will last forever and therefore their resources are a sacred trust which must be husbanded for future generations—that is, the "posterity ethic." Conservationism is rarely an explicit philosophy: the optimal conservationist practices are *de facto* results of these views and practices (although most Hutterite colonies use appropriate extension literature and make contact with specialists in agricultural schools).

This set of institutions and cultural elements differs from case to case, and not all factors lead to conservationism in all groups. In addition, the external forces of the market may force such groups to abuse their resources out of sheer survival necessity, or out of needs to maintain solidarity with each other or with neighbors. And some of the factors are not completely determinative of conservation but only tend to be—for example, consumption austerity does not preclude the possibility, as represented by some kibbutzim and Hutterite colonies, of the establishment of a high *collective* level of consumption, which can exert as much pressure on income, and accordingly on resources, as high *individual* levels. But the conservationist tendencies are very strong; the mix of factors generally does produce more respect and care for physical resources than individualistic entrepreneurial behavior.

The collective agrarian societies show that it is possible for a modern group to develop controls over environmental use on the basis of a self-conscious and articulate philosophy or theology, implemented, of course, by specific institutional practices and forms of decision making that keep the controls operative. Moreover, controls are built into the social system and beliefs in an effective way: they have a clear "sacred" rationale that is reinforced by intensive indoctrination. In individualistic or entrepreneurial systems of resource use, controls have to be levied *against* the individuals or groups by external agencies and forces, and this is always difficult. There is too much room for people to manipulate the system, and the institution breeds dislike and resentment.

In the late 1950s Walter Firey (1957) was concerned with the problem of individualistic resource strategies in his studies of the behavior of agriculturalists and other groups in West Texas using ground water for irrigation. He examined a variety of documents—newspaper editorials, policy statements, farm organization literature, and so on, in an effort to discover the logic and rationale for control of the practice of well drilling, which was beginning to endanger the water table. He found that the language of the statements dealing with the situation always included references to government *regulation* of well drilling and water use, if conservation of water was seen to be important to the welfare of the community. There were few appeals to some higher morality of conservation or to individual integrity. The materials carried an implicit assumption that Texas farmers and industrial water users would not voluntarily curtail their use of water in the interest of conservation alone; they would have to be required or compelled to do so. Firey also noted that the literature that defined the way in which water was to be used as a resource always assumed that the individual had a right to use all of the water he needed without waiting for a group consensus on use strategies. This is perhaps an extreme "Texas" version of entrepreneuring individualism, and in recent years Texas water users, helped by those regulations, have developed more cooperative and cautious strategies, although the problem of abuse remains serious. But the example makes a sharp contrast to the cases of the communal societies just presented, where it is inconceivable that government regulation would be required to curtail abuses of the community's own water supply.

The "Social Limits to Growth"

These ethnic styles of production and consumption contain important lessons and implications for our problem, but they do not focus on the modern dilemma in its pure form: how to control our use and abuse of resources in a world society that is increasingly committed to the proposition of high economic growth rates and their apparent promise of prosperity and gratification for all. The setting of this problem is familiar enough: we all live off each other's backs; what we consume is no longer our own affair but depends on and influences the consumption of everyone. This is true not only for the nations, taken as consumers, but for the individual.

As Fred Hirsch (1977) notes, the distinctions cherished by economists between public and private goods no longer make much sense, just as the belief that resources are there for the taking by the entrepreneur no longer makes sense, when dependence on resources becomes even more dispersed across the world.[9] Out of this problem comes collectivism, political or social, acknowledged or covert, since it means that to meet the demand for equity there is need for control. It means that the simple necessities of life are no longer "free public goods" but are rapidly becoming resources which need to be husbanded and protected. It means that the more insistent the demands and the more attempts there are to meet them the greater the scarcity value of the resource and therefore the greater need to move that resource into the domain of social control.

In the previous discussions I focused on the producer and his decision to use, conserve, or overuse the supply. But in this section we shift our emphasis to the consumer. We are concerned with his demands on the system and how these demands limit the supply and require its control. The proposition to be examined is whether these demands themselves constitute a limiting process, a form of automatic control. In previous passages we have been pessimistic about the possibility of automatic or systemic controls, since our argument was based on a series of behavioral processes that can produce insatiable wants and which cannot easily be brought under control because of insitutional reinforcements. Here we speculate that because of the magnitude of the wants and their attempted satisfaction by a growth-oriented production system, the institutional system itself may eventually have to develop its own constraints. This does not necessarily lend itself to optimism because institutional constraints in this case are equivalent to political challenge and upheaval. The problems are found not only in the hyper-developed countries but also of the developing world, where rising expectations have created insistent demands on an unprecedented scale.

Although the argument emphasizes institutions, it is underlain by behavioral considerations. We are still confronted by the proclivity of humans to want things, to require that material substances and social arrangements be reorganized to supply needs and wants. The engine continues to be driven by the human desire for gratification and the adaptive behavioral process as we have defined it. But once these demands create social values and institutions for their satisfaction, these arrangements give rise to new constraints and opportunities, and these forces begin to generate their own consequences. The process begins to assume the characteristics of a self-generating but also degenerative system, but its automatic qualities are ambiguous since there is widespread knowledge of its workings among the experts. What the experts cannot do is modify the political process to take account of impending disasters. The political system generally lags behind the operations of the economic—the want-satisfying and resource-creating—system.

Reverting for the moment to the arguments in the section on rational choice, we proposed that the root of the problem is to be found in the choices made by the individual. We also observed that from the standpoint of the individual, his wants are either satisfied or not and that this is the foundation of modern market-capitalist economic theory. The possibility that these satisfactions may result in deprivation for all or in the loss of resource capacity is not included as a normal or anticipated possibility. The basic issue is one of scarcity: if my wants are satisfied, they may be so at the expense of yours. This possibility was remote in a world where most people got along on less or where population was small in proportion to the supply of resources. But in a world of increasing population and increasing demands for gratification, it becomes a real and ever-present possibility. Moreover, it is not merely a problem of spreading deprivation but also of environmental abuse. Demands tend to become insatiable; there can be no stable satisfaction level so long as the culture lacks moral restraints on wants.

We should give more attention to the definition of scarcity. Economists focus on material scarcities: shortages of particular commodities or objects that can be produced in larger quantities when the demand exists.

The assumption that scarcities are simply material is the necessary assumption behind the concept of economic growth; growth is an attempt to alleviate scarcities, however they may be defined. Scarcity is always relative to something: I may have a great deal of something until I see that you have more, and then I have little.

Thus scarcity, like feelings of deprivation, is on a sliding scale; it is basically subjective. Therefore, without definitions, there is no end to it; in modern populations the relativity of scarcity tends to work towards an ever-rising scale of wants. Second, scarcity is not based solely on material phenomena. There are several classes of scarce phenomena which do not depend on quantity but wholly on social judgments and the distribution of nonmaterial phenomena in social organization. The classic case is, of course, leadership: only a few can lead or rise to positions of power and prestige because the social meaning of leadership is based on an unequal distribution of roles in a population. The best one can do is try to guarantee a rotation or circulation of such roles, something that is successful only in small communities, where the number of people is not much greater than the number of elite positions. Or, in a nutshell, scarcity rooted in unequal distributions of social phenomena is in a sense not scarcity; it is simply a way to create the meaning or value of something. Another example is fads and the small hobby or participation groups that form around them. They gain their value from the fact that *relatively* few people follow them. Without this snob appeal, they lose meaning and are abandoned.

Another class of social judgments involving a concept of scarcity is the pressure to maintain or attain states of being that become increasingly scarce or hard to obtain because of the very attempt to satisfy them. Solitude and peace of mind become increasingly scarce in an ever more crowded society; as ski slopes become more crowded with skiers, it becomes increasingly difficult or frustrating to indulge in the sport. Automobiles for a time became ever more powerful until, only just recently, in the 1970s, the possibility of using that power on increasingly crowded roads and at reasonable levels of accident diminished to the point where a rollback in the power vector commenced (really caused by manufacturing costs and constraints in petroleum supply—i.e., social constraints).

As these patterns emerge people sometimes exhibit a curious *desire* for scarcity—the opposite of the classical economic theory of the desire to alleviate shortages. That is, while the individual may perceive that something is scarce because more and more people seeking it deprive him of the chance of getting it, he also begins to seek out other things that are rare (scarce) in order to find substitute gratifications. No better example of the subjective-social nature of scarcity can be found. Scarcity turns out not to be based on absolute quantity but on any quantity of anything that is perceived as rare, special, meaningful, etc. The individual is frustrated by scarcity but attempts to alleviate his frustration by finding scarce goods.

This seemingly paradoxical situation is brought about by several forces, but the major fact is probably the fact that social scarcities do not usually have collective impact. That is, not all social scarcities affect all individuals: we select our scarcities, so to speak. The fact that I may be deprived or frustrated by heavy traffic and therefore must take the bus does not mean that I will lose my desire for going on weekend trips in the car. That is, I may use my car just as much as I would anyway and thereby continue to contribute my share to the general disorder produced by automobiles. Or, I may discover that automobiles are a nuisance and stop all traveling; or, if this all happens when I retire and will stay home anyway, then I will not suffer the frustrations associated with growth-induced scarcities. Since in the industrial countries there was by 1990 no large-scale convergence of deprivations, there is no general perception of the general need to reduce the scale of wants and to change the "greed" compulsion to attempt to meet these wants. Hardin's concept of the "tragedy of the commons" proposed that resources may be consumed because individuals are concerned only with their particular share of a resource needed by everyone. When everyone comes to share this view of the right to a share, demand increases to the point of exhaustion of the resource.

This process also generates economic growth. Sometimes this may be seen as socially beneficial and also not necessarily harmful to the resource base. For example, dissatisfaction with processed foods gave rise to the natural foods movement, which supplies "old-fashioned" foodstuffs at high prices to those people who want them. In such an arena the choice and relative abundance is maintained. But for every relatively benign case of this kind there will be many more which generate undesirable consequences in overuse of resources, pollution, increased density, and so on.

Now the central element in this process is the shift of the definition of value from intrinsic quality or social morality to individual gratification. That is, the meaning of consumption in the pre-growth age—which in general is all of human history up until the Industrial Revolution—was provided by either (1) some intrinsic quality like aesthetic complexity or skill—another social scarcity—or (2) the relationship of the phenomenon to some moral or social-consensus component of the culture. Fine art is an example of the former; the parlor recreations of the family group in the nineteenth century of the latter. These types of meaning or satisfaction are not dead, of course, but they have been transformed and overlain by purely material, individualistic-hedonistic, or status-prestige factors. It might be argued that the latter—prestige phenomena—represent the old type of social value, but the difference is that in true social morality the activity or object is given meaning by how it helped or gratified *alter*, other people, the collectivity. Contemporary prestige value tends to be purely selfish, representing only the attainment by the ego of some positional badge or status.

For the time being, the industrial societies must find constraints in the form of government regulation and control, since there is no consensus in a pluralistic culture in which every desire and every concept of scarcity is conceived as equally valid. This introduces the familiar dilemma: while everyone admits that control is needed, the only form the system will tolerate is governmental; yet we consider government control a form of tyranny! We can recall Walter Firey's findings with regard to the Texas well-drilling farmers: the voices of the media and the establishment encouraged individualistic and self-interested use of the water on the one hand and the desperate need for governmental regulation of this behavior on the other. The intermediate process—the need for a genuine cooperative consensus—is ignored. It may emerge, and sometimes it does when things get very bad, but there is no social guarantee, and the record, overall, is not promising. Such a lack of consensus is one of the dangers inherent in the system of individualistic pluralism.

We then have the following alternatives:

1. We can drift towards increasingly severe regulatory mechanisms designed to control our personal consumption, our use of resources, and, eventually, our needs and desires. These regulations will contribute to the growth of huge impersonal bureaucracies—as they already do—which will use increasingly devious manipulatory methods, since polit-

ical values decry direct or overt control. This process is underway in all industrial countries, regardless of the particular form of political economy.

2. We can let things go along pretty much as they are—that is, permit the growth mechanism to continue operating with only moderate development of regulation—and allow for Hirsch's "social limits to growth" (1977) to manifest themselves on the basis of an assumption that in fact they will do so. But perhaps the social limits to growth are simply the regulatory mechanisms and bureaucratic process just described—I rather think they are. As crowding, deprivation, rising prices, and shortages become increasingly severe, the social unrest they create inevitably gives rise to political intervention. The social limits to growth can escape this fate only if:

3. We conduct a search for a new moral definition of wants and the humane use of the earth and its substances. We *must* search for it—it will not spring ready-made on the lips of a prophet, and we may find what we are looking for only after disaster and deprivation have had their effects. Each of the great industrial, high-consumption nations, like each individual, will have to experience privations and frustrations before growth is brought under control, and this will take a long time. Meanwhile, we debate issues and inch forward towards humility and towards reform of our resource policies and practices.[10]

Notes

1. See Bennett 1976a, chapter 3, for discussions of the various disciplinary approaches to human ecology. For an appraisal of various disciplinary approaches to ecology see Dahlberg and Bennett 1986, especially my concluding chapter.
2. For the Japanese case see Bennett and Levine 1976; for the Sahelian case and the general problem of pastoral adaptations, see Chapter 10 of this book.
3. Coelho, Hamburg, and Adams 1974 is a symposium on adaptive processes in behavior and psychology. For the most part, psychologists conceive of adaptation as coping behavior: manipulating the self and the milieu in order to achieve satisfaction. The conception does not concern itself with temporal processes or the impact of coping on the social and physical environments.
4. For a critical introduction to rational choice theory in the social sciences see Heath 1976. See also Herbert Simon's *Sciences of the Artificial* (1969): the mechanisms of quantitative construction of milieu required for planning, regulation, etc.
5. The discussion to follow is a revised version of Bennett 1978a. In particular, the figure has been revised to distinguish the choice function from the temporal resource depletion process.

6. Most of our practical knowledge of behavior in the contexts of uncertainty and risk is derived from economics. For a classical statement see Knight 1921.
7. For an early symposium on hunter-gatherer economies and cultures see Lee and DeVore 1968.
8. For a description of the Hutterites see Bennett 1967, 1977; Hostetler 1974; Ryan 1977. For the kibbutz and other Israeli forms of communal and cooperative settlement see Weintraub, Lissak, and Azmon 1969.
9. Also see Barkley and Seckler 1972, Ophuls 1977.
10. The work of Mary Douglas is especially intriguing in this context. See Douglas 1975, especially part III.

Literature Cited and Consulted

Barkley, P.W. and D.W. Seckler. 1972. *Economic Growth and Environmental Decay.* New York: Harcourt Brace.

Bennett, J.W. 1967. *Hutterian Brethren: The Agricultural Economy of a Communal Society.* Stanford, CA: Stanford University Press.

_____.1968. "The Significance of the Concept of Adaptation for Contemporary Sociocultural Anthropology," *Symposium 7: Proceedings, VIII, International Congress of Anthropological and Archaeological Sciences.* Tokyo. 3: 237–41.

_____.1969. *Northern Plainsmen: Adaptive Strategy and Agrarian Life.* Chicago: Aldine.

_____.1976a. *The Ecological Transition: Cultural Anthropology and Human Adaptation.* New York: Pergamon.

_____.1976b. "Anticipation, Adaptation, and the Concept of Culture in Anthropology." *Science* 192: 847–52.

_____.1977. "The Hutterian Colony: A Traditional Voluntary Agrarian Commune with Large Economic Scale." In *Cooperative and Commune: Group Farming in the Economic Development of Agriculture*, ed. P. Dorner. Madison: University of Wisconsin Press.

_____.1978a. "A Rational-Choice Model of Agricultural Resource Utilization and Conservation." In *Social and Technological Management in Dry Lands*, ed. N.L. Gonzales,, Selected Symposium No. 10, American Association for the Advancement of Science. Boulder, CO: Westview Press.

_____.1978b. "Social Processes Affecting Desertification in Developed Societies." In *Desertification Papers*, ed. P. Reining. Washington: American Association for the Advancement of Science.

Bennett, J.W. and Don Kanel. 1983. "Agricultural Economics and and Economic Anthropology: Confrontation and Accommodation." In *Economic Anthropology: Topics and Theories*, ed. Sutti Ortiz, Monographs in Economic Anthropology, No. 1. New York: University Press of America.

Bennett, J.W. and S.B. Levine. 1976. "Industrialization and Social Deprivation: Welfare Environment and the Postindustrial Society in Japan." In *Japanese Industrialization and its Social Consequences*, ed. H. Patrick. Berkeley: University of California Press.

Coelho, G.V., D.A. Hamburg, and J.E. Adams, eds. 1974. *Coping and Adaptation.* New York: Basic Books.

Dahlberg, Kenneth A. and John W. Bennett, eds. 1986. *Natural Resources and People: Conceptual Issues in Interdisciplinary Research.* Boulder, CO: Westview Press.

Dorner, P., ed. 1977. *Cooperative and Commune: Group Farming in the Economic Development of Agriculture*. Madison: University of Wisconsin Press.

Douglas, M. 1975. *Implicit Meanings*. London: Routledge and Kegan Paul.

Dubos, R. 1969. *A Theology of the Earth* (lecture printed as paperbound volume). Washington: Smithsonian Institute.

Firey, W. 1957. "Patterns of Choice and the Conservation of Resources." *Rural Sociology* 22: 112-23.

Hardin, G. 1968. "The Tragedy of the Commons." *Science* 162: 1243-48.

_____. 1972. *Exploring New Ethics for Survival*. New York: Viking.

Heath, A. 1976. *Rational Choice and Social Exchange: A Critique Exchange Theory*. Cambridge: Cambridge University Press.

Hirsch, F. 1977. *The Social Limits to Growth*. Cambridge: Harvard University Press and Twentieth Century Fund.

Hostetler, J.A. 1974. *Hutterite Society*. Baltimore: Johns Hopkins University Press.

Johnson, W.A., V. Stolzfus, and P. Craumer. 1977. "Energy Conservation in Amish Agriculture." *Science* 198: 373-78.

Knight, F.H. 1921. *Risk, Uncertainty and Profit*. Boston: Houghton Mifflin.

Lee, R.B. 1972a. "Work Effort, Group Structure, and Land Use in Contemporary Hunter-Gatherers." In *Man, Settlement and Urbanism*, ed. P.J. Ucko, R. Tringham, and G.W. Dimbleby. London: Duckworth.

_____. 1972b. "Population Growth and the Beginning of Sedentary Life Among the !Kung Bushmen." In *Population Growth: Anthropological Perspectives*, ed. B. Spooner. Cambridge, MA: MIT Press.

Lee, R.B. and I. DeVore, eds. 1968. *Man the Hunter*. Chicago: Aldine.

Leopold, Aldo. 1949. *A Sand County Almanac*. New York: Oxford University Press.

Martin, Paul S. and Richard GG. Klein, eds. 1984. *Quaternary Extinctions: A Prehistoric Revolution*. Tucson: University of Arizona Press.

Moran, Emilio. 1979. *Human Adaptation*. North Scituate, MA: Duxbury Press.

Ophuls, W. 1977. *Ecology and the Politics of Scarcity*. San Francisco: Freeman.

Ryan, J. 1977. *The Agricultural Economy of Manitoba Hutterite Colonies*, Carleton Library No. 101. Toronto: McClelland and Stewart.

Sahlins, M. 1972. *Stone Age Economics*. Chicago: Aldine.

Schechter, J. "Desertification Processes and the Search for Solutions." *Interdisciplinary Science Reviews* 2: 38-54.

Sheets, H. and Morris, R. 1974. *Disaster in the Desert: Failures of International Relief in the West African Drought*. Washington, D.C.: Carnegie Endowment for International Peace.

Simon, H.A. 1969. *Sciences of the Artificial*. Cambridge, MA: MIT Press.

Steward, J.A. 1955. *The Theory of Culture Change* (see especially chapter 2, "The Method of Cultural Ecology"). Urbana: University of Illnois Press.

Turnbull, C.M. 1972. "Demography of Small-Scale Societies." In *The Structure of Human Populations*, ed. G.A. Harrison and J.A. Boyce. Oxford: Clarendon Press.

Weintraub, D., M. Lissak, and Y. Azmon, eds. 1969. *Moshava, Kibbutz, and Moshav: Jewish Rural Settlement and Development*. Ithaca, NY: Cornell University Press.

Woodburn, J. 1972. "Ecology, Nomadic Movement and the Composition of the Local Group Among Hunters and Gatherers." In *Man, Settlement, and Urbanism*, ed. P.J. Ucko, R. Tringham, and G.W. Dimbleby. London: Duckworth.

4

Ecosystems, Resource Conservation, and Anthropological Research

Introduction

This essay has three main objectives. It is, first, an argument against the persistent dichotomy: nature and culture, man and environment. Second, it describes, by means of some case studies, the complex ways modern humans use and degrade the environment and suggests the kinds of research in which social scientists must engage in order to make a contribution to the unravelling of these complex processes. Third, it speaks for the need for a normative perspective—a viewpoint that takes reasoned positions on the problems of resource use and abuse and proceeds towards scholarly attempts to examine these phenomena empirically.

There is a hypnotic appeal to concepts like *ecosystem*, which give us a comfortable sense of precise and rigorous knowledge of the way the environment works. Less often acknowledged is that if we neglect the major source of influence on the environment—humans and their institutions—this knowledge is of little value. While anthropologists perform studies of subsistence among peasants, municipal authorities struggle with the chemical, geological, economic, and political problems of toxic wastes—with little help from social scientists. Agricultural research provides clever answers to the problems of increasing yields without ruining the soil and water but rarely concerns itself with the problems of

This is an edited and supplemented version of an essay written for the book *The Ecosystem Concept in Anthropology* (ed. Emilio Moran; Boulder, CO: Westview Press, 1985; 2d. ed. 1990). This was the final chapter in the volume and was composed as a wind-up piece, carrying the discussion into philosophical issues and the relevance of anthropology to study of environmental issues in contemporary society. The paper was originally prepared for oral presentation, and this is reflected in its writing style.

decision making among farmers who must make a living and function as members of communities.

We talk about "sustained yield" of resources, a conservationist principle that has attracted little work by the social sciences, other than economics, on how to put it into practice in a competitive and individualistic economy. Entrepreneurial production—rapidly becoming the dominant form of production in the world—is rarely compatible with ecosystemic principles, and thus one wonders, again, if ecosystem and other concepts used by conservationists have any relevance to the real world. This world includes humans who struggle to survive and to realize their goals in a human society and culture. If these factors are not somehow built into our ecological science we are all monuments to futility and elitist pomposity. This view has an acknowledged bias: humans must cultivate more modest aims as well as greater respect for Nature.

This essay contains two general and familiar ideas about the relationship of the concept of ecosystem to human affairs. First, if the human use of the physical environment is to be brought into some kind of balance both human and physical factors must be conceived as a single system, that is, a "socionatural" system in which human needs are redefined so as to sustain the yield of basic resources. As things stand now, human *needs* continue to be defined on the basis of *wants*, and only when these satisfactions are met are adjustments made in resource use in order to reduce exploitative use. This approach generates relative deprivation and consequent escalation of wants. Most of these adjustments, I suspect, simply displace exploitative or destructive use onto some other system. The second and perhaps not so familiar idea is that the most important human factor in ecosystems is not some exotic force or process embodied in biological theory but is basically the purposes and actions of humans in real social contexts; that is, "human ecology" becomes a projection of the behavior patterns of the species.

Politics, social change, greed, profit, self-actualization, ethics, and philosophy are all aspects of the human engagment with the physical environment, and these factors must be incorporated into our understanding of human ecology if we are to achieve a more sustainable use of the world. Human ends must be related to environmental ends; the quality of life must be synthesized with—perhaps politically subordinated to— the quality of the environment. If the term "ecosystem" refers to a dynamic balance between resource and sustenance, the requisites for achieving it are a restructuring of human purpose and a total reassessment of cultural, political, and moral problems.

While these ideas were articulated in the idealistic ecology movement of the 1960s and 1970s, its successor, the organizational environmental movement of the later 1970s and 1980s, largely surrendered them in favor of an acceptance of the political regulation of resource practices. But while the regulatory system has restrained the worst abuses, it has not attacked the fundamental problem: how to control or modify the belief that human demands on the environment have priority over those of all other species. This is a moral and cultural issue and has to be dealt with on that level. The mainline environmental organizations, which by the 1990s had developed into huge operations with multistorey headquarters, budgets in the millions, and employees in the thousands, were hardly in a position to tackle the issues because the basic tenet of a moral approach must be humility and simplicity, restraint of human needs and wants. This "curse of bigness" in the environmental movement was by the 1990s responsible for a growing alienation between the big organizations and grass roots activist groups.

The role of anthropology or any other social discipline in this situation must be dual. First, it must conduct research on the way physical phenomena are absorbed into human systems of needs, wants, and profit-seeking—that is, the "ecological transition." The effort should not be simply an analysis of how humans use physical or natural phenomena to survive and realize their aims (the transformation of Nature into "natural resources") but a normative inquiry obsessed with the question of what environmental costs the transformation process is generating— costs that future generations will have to pay. That is, the human-centeredness of our social disciplines must give way to a concept of systems in which human effort and impact are part of a larger whole. The politics of need and want satisfaction must be included as part of the systems; that is, aspects of culture are to be viewed as part of nature or the environment.

The second role of these disciplines is even more difficult: the need to raise serious questions about fundamental social and ethical values of the twentieth century—in particular, the dominant theme of self-gratification. These values need to be viewed with reference to the costs generated by the efforts to realize such goals. Social scientists should take the leadership in documenting these costs, but even more important is the necessity of finding alternatives. Reduced expectations is the pathway of the rest of the twentieth century; how can this pathway be reconciled with the dominant ethos? How can a culture of mass indulgence be realigned towards a culture of austerity? Above all, how can we create a mass culture more concerned with posterity than with self-gratification in the here and now?

Ecosystems and Human Systems

The modern concept of *system*, originating in mechanical and biological investigations in the 1940s, was originally an arcane notion attracting workers in scientific interfacial fields. By the 1980s the concept became commonplace in many disciplines, including the social sciences, and is extensively used as an analytic concept in applied fields like management and communications. The original philsophical tradition survives in General Systems Theory, a highly theoretical inquiry not to be confused with studies of empirical systems (for a typical treatment see Laszlo 1972).

Ecosystem is simply one of the specialized concepts pertaining to empirical systems and consists of a set of generalizations about the interdependent nutritional and populational processes of plant and animal species living in defined physical environments (Tansley 1935 is the pioneer statement). However, during the 1960s, under the stimulus of the idealistic ecology movement, the concept began to be used by non-biological scientists and commentators in new ways. It was proposed that humans, who disturb natural ecosystems, should model their own uses of the physical environment on that of nonhuman components of ecosystems and should adjust their resource practices so as to insert human activities into ecosystems without strain to the biotic and abiotic components. Likewise, studies have been made in which human institutional processes, like economic behavior, have been proposed as models for ecosystem processes. These various attempts on both sides of the fence have not borne much fruit for either policy or theory, and most efforts are mainly intellectual exercises in analogy (for discussion of this point see Bennett 1976, chapter 6).

The basic ideas associated with the ecosystem concept are expressed by the tendency for natural species to exchange energy in such a manner so as to create cyclical movement. For example, consumption of natural substances and energy conversions among species can result in the dominance of one species or the overconsumption of given substances, but this imbalance gives way, sooner or later, to compensatory phenomena, such as a rise in a predatory population, reducing the numbers of the dominant form, or the bloom of a new sessile plant form which shifts the dominance to a new consuming species. Such cyclical movements, with moving maintenance of approximately stable or average energy budgets, are sometimes approximated among human populations, especially low-energy-using and isolated tribal groups, but they do not begin to describe the major course of human ecological history.

This history was synthesized by Eugene Odum in 1969 in one of the classic papers associated with the ecology movement of the 1960s and early 1970s. In essence, Odum noted that natural systems tend to approach unity or stability in their relations of production to output, subsequent to youthful states where the ratio of production to output was greater than unity. Human systems, on the other hand, increasingly seek maximum output at the lowest possible energy expenditure. Therefore, since human purposes like profit and gratification intervene in and influence the process, unity or stability is never reached; the tendency is for demand to increase exponentially and to require ever increasing amounts of energy. These rising costs of production are concealed or charged to other institutional systems. The classic example is, of course, the cost of fossil fuels consumed in crop production, portions of which are charged to national energy budgets, shunted off to the consumer, or "paid" by the farmer in the form of meager returns on his labor. Thus, the full cost of food production is disguised. While improvements in fertilization, tillage, and other agronomic techniques may appear to lower the environment costs of agricultural production by conserving soil or water quality, these procedures may result in increased environmental costs felt in some other sphere. Individual cases of apparent ecosystemic balance in human activities thus might be illusory when all of the larger systemic processes are considered.

The crucial issue remains how to maintain high levels of production in order to meet social demands. While the ecology movement led to a series of environmental strategies that represent "improvements" in accordance with ecosystemic principles, there has been no fundamental change in social goals—demand remains at high levels, although some erosion has taken place due to scarcities or rising costs (as proposed by Hirsch 1976). The question therefore is whether these high levels of demand exerted by human beings on the physical environment can be maintained without irreversible environmental damage or degradation. That is, can we continue to produce at a high want-satisfaction level and safeguard the environment while doing so?

The theoretical issue, then, of the relationship of ecosystem to the human sphere is simply whether or not human or social factors can be incorporated in balanced, sustained-yield ecosystems. That is, are humans part of ecosystems in the sense that their needs can be satisfied without running down the system? Is there a direct or linear relationship between the magnitude of human demands on the environment and the degradation of this environment? Or is the relationship curvilinear; that is, can degradational processes be modified by superior strategies or technologies and still maintain high yields?

Several considerations arise at this point. First, there is the question of *time*. Obviously, degradation is a temporal process, taking place at different rates and depending on many factors. If you replace one fourth of the forests you cut with seedlings, you delay the time it takes to achieve a state of denuded and eroded land; but if the replacement rate is only one fourth, ultimately the denuded state becomes visible. Yet it is possible to claim, on the basis of replanting activity, that you are meeting some of the conditions of sustained yield. And you can always promise Society (or Nature) that when capital permits you can step up the rate of replanting from one fourth to 100 percent—a noble promise, but one rarely kept.

A second factor, the *circumstances of regeneration* or recovery of an altered natural substance or resource is, of course, also a temporal as well as a material process. No unmodified landscape, once transformed by humans (or by any other species), ever returns to its original state because in a sense there is no such "original state." All habitats, biomes, environments have been under continuous transformation by human beings and other species. However, one can obtain *similar* states: equivalent biomass although with new and different species; or similar or related energy potentials and changes. This constant change and recovery of physical phenomena is itself an aspect of evolutionary change. The human contribution is no different from that of other species; it is simply quantitatively much greater. Moreover, the recovery rates of natural systems altered by humans tend to be slower and the return to earlier states tends to be less promising or certain. In addition, the chance of further intervention during the process of regeneration is always high. Thus the tendency is toward progressive degradation—or exponential curves of increasing output and exploitation. Eastern Mediterranean forests were slowly destroyed over a period of 2,000 years by shipbuilding, goat grazing, firewood, and other uses; they have never recovered. This type of process can be duplicated for countless habitats or ecosystems throughout the world (the Amazonian rain forest is the latest candidate).

But cyclical processes similar to those in natural ecosystems appear segmentally in the human domain. Grazing land offers examples. Here regenerative capacities are often substantial, and what appears to be abusive or degradational usage may turn out, even in a few years' time, to be part of a cycle of use and recovery. The concept of "overgrazing," formulated originally by conservationists with little understanding of the practices of either nomadic herders or sedentary ranchers, ignored the tendency of these people to engage in cyclical resource use strategies. However, secular degradational and erosional patterns exist nonetheless. The conversion of large portions of the North American range to heavy brush cover, often too difficult or costly to remove and to replace with grasses, is a case in point. This example is especially interesting since the brush cover, caused by human abuse of grass, actually represents an increase in biomass over the grass stage. Humans consider it to be a deleterious change for *economic* not ecological reasons. The case illustrates the tendency for judgments about ecological matters to become intertwined with human purpose and value.

All modern uses of the physical environment are mediated by *institutions*. The concept of institution is absolutely crucial to the problem of environment in the contemporary world. However, it is one concept that remains somewhat unfamiliar to anthropologists; indeed, most anthropologists this writer has talked to recently consider the term to be "sociological." This is due to the fact that anthropological theory was formulated on the basis of studies of societies "without institutions"—in a manner of speaking. That is, the formal-legal constituents of rules and purposes segregated by function that characterize the institutions of civilization is a process that was only weakly developed in (formerly) isolated tribal societies. Instead of institutions, anthropologists of the

1920s and 1930s visualized the basic units of social existence as "culture patterns."

If anthropologists wish to make a contribution to the solution of contemporary environmental problems they will be required to use the concept of institution—or to develop their own version of this concept. Such a task includes an objective look at the process of change and reform—a topic very much immersed in the "historical present." For example, the history of the use of the Great Plains by Americans in the past century offers impressive opportunities for the analysis of how institutions shaped environmental successes and failures: the land survey and its irrelevance for natural topography and resource placement, the institution of freehold land tenure in a region demanding collective use and sharing, high-yield cash-crop agriculture on marginal soils, and so on. Even the rehabilitation measures promulgated by the Roosevelt administration as a result of the Dust Bowl can be seen as an example of how the best of intentions in environmental management, if not balanced by an appropriate understanding of human behavior, can make the situation worse. Donald Worster (1979) proposes that soil conservation and other subsidized programs cushioned the fears of farmers so that they assumed that soil abuse would be compensated by federal benefits; consequently, they were free to continue abuse management procedures in pursuit of high yields and profits although the market institutions of the nation forced the smaller farmers to opt for such intensive cultivation.

Some Case Studies

The selection of cases with which to illustrate some of the points already made is based on the writer's own research and consulting activities. The first case could concern Eastern African pastoralism, but since it is dealt with in chapter 10 we need only mention it. The case is especially appropriate because it involves both traditional and contemporary agricultural practices and methods of resource utilization, and, in addition, its history is well known because it concerns the changes associated with colonialism and the transition to modern statehood and associated economic development. It is also of considerable interest for ecological reasons: given the marginal, variable, dry environments of most of Eastern Africa some form of migratory pastoralism was ideally suited to the resources. It provided maximum yield for a modest population with minimal resource degradation. Attempts to "develop" live-stock production using Euro-American methods have experienced considerable difficulty and have contributed to, perhaps caused, aggravated ecological damage.

The first case study concerns the attempt to establish a fishing policy and technology for the U.S. East Coast that would sustain the yield of various species of commercially valuable fish. The concept of sustainability is examined in chapter 7, in a special context, but a few words of introduction to the concept are necessary here.

The concept of sustainability is usually offered as the major objective of resource management systems designed to achieve something like ecosystemic continuity. "Sustainability" is an ambiguous term since it is often not clear whether it refers to the economic product derived from the physical resources or the resources themselves. In addition, every modern resource practice implicates many, not just one, species. Sustained-yield management of forests may assure a continuing supply of trees, but with a diminished or vanished supply of other plants and animals living in the natural stand previous to intensive cutting and replanting. But a certain degree of regeneration is possible even here, providing that intact older stands are preserved as a source of other organisms to replenish the cut-over tracts. But all this is very expensive in terms of contemporary economic arrangements. Labor, time, and other costs must be added to the product price, something the producers are not inclined to do, unless they are required to do so by law or are subsidized by government. Moreover, tax laws and other instrumentalities can also penalize conservationist management schemes. Sustained-yield versions of ecosystems thus become complex matters of costs, prices, profits, laws, and management personnel. The history of forest regeneration on a world-wide basis leaves no room for optimism.

In recent years strenuous attempts were made by the U.S. government to establish sustained-yield management regimes for East Coast fisheries. Overfishing by the multitude of small private fishing boats and companies, particularly in New England, were beginning, in the 1960s, to develop into a classic case of abuse of the "commons": the Atlantic fish school. The evidence took the form of drastic changes in the numbers of fish of various species or the virtual disappearance of some. Of course, pollution and fluctuating ocean temperatures also play a role, and the evidence is not as decisive as one would wish. But, in any case, over-predation by humans was considered to exist. In 1976 the U.S. government promulgated its Fisheries Conservation and Management Act, considered at the time a model of sustained-yield management regulation. Coastal fisheries were extended out to 200 miles, and the general coastlines divided into eight regions. Each region is supervised by a Regional Council, whose membership includes federal, state, and industry representatives. The law requires that fisheries be managed for attainment of what is called *Optimum Sustainable Yield* (OSY), that is, the most you can take and still maintain the fish stocks. This combines both biological and natural factors, plus socioeconomic ones; that is, human activities and needs are supposed to be inserted into the "ecosystem." In essence, this requires some extremely complex trade-offs between fish populations, fish catches, economic costs, and needs of coastal human populations.

The new law and regulatory devices were greeted with optimism by environmentalists but with skepticism by fisheries people. However benign the goals, the law itself made no attempt to define OSY for the simple reason that no one knew how to define it or what types of data to include in the definition. Nor was there any systematic attempt to define the human institutions and activity patterns that modify the physical circumstances. No precedents for sustained yield existed save in the form of seat-of-the-pants management by the fishermen themselves. However, these strategies were site-specific, adjusted to microenvironments and changing physical factors, like wind and water temperature, as well as to social phenomena, markets, and consumption standards. No set of universally applicable criteria existed. In short, the basic information necessary to sustain or manage an ecosystem including human activities in accordance with the law was simply not available in any precise form (see Wilson and Acheson 1981 and other publications of their study for a detailed history and analysis).

Most of the Regional Councils did make an effort to set quotas on total catches, which were adjusted to what little is known about the impact of fishing on stocks and the economic demands of the fishing industry. None of the parties were satisfied with the results: the scientists felt the fish were being depleted; the fishermen resented regulation of any kind; and the Council members acknowledged that they were doing their best but were basically "pinning tails on donkeys." The issue was simply that the optimal fish catches in terms of conservationist standards did not necessarily correlate with acceptable economic returns to the fishermen. That is, a large catch meant only modest income if the catch consisted of species that brought low prices on the market. Taste and preference standards influence the marketability of fish as they do other foodstuffs. Moreover, regulation assumes that the major objective of fishermen is to control and even reduce his own catch.

The study done by Acheson and Wilson showed that the current procedures followed by the Councils were uninformed; they reflected the lack of hard data on the components of the system mentioned earlier. There was no inquiry by the Councils as to what was gained or lost by fishermen when certain regulations or strategies were used. The concept of a trade-off between the demands of the fishermen for income and the species survival of particular fish stocks did not form the basis of the legislation or the makeshift procedures followed. In other words, if human activities are to be inserted into ecosystems, full consideration of the role of various behavioral and socioeconomic factors on the human side need to be integrated with the environmental data. As it stands at present, conservation was conceived largely as a matter of curtailing overfishing, not weaving human interests and needs into the socionatural system. (For related discussions of fisheries problems in Asian contexts see Emmerson 1981).

While conservationists were impressed with the law, the fishermen's attitude might be summarized as a mixture of anger and contempt. Many, if not most, simply ignored the law since it was virtually impossible to enforce due to the lack of precise definitions. Moreover, the concept of OSY, while important, somehow had not attracted the kind of research effort from biologists and resource management specialists it deserved, and there was no more information available by 1981 than in previous years and decades. To establish a sustained-yield regime in a complex socionatural system like coastal fisheries would require an extremely expensive multidisciplinary research program—not to mention innovative thinking and experimentation.

However, the Wilson and Acheson research program was at least a first step—an economic-anthropological partnership between several East Coast universities designed to construct a series of models of local fishing strategies. These models were of two main types: an econometric model of fisheries as composed of small entrepreneurial firms with an emphasis on risk and decision making and an anthropological model based on concepts of adaptive strategy and cultural factors of influence. Some crossover between the models was worked out, but, on the whole, integration had not been accomplished at the time of writing this essay. The chief contribution of the research to our understanding of fisheries as a cultural-ecological problem is the ethnographic information on how small fishermen combine information from social sources, their own competitive interactions, practical knowledge of fish behavior, and so on, to forge their own "seat-of-the-pants" strategies. This is certainly an important first step in understanding the larger system of fishing and the conservation problem, but much work remains to be done.

Once again we are dealing here with the concept of "socionatural system." If human activities are to be inserted into ecosystems, the system itself has to be reconceptualized: it is not a matter of a "natural" system being invaded by human beings but a large, complex system involving an interaction between the physical resources, animal species, and human activities. This requires a shift in values as well: human components must be viewed as analytically equal to environmental components. The tendency to see human needs and interests as separate from and superior to the environmental is what vitiates attempts to develop conservationist and economic management schemes. There is, of course, considerable room for pessimism as to whether these can be implemented given the anthropocentric consciousness of contemporary institutions.

Another example of an attempt to utilize ecosystemic ideas in resource management is that of surface mining of minerals, particularly coal (see National Research Council 1981). The decision in the 1960s to exploit shallow deposits of coal in several Western states received predictable opposition from conservationists, preservationists, sportsmen, and ranchers, whose economic interests, values, and communities would be disrupted by the mining operations. That is, the issues of concern were almost equally divided between physical and social concerns. For a generation the central theme of protest over surface mining has been the visual appearance of the spoil banks following extraction. This concern has taken the form of persistent attempts to obtain legislation designed to require companies to restore the landscape to its "original condition."

The Surface Mining and Reclamation Act of 1977 was the culmination of this campaign; while the act did not completely satisfy its conserva-tionist proponents, it represented a major step in establishing a degree of environmental responsibility on the part of the industry (the Reagan administration issued a revised and weakened set of implementing regulations in 1983). The original law required that a minimum performance standard be adhered to in mining operations which transform the land surface and soils. The term "reclamation" is used in the act throughout, although the word in the past has been more frequently associated with natural "wastelands" to be developed for agricultural or recreation uses. "Restoration" is a more accurate term since the law provided for measures which would "restore the land affected to a condition capable of supporting the uses which it was capable of supporting prior to any mining, or higher or better uses of which there is reasonable likelihood" (SMRA, Sec. 515[b]).

The case also illustrates another important issue: the importance of aesthetic interests in the management of resources and their restoration or reclamation. This factor became one of the most difficult issues in the attempts to adhere to the provisions of the act. Restoration of a mined surface for agricultural uses, industrial or residential development, or recreational purposes are found to be in conflict with aesthetic interests in a great many instances. The preservationist goal is to restore the land to its condition before mining; the value is placed on the scenic appearance or on the "native" contours and vegetation, and since in many cases the basic contours of the land were previously modified by human activities, these goals were somewhat ambiguous. More important is the fact that reclamation of spoils and land levelling for agricultural purposes in many or most regions is more successful if the underburden soil material is left exposed, after a degree of levelling and recontouring, since this material has been found to be more fertile than the original topsoil. If recreational uses focus on water facilities, the rugged spoils contours may be preferable to levelling. In desert regions where the original vegetation was extremely sparse and heavily modified by grazing, restoration to this condition is easily done but this simply returns the land to an extremely low-productivity state.

Analogous to the fisheries legislation, the Surface Mining Act did not define the varying definitions of restoration or reclamation, nor did it base its provisions on research in different landscapes and biomes. Above all, the trade-offs and benefits of different uses of mined land before or after recalamation were not described. Nor were there provisions for involving local people in decisions on the pattern of reclamation. As in the fisheries case, the human activity factor was not included systematically in the specifications. This was to some extent deliberate since the issue was known to be extremely complex, and it was expected that application of the act would develop and vary as experience accumulated. However, insufficient provision for such experimental modification was included. The Reagan administration's modified regulations permitted these flexibilities but also left a series of loopholes that strongly suggest that the real intention was to return to the pre-1977 situation, which absolved companies from responsibility. This may be contrasted to the situation in European countries—Germany, for example—where restoration of mined lands, in accordance with the wishes and needs of local populations, have been a standard provision of law and a budgetary item in mining economies for many years.

The act generated widespread controversy as soon as it went into effect. Questions about its provisions and basic philosophy were asked not only by mining companies, with their obvious vested interests in nonenforcement, but also by environmental groups concerned with the problem of alternative strategies of treatment of the land for different purposes following the mining activity. Community-oriented groups were concerned with the failure of the act to specify clearly that local people should be consulted about the nature of the reclamation or restoration instead of making this a mandatory matter defined by federal regulation. This concern generated enough political steam to encourage various groups in the Carter administration to request the National Academy of Sciences and the National Research Council to undertake a research project aimed at clarifying the whole issue.

Ultimately, two NRC committees were appointed, one of them concerned with technical matters and the other with a fully multidisciplinary inquiry into the role of land, soil, economics, and cultural interests involved in surface mining activity in American society. This committee worked for three years to collect information from published and field sources on the various conditions of surface mining and land restoration in various parts of the country where the activity was taking place—in particular, Appalachia and the northern Great Plains. The result was a report (NRC 1981) while, while suffering from the usual ills of research-by-committee, nevertheless managed—for the first time—to define officially the problems of surface mining both in terms of sociocultural factors and purely economic and technological factors. That is, the report was a kind "cultural ecology" of surface mining. It was not reviewed as such by the *American Anthropologist* because anthropologists do not identify cultural ecology as anything that exists outside of their specialized arena of research subjects (tribals, peasants), but it is a document in the field nevertheless. As such, it indicates the magnitude of the costs of socionatural research, in particular, the cost of assembling a thoroughly multidisciplinary team of expensive experts to work for three years to produce something like a general-systemic model of a complex instrumental activity; moreover, we are faced with the fact that such cost can be borne only by the government.

As one who participated in the work of this committee, I can testify to the fact that anthropologists were listened to carefully and that the anthropologists listened carefully to the economists and technical people. The work of such groups as the Anthropology Resource Center, which published a report on the impacts of energy development on Amerind reservation groups (Jorgensen et al. 1978), was taken seriously, and representatives of that research effort were asked to make presentations to the committee.

This case illustrates the way *ecosystem* becomes absorbed into a matrix of human intentions, values, and economic activities. The goal of simply returning a landscape to a *natural* state is largely meaningless since it is difficult to define the nature of the previous state and its value to humans. Once a physical environment has been altered, questions of relative costs and benefits immediately arise. If in a pluralistic society there is no general consensus on the array of costs and benefits, then these must be determined through a complex social process involving dialogue between various groups. Each of these groups, with its distinctive uses of the land, may have a different definition of what constitutes a balance between human interests and those of the environment. Biological standards of ecosystemic functioning are thus not sufficient to decide the case. Once again, the system must be reconceptualized as a socionatural entity in which humans are defined as responsible components with other components of the system. This means subjecting human interests to a dispassionate scrutiny and making hard choices between those interests. Thus, systematic thinking in the resources field becomes a political process as well as a sociopsychological one.

Concluding Remarks

These considerations raise some important issues concerning how ecological science is to be used in practical environmental affairs. Ecosystem is one of those concepts that seems to acquire a life of its own: once the concept had proved its usefulness as a way of analyzing interdependencies and processes among living species and physical phenomena, "ecosystem" became a reality: ecosystems existed (as with the discovery of "culture," which, once named, existed). Hence we are persuaded to search for and *find* ecosystems, and their properties are likely to be idealized. In the early idealistic ecology movement the fact that some subsistence tribal societies were represented as approximating ecosystemic homeostatic properties was the occasion to recommend similar behavior for modern society, ignoring the fact that modern society operates on entirely different principles of resource use and with differing social and economic power magnitudes. While the exegesis based on the ecosystem concept formed a significant critique of the destructive practices, it could not supply remedies.

The remedies, as the later organizational environmental movement and its experiments in regulation and legislation has found, lie in everyday institutional forms and behavior. Ultimately the meaning of a total ecosystem is to be found in ourselves, not in Nature. If we are to engage Nature in some sophisticated and constructive way we must study ourselves as much as we study Nature, perhaps more. Socionatural system, not ecosystem, is the appropriate concept for environmental analysis on the human level, since it incorporates both members of the relationship.

Several research tasks have high priorities. In my opinion, one of the highest concerns the way different organizational forms and institutions establish high probabilities for specific resource practices. Are cooperative forms more conducive than competitive ones to resource conservation? Are collective property institutions, like those of the Hutterian Brethren (see chapter 7), more congenial to a sense of guarding resources for posterity than individualistic frames? Are market pressures and profit motivations more exploitative than centrally planned systems? A carefully conceived and planned comparative study of these institutional forms, with systematic variation in other variables like population, climate, crops, and extractive modes of utilization, might begin to give us the information we need. The need for this type of information is critical in Third World countries where development programs in agriculture and industry have wrought havoc on the physical environment.

A second major task concerns the way societies allocate and control their use of resources. This task must begin with research on the institutions and organizations that any society have available to make resource decisions and organize the transformation of these resources into products or energy. How resources are used and distributed is governed, as noted earlier, by sets of rules which are as yet only generally understood. Intensive research needs to be done on particular strategies of research utilization and transformation: mining, petro-chemicals, cropping, fisheries, timberlands, and so on. Such studies must include the politics and economics of the institutional system, as well as cultural values and habits which influence the power structure. Anthropologists have a vital role here since their ethnographic case-study method can be easily adapted to such research. Prototypes already exist: the accumulating material on African pastoralists in the development process is an example (see chapter 10).

The problem, however, is not one a single discipline can solve. A concept like socionatural system is the key, and this concept would require intimate collaboration among several disciplines in order to be effective as a research frame. So the main problem of defining cultural ecosystems becomes one of overcoming the social and cognitive barriers to collaborative work by people from different branches of scholarship. A socionatural system concept requires a structure of cognitive interdependence among people who at the present time are required to find their rewards in life largely in the form of personal intellectual satisfaction and the prestige gained by impressing colleagues. The reinforcement of this segregative social process by the structure of the modern university is one of the more depressing aspects of the problem. The most recent attempt to cope with this problem is Indiana University's Anthropological Center for Training and Research on Global Environmental Change, an interdepartmental venture originally planned and encouraged by anthropologist Emilio Moran (and officially announced as this manuscript goes to press in the summer of 1992). This endeavor has a structure similar to the programs introduced at many universities during the 1960s and 1970s, nearly all of which had disappeared by the 1980s.

As things stand now, intimate relationships among disciplines are largely interdicted by the structure of the professions and the universities (see Bennett 1981, 1986). This sort of work can occur only in organizational settings outside universities or in sheltered zones inside the institutions, like research institutes with outside funding. Government agencies are responsible for much constructive work of this kind, but this era may be drawing to a close due to financial constraints. Integrative research and scholarship, related to the pressing environmental problems of the age, will have to depend largely on enterprising and ethusiastic individuals who band together and attempt to overcome the antiquated institutions that imprison them. Interdisciplinary research on socionatural systems is the main survival task of science; yet it is the one thing our vaunted establishments of learning and knowledge find most difficult to sponsor. To realize the goals of scientific integration and system management of resources we must change the arrangement of cognitive categories in the human mind and the social forms these create. This is a formidable task indeed.

Literature Cited and Consulted

Bennett, John W. 1976. *The Ecological Transition*. New York: Pergamon Press.
_____. 1981. "Social and Interdisciplinary Sciences in U.S. MAB: Conceptual and Theoretical Aspects." In *Social Sciences, Interdisciplinary Research and the U.S. Man and Biosphere Program*, ed. E. H. Zube. Workshop Proceedings, U.S. MAB, Dept. of State and the University of Arizona, Tucson.
_____. 1986. "Summary and Critique: Interdisciplinary Research on People-Resource Relations." In *Natural Resources and People: Conceptual Issues in Interdisciplinary Research*, ed. Kenneth A. Dahlberg and John W. Bennett (Boulder, CO: Westview Press).
Cernea, Michael. 1981. "Land Tenure Systems and Social Implications of Forestry Development Programs," World Bank Staff Working Paper No. 452. Washington, D.C.: World Bank.
Emmerson, Donald K. 1981. "Rethinking Artisanal Fisheries Development." World Bank Staff Working Paper No. 423. Washington, DC: World Bank.
Hirsch, Fred. 1976. *Social Limits to Growth*. Cambridge, MA: Harvard University Press.
Jorgensen, Joseph G. et al. 1978. N*ative Americans and Energy Development*. Cambridge, MA: Anthropology Resource Center.
Lazlo, Ervin. 1972. *Introduction to Systems Philosophy*. New York: Gordon and Breach Science Publishers.
National Research Council. 1981. *Surface Mining: Soil, Coal, and Society*. A report prepared by the Committee on Soil as a Resource in Relation to Surface Mining for Coal. Washington, DC: National Academy Press.
Odum, Eugene. 1969. "The Strategy of Ecosystem Development." *Science* 164: 262–69.

Tansley, A. G. 1935. "The Use and Abuse of Vegetational Concepts and Terms." *Ecology* 16: 284–307.

Wilson, James A. and James M. Acheson. 1981. *A Model of Adaptive Behavior in the New England Fishing Industry*. University of Rhode Island and University of Maine Study of Social and Cultural Aspects of Fisheries Management in New England. Report to the National Science Foundation, vol. III.

Worster, Donald. 1979. *Dust Bowl: The Southern Plains in the 1930s*. New York: Oxford University Press.

PART II

Field Studies of Resource Management

5

The Social Ecology of Japanese Forestry Management in the World War II Period

The Social-Historical Background

Japan, down to and during World War II, was a cultural hybrid, possessing many of the features of a centralized feudal nation (resembling, say, France in the fifteenth century) along with the structures and energies of a twentieth-century industrial society. Although Japan possessed many of the cultural features of a medieval society, she also had the beginnings of modern technology. Japan's visible social structure looked medieval, with a sword-bearing knighthood, but at the same time it displayed stirrings of a labor movement and popular representation. This mélange of historical anachronisms was dismantled and radically reformed under the guidance of the Allied Occupation (1945–1951). While many of the traditional features have persisted into the 1990s, sometimes as ceremonial "heritage" activities, the economic and sociopolitical structure of the country has turned toward the modern industrial-democratic pattern. Thus, some of the social organizational features described in this chapter, while still viable in the late

---

I include this piece since I believe it is a pioneer attempt to deal with social aspects of resource management. The original work was done on assignment as a staff member of the Public Opinion and Sociological Research Division of the Japan Occupation in order to provide a basis for certain reforms in forestry management undertaken by the Occupation and the post-surrender Japanese Ministry of Agriculture and Forestry. The original research included social fieldwork and technical studies of forestry and timber production in several regions, one of which is represented by the data presented in this chapter. This essay is a synthesis and rewriting of three chapters in the book *Paternalism in the Japanese Economy* by John W. Bennett and Iwao Ishino (Minneapolis: University of Minnesota Press, 1963). Ishino was responsible for the materials on the *oyabun-kobun* system that are reviewed in the chapter. The materials on the local forestry "boss system" also were published in my 1958 article, "Economic Aspects of a Boss-Henchmen System in the Japanese Forestry Industry" (*Economic Development and Cultural Change* 7, 13–30) (Bennett 1958).

1940s when the writer researched them, have now been abolished or considerably changed as a result of altered property relationships, entrepreneurship style, and labor-management reforms.

The particular features discussed here in the context of forestry resource management at the local level focus on distinctive "familial-feudal" patterns of economic organization.[1] Prominent among these was a pattern of social relations called by the Japanese sociologists and anthropologists the *oyabun-kobun no kankei* (literally, "father-status/child-status relationship") (see fig. 5.1A). The phrase is a catchall term for a large variety of hierarchical relationships in many occupations and institutions that retained patterns of premodern Japan: rural economic activities, local politics, professor-student relationships, criminal gangs, dockyard workers, the urban construction business, farm tenancy, and local fisheries. The basic pattern of these systems was hierarchical, based on a series of dyadic relationships between superiors and inferiors, the cultural flavor of which partook both of feudal lord-vassal and familial parent-child relationships. Inferiors owed loyalty to superiors, and the latter owed protection and job security to the former. Older persons were generally subordinate to younger.

As in the Japanese (and Chinese) traditional family and kinship systems, the eldest son was the inheritor of authority, and the male line was considered the effective line of descent. "Descent," of course, in purely instrumental contexts was fictitious, but, to preserve the symbolic ambience of kinship, modified versions of kinship terms were often used to connote the relationships, and specialized induction rituals were often required when new workers or group members were taken on. These observances had strong elements of subservience, protestations of undying fealty, and the like, featuring distinctive Japanese familial-feudal symbols. Many of the groups were de facto exploitative labor gangs; others were benevolent groups in which the *oyabun* was a genuine father-figure, taking good care of his employees, some of whom, of course, were in fact kin. Figure 5.1B illustrates the terminology of a typical elaborate *oyabun-kobun* system, found in the 1940s in Japan, associated with road work and other construction.

Another important aspect of this system of instrumental relationships was the deliberate use of it by Japanese modernizers to foster economic security in a country undergoing rapid economic transfor-

Figure 5.1
STRUCTURE OF AN ELABORATE RURAL OYABUN-KOBUN ORGANIZATION
A. "Status Generations" or Status Terminology Hierarchy

O-OYABUN		o-oyabun	
OYABUN	ojibun	oyabun	ojibun
KYODAIBUN	anibun	EGO	ototobun
KOBUN	kobun	kobun	kobun
MAGOBUN	magobun magobun	magobun magobun	magobun magobun

B. Terms of Reference

Status of Ego	Status of Alter	Ego's Term of Address for Alter
oyabun	kobun	*omae* (you) or by personal name
oyabun	ojibun	*omae* (you) or by personal name
ojibun	oyabun	*oyakata* (respectful parent)
kobun	oyabun	*oyakata*
kobun	ojibun	*ojisan* or *ojiki* (uncle)
senior kobun	junior kobun	*omae* (you) or by personal name
junior kobun	senior kobun	*niisan* (elder brother)
oyabun's wife	kobun's wife	*nee* or *ane* (elder sister)
kobun's wife	oyabun's wife	*neesan* or *anesan* (elder sister plus the suffix *-san*, designating formal or respect relations
oyabun	kobun's wife	*X-san tokono ane* (elder sister of Mr. X's place)
kobun	oyabun's wife	*anesan* or *neesan* (older sister)
oyabun	kobun's child	child's first name only' no *-san* suffix added
kobun	oyabun's child	child's first name plus *-san*—a sign of respect for the father

mation. The prewar Japanese solution to problems created by a growing population was to permit an indefinite expansion of employment in order to divide the available jobs among the largest number of workers, especially in sectors of the economy where modern entrepreneurship was inconvenient or impossible to achieve; that is, the use of familial-feudal relationships as a substitute for modern social and employment security measures. To some extent this still exists, although the traditional systems are greatly modified, and the government has gradually introduced more of the universalistic security programs typical of contemporary industrial welfare societies. In any case, in prewar Japan one found innumerable small, family-owned enterprises, the padding of employment rosters, proliferation of small-scale factories and shops, and the boss-worker hierarchical groups described in this chapter.

The Prewar Japanese Forestry Industry

The forest and wood-products industries provided examples of all these patterns. Being almost entirely rural in locus, operating with little capital, and replete with small productive and labor units, it offered abundant opportunity for the development of "boss" systems of control. Such systems tended to concentrate scarce capital—especially in periods of economic distress—in the hands of local magnates and labor suppliers who disbursed it according to need and hierarchical precedence.

Japan has been known to Western conservationsists as a society in which intensive utilization of available resources was for centuries coupled with intelligent conservationist practices. The conservationist attitude has been regarded as rooted in the Japanese approach to Nature: that reverence or an aesthetic appreciation of natural landscapes, or landscapes made even more carefully "natural" by the hand of man. Conservationist practices were prominent in the sphere of forestry, since the Meiji period Japan's use of wood was extensive and forests were important in watershed protection, erosion control, and hydroelectric power. Accompanying these uses of the forests (which are in the mountains, since all available level land has been under cultivation for centuries) are deep-seated aesthetic and supernaturalistic attitudes regarding forests and mountains. The woods and hills are the abode of powerful divinities, often served by famous shrines, and hermit priests may roam the byways. Traditionally, man invaded the mountains and cut the trees only through necessity, but with care and circumspection.

Science made its contribution to this culturally reinforced conservationism during the Meiji Restoration (ca. 1870s, i.e., early modern Japan). German foresters taught the Japanese how to cut trees and plant seedlings according to modern practice, and enforcement was put in the hands of the police, who kept records of all trees cut and required farmers to get seedlings from nearby government agricultural offices. Either native conservationism had not been as prevalent as is usually thought, or the government sale of communally owned forest lands to private owners during the Meiji period had resulted in laxity. In any case, with German help the Japanese developed the system called by modern foresters "sustained yield management," that is, cutting no more trees than are reproduced by natural seeded growth or by planting. Before World War II the Japanese imported as much as 60 percent of all their timber simply to avoid the overcutting of their own forests (a practice which continues into the 1990s). During and after the war, when Japan was cut off from overseas supplies, domestic forests had to serve all needs and thus were severely depleted by, first, the demands for timber by the armed forces and, later, the need to rebuild bomb-shattered cities and to supply the Occupation and regenerating Japanese industry.

The prevailing pattern of ownership of forests in Japan since the Meiji period was one of many small tracts of land held by individuals living in the immediate community.[2] This was a recent trend, since before the Meiji Restoration a majority of forest lands were owned by the community itself and cooperatively managed. This older system of communal ownership, coupled with the attitude toward nature described earlier, created the Japanese conservation system. In the late nineteenth century political and commercial pressures led to the abolition of the communal ownership system and most forest lands were divided between Imperial control ("national forests") and individual local forest owners. The division of lands was complex, and even owners with considerable acreage generally did not own contiguous plots but rather several small areas scattered over a region. In addition, a number of very large forest estates remained in the ownership of a few Shinto shrines and Buddhist temples. With most Japanese forests in the hands of individual owners or religious groups, general economic fluctuation tended to result in a fluctuating rate of cutting, with severe exploitation appearing, generally, in periods of economic difficulty.

At the time of the study (and still to a large, but decreasing extent), the Japanese were more dependent upon their forests for vital industrial and domestic materials than the people of any other modern industrial nation. In the historical sense this simply represents the persistence of preindustrial means of satisfying needs for construction materials and heat energy. While Japan developed water power for industrial and public utility uses, and her steel and concrete industries for the construction of public buildings, the domestic population continued to build wooden houses and heat them with charcoal, just as they had done for centuries, without government interference. As time went on, wood for rayon, newsprint, railroad ties, and a dozen other purposes was also supplied from Japan's forests, although some of Japan's timber needs were always served by imports.

Forestry Economy at the Local Level

Aside from these various domestic and commercial uses for timber, Japanese forestry use, by providing extensive employment and free raw materials for the peoples who lived in the mountainous areas, amounted to a sustaining and recycling system. During the Tokugawa and earlier periods, when forests were largely communally owned, the economic benefits were extensive and profitable, since the mountain people managed and lived off their own forests. However, after the nationalization of some communal land and the disposition of the rest to private owners it became much more difficult for local people to live off the forests. However, the system was by no means dead; niches or subsystems that developed in the late Meiji period and survived into the early postwar period are described below.

The first of these subsystems was found in the commercial softwood (cryptomeria [*sugi*] and pine [*matsu*]) timber industry, which included the owners of forests, the dealers in timber, the sawmills, the wood products factories, many small workshops, and the laborers connected with all of these. This industry was by far the most important economically, and included 70 percent of all persons engaged in forestry—full or part time—for a living.

The second subsystem was represented in the collection and processing of wood and charcoal for fuel for heating and cooking. In the past, virtually all heat energy in Japanese homes and small business establishments and many schools and public buildings was furnished by charcoal. It was not until the postwar period that kerosene and propane stoves and heaters began making substantial inroads on the use of charcoal. In the early 1950s a substantial fraction of Japanese motor vehicles were still running on engines powered by hardwood or charcoal lumps. Fuelwood is all hardwood in Japan; hence the fuelwood system is distinct from the commercial softwood timber industry in that its products are handled differently down the line. However, there exist some economic ties. One of the groups from the softwood timber industry usually involved with the fuel system comprised those forest owners who happened to own stands of hardwood, from which were collected the materials for charcoal. Other than these, a few farmers owned small tracts of hardwood coppice, a ubiquitous forest type in Japan, consisting of dense growths of hardwood tree-bushes, resulting from recurrent cutting of the tree trunks. The processing group consisted of hardwood collectors, full or part time (some of them farmers seeking to augment their income); small charcoal kilns, often operated by collectors; the large fuelwood dealers, who operated large commercial charcoal kilns; and, finally, charcoal dealers operating small shops. Another link with the commercial timber system was sometimes established between the large kiln operators and dealers with sawmills, where hardwoods were processed for special furniture or lumber, the scraps being purchased for fuel.

The third subsystem was associated with the collection of forest litter and sawmill refuse and its sale to a variety of small processors. The collectors included a few families who did it as their sole means of support, but the majority were part-time farmers, laborers, and lumbermen who sold the material as a means of augmenting their income. Farmers also would use the leaves as compost for their fields, while other collectors sold the materials to bark-shingle makers, incense makers (some Japanese incense is made from cryptomeria bark[3]), makers of baskets and containers, villagers, and others who would use sawdust, shavings, or branches as firewood. Most of the collecting in forests was done with the permission of the forest owner or the manager of the forest, since the cleaning of the forest floor was regarded as a desirable service. However, in the economically tight period of the study, forest owners were beginning to charge farmers for the leaves they collected as compost, a practice resented by the farmers.[4]

These three subsystems of forestry enterprise were based upon the natural ecology of the region in Tochigi Prefecture (central interior Honshu, the big island) where the research was conducted. The area was characterized by a number of steep-sided valleys in which streams drained the mountains and hills to the West. As one went upstream, forests increased in size and economic importance, since agricultural land—level land—was scarce. In the downstream area were found the sawmills and wood factories, and the headquarters, in small towns and Kanuma City, of the business establishments of the forest industry. Each river valley also made up a political entity, or *mura* (incorporated settlement, somewhat comparable to a township in the United States). The divisions of the industry to some extent were allocated within these *mura*; that is, each *mura* had its own commercial timber, fuelwood, and collecting systems, although one or two businesses which had emerged in the postwar period linked a few of these *mura* industries in larger combinations. But by and large the forest industry, however regional in scope, was based on localized economic relationships, a pattern that was specifically and insistently approved in interviews with persons representing every type of economic operation.

Moreover, these local relationships were characterized by strong traditional ties between the various agents in the economic process: timber dealers who for years had purchased stands from the same forest owners, lumbermen who always worked for the same dealers, farmers who for generations had collected litter from the same forests, sawmills that had always processed the trees from the same small locality, charcoal kiln operators who had for generations burned hardwood from the same forest in the same spot, and family-owned workshops that subcontracted from the same factories and sawmills. The basic socio-economic units also tended to be small: family operations were the general rule and relationships among these groups and among members of any one group were based on a system of mutual obligation and loyalty. At various stages in the development of these relationships, ceremonial elements and traditional values were used to sanction the transactions. Complex hierarchies of mutual economic dependence were thus established, which lent the forestry economy of the region a strong traditional flavor.[5]

These networks of hierarchy and obligation uniting the many small groups engaged in forestry economy served needs other than profit. Timber dealers supported their lumbermen workers out of their own pocket in periods when tree purchases were few; farmers caught in a tax squeeze could collect litter and sell it to fuel wood dealers; persons out of a job could hire out at nominal wages to a sawmill owner if they had a relative who was an old or trusted employee. The spreading of employment opportunities *via* part-time work in the forest industry had become, by the time of the study, a common and complicated phenomenon—so much so that employment statistics for the region were very difficult to collect and interpret.

While the entire system was based on a series of small enterprises, it was also possible for ambitious entrepreneurs to manipulate it in such a way as to establish combinations. The very network of small enterprise units, depending as it did upon traditional and personalized ties, could be organized into one large enterprise if the entrepreneur knew how to manipulate the unitary sets of obligations and loyalties.

In essence, such entrepreneurial systems were fused with the power structure of these relatively remote mountain communities in which forestry represented the only available source of employment. Typically, in prewar Japan and to some extent in the contemporary period, each community or *mura*, and even each *mura* district (*buraku*) was dominated by an elite clique consisting of the *mura* mayor and the principal forest and farmland owners. This group was charged with the responsibility to supply timber for military or war production use.

Japanese Forest Industry in the Wartime and Early Postwar Periods

By the time of the opening of Japan's engagement in World War II (the "Pacific War" in Japanese nomenclature) a system of government procurement of timber for activities associated with Japan's military involvement with China had evolved. This system, strengthened and refined during the Pacific War, was essentially decentralized, in accordance with the government's reliance on voluntary compliance with national aims. The ministries involved in war production along with the Ministry of Agriculture and Forestry established priorities for timber uses and required the prefectural departments of forestry to monitor the cutting of local forests. Each prefecture was required to establish a Forest Management Plan (FMP) which established quotas for cutting and timber processing and delivery. Each *mura* was required to set up a Forest Owners' Association, and these FOAs were given quotas for cutting based on the demands from the national agencies and also on the basis of available cuttable stands in the locality. The membership of FOAs in each community included the *mura* mayor, the largest forest owners, and other local elite, the whole representing the top echelon of the local power structure. The system functioned efficiently, and the war effort was never short of timber. However, the demands for timber, plus the cessation of timber imports, meant that the timberlands entered a phase of overcutting and abandonment of the earlier conservationist program, based as it was on a more modest set of demands.

With the end of the war the needs for timber mushroomed. The reconstruction of bombed-out cities, the rise of a vigorous free publishing system with its need for paper, and many other needs for wood resulted in extreme pressure on the forests by the early 1950s and thus in a change in the management of Japanese forests. While regrets were expressed by everyone—bureaucrats, forest owners, and timber dealers—it was not denied that the Japanese had abandoned most of their careful conservationist practices and were engaged in serious over-exploitation of forests. The situation was made the object of considerable study by Japanese and Occupation agencies, in order to ascertain the precise circumstances and the local variations in the picture and to plan for improved replanting and conservation. The general causes, of course, were understood by all: rising population (especially in mountain regions), pressures and fluctuations in the timber market, economic insecurity and taxation, and a decline in the supply of cuttable trees. Moreover, such factors were all related, being "effects" of each other's "cause."

As a result of rising population in the forested regions there were more people than could be conveniently supported by a volume of timber suitable for sustained yield management practice. The computation of such a figure was difficult, since, as we have seen, a marginal living could be derived from the forestry economy in many different ways, not all of which required the cutting of timber. However, the largest increment of the population of forested areas in Japan was supported by commercial lumbering operations, and before World War II this population had reached an optimal level if sustained yield was to be maintained. Any increase, especially if inflation occurred, would be bound to force an increase in the cutting of forests. In 1951 some 1.44 percent of Japan's population lived in forested regions, and, according to labor force statistics, about 500,000 persons listed forestry as their major occupation. About an equal number lived indirectly or partly off the forest economy. The figure of 500,000 could not be compared directly with prewar figures, since Japanese labor force statistics were not collected in that manner in the pre-World War II period, but estimates placed the prewar total at about 300,000 and the number of persons partly supported by forestry at about half the postwar figure. In the region studied, the number of workers holding or seeking jobs in the forest industry had nearly doubled from 1946 to 1950; likewise, the number of commercial timber dealers operating in the region studied by our research group was double in 1947 what it had been in 1939.

A booming timber market in early postwar Japan was created by the reconstruction of bomb-damaged urban areas. While a number of individuals attempted to encourage construction with materials other than wood, and many suggestions along this line were made by both Japanese and American architects, the practical situation, and the attachment of the Japanese for their traditional wood architecture, proved too strong to permit the development of an active program designed to provide wood substitutes. Since timber imports at that time were financially out of the question, domestic forests had to serve the need. The result was a tremendous boom in the timber supply and wood products manufacturing industry. Prices soared, and large numbers of timber dealers, factories, and lumber yards sprang into existence, creating new opportunities for persons who had been thrown out of work by the general economic decline or who had been demobilized or repatriated. Forest owners, caught in the postwar financial inflation, sold forests to take advantage of the high prices, and the dealers put great pressure on them to do so. Workers moved into the mountains, as tales of the jobs to be had in the forests and mills spread into the cities.

When the lumber market gradually contracted, beginning in 1950 as monetary deflation, credit control, and a slackening of construction had their effect, further pressures developed. With a decline in the price of timber, dealers attempted to buy up whatever they could find. Owners, faced with reduced income and high taxes, sought out dealers in order to sell trees even at a sacrifice in order to get cash—although in other cases taxes curbed cutting, when owners feared investigation by tax commissions concerning the extent of their timber sales to dealers. Behind this activity lay the need to keep the excess labor force employed, a need which stemmed in part from attitudes of paternalism and loyalty in the employer-employee relationship.

From a financial standpoint the ideal arrangement in the mountainous regions was a balanced combination of forest and farmland, and the most prosperous families usually maintained this balance in prewar periods. However, the Occupation-period Land Reform disturbed this pattern, since every farmland owner was required to relinquish all but a few acres. Of course, in areas where the land was hilly and little or no farming was possible there had always existed a few old families obtaining all their income from extensive forest holdings. In the postwar period the pattern was modified further by the fact that urban corporations had started to take advantage of the general poverty and buy up tracts of forest land, introducing a significant factor of absentee ownership into many forest communities.

Atomization of ownership had been present not only with respect to forests, but also in many segments of the wood products industry. The making of *geta* and other wooden footgear, *tategu* (interior house fittings), wooden utensils for household use, and furniture of all kinds was done in factories, but also to a large extent in small, family-owned shops. In 1950, in the region studied, about 50 percent of all production of these commodities came out of such shops. In the postwar period the number of these shops had increased greatly, as one response to the need for support of a growing population. Wood products produced in the shops command a higher price than factory-made articles, but so low in times of economic distress as to lead to a near-starvation existence for the family operators. During the period of the study, Kanuma City, the center for wood manufacturing in the region, had three streets, each four or five blocks long, lined almost solidly with wood workshops, many of them shabby, poorly equipped, and in general showing the signs of economic marginality. Income and expenditure figures collected from several bore this out. Even with the high prices obtainable during the period of reconstruction inflation and taxes made the existence of many, probably most, of these families a marginal affair. Many had gone to work for local wood factories during exceptionally tight periods but would return to the family shop when conditions improved.

A Local Forest Industry Boss-Entrepreneur

The entire wartime and postwar system, with its pressures and opportunities, working through the traditional systems of the elite authoritarian power structure of these forestry communities, gave rise to a pattern of vigorous entrepreneurship that required investigation before new conservation regulations could be established. In essence, the system was simply a projection out of the traditional hierarchical patterns.

The research project selected one major boss-entrepreneur for study, since the contemplated changes in regulations governing forest use and conservation and labor relations would affect the power and activities of such men and their families and the various echelons of *kobun* or henchmen attached to these men. While prewar and wartime Japanese society has been described as a homogeneous, monolithic structure, in fact it consisted of a mosaic of hundreds of virtually autonomous communities and activities linked by complex deals and mutual backscratching arrangements—as are most social systems with a heritage of "feudal" or pre-industrial—*noblesse oblige*—values. Therefore any government regulation concerning the use of local resources would be monitored and manipulated by the elite group in power, and this usually meant the negotiation of covert violations, accompanied by bribery, mutual favor granting, and the like.

The particular "boss-henchmen system" selected for study in one *mura* in Tochigi Prefecture was headed by a vigorous man in middle age born into a small farm family but who nevertheless had become a favorite of the dowager of a large extended family that owned forest land and a famous private shrine used by farmers from all over central Japan as a place to find protection against fire (the curse of the wooden, thatched farmhouses).[6] This woman appointed him manager of the considerable forest estates of the shrine and also set him up in several of the small forestry businesses like charcoal-burning. He also functioned as a private timber dealer, seeking out cuttable stands and selling them to mills and wood products shops, as well as to government procurement officials.

Eventually "Mr. Harasaki" (as we called him) rose to the positions of mayor of the *mura*, postmaster, and chief of the Forest Owners' Association (FOA), a key wartime institution which the Imperial Ministry of Agriculture and Forestry required every community to create in order to provide a channel for administering taxes, cutting regulations, and, above all, procurement of timber. The combined role of mayor and FOA chief gave Harasaki almost complete control over most decisions affecting lumbering and conservation during the war and early postwar periods. In addition, his management of the vast shrine forests in the mountainous uplands of the *mura* meant that he also had control over most of the labor force. In fact, he asserted his role as the local boss by outfitting lumbermen and sawmill workers under his direct control with a heavy-duty cotton *happi* coat with his name prominently stencilled on the front. By the middle of the war he had assembled all his various forestry interests into a single company, with his eldest son as president. His various activities, political and economic, had permitted him to acquire title to a respectable acreage of timber as well as the paternalistic control of a hundred or more laborers—which meant a percentage "take" from the wages and absolute control over the jobs they were assigned (to keep his workers busy he could assign them to various forest workers and wood products shopkeepers). (Incidentally, the Harasaki family maintained its control of community affairs as late as 1992, when a descendant of the "boss" became mayor.)

Operations of the FOA under Harasaki exemplify the way these local magnates could manipulate forest conservation and use. Under the wartime rules, the number of trees cut on any tract had to be reported to the Prefectural Department of Agriculture and Forestry for taxation and conservation purposes, but the local agency in charge was the FOA, and if this organization was dominated by a cabal consisting of its chief and the four or five largest forest owners, it was possible for these people to report whatever amount they chose. And records showed that they had consistently underreported cutting, meaning that their taxes were less than they should have been and their profits greater. Such activities meant that Harasaki gradually assembled a backlog of mutual obligations and favors that cemented his power and control of the entire system. Although the government departments sent agents into these mountain districts to check on this kind of activity, the remote and not easily accessible upstream areas where most of the cutting took place made it difficult to maintain adequate surveillance.

Harasaki's operations, as the research team analyzed them from fieldwork and analysis of available records, typified the early modern, post-Meiji system of forestry management in these mountainous areas described earlier: control by the local elite plus paternalistic exploitation of the labor force. The system permitted reasonable sustained yield through natural replacement and seedling planting. However, this did not prevent serious overcutting and overexploitation of the forests by Harasaki and his "gang" (*batsu*), as some of the local people called it, when prices were high and the possibilities available.

A Local Labor Team

The research team also selected a typical group of lumbermen for study of the system at its lowest level. The group was called by the local people a *nakama*, a common word simply meaning "group" and connoting intimacy and solidarity. This system of teams of laborers— in this case, lumbermen—was referred to by Japanese sociologists as the *kumi* or *ko-kumi* method of employment and labor, which involves the hiring of workers for any type of job as unit crews rather than as individuals. Such *kumi* in labor-boss organizations had a hierarchical structure. However, *kumi* of the *nakama* type were cooperative teams composed of social equals all skilled in a particular job, with a senior or otherwise responsible member as a leader and negotiator. Groups of this kind were attached to employers in the de facto status of family dependents; in such cases, the sociologist could refer to the *kumi* as a "patron-client" group.

In general, the *kumi* were found commonly in those sectors of Japanese economy dependent on relatively unskilled labor, or where the business was small and locally organized and did not require a large, permanent body of employees. Occasionally the system appeared in the small factories, where an entire department could consist of a *kumi*, although these cases seem to have been infrequent. The essential function of the *kumi* was carried out in economic situations where labor was intermittent and where the crew could easily be transferred from one employer to another as work became available.

Nakama specifically referred to crews of lumbermen in the upstream areas where lumbering was virtually the sole occupation. Members of the *nakama* all lived in the upstream *buraku* districts and whenever possible worked exclusively in their own locality. Each *nakama* was primarily affiliated with one timber dealer, who usually lived in a different district of the community. It was this dealer-patron's responsibility to keep his crew employed, although he often transferred the crew to other dealers for work when he had none to offer. Thus the *nakama* was not necessarily bound to the patron with traditional ritual or moral ties. However, Harasaki's control of the local forestry industry meant that all *nakama* in the area were obligated to give his jobs precedence. Instances where *nakama* were transferred to other dealers were noted, but this happened only *after* permission was obtained by these dealers to operate in the boss's territory.

Lumbermen's *nakama* in the district studied were composed almost entirely of young men in their twenties or thirties, most of whom were married and had one or more children. The number of men in the groups varied from five to twenty, depending on the amount of lumbering work available in the locality, the availability of other jobs, and various other factors to be noted later. *Nakama* generally consisted of a small core group of three to five men, along with a younger, peripheral, more mobile group of up to ten men. These latter could in some sense be thought of as apprenticed lumbermen, or as men not firmly committed to lumbering as a calling. The core group included the *nakama* leader, who was always a man of about forty years of age, usually the oldest member of the group. During the research it was found that typically within a group of average size (about twelve) at least half of the members were relatives by blood or marriage. *Nakama* members were regarded as experts on the *buraku* forests and as serious, humble, hardworking, local men with close ties to the traditions and interests of the locality. While lumbering as an occupation was considered by people in the downstream as having relatively low prestige, in the upstream forestry areas the *nakama* lumbermen were considered to be men of quality, a proletarian elite.

The duration of a particular *nakama* was sometimes difficult to determine. In two cases studied fairly extensively, continuity of membership seemed to have existed for about fifty years. That is, within the particular *buraku* these two *nakama* had a long record of transfer and succession from father to son, friend to friend, relative to relative. In other cases *nakama* were only two or three years old. Some *nakama* seemed to be dissolving during the period of study, as lumbering tapered off because of a growing shortage of timber. More important than the duration of specific *nakama* is the fact that the principle of employment involved was very old and available for use whenever economic conditions required. Composition and number of groups, as well as various aspects of the roles and behavior associated with the system, varied by situation.

The informants stated that the *nakama* were simply the most expedient and commonsensical way of handling the job of lumbering. Examples: "they are natural things"; "they just form naturally, because that is the most sensible way of getting timber out of the forest"; "it is easier to have lumbermen work in groups because of the nature of lumbering—there has to be cooperation and a lot of knowledge about the forest." Others noted the fact that lumbering is a very dangerous occupation, and that dealers preferred to hire men with a background of cooperation so as to reduce the accident factor. In no case was the formation of the *nakama* attributed to cultural traditions or special values.

Whatever the circumstances surrounding the formation of *nakama*, it is clear that in cases investigated the group was perpetuated on the basis of a combination of locality ties, blood or affinal relationships, and friendships. New groups, or older groups recruiting new members, utilized all such connections to acquire members. The following verbatim account of the recruitment and severance procedures by the leader of one *nakama* may be taken as typical:

> Usually, in this *buraku*, a group starts with a few friends. Then relatives will join the group. First two or three persons will get together, then because the work can't be done by so few, relatives will be called in. If there still aren't enough workers for a particular job, temporary workers are hired. People come and go, but usually the original group and some relatives will stick together. But anyone can leave if he wants to—to get a lumbering job nearer his home, for example. Of course, there's a sense of *giri* [customary obligation to the leader and the group], and if a man wants to leave he has to talk it over with the others. There isn't any ill feeling if he talks it over. And he can come back here again if he wants to. Sometimes we ask the man to find a

replacement, too. As long as his leaving doesn't interfere too much with a job we have, it is all right to go.

The principal significance of the *nakama* system of lumbering for conservation lies in its "knowledge of the forests" mentioned in the quotation. Since these men were born and bred in the district and did most of their work there they were in a position to inform the timber dealers and sawmill operators about the stands best available for certain purposes and stands that had best be left alone due to immaturity, disease, or some local political reason. Harasaki and his subordinates treated their *nakama* lumbermen very well because of this essential information-supplying function—a function extraneous to the employment arrangements.

Studies of the pattern of stand-cutting in the upstream districts, where most of the traditional, locally oriented *nakama* functioned, suggested that less damage had occurred to the forests during the heavy cutting period of wartime and early postwar years than in the down-stream districts, where *nakama* were not as well organized or as locally oriented. Whether this is evidence for a conservationist role for these labor teams was not definitely known, but the research team was inclined to think so. Cases were found where *nakama* leaders were considered to have a "territory," that is, to be informal experts on the stands in their district and persons to be consulted by anyone who had designs on particular cutting operations. In light of contemporary propositions associated with the "common property" movement in economic development theory (see chapter 7) it would seem to follow that localism of any kind—ownership, supervision, familiarity—can, *under appropriate circumstances*, function to promote conservationist strategies. In cases where the relationship between patron and *nakama* was a close one and regular monthly salaries were given the lumbermen whether they worked or not, the patron and the *nakama* leader-worker operated as a team, the latter informing the former about likely stands and then accompanying his boss to the stand to work out plans for cutting and conservation.

Reverting to the theme of traditional social organization in instrumental contexts, figure 5.2 reproduces the terminology assigned to various functionaries in a typical *nakama* patron-client system, which exemplifies a simplified and attenuated version of the *oyabun-kobun* system of the elaborate type shown on figure 5.1.

Figure 5.2
Terminology of a Typical Nakama Lumbermen System

Japanese Term	English Translation	Description
	The Patron of the Nakama Team	
zaimokuya	"timber dealer"	The *nakama* leader would call him by his personal name or by respectful terms terms for "boss."
	The Nakama Team Leader	
daihyosha	"representative"	A term of address used by dealers and workers when talking to the leader, or a term of reference used in describing the leader's role in mediating between dealer and *nakama*.
sewayaku	"foreman"; "helper"; "intermediary"	Also a term of address or reference. However, this term is used in talking about the instrumental role of the *nakama* leader in actual lumbering operations.
oyakata	"parent-person"	A term of reference, never used in the presence of the *nakama* leader and felt to be archaic or jesting.
	The Worker Members of the Nakama	
wakaishu	"young people"	The usual term of reference used by the leader when speaking of workers; the leader is almost always the oldest member of the group, and a third to a half of the group are relatives of him.
rodosha	"workers"	Most commonly used term of reference and address for worker members. Used by everyone. Purely descriptive.
kobun; kobata	"junior-status";	Term of reference used by "child-person" dealers and sometimes by workers themselves, but usually in jest.

(Note also that the timber dealer usually referred to the entire *nakama* by such phrases as "my own workers," "my families," "my gang.")

The two or three terms derived from *oyabun-kobun* were not customarily used as both terms of reference and address. They were, in most cases observed, terms of reference only. *Oyakata* was never used to refer to the leader in his presence. *Kobun* and *kokata* were primarily terms of reference, but on several occasions the *nakama* members referred to each other or to themselves by this term, although in a jesting spirit.

Despite the attenuated character of these kinship-derived terms and the absence of a formal simulated kin structure, the rudiments of the *oyabun-kobun* relational pattern were visible here. The terms themselves were used in symbolic context; that is, they were used whenever the informants were discussing the general solidarity and interactional features of the *nakama*, as against its purely instrumental or task functions. It was clear that, in a diminished way, the informants were thinking of the *nakama* in terms of the basic *oyabun-kobun* model, even though they were well aware of the fact that the system could not be considered a full-fledged example of that structure.

The timber dealer-patron of a given *nakama* was always referred to by the *nakama* members as employer or boss (*kashira*), and in no case did any informant in any status or locality refer to the dealer as *oyabun* or *oyakata*. It was recognized that the relationship between dealer and *nakama* was that of "patron-client" and not "boss-henchman." When *nakama* contained blood and affinal kin (*shinrui*), as they almost always did, relatives addressed one another by customary terms or by name. No special usages were noted. The kinship aspect of the *nakama* was, in effect, a bilateral kindred composed of male members only, interacting as equals—that is, on the *kumi* rather than on the hierarchical, patrilineal extended family pattern. But the *nakama* as a group in the larger forest industry system had elements of subordinated dependency.

Other Factors in Forest Exploitation

The preceding vignettes give a general idea of how a renewable resource—trees—were managed at the local level in prewar and early postwar Japan and how, given stable demands for trees, the system might have operated to encourage or facilitate a sustained-yield policy. However, various aspects of lumbering technology and practice, as well as the social organization of the system, contributed to overcutting in the postwar period. For example, "skid trails" (*sori michi*) were vital to getting the cut timber out of the steep wooded slopes. Once a particular trail had been constructed, owners interested in selling timber and dealers interested in cutting and buying it would take advantage of the existence of such a trail and immediately heavy cutting would spread through the locality. In prewar times owners were extremely cautious in allowing the construction of trails, but in the postwar preiod the need for money, accentuated by the forced surrender of much of the farmland owned by forest owners, reversed the attitude. To a considerable degree, the reform of agricultural land in Occupation Japan had a deleterious effect on forests.

The extent to which the entrepreneurial boss system functioned to promote excessive cutting beyond the point where remaining trees could seed new growth was also examined by researchers. The general results suggested that the boss system cut both ways: in some instances the rigid control over timber cutting and sales (in Mr. Harasaki's locality) led to controlled exploitation, but in other cases just the opposite would occur. One of the former cases involved the "invasion" of Harasaki's territory by a timber dealer from an adjoining community who was considered to be a kind of semi-detached "*kobun*"[7], that is, a henchman with weak ties to Harasaki. This man negotiated a deal with a forest owner whom Harasaki considered to be in his circle, and one who collaborated in the activities of the local FOA. Harasaki stopped the deal by the use of ceremonial force: summoning the renegade dealer to his house and forcing him to participate in traditional humbling rituals of apology. The trees were not cut, to the chagrin of the owners, whose attempt to get around the boss was thereby defeated. Several similar instances were recorded, indicating that the boss control of the forests could result in a more or less careful husbanding in order to maintain the supply. But the reasons had little to do with conservation or ecology; rather, it was a matter of sustaining local authority and power.

Examples of the opposite tendency—the way the system promoted excessive cutting—were already mentioned in the case of the skid trail. But the most common situation involved the cutting of timber in excess of the FOA plan for financial reasons and concealing the results by falsifying records. The most frequent method was simply to underreport the volume of timber actually removed. In many cases it would be found that the *age* of the trees was also underestimated. This was done for the purpose of rendering plausible the underestimation of the volume. The lower the volume of timber, the less the amount of cutting tax charged to the owner. Thus, in one case trees on one tract (the area surveyed was approximately correct as given) were recorded in the precutting survey as being twenty years old (incidentally, about ten years too young for effective use), and the volume of timber estimated in trees on an area of this particular extent was given as 240 *koku* (one *koku* equals about ten cubic feet)—which was too low an estimate for trees of this age on a tract this size. However, in the FOA report of the actual volume cut, the volume was given as 700 *koku*, which was reasonable in light of the false age. Now, it was determined that the trees were actually *thirty* years of age. Trees of *this* age on a tract of the size known would have produced 700 to 1,000 *koku*. Hence, about 300 *koku* of timber were simply not reported. In another tract in the same purchase it was found that the type of forest cover was misrepresented: a stand of *sugi* mixed with hardwood scrub was listed as "coppice," which would imply that the cut wood would be low in volume and usable for firewood only. In actuality the tract produce a sizable volume of commercial cryptomeria timber.

The price paid for lumber was also underestimated. Such underrepresentations of price would have a desirable effect on the owner's and dealer's tax reports. During the period in which these manipulations were common, most of the people in the forestry economy, from lumbermen to owners, and the ordinary dealers, were having a hard time paying taxes on the lumber they *did* report. Obviously the large entrepreneurs profited most.[8]

The research team also examined the social organization of persons involved in some of the skid trail episodes, where the construction of a trail triggered a series of cutting sprees. It was found that blood and affinal kinship played an important role. In one case, ten forest owners were involved in a series of stand clear-cutting centered around a particular trail. Of these, only one was an absentee owner and had no kin ties with any of the others. The other nine owners were all related, and all of them were tied by obligations to Mr. Harasaki or his henchmen and companies.

The sale of the trees and subsequent evasions of regulations were in large part carried out in the atmosphere of a closely interacting group of relatives and associates. Thus most persons involved in the transactions were parties to the operation; nobody could possibly have been hoodwinked. It is necessary to consider economic transactions in an atmosphere of this kind not on the model of free, individual agents but from the standpoint of a collectivity, acting in its own interest.

An intimate collectivity, engaged in such deals, requires the services of go-betweens. These people functioned in two ways. First, in four of the six purchases the initial approach to the owner was made not by the dealer actually buying the trees but by a special go-between who collected information for the dealer on the owner's views and thereby permitted the dealer to work out an initial contract for bargaining purposes. Second, the go-between system also functioned in connection with the custodianship of skid trails. One of the Harasaki negotiators was the custodian of the first trail; others acted in this capacity for the other trails. The trail custodian had to be consulted by the dealers while arranging the deal, and he also provided the principal message center for lumbermen and dealers. The lumbermen teams (*nakama*) were expected to get in touch with the man in charge of the skid trail when they became aware that a stand of trees near the trail could be cut. The custodian would then relay the information to the dealer with whom the team usually worked or to some other dealer if the team was not closely bound to a particular one.

The go-between institution was a mediating device between the associated kin groups of owners on the one hand and the dealer group (and their business connections with timber companies, mills, etc.) on the other. Since decisions in these transactions were usually collective and not individual, the bargaining was complicated and a go-between was needed to keep the parties informed while avoiding direct negotiations until the time was ripe.

Conclusions

Japanese attitudes toward forests have been considered by many to reflect the cultural value of conservationism—a partnership between man and nature or a reverence for the bounties of nature in a society constrained by geographic isolation and limited natural resources. Presumably such values guided the Japanese in their centuries of social isolation, up to and during the Tokugawa era, when, as a matter of national policy, it became necessary to husband resources.

In the modern, post-Tokugawa era Japan changed from isolation to industrial expansion and an international trading policy. During the first three decades of the twentieth century this policy was carried on simultaneously with the older patterns of careful resource conservation. For example, even in the face of of the abundance of Japan's forests the country imported a large proportion of timber in pre-World War II years. During the war, this policy could not be followed, and Japanese forests experienced a heavy drain on timber to meet military needs. In the postwar period this drain continued as the cities in need of rebuilding and the Occupation forces demanded large quantities of lumber.

In the forestry communities numerous adjustments were made in the order to supply this timber. Local conditions of unemployment and surplus population accelerated forest exploitation, since it was necessary to support this population. Financial and taxation conditions had similar effects. The institutions and arrangements functioning to exploit timber lands were not novel, but consisted of the old ones, simply adapted to a different pace of enterprise. Local forest owners seemed to have regretted the need to cut their trees to a point where yield was not sustained, but on the other hand they seem not to have resisted this necessity when their financial position required it.

The various social patterns visible in the case of exploitation described in this chapter were the familiar ones of the mountain community: kinship ties, boss-henchman and patron-client groups, go-betweens. The important values involved were those of extended family, hierarchical sibling order, *noblesse oblige*, and deference to the superior—all features familiar to students of Japanese familial-feudal organization. These values were mobilized by entrepreneurs in the postwar period to obtain a larger flow of timber, whereas in previous epochs these same values had operated to husband the trees and maintain the local forestry economy at a level that would just satisfy the local needs.

But the familial-feudal value system was essentially neutral with regard to questions of the conservation of natural resources and aesthetic aspects of man's relationship to Nature. When it became necessary to develop the forestry economy the system adjusted itself without conflict. That is, obligations to support the local population in accordance with feudal-like paternalism, as well as actual economic pressures, superseded cultural values of conservationism. Moreover, systems of enterprise like that of the boss-henchman are inherently well adapted to exploitative ends. The power-seeking element within them permits expansion when external conditions encourage it.

The relative ease with which traditional cultural values in Japanese society could be put aside, so to speak, for purposes of economic development has been one of the persisting features of Japan's modernization. At the same time, the ability to preserve such values and put them back into effect when conditions permit may be an equally enduring feature of the Japanese scene.

Afterword, 1991: The Japanese Environmental Situation

In the background of this chapter lies an essentially dual or contradictory character of the Japanese attitude toward the physical environment. In the later postwar period accumulating industrial pollution resulted in vigorous citizen movements. These were triggered by two major disasters: the Minimata episode, involving the poisoning of many members of a community by mercury discharged into a river by a local factory; and the *itai-itai* disease caused by cadmium poisoning in another community. These and other scandalous episodes illustrating the production-at-any-cost attitude of Japanese industry led, by the 1960s, to some of the most stringent antipollution laws in the world. And these disasters were simply repeats of a much earlier episode in 1878, when copper poisoning from a mine in Tochigi Prefecture, not far from the scene of this chapter, led to a major disaster, causing disease, death, the abandonment of hundreds of farms, and finally a march of militant local farmers on the prefectural capital. Cleanup was then accomplished.

On the other hand, recent laws and the heightened public consciousness has not led to as vigorous or sustained an environmental movement in Japan as in the United States and other countries. Japan's version of the U.S. Environmental Protection Agency, established after the Minamata and the other disasters, has little force and authority. As of 1990 it has never closed a factory for violations of pollution or toxic discharge and has never disapproved or cancelled an industrial or any other type of project. Little or no activity concerning endangered species or other environmental matters not associated with pollution exists, although a number of organizations have been formed. No single group, like the Sierra Club in the United States, functions as a flagship organization or has major public renown and prestige.

So far as the Japanese forests are concerned, the resumption of timber imports in the 1960s helped to protect against heavy exploitation, although the damage done to the trees in the periods described earlier in the chapter has never fully been undone, since, despite imports, cutting in this booming consumer culture remains heavy. Regulations introduced in the later Occupation period did induce some controls over the worst abuses and made it difficult for independent entrepreneurs like Mr. Harasaki to gain control over entire forested regions. In general, as Japan has entered into its full-blown capitalist-industrial era the problems of protecting natural resources against exploitative interests are similar to that of the United States, and the need for government regulation becomes acute. Such regulation appears to be the only effective way of introducing some control. The days of localized, socially systematized conservation are long past. Outside ownership of forests by corporations continues to grow; local voluntary conservation gives way to commercial tree-farming. National forests, like those in the United States, are subject to pressure from the "interests." The many sideline activities and industries described for the prewar period are mostly gone, and local people must earn their livelihoods in industrial labor. Mountain communities suffer a steady loss of population. Pilgrimages to the mountain shrines, once a serious venture, has gradually merged into holiday tourism.

Notes

1. The following works provide introductions to traditional Japanese familial-feudal social organization and the *oyabun-kobun* system: Nakane 1967–1970; Smith 1959; Fukutake 1967; Mogami 1937; Odaka 1955; Tanaka 1955; Government Section, SCAP 1947. Orchard 1930 is a pioneer study of Japan's modernizing economy and contains valuable material on the role of traditional social organization. Dore 1973 contrasts the Japanese labor-management style with the British.
2. For descriptions of Japanese forestry ownership, management, and conservation down through World War II see the following: Japan FOA 1959; Nuttonson 1951; Ackerman 1953; Natural Resources Section SCAP 1949; Ikeuchi 1948.
3. *Sugi*, or cryptomeria, is known in the Western world in the form of the huge trees lining the entranceways to Japanese shrines and temples, but it is also the standard commercial softwood timber, comparable to Ponderosa pine in the United States in its texture and uses and to Southern Yellow pine in its rapid growth habits.

4. The research team attempted to obtain estimates of the number of persons supported by various means on given tracts of forest land. Since the arrangements
made between forest owners and litter collectors and the like were highly informal
and personal and not measured in terms of the income or cash value of the work,
it was difficult to get precise data. One of the more verifiable was the following.
The owner had twenty acres of forest and about an acre of rice paddy. He estimated
that the forest land supported only half of the eight members of his family; the rice
the other four. In addition to these four family members, he estimated that the forest
land alone supported another twenty-five persons, in whole or part. This twenty
was broken down as follows: five persons bought hardwood from the owner from
the coppice portion of his acreage to sell in town for firewood; about fifteen other
persons worked part of the year for the owner in trimming, planting new trees, and
performing other maintenance chores; the final five persons were farmers who
collected leaf litter for composting their rice paddies. The owner emphasized that
this figure remained pretty stable from year to year.

5. The "traditional flavor" of the system was, however, only part of the story. The
forestry and lumber business was operated by economic as well as cultural methods
and objectives. In almost every context—employment, tasks, financial practices,
negotiation—there appeared what could be called "dual sanctions": that is, a
traditional cultural rationale as a well as a purely economic justification. Two
examples: (1) Dealers always made efforts to obtain their lumbermen from the
buraku in which the particular stand of trees they had purchased was located. When
asked why, they replied in most cases that it was more economical that way, since
the local people would work for less, not requiring transportation money. But in
some cases the dealers would volunteer a second reason which had to do with
traditional aspects of the situation: for example, "it is important to work with the
local people because it is a matter of *ninjo* [human feelings, considerateness]."
That is, by dealing with the local people you pay your respects to the social
system—and incidentally assure good will for your business in the community.
(2) In several cases respondents pointed out that the shift from the formerly
prevalent communal ownership of forests to individual ownership was a necessary
economic measure, given Japan's program of economic development since 1870,
and a necessary institution because of changes in Japanese traditional culture, or
"national character" as one forest owner put it. These dual sanctions might be
analyzed as the result of social change; that is, the traditional sanction for a given
activity represents the older state of the activity, the rational or economic sanction
the contemporary changed aspect. However, long before Japan underwent economic development she possessed institutional patterns which stressed individual
accomplishment and the utilization of traditional ideology as a rationalization or
support for such activity.

6. This shrine is an important and famous institution of the region. It was originally
the private shrine of ancestors of the owning family and was dedicated to the family
clan deity. It was still owned by the family in the 1950s. The shrine was founded
by a *yamabushi* ("mountain priest") possibly as early as the eighth century A.D.
These priests used to wander in the remote mountainous regions of Japan in search
of spiritual enlightenment and solitude. According to legend the shrine was
founded by Ennogyoja, the eighth-century *yamabushi* who established the custom
of mountain worship. The founder of the family was said to be one of the two *oni*
(ogres) who served Ennogyoja. During the Tokugawa period the shrine was visited
by pilgrims on their way to a nearby holy city and became of the important

subsidiary places of worship in the area. The principal deity, Tengu, the popular long-nosed god of Japanese folklore, was probably added later, although some claim that it was the original family god. The shrine is particularly popular among farmers of central Japan, who feel that the deity has the virtue of increasing crops and protecting the worshiper against fire and theft. In 1949 forty persons were employed at the shrine, and the establishment obtained a large yearly income from donations and concessions.

7. I use quotation marks around "*kobun*" in order to indicate that the use of the term by local people was metaphorical. Harasaki himself was often called "*oyabun*" in a similar spirit. More commonly, Harasaki was called *kashira*, which simply means "boss" or "head," although in other contexts it can mean "firewarden," an important local official in Japan down through the nineteenth century.

8. In addition to the falsification of records, much cutting took place by black market dealers who entered into collusion with the market owner and arranged with him not to report the sale.

Literature Cited and Consulted

Ackerman, James. 1953. *Japanese Natural Resources*. Madison: University of Wisconsin Press.

Bennett, John W. 1958. "Economic Aspects of a Boss-Henchmen System in the Japanese Forestry Industry." *Economic Development and Cultural Change* 7: 13–30.

Bennett, John W. and Iwao Ishino. 1963. *Paternalism in the Japanese Economy: Anthropological Studies of Oyabun-Kobun Patterns*. Minneapolis: University of Minnesota Press. [New edition: New York, Greenwood Press.]

Dore, Ronald. 1973. *British Factory and Japanese Factory*. Berekeley: University of California Press.

Fukutake, Tadashi. 1967. *Japanese Rural Society*. New York: Oxford University Press.

Government Section, GHQ, Supreme Commander for the Allied Powers. 1947. *Report of the Oyabun-Kopbun Subcommittee*. Memorandum for the Control Coordinating Committee, Economic and Scientific Section (mimeographed).

Ikeuchi, Hajime. 1948. *Report of Survey Research in Forestry Communities* (by the Public Opinion Research Institute of Tokyo). Tokyo: Japan Forestry Association.

Japan Forest Owners' Association (FOA). 1959. *A Century of Technical Development in Japanese Agriculture*. Tokyo.

Mogami, Takanori. 1937. "Oyakata-Kokata," in K. Yanagida, ed. *Sanson Seikatsu no Kenkyu* (Research on Life in Mountain Villages). Tokyo: Iawnami Shoten.

Nakane, Chie. 1967. *Kinship and Economic Organization in Rural Japan*. New York: Humanities Press.

_____ . 1970. *Japanese Society*. London: Weidenfeld & Nicholson.

Natural Resources Section, GHQ, SCAP. 1949. *Important Trees of Japan*. Report no. 119. Tokyo.

Nuttonson, M. Y. 1951. *Ecological Crop Geography and Field Practices of Japan: Japan's Natural Vegetation and Agro- Climatic Analogues in North America*. Washington, DC: American Institute of Crop Ecology.

Odaka, Kunio. 1950. "An Iron Workers Community in Japan" *American Sociological Review* 15: 186–95.

Orchard, John E. 1930. *Japan's Economic Position: The Progress of Industrialization.* New York: Whittlesey House.

Smith, Thomas C. 1959. *The Agrarian Origins of Modern Japan.* Stanford: Stanford University Press.

Tanaka, Shinjiro. 1955. "Oyakata-Kokata Relations in Rural Communities: Past and Present." *Nihon Minzokugaku* 2: 89–94.

6

Ethnographic Research on Allocation and Competition for Land and Water in the Canadian Great Plains

Backgrounds

Agricultural research in North America, for most of its history, has been devoted to the goal of increasing production. This emphasis led to the neglect of two topics: the environmental consequences of agricultural technology (including chemicals) and the social behavior of people engaged in production. Farmers were viewed to some extent as undependable components of the market system, since they could not be relied upon to use the techniques and strategies that research had shown would produce the best results at the least cost (see Bennett 1986). This narrow view of the nature of agriculture developed in the first quarter of the twentieth century, as "farm economics" gave way to "agricultural economics" and as the old extension stations and services became thoroughly integrated into the land grant universities with their huge agriculture departments (Bennett 1982, 7–10). Farming, which had been seen in the nineteenth century as a worthwhile human endeavor carried on by sturdy yeomen, was turned into a branch of the business world. Since the burgeoning "science" of economics increasingly took over the

This chapter presents case studies of how farmers and ranchers obtained their land and water resources in a Western North American region, in particular, a 4000-sq. mile region of southwestern Saskatchewan, adjacent to the international boundary. The work was accomplished as part of a fifteen-year research program known as the Saskatchewan Cultural Ecology Research Program (SCERP) and was published in several books and many scholarly papers in the 1960s through the early 1980s. The principal sources for this chapter are chapters 8 and 10 of the book *Of Time and the Enterprise: North American Family Farm Management in a Context of Resource Marginality* (Minneapolis: University of Minnesota Press, 1982). (Other publications on SCERP research are added to the bibliography at the end of this chapter.)

responsibility of setting standards of performance and profit, the principal aim of agriculture came to be one of increasing production without much concern for the "externalities" of the activity: for example, the costs of resource degradation, or the costs to the farmer of commodity price fluctuation. The latter issue led, by the 1890s, to vigorous agrarian protest movements. However, the environmental costs of growing rationalization of farming did not begin to be an issue until the ecology movements of the 1970s and 1980s and its offshoot, the "alternative agriculture" movements, got under way (see, for example, Lockeretz 1986).

The picture by the early 1990s was mixed: "family farms," the grass roots basis of North American agriculture for two centuries, were giving way to corporate agriculture; agricultural research was increasingly aware of environmental problems and began to link up with the alternative agriculture experiments. But, at the same time, the corporatization of farming meant, in many instances, even less concern for resource conservation and pollution than had been the case under family-farm operation. Moreover, research on production began to suggest that corporate farming was even less productive and had higher external costs than the family type.

This North American system of capital-intensive agriculture, with massive inputs designed to increase production and reduce costs of operation, was attempted across the continent, with little regard for climate, soils, or topography. The procedures were best suited to Eastern and Midwestern states and provinces with their rich, forest-derived soils, longer growing seasons, and twenty- to thirty-inch rainfalls. The states and provinces also possessed most of the largest and most influential agricultural colleges and experiment stations. From the 1890s through the 1920s students from these schools formed the first cadre of professors and scientists in the new experiment stations in the Great Plains.

Moreover, the turn-of-the-century settlers of the Northern Plains commonly spent months or even years in Ontario or the Midwestern states, resting after long transatlantic voyages, staying with relatives, or attempting to find suitable farmsteads. By the time they reached the Plains they were habituated to the family-farm concept of agricultural production. This ideal was also that of the politicians and bureaucrats in Washington and Ottawa who framed the homestead regulations. Since no one had any knowledge of the magnitude of the variability and marginality of the resources of the Northern Plains, the regulations were

Peter A. Russell, Ph.D.
History/Economics

Box 189
2552 Trans Canada Hwy. N.E.
Salmon Arm, B.C. V1E 4N3

Tel. (604) 832-2126 Loc. 217
Res. (604) 832-0544
Fax (604) 832-4368
E-mail:parussell@okuc02.okanagan.bc.ca

OKANAGAN
UNIVERSITY
COLLEGE

initially framed on the assumption that the rules of the game that allowed for successful production and farm income in the East and Midwest would work in the West.

Thus, the first homestead allotments were set at 160 acres, an absurdly inadequate amount for even simple subsistence farming in the West. The size of the tracts were soon enlarged by various provisions. But, in any case, farm units became ever larger, as droughts, economic depressions, and other intermittent and often unpredictable circumstances made farming increasingly difficult; and as farmers gave up or turned to cattle as their main crop, their neighbors expanded. "Enlargement of unit" became, for several decades, the only effective means to combat the uncertainty and marginality of the physical and economic environment—and despite great improvements in the knowledge of cultivation and plant varieties, it still is.

Many ways of dealing with soil-blowing and moisture shortages have evolved, but basically the problems are insoluble so long as friable soils are overused or market pressures induce the cultivation of soils that should remain in grass cover. But even the latter has not prevented severe erosion, as the livestock markets have encouraged overproduction and overgrazing. The basic problem is the system of capital-intensive production—granting that many improvements have been made in farming and management techniques. And the record of resource management in the centrally planned agriculture of the semi-arid grasslands of the former Soviet Union is no better.

Thus behind the discussions of social aspects of production activity in this chapter lie a series a series of physical and institutional imperatives that can be considered to function as constraints on farmer behavior, requiring certain kinds of responses and discouraging others. Suitable strategies for maintaining crop and animal yield and income are subject to modification depending on the particular resource configuration in regions and on individual farm units. Thus there is a considerable element of chance: the ability to follow the rules of the game varies by all of these circumstances and, finally, by the skills and interests of particular farm operators. Success at farming is measured not only by income satisfaction but also by strategic behavior on the part of the farm operator and his family members—assuming that the "family farm" is still the instrumentality of production.

These "imperatives" consist of familiar patterns of economic activity in North America. *Land* was, and still is, allocated according to the principles of the institution of private property or, more precisely, freehold tenure. Land tends to be valued on the basis of what it would bring in an open sale to a private individual. However, in the West this basic institution has been modified or supplemented by other types of tenure: the leasing of government-owned land, renting of land from individuals, cooperative or joint ownership and/or management of agricultural land, or fee-paying for the use of government land. The allocations of *water*— that precious resource in the semiarid West—were based on various doctrines described later in this chapter. However, various modifications of the doctrines in areas where government-financed and constructed water schemes introduced different types of assignment. Despite these changes in the historic capitalist institutions of land and water tenure, the underlying values or expectations emphasize private ownership and rights. For example, even in the case of government-owned leased grazing land the lessee is entitled to sell his improvements, providing, of course, that the lessor approves of the transfer of the lease to the new "owner."

The basic assumptions concerning resource conservation include the idea that when an individual has control—if not outright ownership— over resources he will guard their productivity. This value is in turn based on the assumption that the traditional father-son succession procedure guarantees that the father (or present owner) will make sure that his son (or successor) is provided with a viable enterprise. That is, private entrepreneurship is supposed to contain an inherent conservationist philosophy. This belief, of course, is less operative when the resources are subject to market mechanisms that make it less likely that the present owner really cares about the condition of his land. The urge to extract one's "equity," or invested cash and sweat, can result in exploitative use with little concern for successor operators.

Studies of Leased Grazing Land

As we have suggested, the history of livestock production in most Western states and provinces is based on changes in land tenure. And land tenure, in turn, was based on the existence of a land survey that could permit clear demarcation of tracts. Everywhere in the West the first agricultural users of the land were cattle and horse raisers who were little concerned with ownership since the land they used was unfenced and unsurveyed range, subject to understandings and agreements between the users—as range was, and still is, in parts of Asia and Africa under control by migratory herders (see chapter 8). Livestock were rounded up at intervals as a joint undertaking by all the raisers functioning as an association or informal cooperative body.

Land surveys were undertaken in the West when it became evident that the land had to be opened to farmer settlers. As settlement decisions were made the surveyors moved in and laid out the land in a rectilinear grid, ignoring topography and watercourses. This grid was based on one-mile square units, called sections, and a township consisted of thirty-six sections—and so on. The system was based on the British land survey, and was designed to permit easy determination of property ownership and also to facilitate the plotting of government jurisdictions. It had, as suggested, little or no ecological relevance.

The livestock raisers had to conform to this system, which meant the creation of fenced tracts called "ranches," many of them wholly owned. The majority, however, at least in the Saskatchewan region researched, consisted of large tracts leased to the operator and a small tract, sometimes little more than a quarter-section, owned as a homestead and containing the ranch buildings. These new surveyed and fenced ranches changed the scale and technology of livestock production, requiring attention to range and water conservation and ownership rights.

From time to time portions of former rangeland that had been opened to homesteading were reclassified as range since it was found too dry, high, or rough for farming. This process of revision of and reversion to earlier forms of land use, a consequence of thee blanket grid land survey system, continues, as instrumentalities like grazing cooperatives, community pastures, government-owned rangeland in the United States, and planned water and land development schemes appear and change.

The difficulties of grain production in the semi-arid Northern Plains led eventually to demands by the remaining farmers for access to large tracts of grazing land. Consequently, in Saskatchewan, with a strong cooperative tradition, portions of large ranches were reclassified as leased land and opened to farmer bids or made available for grazing cooperatives benefitting small ranchers as well as farmers. This system also to some extent protected grazing land from speculative pricing. In the United States somewhat similar systems evolved, but the majority of government rangeland is made available to ranchers on a fee basis—a system that by the 1980s had become a political and environmental issue since the low grazing rentals encouraged overgrazing. In any event, straight grain farming has given way nearly everywhere in the Northern Plains to mixed ranching and farming on medium-sized tracts. Large-scale grain production is found only in especially suitable regions of Montana and the Dakotas and, in Canada, in areas like the Regina Plains or parts of southern Alberta.

During the 1960s, grazing leases in Saskatchewan were awarded to livestock producers on a uniform thirty-three-year basis. This tenure represented a simplification of a confused system inherited by the Cooperative Commonwealth Frederation (CCF) government in 1944 (Lipset 1968). According to the simplified procedure, leases were assigned to suitable individuals upon application when the land in question was posted as available for lease. Leases could be transferred by bequest to a legitimate heir, although the Lands Branch of the provincial Department of Agriculture might attempt to modify the arrangement when the heir was manifestly incompetent. Assignment of leases to any new lessee was made by a board of impartial citizens, who were required to review the individual's serious intent to remain in agriculture in the locality; his general competence as a farmer or rancher; his need for the particular lease; and evidence of his ability to stand on his own feet in the near future, if not immediately. These criteria emphasized individual competence and stability of residence; persons with these capacities had a better chance of getting a lease than those without.

Low rental fees were charged on grazing leases: an average of $.075 per acre for all lands, but $.155 for the best grazing lands. These small rental costs made it possible to operate a livestock business with great economy of cost of basic resources (as is still the case in both Canada and on "public lands" in the United States). The lessee was required to obey certain rules concerning his use of the land. He could not cultivate a grazing lease and sell the crops; he could not permit anyone else to pasture livestock on his lease; he had to maintain a certain carrying capacity—that is, he could not overgraze by letting too many animals use the land. He could "sell" his lease to a private buyer; however, in reality he could sell only improvements like buildings and irrigation as well as, of course, the deeded pieces. The seller also had to stay within 20 percent of a certain price-value for the improvements and deeded land, as assessed by a representative of the Lands Branch. Leases were also allocated on the basis of a definition of "economic unit"—a technical term defining a situation in which production and resources are in balance, or a ranch just the right size for the amount of labor that the applicant can supply to work it. And the government had to investigate the prospective new lessee before transferring the lease to him.

Thus, the lessee had the right to will his lease to an heir and to "sell" the lease, or at least what amounted to his accumulated equity in it, to an approved buyer. He could pasture his own cattle, but not those of others, and he had to keep the lease in good condition. His tenure was therefore mixed: he had some of the rights of outright ownership, but the government retained control over his treatment of the property and also over its ultimate disposition.

Everywhere in the West cattle ranching evolved on the basis of low grazing rentals. The savings created by these low resource costs allowed the rancher to improve his breed of cattle, repair his house, educate his children, or just save his money and bequeath it to his family. Saskatchewan ranchers were not very well off until after World War II, because low prices for cattle during the 1930s had built up large debts; hence, the low grazing rentals also served to tide the rancher over during a period of disastrous drought and economic depression.

Despite the economy of the operation, the institution of leased grazing land was resented by the majority of Saskatchewan ranchers, who regarded it as an invasion of their rights of private property. The appeal of land everywhere is based on its image as a "private place," a locus in space on which the farmer and his family live out their lives and carry out their business as they see fit. Their resources are supposed to be their own, to do with as they please. If land is rented, it is defined ideally as a small or accessory tract, often not as productive as the titled land, and is viewed as disposable if its management is overly time-consuming or expensive. That is, the culturally normative conception of using land other than "owned land" featured the notion of a disposable investment.

However, if most of one's livestock is actually raised on government land, the government has an interest in the raising of the animals, since it is concerned with the condition of its land and what happens to it during its use for grazing. In one sense, the Saskatchewan rancher or farmer leasing land could be considered as an agent of the government who is compensated for his care of the land by being permitted to keep the profits from raising his cattle.

The basis of rancher opposition to the institution of leased land, in the face of their realization of its obvious economy, was found in two attitudes toward land. The first of these is that of usufruct or use-right, a form of land tenure common in tribal societies and especially in the institution of territorial rights among hunters and herdsmen. It was likewise important on the open-range cattle frontier, with its communal grazing controlled by Roundup Associations. In usufruct tenure, the group or person has a property right over the land so long as he uses it. Thus Saskatchewan ranchers sometimes conceived of their tenure as implying the *right* of the individual to treat the land as he pleases, so long as he is in actual use-possession of it.

The second attitude concerned the right to own the land without fear of risking its withdrawal—that is, the need to confirm the right of private property. In this conception, opposition to leasing took the form of resistance to the institution of leasing itself and anger about the occasional nonrenewal of ranch leases and their transfer to farmers in need of grazing land. The ranchers held that, as private entrepreneurs, making their own living on the land, they should have the right to own it in clear, inalienable title, and not have to lease it from the government, risking its withdrawal. One other argument frequently given in justification of this view was that a man will not take proper interest in maintaining or improving his land if he does not have a deed to it. In fact, however, most ranchers observed proper caution in grazing and followed the government rules on carrying capacity and the like, since these regulations were on the whole in their own interest.

We noted earlier that, in one sense, the rancher did have a "deed" to his land. When he died, he could bequeath his lease to a "bona fide relative," providing the relative was an agriculturalist. The ambiguity of the rancher's attitudes on tenure rights thus had a partly realistic basis in inheritance practices: the operator *did* have a kind of title; his use-right *was* strong in the area of testamentary succession. Thus, the values of individual property rights and family continuity, exerted through political pressure on legislators and bureaus, had led to modifications in the extent of bureaucratic control over land in government title.

Ranchers invoked either the usufruct concept or their philosophy of property rights when they discussed the problem of "security of tenure," the standard phrase referring to how certain a leaseholder can be of keeping the lease indefinitely, within or beyond the thirty-three-year period. The rancher would point out that he had lived on this leased land (in many cases, his father or other relative had lived there before him), raised children and cattle on it, developed its potential, husbanded its grass, starved for it, admired its scenery, and so on—and yet he had no permanent or legal title to it.

The Lands Branch looked at this matter very differently. Secure in its basic control of the land, it took the position that the leaseholder was awarded the use of the land only so long as he handled it according to regulations. His use of the land thus entailed responsibilities as well as rights. It was this idea of "responsibility" that the leaseholder did not appear to grasp. He might acknowledge responsibility to local custom or to his own conscience, but rarely or reluctantly did he feel that he owed any to the government, which has no "right," in the ethics of individualism, to demand responsibility from the individual.

Thus, one government official explained to the writer:

> A grazing lease is not only a matter of land, control given to the individual, but is also a privilege for the use of that land. The rentals are extremely low, really a subsidy of the operator for raising livestock, and we feel under those circumstances that we have the moral as well as the legal right to define the lease as a privilege and a responsibility.

It was this very "privilege and responsibility" that the rancher leaseholder did not like to acknowledge.

Attitudes of the farmers toward leased land differed substantially from those of the ranchers. Farmers had been acquiring leases for a period of only about twenty years; they usually obtained them in small parcels, to assist in the partial conversion to livestock production. Farmers used considerable political pressure to obtain this land and regarded it as their right and proper share. Farmer identification with the CCF government was strong, and they viewed leased land as a kind of gift from "their" (farmer-oriented) government. This difference in attitude, and the fact that farmers were latecomers to the livestock industry, established competition between ranchers and farmers for leased grazing properties.

Competition for Leases

We noted that ranches with the majority of their land in leases could be sold, providing the sale price was no more than 20 percent of the Lands

Branch assessed value of the deeded properties and improvements, and subject to approval of the Branch. These regulations had the effect of thrusting the Branch into the process of land sales in the local communities. The effects of this intervention are discussed below.

In general, most sales of privately owned agricultural properties in southwestern Saskatchewan were made to local people on the basis of kinship, friendship, or complex business relationships involving favors granted and repaid. Leased land was also subject to this practice before new regulations came into effect in the 1950s. Before that time, leases could be transferred to any person the lessee indicated; government approval was perfunctory. With new regulations, the Lands Branch could exert more control over the price of the property and the person to whom the ranch was sold. This had the effect of opening up the sale to outsiders who might think they could qualify for the lease or who believed that they had some political influence with the Lands Branch.

The buyer of one ranch was a wealthy man from an Alberta town, whose political influence enabled him to get the Lands Branch to approve assignment of the lease to him over other candidates, some of them local. In all other transactions over a fifteen-year period, however, ranches were transferred to buyers in the immediate ranching and farming districts. Competition was keen among these local people, and prices inevitably went up. This put great pressure on the 20 percent limit, and price increases appeared in the form of "under the table" agreements between seller and buyer to pad the price of the ranch. The official price would be within the legal limits; the unofficial price would be higher. Ingenious means were worked out to permit the buyer to increase his offer: interest-free loans, gifts of livestock, transfer of bonds or other securities, or simply unrecorded cash payments. All of these were technically illegal.

One consequence of all this was to make the sale of a ranch a complex and largely secret ritual. To some extent, sales of large properties everywhere have this characteristic, but lease regulations were the specific cause in the Saskatchewan case. Many of the dealings in prospective sales took place in secret, long before the government agents were called in, and buyer and seller consulted at length to determine how to arrange things so that the government's favorable decision on lease transfer could be guaranteed. In short, the government intervention had the effect of driving ranch sale transactions even more into the domain of covert social relations than they had been previously.

Leases could also be "put up" for open application, as when a rancher died intestate, or when nonoperation of the ranch forced the government to reappropriate the lease. In such cases, a notice of availability of the lease was printed and posted in government offices in Regina and in the locality. Applicants could then submit their requests, with all necessary information, and the Lands Branch would choose among these on the basis of criteria described earlier. Since most leases were transferred to new lessees either by sale or by testament, this procedure appears to have occurred rarely, and then usually only in the case of small tracts.

About every fifteen years, however, at least one large lease went up for open application. This usually became the occasion for strenuous local competition. The fact that such a lease would be available was usually known throughout the community before the government posted the opening. The local etiquette required that everyone interested in the lease should wait until the posting was made before submitting an application. In almost every case we examined, however, at least one local person was anxious enough to obtain the lease to attempt to get a head start on his neighbors and friends. This involved setting up consultations with politicians from whom one might have some reason to expect a favor—usually a word with the Lands Branch—or it simply meant writing a letter to the Branch, stating that it was common knowledge that the lease would be posted, and that the writer was unusually well qualified. This was called "jumping a lease"; if more than one person was involved, the entire episode would be called a "lease war."

The "lease war" could also continue on into the period of public notice and legal application. One locality was settled with a number of small and medium ranches, all of them too small for income-satisfying operation, all their operators anxious to obtain additional grazing land. Several large ranches were adjacent to the smaller places, and one of the large ranches became available for lease due to the fact that its owner had died without an heir, and the ranch was being illegally grazed by a former friend. (Actually, there was a claimant, a relative, who "permitted" the rancher friend to "operate the ranch for him" but who was really grazing his—the friend's—own cattle.) The government finally disallowed this rather typical circumvention of lease regulations. The neighbors knew about this arrangement, of course, and at least two had reported it to the Branch by letter.

As soon as it became known that the Branch would investigate, the "lease war" was on. Nearly all the smaller ranchers made application, and one or two had done so long before the lease was posted. One of these resorted to political intervention and was successful in obtaining an informal promise of a substantial portion of the lease. Later, of course, he submitted a pro forma application. His "lease-jumping" earned him virtual ostracism from the ranching community for a decade. His right to and need for a lease was not questioned; the offense was his prior negotiation, conducted in secret, without the knowledge of his close friends and neighbors. The rest of the lease in question was divided among three of the other smaller ranchers in the district. Thus the Branch endeavored to strengthen four marginal enterprises by breaking up one large lease.

Leases and Kinship Relations

In all the larger families of the region—both ranchers and farmers— there existed a history of considerable father-son and brother-brother conflict. In each of these cases involving large properties and large families, these familial stresses led to difficulties in the transfer of property at the death of the operator and also in the management of the ranch as an enterprise. This situation, by itself, was not the consequence of lease-transfer regulations; but the fact that the government entered these cases as an interested participant resulted in a change in the method of property transfer and the relations among family members.

In the fifteen years preceding the study on our sample group of thirty-six ranches, most of them linked by kin ties, the Branch was known to have participated intimately in four major cases of difficulties between relatives over inheritance and disposition of leases. Briefer involvements were recorded on three others. With regard to the problem of inability of relatives to cooperate over the management of existing separate leases, one case involved major government intervention in this same period; lesser degrees of intervention were reported in three other cases. We were told of one other major case in which family difficulties over leases and related matters predated the present government, making four altogether in a period of a little more than twenty years. Less specific data were secured on cases going back fifty years or more in the region. It seems reasonable to conclude that family troubles involving leases were fairly common and that the government's role in resolving the issues was a significant one.

Retirement, Succession, and Property Division

One of the principal styles of family management on the early ranches (1885–1900) was an informal partnership between a father and one or more sons. The arrangement between the men was not formalized either because the practice of leasing land did not exist in earlier days or because the ranch was located in a district where homesteading was improbable and the question of security of tenure or difficulties over transfer of leases would not be likely to arise. Under these relaxed conditions, father and sons could carry on a cattle enterprise with little thought of the future disposition of the property; it was assumed that the ranch would be taken over by one or more of the sons. Relations between father and sons were such as to make planning for the future—setting forth a clear, rational choice as to which of the sons would take over—very difficult. Consequently, the decision was allowed to develop slowly. Typically, some of the sons would lose interest in ranching; they would have arguments with fathers or brothers and leave the premises to the survivors. The relaxed regulations of the earlier days made it possible for family relationships to influence ranch management in this way.

As lease regulations became tighter, and particularly as the Lands Branch developed regulatory principles that pertained to rational management and economic viability, these informal attitudes about the succession issue had to change. In one case, the first-generation proprietor of one of the larger ranches had educated his sons in the practical tasks of ranching by the traditional apprenticeship system. The sons were given no training in skills other than ranching, and it was understood in the family that the sons would continue in the business after the father's death. Before the lease renewal came due, the father wished to split up the ranch among his three sons, in conformity with the old customs of informal multiple inheritance. The government, however, refused to permit the division of the ranch on the grounds that the segments would be too small and therefore would be "uneconomic units." The three sons, with the father still on the ranch, tried to operate it jointly. There were numerous quarrels and difficulties, and finally the eldest of the sons left and bought a ranch in Alberta. His share in the ranch was bought out by the two younger brothers. The two brothers then tried to work together, but this arrangement also failed. The middle brother had a disagreement with the father, left after the young brother said that he would buy out his share, and became a laborer in a local town. The youngest son lived on the ranch with his father and his wife and children into the 1950s, then made a legal agreement with his father to purchase his father's share in the ranch. The father retired to town.

Under earlier Saskatchewan governments, the divided arrangement would probably have been approved. In the 1960s, however, the Branch disapproved of the multiple inheritance and the splitting up of the ranch. In this case, the termination of the lease forced a decision on the family that, in the old days, would probably have been reached more casually and on the terms proposed. In the past, notification of the government would have been a detail; in the contemporary era, it was a fateful step. The Branch's apparent refusal to countenance a traditional multiple succession triggered a series of family quarrels that ended with one son taking over, and it prevented the fractionization of grazing properties.

In another case the lease was not terminating. The father was advised by his lawyer to make an agreement with his two oldest sons, because he was aging rapidly and might die before a settlement could be made. One of the sons was established on a small ranch in the region that the father had bought for him out of savings. He proposed that the other son be established on one half of the old ranch, with the father operating the remaining half. While the sons would be assigned half the leases, the two would operate the entire spread as a single unit. When the father died, the other son could sell the small ranch he had bought and take the father's place.

This proposed arrangement was not approved by the Branch because there was chronic conflict between this father and his sons. The Branch therefore took the position that if the father and son could not agree on the management of the ranch and refused to cooperate, the government would be confronted with two economically marginal ranches. Two principles of government lease regulation are visible here: one is the formal and announced policy of maintaining "economic units," that is, the government's desire to maintain indirect control over agricultural quality. The second is an entirely informal policy that does not appear in the printed regulations: the disapproval of lease assignments on the grounds that family disagreements would result in deterioration of operating standards. In this sense, the Government took a stand on a particular aspect of kinship relations: the classic father-son conflict pattern in ranching families. Doubt was also thrown on the possibility of the two sons coming back together after the father's death. Finally, it was observed that the old ranch could probably not support two families, at least in terms of the sons' operating methods, which were known to be only moderately efficient.

In a third case a rancher of established reputation and skill managed the ranch that his father had willed to his surviving wife, the rancher's mother. On her death, the mother willed the ranch not to the son alone, but to all her children, some of whom had financial troubles. A formal partnership was arranged among these people. The operating brother informed his partners after a time that the ranch could not be expected to furnish them all with a living, but they were unable to come to an agreement among themselves on how to settle the issue. Their interference with the management of the ranch was also seriously affecting its productivity. The rancher finally consulted the Lands Branch, which advised him that he could either sell the ranch to an outsider or buy out the other family members. The government refused to transfer the lease to any other member of the family, since none of them were established ranch operators. The rancher tried to buy out the other members, but disagreements prevented them from concluding a suitable arrangement. Therefore, he took the alternative of selling to an outsider and dividing the proceeds among the partners.

In this case, the ranch had been willed to a large number of warring relatives, who could come to no agreement about management. The government's action apparently prevented what would have happened in an earlier time: a prolonged period of declining and increasingly disorganized management. The rancher, in this case, was not prevented by the Branch from doing something that he wanted to do; rather, he was assisted by the Branch in making the only decision that would permit the ranch to continue as an economic unit. This decision was to sell to an outsider of established reputation—a young man, son of another rancher in the region, who needed an enterprise to support his new wife and child. The decision was greeted with sadness by neighbors, who regretted the fact that one of the pioneer ranches in the region was passing out of the control of the original family.

Kinship Paternalism

This region of Saskatchewan, like all Western ranching societies, had a patron-client system that permitted young men to "bind" themselves to a benefactor, who provided them with money or facilities in return for labor and general loyalty. This institution included nonrelatives as well, but we are concerned here with a case of *kinship dependency*. A total of five cases with generally similar dimensions and problems were found to have occurred during the ten years preceding the study, in the sample group of thirty-six ranches.

In this case, a young man was staked by his wife's uncle to buy a small ranch adjoining the uncle's ranch. The arrangement was devised in order to help the young man and his wife, who was the niece of the older man, and also to help the older man, who was aging and unable to operate his place alone (but unwilling to give up). The older man was a bachelor, and hence he had no children of his own to help get started. The Branch assigned the lease of the adjoining ranch (which had been owned by a nonrelative) to the young man with some reluctance, since he did not have much of a record in agriculture. The transaction was allowed to go through, however, since the uncle was a first-generation member of an old and respected ranching family in the region.

After the young man took possession, a series of reciprocal transactions took place between him and the uncle. While some of these were beneficial to both, the uncle probably received the lion's share in the form of labor needed to run his own ranch. The transaction that finally attracted the attention of the government was the following. The uncle asked the young man to pasture some of the uncle's horses on the young man's lease in return for letting him pasture his cows on the uncle's lease. The advantage to the young man was that his cows could be serviced by the uncle's bull, thus saving him the price of a bull for his cow herd. This was a respectable saving, since a good bull cost about $500 during this period, and he had almost no resources other than those extended by the uncle. On the other hand, the uncle's herd of horses ate almost twice as much grass as the cows, so it is doubtful if he saved much in the long run. The young man complained to neighbors and friends about the transaction, but accepted it since he was in debt to the uncle.

A key government regulation concerned the requirement that a lease-holder could graze only his own livestock on his land, unless special permission was granted—and then for periods of one year only. In the casual tradition of ranching, the reciprocal grazing transaction was planned and carried out without the Branch being notified. This may have disturbed the young man, who was aware of the fact that the Branch was more vigilant than it had been in the past, but he gave way before the uncle's belief, carried forward from an earlier period, that no one would ever know the difference.

Apparently, the Branch was informed about the arrangement by the usual route. A neighbor wrote and complained, saying that leased land in the district was short in supply and could be used to better advantage by himself and others. He noted that the young man, while reasonably energetic, was not really interested in agriculture, and that, if he was willing to violate regulations, perhaps his lease should be given to someone else.

The Branch investigated, confirmed the existence of the arrangement, and wrote the two men, asking if the information was correct and requesting an explanation. The men put the matter in the hands of a lawyer who specialized in such cases. The lawyer wrote to the Branch, saying that the young man was dependent upon his relative and had to return the favors granted, since the old man did not have adequate help. He cited other cases in the region in which a favorable decision had been given on such arrangements and explained that the failure to request permission was an oversight. In the same letter, the lawyer forwarded a routine request to permit the young man to cut hay on his lease and sell a portion of it to his relative, who needed it. The government decided to grant permission for the grazing transaction (and also the hay-cutting) for the current year only, not subject to renewal. The Branch took the position that, even if the young man held the lease for several years, he probably would be no closer to "establishment" than he had been in the beginning. The Branch also noted that it probably would not have been satisfied with the young man's management ability and would have doubted if he was really interested in agriculture. There may have been an implication here that the government was aware that the young man was not a very good farmer-rancher and would probably like to get out, but that he was involved in a dependent relationship with a relative. The young man actually did sell the place, one year after this incident, and returned to his trade of auto mechanic in a nearby town. The land was bought by another young man not related to the uncle.

In this case, we see how the regulations were utilized to (1) enforce the policy of pushing leaseholders toward independent entrepreneurship; and (2) encourage uninterested operators to leave their enterprise and sell to a more qualified person. In discussions, officials pointed out that restrictions of grazing exchanges to one year could be based on the fact that while reciprocal grazing arrangements between father and son could be defended, those between other relatives could not. The Branch felt that the "primary family" deserved to enjoy exceptions to the rules, but it did not approve of the privilege for extended kin groups. Incidentally, nothing in the regulations forbade lease transfers or sharing of grazing land between fathers and daughters, although this was very rare.

Favors extended to the "primary family" were defined in informal policy statements in the following manner. The Branch looked with favor on all cases in which fathers and sons permitted their livestock to graze on each other's lease so long as this was part of the procedure for getting the younger man started in ranching. The father, in such cases, had to be an active cattleman, and not retired; if he was retired, the practice was held to be in violation of the regulation. A Branch official stated "We want to encourage natural succession and allow exceptions of the rules in order to permit this." "Natural succession" was the Branch's term for a father-to-son (or father-to-daughter) transfer of lease assignment, that is, single rather than multiple inheritance.

In any case, the informal policies developed by the Lands Branch on kinship ties suggest that government bureaus dealing with family enterprises are required sooner or later, to develop policies on the applicability of regulations to certain classes of kin.

Political Activity and Grazing Cooperatives

Reference was made earlier to campaigns by farmers to obtain grazing land for their expanding cattle industry. Local agitation among farmers over grazing land had a long history in southwestern Saskatchewan, dating back to the 1920s, and the activity was, of course, intensified with the accession of the CCF—the "farmer's government"—in the 1950s.

Much of this agitation took the form of campaigns for grazing cooperatives—groups of farmers with a joint lease, working together to maintain
the facilities, but owning their cattle individually. "Farmers" is not meant
literally; the real factor was size of enterprise, and some of the members
of grazing cooperatives were, in fact, small cattle ranchers. Such groups
would attempt to find land where they could and would then persuade
the provincial government to award them a lease or to assist them in any
way possible to purchase a substantial deeded tract. Each of the grazing
cooperatives had a different land tenure history. One co-op was wholly
deeded (local farmers managed to combine, form a co-op, and buy out
the owner of the single largest wholly owned ranch in the region); another
was formed out of a portion of a large lease detached from the rest and
denied to its former rancher lessee when renewal came up; others were
combinations of leased tracts and purchased land.

The political activity needed to obtain leases can be illustrated by the
following interview material, remarks made by one of the founders of
the co-op formed out of a single large lease tract detached from an old
ranch.

> Well, in 1950, it was, a little while after they passed the law—we started working on
> the idea. It really got started this way: one day that Lease Inspector was going through
> my yard here to get next door, and I asked him if there was any chance of us fellas
> getting a lease for a co-op around here. The Inspector said he thought so, because he
> knew that the X lease was going to be cancelled and put up for bids, because it wasn't
> being run right, just sitting there. He put me wise to contact the Department [of
> Cooperatives], this Extension office, and the Ag Rep here. So I did. Anyway, they
> came out to see us, and helped us organize a board of directors and apply for help
> under the cooperative law. I picked out the men around here who needed the cattle
> the most [all farmers with small acreage, just hanging on]. They were the younger
> fellas too, getting started on these small places. That's the main thing on these co-op
> pastures, to give the young fellas a start, because it's getting harder for them all the
> time. Around here lots of them just didn't stay around because their fathers didn't
> expand, so the Hutterites came in and bought up the land. Anyway, we applied for
> the lease and got it. Later on, when the Y place was being sold down south, we jumped
> in there and applied for a piece of the lease, and after quite a fight we got it. This gave
> us 13 sections, and now we got 14 fellas in the co-op now. It took a lot of work to get
> them last 8 sections from the Y place—I kept asking around in town every time I went
> in, trying to find out when it was going up for sale, and asking when Mr. Jones from
> the land bureau was going to come into town to hear the men [prospective buyers]
> who wanted it. We wrote him a long letter—several of them—telling him we wanted
> it. Finally I got the word he was coming to town so I ran in in a hurry, saw him at the
> hotel, and he told me to keep out of the meeting, that he had our need in mind. Well,
> I waited around, and finally they came out of the meeting, and Herb Jost, he came up
> to me and really looked at me, mad as the devil. Then I knew he got the place, but we
> got our 8 sections!

No sir, you don't get these co-ops by just hoping, you got to work. I forgot to mention that Stan Stanko's daughter, Nellie, she is a secretary in Regina for a Member, and she helped us by getting us information on what leases would be up, and about the new law.

In some respects, the grazing cooperative typified the tendency in Saskatchewan, especially among farmers, to get together in order to obtain the resources one needed; but, at the same time, the cooperative reaffirmed the basic adherence to private property institutions. By the time of the study, the grazing co-op had become a social institution as well as an instrument for resource acquisition and production. For this reason, some descriptive details about the co-op's activities may be of interest.

The structure of the organization emerged most clearly in the annual roundup and branding operations on the co-op pasture. These sessions also provided opportunities for observing relationships between farmers and ranchers, since often the neighboring big ranchers participated as helpers and friends in the activities. They were intensively social events. The women supplied lavish picnic lunches, the young people had opportunities for courtship and play, and neighbors could plan various cooperative exchanges and social functions for the coming months.

Grazing cooperatives recruited a new member by vote when one of the original group dropped out. Fees for lease rentals, maintenance of fences, a fence rider and herder, and the bull herd were charged annually. Each member was allowed a given number of cattle, the number adjusted occasionally in accordance with improving or deteriorating pasturage. In times of drought, the number was supposed to drop, which could cause hardship for the farmers who depended heavily on cattle during these very periods. The average yearly expenditures of a grazing cooperative were about $7,000, and most co-ops in the region met these expenses without deficits during the 1950s and early 1960s, a period characterized by generally high prices for cattle and good moisture conditions. Brandings and roundups were carried out jointly by all members, as they were in the old openrange roundup associations. Financial assistance from government averaged $6,000 per co-op per year during the decade of research. This figure covered assistance for fencing and corral construction mainly, and the amount tapered off in the 1970s to about $5,000. The amount of annual assistance to a given co-op was as high as $10,000 in the early 1960s, when most of the cooperatives were formed, as they required considerable assistance for establishing new pasturelands and fodder facilities.

The avowed purposes of the grazing cooperative, as stated by the farmer whose remarks were quoted earlier, were to promote income stability through diversification and also to strengthen the younger farmers who needed a better start. There is no doubt that the first of these objectives was continuously met by the operation of the co-op. The second, however, tended to change as time went on. In one of the regional co-ops, no younger man had been admitted for several years, and two sons of members were turned down in favor of two older neighbors when an opening occurred. In another, with twenty members, there were five father-son pairs, or half the entire membership, demonstrating that kinship was an important factor in admitting young men. In a third, 80 percent of all members were relatives in the male line. (Because of the predominance of a single family name, this co-op was known humorously as the "Lenko Family Ranch.") In one co-op, a member led a campaign to introduce a point system for entrance, which would have had the effect of keeping relatives out, but after a one-year trial this system was voted out.

Aside from the tendency for the co-op to exclude the younger men, their chief problem concerned the pressure to increase the herds of members at the expense of the total number of members. According to lease regulations, evaluated carrying capacity of the land determined the total number of stock, hence the only way the individual farmers could increase their herds was to reduce the membership. In one co-op that started with twenty-five members, the number had dropped to twenty-two in the fourth year of operation. The farmers who dropped out were not replaced, and their herd allotments were divided among the remaining members. Others showed comparable drops. The co-op thus could become an instrument for private gain among a group of neighbors—that is, local control over possible tragedies of the commons.

The essential feature of the grazing cooperative concerned the assignment of a lease, the ownership of deeded land by a group of neighbors who then combined their efforts to maintain the resources needed for their own separate enterprises. This system worked well, in contrast with another means of collective-use effort, the *community pasture*. The creation of these latter facilities involved preliminary political action campaigns by farmers and small ranchers in need of additional grazing land, but they were operated by federal and provincial governments as grazing facilities with irrigated forage production and sometimes bull-breeding stations.

Although the pastures were operated by the government, so that farmers could obtain no equity in them, farmers using them occasionally displayed collective sentiment—"our pasture"—and recognized them as vital to the economic well-being of the community. From the cooperative point of view, this attitude had its virtues, but also, from the standpoint of the government agency supervising the pastures, its liabilities. Thus, most of the problems described as typical of the grazing co-ops were also found for the pastures. Pasture patrons sometimes conspired to adjust the size of their herds up or down, despite the regulation that allots each patron the same number; they sought to curry favor with the pasture manager in order to obtain lucrative custom contracts for haying; and they exerted pressure to keep some men in and others out. Most of this activity went on behind the back of the manager and was in violation of the regulations, whereas in the co-op it took place in the "legitimate" context of the business meeting and represented group decision.

Such particularistic maneuvering led to results similar to those noted for the grazing co-ops. Young men tended to be excluded from patronage by various techniques. For example, when a vacancy occurred, neighbors could get together and write letters to the agency supportive of one of themselves and speaking against a prospective new member. Or, on the other hand, when the regulations were changed so as to expel certain categories of patrons—such as old-age pensioners—complaints were so loud, and political pressure so severe, that the rules had to be modified. Thus by the 1960s, perhaps a majority of patrons of the pastures were the most persistent and energetic, but not always the best, middle-aged farmers in their districts.

While the pastures made it possible for farmers to supplement and stabilize their income and hence to remain in agriculture, the effect of the pastures on the economy was to increase livestock production among a group of small producers who had come to depend intimately on this type of production. Consequently, when cattle prices fell or drought forced herd reductions, these farmers were thrown back on their original grain income. This strengthened the farmers' determination to acquire private grazing leases, which could be done only by having them reassigned from ranchers. The ranchers were aware of this relationship between community pastures and the farmer campaign for leases and consequently criticized the community pasture system. Most ranchers and their professional association, the Saskatchewan Stock Growers' Association, felt that government should turn the community pastures into self-supporting cooperative ranches or grazing cooperatives.

In any case, local grazing cooperatives had advantages over government-managed facilities. In the latter, the individual patrons had collective sentiment, but no general collective responsibility: they were free to combine against regulations, exert pressure as individuals, or seek special favors. In the co-ops, the responsibility was joint and definite, and regulations had to be worked out by discussion and vote. The co-op "owned" its land and benefited from its equity, even though title was kept by the government. The pasture patrons simply used the land, and had little sense of ownership and respect for it. In only one of the several community pastures of the region did the patrons have something of a collective existence—and it was this pasture that had the most intensive neighborhood effort behind it in the beginning.

Water: Private Rights and Public Irrigation

Water is the most important limiting factor in Western agriculture. Its scarcity and its geographical variability make it an increasingly prized resource as population increases and as development proceeds. In many parts of the West competition for surface water was reaching a point of saturation by the 1970s, as individuals insisted on full use of water rights that collectively exceeded stream flow or as plot-renters on the public irrigation schemes exceeded their allotment of water. Still, these instances did not pose as serious a problem in Saskatchewan as they did in parts of Texas or Arizona, where competing uses for water among urban, industrial, recreational, and agricultural users have created serious shortages and the need for rigid regulations. Moreover, groundwater resources were virtually untouched: there were no irrigation schemes based on deep wells, and the only major use of the abundant ground water from the southwestern Saskatchewan Cypress Hills aquifer was the domestic supply for the region's principal service-center town.

Water Rights

Betty E. Dobkins, in a presentation of the historical development of water laws in Texas (1959, esp. chap. 1), distinguishes between three types of legal arrangements governing the use of water in North America: the riparian rights laws, the doctrine of prior appropriation, and the "administrative type." The first of these systems developed in England and became part of the common law. It was based on a humid environment where access to land was more important than to water. Each holder of a riparian right had equal rights to the water flowing by his property, providing that he returned the water to the stream after using it. The water was seen, therefore, as a usufruct, not an object of outright possession. Such a concept was appropriate to an early industrial economy in which the most intensive use of water was to turn the wheels of grist mills.

In arid and semiarid western North America, the riparian doctrine was unworkable for several reasons. First, irrigation, which became the major use for stream water in the West, reduces the amount of water available to downstream users, because some of it is absorbed by the soil or evaporates; hence, the usufruct concept of water could not apply in toto, although it could be assumed that *some* of the diverted water would be returned to the stream. Second, riparian rights require stream frontage; in the West, canals provide irrigation to people without frontage. Third, riparian rights assume constant or nearly constant stream flow. This is a condition met with in humid lands, but not in the West, where many streams are greatly reduced or even completely dry except for the spring flood period. Obviously, riparian rights could not be applied in the West, and modifications began to develop with the beginning of settlement.

The second type of water law, that based on the doctrine of prior appropriation, is really a complex set of procedural modifications of the common-law riparian conception in use by Western states and provinces. These laws have the following characteristics: (1) They specify that water shall be used for *beneficial* purposes—in contrast to the riparian conception of "any *reasonable* use." That is, the water must not be used casually: in rural areas, this usually means that it must be used for agriculture. (2) The laws provided for the reduction of volume of water by irrigation diversion and absorption. (3) The new laws also held that the first persons—settlers—to put the water to beneficial use had rights to it ("prior appropriation"). Thus, the first settler on a stream would have

Water Right No. 1; the next settler, No. 2, and so on. In many cases, the amount of water to be diverted is specified in each right—usually expressed in terms of acre-feet, or the amount of water necessary to cover an acre of ground to the specified number of feet. (4) In the old riparian conception, water could be taken at any time of the year; in the prior-appropriation modifications, the period of permitted diversion is often specified, and, if the water is not taken at that time, it is forfeit. In general, the prior-appropriation rules hold that there is no absolute right to water; it is qualified by the amount available, and is shared, in turn, by a group of neighbors on the basis of priority and time of year.

These modifications of the old common-law versions of water rights had been worked out in the United States by the 1870s, and thus were available to the Canadians when they wrote their water laws a decade or so later (see Gisvold 1959). Saskatchewan's first water rights laws were written in 1882, when the area was part of the old Northwest Territories. The first rights under these laws were granted in the southwestern region in the early 1880s. Two families still living in the area in the 1960s held their original No. 1 right on their frontage creeks, rights dating from the 1890s. Water rights remain with the property, of course, and subsequent owners or lessees acquire them in the transaction, although a separate action of transfer must be made, as in the case of leased grazing land.

Water rights, therefore, constituted the oldest system of government regulations governing the allocation and use of natural resources in Saskatchewan. Since water is vital for winter forage production, ranchers regarded water rights as personal property (which they really were not), and also as an inalienable part of the ranch as a *private place*. Low-numbered water rights were also a prestige item—whether or not the person holding them had acquired them through inheritance from the original applicant. Dobkins' third type of water law—the administrative—is a development out of the prior-appropriation laws that appeared relatively recently in the form of irrigation projects financed by the government.

Saskatchewan's water laws represent combinations of prior appropriation and administrative regulations, although they had not evolved to the highly explicit stage as represented by Colorado laws (Dunbar 1948). However, in contrast with Montana, where nearly every dispute over water rights is brought to court in the form of a civil suit, in Saskatchewan disputes were resolved in nearly all cases by administrative intervention.

(Down to 1968, only one case in twenty-five years had been brought to court; Montana courts were chronically full of cases.)

In any case, water rights in Saskatchewan were granted to individuals, and, whatever their actual status in law, they were regarded by local people as equivalent to a title to water. This impression was strengthened when a farmer or rancher decided to build a check dam in a drainage coulee leading into a main stream and requested a water right to permit the impounding of water. If he received the right, he believed that he had received title to a certain *amount* of water, although legally he had only the right to *use* a certain amount. Similarly, when a man with a right diverted floodwater in spring to irrigate his hay field, in his view he had simply taken what was his by legal possession. This local conception of water ownership was repeatedly demonstrated when ranchers took water out of the creek *after* the spring flood, justifying their action by saying that they did not "take all the water that was coming to [them] during spring." According to the regulations, they forfeited this water if they did not take it when allowed; thus, they had no *title* to water, only the *right to appropriate some for beneficial use, at the time specified*. While the actual quantity was specified, this was not as important to the rancher as the right of possession. The legal principles involved were regarded by the local ranchers as hairsplitting.

When water rights granted to individuals were used for irrigating their own hay fields by diverting creek water into ditches running through their property and then back into the creek, individual rights and irrigation practices merged into a single system. Difficulties arose when an individual without creek frontage applied for a right and sought to dig a canal through someone else's property, but these matters were usually settled by administrative decision by the provincial water agency and by personal negotiations between the parties concerned. More complex problems emerged when the system of private water rights had to be combined with a community or watershed irrigation program, in which large amounts of water were impounded in reservoirs for use in public irrigation plots used by a large number of agriculturalists. Here the individual holders of rights faced the necessity of sharing their water not only among themselves, according to the specifications of their rights, but also among an even larger number of people who did not live near the creeks. Under these circumstances, there was a basic conflict between individual use and public or collective use.

Conflict over Water Rights[*]

On the Saskatchewan ranching frontier of the late nineteenth- and twentieth-century water rights were a matter of simple request. A man routinely asked for a right, and he received it with no difficulty. Ranches were few, and water, therefore, relatively abundant. Irrigation was elementary: a ditch or two to run spring floodwater onto a field, where it was permitted to soak into the soil, drain into old oxbows along the creek, or drift into hollows. Too much water was diverted, and too much of it was lost from the creek; but since users were few, there were no complaints. During the 1960s, many of the older ranches were still using the original ditches built by their fathers or grandfathers, and the ranchers resisted attempts by the government agencies to get them to rebuild the ditches or properly level the fields so that water could be used more efficiently.

As the older ranches were broken up, and portions of formerly homesteaded land were opened to small leases, the number of ranches increased, and water rights were granted to permit irrigated hay production. From 1900 to 1963 the rights on one major creek increased by nearly six times and on the second creek by more than five times. All these rights were for spring flood irrigation, except about four or five for each creek, granted in the 1960s, for pump extraction of water, used mostly for sprinkler operation. The factors of increase noted for these two creeks were duplicated for the others in the region, proportionate to the amount of water available or to the number of users. (The greatest increases in numbers of individual rights occurred, of course, along the creeks with largest volume of flow.) About 5 percent of the increase in water rights on two major creeks in the study area could be attributed to additional rights given to existing older ranches, who had found the time and funds to develop their irrigation schemes beyond the original ditches—including stock dams and other water-impoundment schemes on the branches.

By the 1960s the provincial water agency believed that if all holders of water rights would take all the water coming to them in the specifications for their rights, most of the major creeks would go dry, and the storage reservoirs for the community irrigation projects would be dangerously depleted. The situation was saved by the fact that aging or carelessly maintained ditches on over 10 percent of the ranches took

---

[*] Additional material on this case study will be found in chapter 8.

much less water than was due the right-holder, and also that many ranchers with more than one right were not using all of these. Thus, the ranchers'conservatism about water development, *against* which the agricultural extension agents occasionally propagandized, paradoxically probably helped the whole system to operate without serious depletion! A provincial water official remarked,

They hang onto those water rights—they won't let go. They can't cooperate with each other on water, but still these are all friendly neighbors, good, nice people, they'll help each other on anything, get together in the roping club, fight for schools, but when it comes to water it takes the government to settle the fights!

In studying cases of friction between neighbors traceable to water rights, we made an effort to obtain knowledge of the frequency and magnitude of these difficulties. We noted that they fell into two large classes. The first category included difficulties between immediate neighbors on a particular creek, resulting from suspected irregularities in taking water. Such difficulties, a longstanding feature of the social scene, dated from about 1910, when the number of water rights began to increase. The second category of difficulties, of more recent origin, stemmed from the tendency to overuse particular creeks as a result of new methods of pumping water, new private irrigation schemes, and clashes between private and public irrigation systems. These latter difficulties were considerably more complex than the former, since they involved chains of reciprocal accusations.

We shall describe the chronic neighborhood quarrels first. On one of the major creeks it was determined that every rancher among the fifteen using water from this creek had accused or suspected his immediate neighbors of violating their own water-right acre-foot allowances at least once in the thirty years preceding the study. During the four years of research, there existed four cases of neighbor competition and suspicion, involving a total of eight ranchers. Other quarrels were quiescent. None of the parties to the existing disputes had reached the point of open break; all of them were on reasonably friendly, if not intimate terms, and work exchange on haying and branding took place among most of them.

These disputes centered on practices that a neighbor regarded as violating the reciprocity of water rights:

Now you take W. next door [actually, three miles upstream]. He went ahead and diked that flat next to the house and is putting water on it. He has a couple of rights up there, but he hasn't got one for that flat. He don't know nothin' about water, and he puts it on heavy. I don't know why he don't get a better crop, Lord knows he puts enough water on it! Anyway, in the spring he lets so much out there isn't enough [in the creek] to get into my ditches.

The facts were generally correct, except that the informant did not note (or may not have known) that the neighbor had applied for a right for his hay flat, but, due to bureaucratic delay, had not yet received it. A determined man, he went ahead with the project, since he needed the hay. Another informant remarked,

Last year this happened again. These three little fellers up above me—they're stealing water right and left. Two of them has bulldozed out a bunch of stock dams without getting rights [actually, one of them did have a right] and the other one, he's digging ditches all over his place. What can you do? I went ahead and built a dam too; it's a dog eat dog around here.

An important aspect of the disputes concerned the fact that moral conceptions about neighborly reciprocity and sharing were mixed with accusations of violations of water-right specifications. Whether the person involved actually had a right or not was less important than the fact that his use of the water was reducing the amount available to downstream users. This conception is reminiscent of the old common-law riparian notion of an equal amount available to all, although reduction of stream volume by water use is an accepted principle in the Western modification of riparian law. However, the precise legal dimensions of the situation were less important to these ranchers than the notion of fair play among neighbors who depend upon the same limited resource.

Only one informant among the many interviewed on this problem recognized that the conflicts were inherent in the system of private rights, and not in the character of the people involved in water use. The more typical views were represented by the remarks of the man quoted above, who resorted to similar "thefts" in self-defense; this type of retaliatory practice was common, and most people involved in water-rights struggles engaged in it. The single exception stated that quarrels would continue so long as the system of private rights was in existence:

Sooner or later they have to change this business of private rights. In the old days anyone could take all the water he wanted, and there wasn't enough places to matter. But now we're all fighting over the same water, and there isn't enough of that.

In general, "thefts" of water increased in the 1950s and 1960s as the number of ranchers and cattle farmers increased, and as costs rose to the point at which intensification of production was required to obtain income satisfaction. New methods of pasture development and irrigation began to take hold, and many of these were inoperable with existing ditching systems. Hence, enlarged ditches and pump-sprinkler systems began to appear, some surreptitiously, since the water rights were not adequate to permit these developments. A common practice was to run the pumps after midnight, when neighbors were assumed to be asleep. Deepened or enlarged ditches could be permitted to grow heavy weed crops to conceal their capacity. Or gates would be opened in broad daylight, on a Sunday, and lookouts posted. But it was difficult to fool the neighbors. They would carefully watch the flow of the stream past their property and could tell immediately if a new diversion had taken place. On one creek government measurement of flow had to be constantly maintained in order to be certain of sufficient water to take care of the American share, agreed upon by international treaty, since the creek, really a small river, supplied water to the Milk River, flowing into the United States. It was, however, on this creek that the largest number of clandestine water diversions took place, as a result of increasing development on the ranches and farms.

The practice of taking water in quantities or at certain forbidden times was in part a reflection of the lack of proper land leveling—the most expensive aspect of irrigation. A ditch can be dug by the rancher or farmer himself, at minimal cost, with tractor and scraper; land leveling requires special equipment and technical skills, and it cost about $100 an acre during the period of study. Government officials stated that if all the flood schemes were properly leveled on the major creeks "thefts" would be unnecessary, since the allotted amount of water would be used more efficiently, but they admitted that the only solution would be abrogation of all private water rights and a government-financed watershed development plan in which all farmers would be allotted irrigated land to produce their feed.

Community Irrigation Schemes

The setting was the Cypress Hills, a major erosional remnant mainly in southwestern Saskatchewan, an elongated east-west elevation reaching over 4,000 feet in some places, parts of which were never glaciated. The Hills run more or less parallel to the international boundary, the crest about 90 miles north of the line. Water flows down both slopes: the North Slope drains into the Saskatchewan River and Hudson's Bay; the South Slope eventually into the Milk River and its tributaries and finally into the Missouri River. One major irrigation scheme occupied each slope.

The North Slope project received its water mainly from two major creeks, both of which had old private ranch flood irrigation schemes based on pioneer water rights. The water was apportioned between the private schemes and two reservoirs constructed at the lower end of the slope. Below these reservoirs the water flowed into an extensive irrigation tract, consisting of plots for forage crops constructed and maintained for the benefit of small rancher and cattle-grain farmers, who rented them from the federal government agency that built and maintained the entire system.

The South Slope project, jointly built and maintained by both the provincial and federal governments, used the water from one major creek and also a large natural lake or drainage basin for smaller creeks and snowmelt runoff from the Hills. Like the North Slope, these water sources were tapped by private schemes. The water drained off into the Whitemud River, a northern tributary of the Milk, and international agreements had allotted shares to both Canada and the United States. This situation was an inevitable source of difficulty since it was difficult to persuade the Canadian ranchers and farmers to accept limits on all this water flowing through their property and country.

Both projects were large in scale, complex in construction, and the source of continual argument. The initial round of problems concerned the fact that in order to build the schemes the government agencies had to buy, eliminate, or use many of the private schemes, providing compensation or equivalent water service. This took about a decade to accomplish. The second arena of problems concerned the conflict between the plot holders at the base of the North Slope project and the ranchers and farmers above them. The former continually accused the latter of taking more water from the system than their water rights, modified by agreement with the project agency, entitled them to. A third arena of conflict concerned competition between the private water-rights holders along the creeks. Since the project, in order to maintain adequate supplies in the storage reservoirs serving the new plots, had to change allotments (even though assistance was given the users to redevelop and improve their ancient schemes to operate more efficiently) the rights holders felt that their right to whatever water they needed and at whatever time—attitudes described above—was being abridged by the government. Consequently, a pattern of competition developed between the holders, some of them "stealing" water—in the views of the neighbors—by various means. A fourth pattern of resentment and complaint was jointly manifested by all water users on the slope and the plot holders on the base of the slope, who felt that water drained off the plots, which continued several miles further north to provide still another irrigation project on a federal community pasture, should be kept in storage for more frequent waterings on their schemes and plots.

We investigated various instances of complaints and conflict. As we noted earlier, in contrast to the situation in Montana and North Dakota, where U.S. law permits private suits and other litigation between water users, in Saskatchewan most problems were resolved by "jawboneing" between the government water agencies and the various parties involved. A conflict between two or more individual water users on the developed creeks and the lake on the South Slope usually began with letters of complaint about water thefts, illegal sprinkler pumps, clandestine gate openings, and the like. These letters could be written by people who otherwise were considered good friends, cooperating on farm and ranch labor, and who might even have kinship connections. The agencies would then send a representative to investigate the activities and, eventually, to persuade the malefactor, if the allegations were true, to cease and desist.

Still other problems developed down on the "flats": the big scheme for forage production for small ranchers and farmers on irrigated plots on the North Slope. When the facility was completed and opened for application, very few operators did so, and the federal agency, desirous of getting the scheme functioning, awarded plots to a number of individuals engaged in marginal occupations and casual labor in the nearby town. These men saw an opportunity of augmenting their incomes by raising hay to sell to farm and ranch operators elsewhere, since the rental charge was nominal. Once a plot was awarded, it could be withdrawn only if the renter could be shown to abuse the privilege in some way. However, once the scheme was in operation, the operators for whom the scheme was designed realized its advantages, and agitation to expel the marginal plot renters in favor of authentic farm and ranching enterprises developed. By the early 1960s the plots were providing winter feed for 160 enterprises carrying 13,000 head of cattle, but if the marginal operators could be excluded, these figures could have been increased by a third or more. In addition, some of the farmer and rancher operators using the plots began to negotiate transfer of their plots when circumstances warranted, to relatives and friends—a situation comparable to that described for the grazing cooperative memberships. Similar problems were found for the irrigated tracts on the South Slope projects.

Conclusions

These cases from Saskatchewan concerning conflict and competition for water and land are examples of what happens when a system of individual enterprise, based on a common resource, is intersected by public regulations designed to equalize access to that resource. North American entrepreneurship encourages the agricultural operator to develop his resources to a level providing the largest possible yield at the lowest cost. The government agencies involved in these cases used this theme in their propaganda leaflets and instructional programs, in an effort to induce farmers and ranchers to take advantage of the opportunities afforded by the enhanced resources. The results helped the local economy but also increased the number of enterprisers desiring to benefit from the facilities. Within a decade or two both land and water, but especially the latter, became scarce. The existence of the private irrigation schemes (which politically had to be retained or duplicated but are now sharing water with the new irrigation schemes) meant that competition for water increased. Water is a finite resource; there is only so much to go around (although one of the uncertainties in the situation was the moisture variability of the northern Great Plains, which means that in some years the reservoirs and streams were overflowing while in other years they were virtually dry). Thus, government intervention in such an environment does not eliminate uncertainty and risk and competition for resources and in some cases intensifies them—although at the same time it also enhances access to them. The same effects are now seen all over the world, as economic and agricultural development schemes have been introduced—or imposed on—indigenous societies.

While the basic patterns of interaction are similar in all such cases, cultural content differs. For example, in these North American cases blood and affinal kinship do play a role, but they are not as significant as they would be, for instance, in a Latin American or East Asian agrarian context, where kinship ties are more pervasive in resource allocation. Such differences of emphasis and detail can be crucial in development projects, where even a single unknown factor, if ignored, can make the difference between success and failure of the project.

The North American case has, as already implied, distinctive characteristics attributable to the major values and behavior patterns associated with private entrepreneurship. This system presumably thrusts the onus of success on the individual. In reality, individual small entrepreneurs cannot function alone. They require assistance and support not only from neighbors and relatives but also from governments—whether they acknowledge it or not. There is, then, a constant interplay between the public values of these institutions—the way the bureaus are supposed to handle practical issues and regulations—and the private values and practices that evolved in particular localities.

In sociological jargon, "universalistic" values intersect "particularistic" values. *Universalism* refers to the strong tendency in democratic-capitalist societies toward treating everyone alike or giving everyone the same opportunity, an institutional pattern which may not be practiced in all cases, but which had a powerful influence on social and political attitudes. *Particularism*, on the other hand, refers to the treating of individuals as individuals, that is, in terms of a definition of their rights and obligations based on their particular characteristics: kin group membership, age, education, skills.

So the government bureaus must contend with the particularistic definitions of rights and privileges evolved in the culture of the community, and eventually this means that regulations begin to acquire exceptions or modifications based on these factors—as we saw in the case of kinship elements embedded in the application of land leasing regulations. So far as the local social systems are concerned, the insistence of bureaus to adhere to their regulations can result in, for example, the writing letters of complaint about water thieves, people who may be your neighbors and friends. But by writing such letters and keeping the infractions out of the sphere of personal relations the particularistic relationships are protected—at least to a degree.

Aside from implications for the social system itself, the arrangements described in this chapter also provide an example of the way natural substances become connected to social organization and cultural values, that is, an example of a "socionatural system" in operation. Human beings, their institutions and patterns of social organization, and the natural world form one interrelated system of action and decision.

Literature Cited and Consulted

Bennett, John W. 1982. *Of Time and the Enterprise: North American Family Farm Management in a Context of Resource Marginality*. Minneapolis: University of Minnesota Press.

_____.1986. "Research on Farmer Behavior and Social Organization." In *New Directions for Agriculture and Agricultural Research*, ed. Kenneth A. Dahlberg. Totawa, NJ: Rowmans Allenheld.

Dahlberg, Kenneth A., ed. 1986. *New Directions for Agriculture and Agricultural Research*. Totawa, NJ: Rowmans Allenheld.

Dobkins, Betty E. 1959. *The Spanish Element in Texas Water Law*. Austin: University of Texas Press.

Dunbar, Robert G. 1948. "Water Conflicts and Controls in Colorado." *Agricultural History* 22: 180–86.

Gisvold, Per. 1959. *A Survey of the Law of Water in Alberta, Saskatchewan, and Manitoba*. Publication 1046. Economics Division, Canada Department of Agriculture, Ottawa.

Lipset, Seymour Martin. 1968. *Agrarian Socialism: The Cooperative Commonwealth Federation in Saskatchewan*. New York: Doubleday.

Lockeretz, William. 1986. "Alternative Agriculture." In *New Directions for Agriculture and Agricultural Research*, ed. Kenneth A. Dahlberg. Totawa, NJ: Rowmans Allenheld.

Reisner, Marc. 1986. *Cadillac Desert: The American West and its Disappearing Water*. New York: Viking.

Worster, Donald. 1985. *Rivers of Empire: Water, Aridity, and the Growth of the American West*. New York: Pantheon.

Publications of the Saskatchewan Cultural Ecology Research Program Relevant to this chapter

Bennett, John W. 1966. "Ecology, Economy, and Society in an Agricultural Region of the Northern Great Plains." In *Social Research in North Amerrican Moisture Deficient Regions*, Contribution No. 9 of the Committee on Desert and Arid Zones Research, American Association for the Advancement of Science. Las Cruces: New Mexico State University.

_____.1967a. "Microcosm-Macrocosm Relationships in North American Agrarian Society." *American Anthropologist* 69: 441–54.

_____.1967b. "Social Adaptation in a Northern Plains Region: A Saskatchewan Study." In *Symposium on the Great Plains of North America*, ed. C.C. Zimmerman and S. Russell. Fargo: North Dakota State University.

_____.1968. "Reciprocal Economic Exchanges Among North American Agricultural Operators." *Southwestern Journal of Anthropology* 24: 276–309.

_____.1973. "Adaptive Strategy and Processes in the Canadian Plains." In *A Region of the Mind*, ed. R. Allen, Canadian Plains Studies No. 1. Regina: Canadian Plains Research Center.

_____ . 1975. "Characterological, Institutional, and Strategic Interpretations of Prairie Settlement." In *Western Canada, Past and Present*, ed. A.W. Rasporich. Calgary: McClelland and Stewart West and the University of Calgary.

_____ . 1976. *Northern Plainsmen: Adaptive Strategy and Agrarian Life*. Arlington Heights, IL: AHM Pub. Co.

Bennett, John W. and Cynthia Krueger. 1966. "Agrarian Pragmatism and Radical Politics: The Fate of the CCF." Supplementary chapter in Lipset 1968.

Kohl, Seena B. 1976. *Working Together: Women and Family in Southwestern Saskatchewan*. Toronto: Holt, Rinehart and Winston of Canada.

_____ . 1979. "The Making of a Community: The Role of Women in an Agricultural Setting." In *Kin and Families in America*, ed. A.J. Lichtman and J.R. Challinor. Washington, DC: Smithsonian International Symposia Series.

Kohl, Seena B. and John W. Bennett. 1965. "Kinship, Succession, and the Migration of Young People in a Canadian Agricultural Community." *International Journal of Comparative Sociology* 6: 96–116.

7

Social Aspects of Sustainability and Common Property: Lessons from the History of the Hutterian Brethren

Introductory

This chapter concerns the history and socioeconomic development of the Hutterian Brethren, a sixteenth-century Anabaptist sect practicing a comprehensive form of communal property. The experiences of Hutterites have implications for other agrarian communities organized on cooperative or communal principles. They also may shed some light on problems of common property and sustainable development projects in Third World countries. The historical contrasts are considerable: the Hutterites are survivors of a late medieval form of dissenting Christianity, but they are also practitioners of large-scale, efficient grain and livestock agriculture in the Northern Plains of North America. On the other hand, the institution of "common property" is a late twentieth-century concept

---

This essay, written especially for the book, is based on a series of research ventures concerned with communes and cooperatives I undertook beginning in the 1960s. A bibliography of the main items is appended to the chapter. The principal source is my book *Hutterian Brethren: The Agricultural Economy and Social Organization of a Communal People* (Stanford University Press, 1967), which reported on field work in twelve colonies in western Canada during parts of several years in the 1960s and early seventies. A second source is my work on agricultural cooperatives performed for the Land Tenure Center of the University of Wisconsin in the 1970s and 1980s, which was preceded by a 1966 observational tour of such organizations in the Far East and India under the auspices of the Agricultural Development Council. That tour began in Israel, where I lived for a time in a kibbutz community of the "left" federation of the movement, which is organized in a thoroughly communal fashion. At the invitation of the kibbutz leadership, I delivered a series of lectures on Hutterian communalism. Portions of the chapter were developed from notes for a paper delivered to the annual meeting of the International Association for Common Property in 1990. The writer acknowledges the assistance of Benjamin Kohl on bibliographic matters.

referring to collective management of physical resources for conservationist purposes in Third World agrarian communities.

Certain features of collective organizations are timeless in the sense that all people attempting to practice them will experience similar problems. However, the study of Hutterites and other communal and cooperative communities cannot tell us all we need to know about common property and its effects on the sustainability of resources. The writer considers the Hutterian colony—perhaps along with the Israeli kibbutz—the world's most comprehensive form of common property and thus an extreme case. This case therefore provides theoretical ideas concerning social development and change but probably few immediately applicable to organizational techniques.

Among the general themes of this chapter are the dynamic nature of resource management systems, their interlock with social organization and cultural values, their dependence on and interaction with exogenous institutions, and the difficulties of generalizing about causes and consequences created by such features. Another is the influence of individual behavior on resource and management systems and the way the rules and constraints can be modified by individuals seeking rewards.

Concepts of Sustainability and Common Property[*]

Since the early 1950s, the objectives of economic development have been expressed by a series of catchwords or phrases, each denoting a decade or so of practice and theory (e.g., Chilcote and Jackson 1983; Gamani 1990; Norgaard 1988, in III). The 1950s featured Industrial Development, which was soon superseded by Agricultural Development; by the 1970s the catchword was Poverty, which soon gave way to Basic Needs. And by the mid-1980s Sustainability joined the roster. The term represented an important awareness of the need in development work to obtain an economic regime that could be supported indefinitely and initiated by planned development projects. The term was associated with changes in policies of development and agencies requiring scrutiny of proposed projects in order to ascertain implications for resource conservation and social continuity (e.g., Barbier and Markandya 1990; von Weizacker 1991, in III). Thus, sustainability came to refer to the main-

---

[*] The bibliography for the chapter is divided into three sections; cited items include a Roman numeral referring to these.

tenance of productivity of a resource base and also to the stability of a particular socioeconomic regime that supported this. In fact, the use of the term "sustainability" in book titles could imply either one or both of these objectives, and in some publications it was necessary to study the document carefully before the precise emphasis could be grasped.

A problem obscured by varied meanings of "sustainability" lies in the fact that demands made on any resource base vary continuously by population and levels of income satisfaction. That is, a particular scheme conferring resource sustainability is designed for and will function only at particular levels of demand, and demand increases when population and wants/needs do likewise. Like other theoretical concepts relating to economic development, sustainability was often used or discussed without reference to the temporal dimension and the changing magnitudes of the factors influencing demand (e.g., Tisdell 1988; Redclift 1987, 1991, in III).

From the standpoint of ecological research, the sustainability concept was probably derived initially from studies of island ecosystems. Such studies (see Beller 1990 in III for a review) were among the very first research that included humans are part of the environmental matrix. Islands were attractive to ecologists since they were clearly bounded and the more isolated cases demonstrated processes and factors that could be relatively easily controlled in experimental ecological change programs. "Sustainability" in such studies came to be defined as maintenance of species and the closure of food chains, with measurable human input.

The concept of common property—another catchphrase associated with 1980s and 1990s development theory—centered on the concentration of ownership or control of the resource base within a group of resource users who are expected to manage the resource as a collective undertaking (e.g., McKay and Acheson 1987; Swaney 1990, in III). This definition has some important implications. The first is that the resources under collective control are barred from access by other individuals and groups; that is, it is a way of excluding some potential users and thereby controlling impact on the resource. Second, the degree of access by both members and nonmembers is variable: each common property system may have its own rules of accessibility. Third, obtaining membership in a common property organization can be easy or difficult: constrained by particularistic criteria (like age, sex, or kinship status) or subject only to simple, universal criteria (like citizenship). Fourth, most local common property systems must function within larger institutional contexts, like markets, trade associations, or government bureaus, that present a variety of constraints and opportunities. Few common property systems exist in an economic vacuum—a reason why typologies and abstract generalizations concerning both sustainability and common property systems are not very useful (e.g., the kinds given in Oakerson 1986, in III).

The relationship of resource conservation and common property institutions is theorized as close, based on the proposition that when a group of resource users has joint title and responsibility they will be disinclined to abuse the resources (Wade 1987, in III). The essence of the argument is that collective management induces a conception of sustainability of resources for the benefit of posterity. This proposition, like some other ideas in the development field, is subject to many qualifications, not the least of which is that the treatment of resources is rarely dependent exclusively on the users but also on external forces and agencies. If a significant fraction of agricultural production is for the market, the financial conditions created by the market mechanism will certainly influence the extent to which the resource base is used or abused, a variable accompanied by factors in any local social system that function as constraints and/or facilitating factors.

Forms of Collective Organization

The chapter deals mainly with one form—the commune, and, specifically, the Hutterian colony. Communes or communitarian societies are assemblages of human beings seeking to live modestly and avoid personal possessions and to maximize affiliative social relationships (Bennett 1975, in I; Erasmus 1977 and Hillery 1968, in IIC). However, before we concentrate on the Hutterites we must attempt to place them in larger perspective. The traditional dichotomy, of course, is individualistic vs. collective social organization—a distinction that arose mainly because societies with dominant individualistic values came to decisive prominence and power with the spread of capitalist industrialism in the eighteenth century. Prior to that time, most societies were pragmatic matrices of various forms of property and social organization, individualistic and collective. It is generally considered that, over the long haul of *Homo sapiens* history, collective or affiliative forms of organization dominated.

Individualism and individual liberty are associated mainly with modernity, democracy, and prosperity.

For our purposes, collective forms of organization may be classified into two main types: the cooperative and the communal (see Bennett 1977a, especially diagrams, in I). This classification, however, is simplistic; in actuality, real organizations are established on the basis of a mixture of features. These main features are as follows:

1. How is membership obtained or created? By application, recruitment, common descent, or mixtures of these?

2. Functions of the nuclear family of parents and children: to what extent is it granted autonomy by the larger community?

3. Who socializes and educates the children? The family, or the community?

4. How is consumption regulated? By shares of available income, by distribution of goods by the community, by informal individual purchase or manufacture?

5. If there is an economic surplus, what happens to it? Is it shared, equally or unequally, among the members? Invested or saved?

6. How are members remunerated for their services and labor? With cash, credit, or communal distribution of needed goods?

7. How is access to the pool of productive resources and capital goods controlled? Available to members only? To outsiders on arrangement? Are individual members free to use resources for their own production?

8. Does the organization have a central ideology to which everyone must subscribe? Is this ideology religious or secular in nature?

9. How does the group define its relationship to the outside world? Exclusionistic or participative?

Communities and organizations might be considered to fall along a continuum, with cooperative forms at one end and communes at the other. Thus if an organization limits the power of the nuclear family to raise and educate children, giving up many functions to the community as a collectivity, if it regulates consumption as rigorously as possible, prohibiting or severely limiting personal possessions, if the income-producing activities are concentrated in the same place as the domicile and the proceeds kept inside the organization and used for production and consumption, if members are given as remuneration only or mainly their living and their retirement, if access to the resource pool is limited strictly to members only and then only as a collectivity, and if there is a central ideology to which all members must strictly adhere—*then* one may define the group as a *commune*. Departures from this model can be considered to define the other end of the continuum—for example, if members hold shares in the proceeds as equity or are paid wages, if education and socialization are minimally supervised, and if access to resources is mainly given to members but can be opened to outsiders under certain circumstances, and so on—then one can speak of a *cooperative*.

But this listing of criteria ignores qualitative or cultural variables that exert independent influence. One of the most important of these is the nature of the central ideology: if it is religious, that is, uses "sacred" or absolutist criteria, it will affect the strength of all other sanctions upholding the various features. That is, deviance will not be tolerated because it is an offense against the absolute. This criterion is one of the main distinctions between the Hutterian colony and the Israeli kibbutz: the former is sanctioned by complex and deeply held religious beliefs; the latter by a historical-secular ideology that allows considerable latitude for infractions and a much greater freedom for members to participate in exogenous organizations. Thus, the structure—the organizational pattern—of the two communes is virtually identical, but the sociocultural ambience and the role of the individual in the group are very different. And this also helps to define the nature of cooperatives: since their ideology is secular-pragmatic and since they hold shares, members are motivated mainly by self-interest, and this of course lends a flexibility and informality to participation in the community that the true—especially the religious—commune, with its stricter sanctions, lacks.

But what happens when some of these polar criteria are mixed? For example, in Israel the cooperative sector is represented by a number of *moshavim*—communities that vary among themselves with respect to various criteria (see various items on moshav co-ops in IIB). The *moshav ovdim* has communal features, that is, the productive resources and equipment are communally owned, whereas the *moshav shitufi* allows its members considerable personal property as well as some tools and equipment and, in addition, allots land to individual families to raise gardens and part of the commercial crop. And so far as communes go, we have already noted the modified communalism of the kibbutz as compared to the Hutterian commune. But there are also gradations among the various kibbutz federations—the communal model described above really applies mainly to Kibbutz Ha Artzi, the "left kibbutz" movement and the most communal of the lot.

Another factor concerns the degree of self-sufficiency sought by the community, or, more precisely: are the economic activities of the organization comprehensive, or does the community agree to consider only certain aspects as subject to collective rules? Typically, the commune seeks to universalize its activities, to consider them all under the rules of communal or common property and collective effort. Cooperatives, on the other hand, can specialize in single sectors—production, consumption, marketing, crops, craft manufactures—leaving the members to engage in their own activities or social circles outside of the designated sphere of effort. In other words, the more a community insists on the commonality of its property and its right to define the roles of its members, the more "communal" it can be considered.

Still another criterion that is difficult to define precisely is the attitude of the organization toward posterity. This is a reflection of ideology, the nature of socialization, and the way property is managed. The ideal commune is deeply concerned for posterity since it considers its way of life absolute (sacred) and the community eternal, a decisive investment in the true path. It therefore has a strong incentive to guard its productive resources—soil fertility, water supply, and so on. The cooperative may have some of these objectives, but the generally pragmatic attitudes and/or the partial or segmented nature of the targets of cooperation make it less concerned—or perhaps less sanguine—about future generations.

A final key feature is individual equity, an issue present in some form or other in all collectives. Members are always concerned about their individual or familial welfare in the event that the community fails, because organizational failure of collectives is frequent enough to create anxiety. The issue is typically weakly developed in communes and strongly so in cooperatives. In fact, it represents the most common reason for the dissolution of cooperatives (see Cooperstock 1961, IIC, for a classic case of an agricultural co-op with communal features that declined because of equity demands). And, of course, the degree to which any collective is prone to dissolution is directly related to the expectations of its members; if the expectation that the pooled resources will be guarded or conserved is weak or uncertain, then the collective is more likely to fail, while a stronger sense of confidence in the communal resource-use system can be a factor in the healthy longevity of a collective endeavor since participants are more likely to concern themselves with the future of the collective for posterity.

Hypertypical Communalism: The Hutterian Brethren

Despite the deficiencies of descriptive typologies, it may be possible on the basis of performance alone to characterize the Hutterian Brethren and their communal settlements as *the* classical type of common property institution. A brief account of the history of Hutterian society and its religious reinforcements therefore follows. The reader should be advised that the chronology has to be fudged, since much of the Hutterian system that evolved in the late sixteenth century is still operative today. Consequently, we will shift, often without warning, between historical and present-day contexts (for Hutterian history see Friedmann 1961; Gross 1965; Hostetler 1974; Peter 1987; Horsch 1931, in IIA).

Repeatedly throughout the Middle Ages and into the Renaissance small bands of Christian dissidents gathered into sects featuring some form of group ownership of property and extreme versions of equality and humility, basing customs on an imperfect knowledge or memory of early Christianity (see Hobsbawn 1965; Cohn 1961, in IIC) and generally representing revolutionary postures vis-à-vis the elite. The New Testament has numerous references to the sins of greed, avarice, accumulation, and exploitation of others. Another well known doctrinal source was the passages in Acts II that describe Christ's followers surrendering their personal property as proof of their decision to accept him as Messiah (for the Hutterian exegesis of communal property and simplicity of life-style see Friedmann 1960; Hutter 1964, in IIA). With the translation of the Bible in the sixteenth century it became possible for much larger numbers of people to have access to such ideas—people who also had severe grievances with the established social and economic order. Europe was becoming industrialized and urbanized: the medieval simplicities of communal peasant life and egalitarian craft guilds were disappearing as society became divided into groups and strata on the basis of wealth and occupation. These early manifestations led to open revolts among peasantry in the fifteenth century, and by the sixteenth century, with the victory of the Lutheran Reformation, incentives for revolt and religious innovation were greatly strengthened. The century seems to have been one long sectarian uproar, with social and economic reforms advocated in the guise of religious reform.

There were, in fact, two Reformations: the Lutheran is well known; the other, more obscure, has been called the Radical Reformation (Williams 1962, in IIA) or the Second Reformation, because it followed (and of course was influenced by) the Lutheran. However, the Second did not—at least in the beginning—take the form of a major reformed church, that is, a reform of established Catholicism. The Second was a new-old form of Christianity in the views of most of its leaders: a *return* to the doctrines of the early Christian communes, features which both Catholic and Lutheran churches had abandoned. The Second was therefore offered as a decisive cleansing of the Christian spirit. And its doctrines were "radical" because they challenged the emerging bourgeois socioeconomic order, which was seen as the source of corruption of the Christian spirit.

The Second also came to be called the Anabaptist Movement because its adherents rejected the doctrine and practice of infant baptism, which they viewed as a way for the established Protestant and Catholic churches to insure their social and political dominance—that is, by creating adherents out of infants too young to have any intelligent say in the matter. Since the adult converts to the Anabaptist sects underwent a second, adult baptism, the Greek-root term *anabaptism*, "again-baptized" (in German, *Wiedertaüfer*), came into use by opponents of the movement. Anyway, the idea was to reserve membership in Christ's legions to persons who were sufficiently adult to be able to make a conscious choice or confession of faith. There has been considerable argument among historians of Anabaptism as to just how important the infant baptism issue really was, with a kind of consensus forming around the proposition that it was probably of lesser significance than the socioeconomic doctrines and practices. Nevertheless, for the outside world it became a major symbol of Anabaptist dissent.

These concepts were the subjects of constant internal debate and revision, and Anabaptism evolved as a converging expression of doctrines preaching a more basic or early Christianity. Using the Hutterites as an example, Karl Peters calls the process one of "doctrinal drift" (Peters 1987, in IIA). Among the primary features of the doctrines were communal property, an austere life-style, the renunciation of all forms of militarism and military service, and condemnation of a stratified social system, a formally educated and paid clergy, and a wealth-owning centralized church. These elements were dealt with frequently in doctrinal disputes, but persecution also helped define the movement; groups at odds over theological issues sometimes united against a common enemy. After a century of sectarian competition, formation, and persecution the Anabaptist movement came to focus on four principal sects: the Mennonites, with origins in Germany, Austria, and parts of Switzerland; the Swiss Brethren, whose doctrinal constitution is identical to the Mennonites; the Amish, who are ultra-conservative Swiss Mennonites; and the communal Hutterites. If one is interested in simplifying the classification, we can speak of just two: Mennonites and Hutterites. From the standpoint of basic theological tenets, there are really no significant differences among the sects; the important distinguishing features are patterns of daily life, economic practices, and the way the community and individual worshippers relate to the majority society or "The World." The Amish, for example, have their own expanded religious communalism: districts under the control of "bishops" with their own churches, marriage within the sect, and so on; but they lack the community nucleation—the *Bruderhof*, as the Hutterites called it.

The Hutterites are the only group of the surviving Anabaptist Reformation that practiced, and still practices, the complete "community of goods" (*Gütergemeinschaft*) and also lives in secluded village colonies or communes. All of the Hutterites now reside in North America—paradoxically the home of the world's most individualistic social system. Hutterites therefore exist on two historical planes: they are relics of the sixteenth-century religious revolution and descendants of sixteenth-century Anabaptist sectarians who used religion to establish a communal frame of life; on the other hand, they are large-scale, highly mechanized agricultural entrepreneurs in the Northern Plains of North America in the twentieth century, competing with each other and with neighboring farmers and ranchers, and constituting, in their several localities, a major ingredient in the regional economy (see Bennett 1967, in I).

The people who later became "Hutterites"—or *Hutterische Brüdern*—originated in the Austrian Tyrol, along with other Christian groups with differing combinations of the dissenting doctrines mentioned above, few of which could be called "sects" in the early part of the fifteenth century since their doctrines were not fixed. The Austrian Tyrol was under the control of Catholic nobility who were inclined toward persecution of heretical and dissenting groups. Thus many of these groups moved southward into the district of Moravia, now part of modern Czechoslovakia. The people called Hutterites came together in Moravia under the leadership of several outstanding activist-theologians, of whom Jacob Hutter was the best known. The several small bands that Hutter assembled eventually received patronage from the Lords Kaunitz, a wealthy Moravian noble clan who owned many large estates. Hutterites were offered the opportunity to become managers—stewards—of these estates.

Hutter's ability to mate religious doctrine with practical social and economic arrangements was a crucial factor in the emergence of the Hutterian system. Hutter and his associates came to realize that if the central Anabaptist ideals were to be implemented, it would be necessary to effect a certain withdrawal from the outside world but at the same time learn to beat the world at its own game, so to speak—that is, to be economically successful. The structural expression of this combination was the *Bruderhof*, known in North America as the "colony": dwellings located in the center of agricultural fields, barns, and shops. The generalized model was the typical medieval closed peasant village with some overtones of the monastery. The colony settlement system was chosen because, as suggested, it was a way to accomplish particular goals: to practice the community of goods and also to permit mutual surveillance in order to ensure an austere, egalitarian lifeway. That is, Hutterites were not only expected to relinquish personal property but also to *share* equally in this voluntary austerity and to forego any reward other than the guarantee of a secure life.

In the early days of the sect this strenuous commitment to egalitarian sharing was a matter of voluntary action on the part of the adult convertees, but as the sect matured and the population of Bruderhofen increased such commitment had to be continuously generated through child socialization. And this aspect of the system distinguished it from the monosexual monastic communities where families did not exist. Similar arrangements had been tried by Albigensian and Waldensian heretical groups in the Middle Ages, but not on the scale attempted by Hutterites. By 1621, after about a century of growth, there existed in Moravia some 102 Bruderhofen with a population of between 20 and 30 thousand inhabitants (Hostetler 1974, 29, in IIA)—a magnitude never reached again until the 1970s and 1980s, in North America. The rapid growth and prosperity of the modern colonies speaks for itself: Hutter and his people had found something quite effective in the way of community organization.

This organization is the more remarkable for the fact that the colony system was politically a kind of totalitarian society, where every member was (and is) watched carefully to ascertain his loyalty and adherence to the rules. If infractions occur, immediate sanctions can be applied, including the potent one of requiring the malefactor to make a public apology in council sessions. Ostracism and expulsion were used for severe or recidivist cases. Every member of a Bruderhof shared in the possessions and wealth of the group, and every member renounced personal accumulation of possessions. This meant that basic features of the social order of late Medieval Europe were discarded: the feudal system, the duties to the Church and State, military service, and taxation. These were the rewards for accepting the surveillance and the simple life.

No other Anabaptist group created a successful Bruderhof system— although all of them preach consumption austerity and avoidance of the corruption and greed of the world. The Mennonites have a formally trained and ordained clergy on the Protestant model, but from the Hutterian viewpoint as soon as a Christian lived in his own house, bought all his tools and possessions on the market, and accepted an ordained minister as his spiritual advisor, he was falling away from Christ. And, of course, an individual family, living in its own small house, cannot really practice the *Gütergemeinschaft*.

As mentioned earlier, the social and intellectual withdrawal from the world into self-contained communities was accompanied by an active and engaged economic posture. The combination of the two created a remarkable bureaucracy, the modern version of which is illustrated in figure 7.1 (a revised version of diagram 3 in Bennett 1967). This contemporary system is a simplified version of the organization of some of the large Bruderhofen which had a variety of craft manufactories as well as agricultural activities. That is, the instrumental organization required in order to maintain loyalty and obedience to the strict norms— especially avoidance of private accumulation—plus the need to organize, manage, and maintain a diverse array of productive activities, gave rise to a complex structure which is more or less replicated in even the smallest colonies. There has been a certain amount of debate among the analysts of Hutterian sociology as to where the Brethren got this system (e.g., see Peters 1987, chapter 1, in IIA), but the question is mainly rhetorical. Such complex organizational systems were common in Medieval and late Medieval Europe in monasteries and the large estates of the nobility. Once established in Moravia, as stewards and resident farmers and craftsmen on estates, the Hutterites simply did what came naturally. Moreover, the original group, while peasants and tradesmen were in the majority, included educated professionals who would have had the knowledge and skills to help refine the managerial arrangements.

The extreme diversification of the Bruderhof economy—so attractive to the Moravian nobility—seems to have been created in part by a need to keep the population busy, considering that it consisted of convertees from just about every trade found in the sixteenth century; the epistolary and historical literature of the period list at least forty. In the second place, this diverse array of craftsmen and clerks represented just what the system required in order to survive with a maximum degree of separation from external society. And in their North American phase Hutterites have been economically successful because their tradition of diversification permitted them to avoid overspecialization in grain or cattle, the two major Great Plains crops with fluctuating values which are responsible for chronic farm bankruptcies. (However, by the mid-1970s some of the colonies in the dryer parts of the Northern Plains began to specialize in high-volume mass-market crops like turkeys and hogs, often on a contract basis with large suppliers and supermarket chains. Economic conditions encouraged this change, but the colonies will shift back to a more diversified production regime if these conditions altered. The diversification/self-sufficiency ethic in Hutterian economics is deep-rooted.)

The *Gütergemeinschaft* was, as noted, based on Christ's command to his followers to divest themselves of their worldly goods. However, the community of goods has played an extremely important role in Hutterian economic organization and financial affairs. The practice really contains two elements: the moral command to avoid the accumulation of personal possessions and the equally stringent command to live simply and austerely—as did Christ and his disciples. The combination of the two gave rise in many medieval Christian groups like the Franciscan order to the concept of "poverty": the individual friar—or any Christian—should be *poor*, since the poor shall inherit the earth (see Little 1978, in IIC).

However, the Hutterian system was not really based on the concept of poverty but rather communal property, that is, the collective, the colony, could—can—be wealthy, but its individual members *must* live a life of simplicity and piety. The collective wealth of the colony goes into investments in equipment, machinery, and buildings, but not individual possessions. A modern, well developed colony in the Northern Plains can be capitalized at two or more million dollars, and a large Bruderhof in Moravia in 1600 would have had a comparable value; but in both cases these are collective equity valuations, not a measure of disposable wealth available to individual members.

The ideals of the *Gütergemeinschaft* are one thing, but the actual distribution of various forms of property is another. While the collective ownership of the basic productive resources—land, water, tools, seeds— was universal in the Bruderhofen and also in the modern colonies, the property used in the domestic sphere shows some variability from community to community. The typical Hutterian dwelling apartment is sparsely furnished, but often with beautifully made natural wood furniture. The kitchen equipment is always collectively owned, as are all farm machines and tools, but the quantity and property concepts of household furnishings vary to some extent from colony to colony. A few basic items, like a clock, a bed, and a blanket chest, are community property and are issued to married couples, but tables, desks, chairs, dressers, and so on are often personal property, handcrafted or refinished items given to the married couple by relatives and subject to testamentary disposition to kin upon death. There is variation in strictly personal items like razors, mirrors, books, keepsakes, and the amount of these varies by colony and even by family within colonies (and when a colony is troubled these items tend to increase in number). In other words, the absence of clear rewards for individual performance or need is a source of anxiety, and Hutterites loosen their strict rules against accumulation when morale is shaky. In this sense, one might speak of using permissiveness over items of personal property as incentives or rewards for tolerating the overall communal property system. Much the same can be said of the stricter kibbutzim.

In any case, property is a constantly emerging phenomenon, and, like everyone, individual Hutterites are in a sense always engaged in creating private property. Appropriation of odd items—scraps of wood, an old chair that can be refinished, or a piece of machinery or tool that the chief mechanic said one might take home, magazines or books presented to

Figure 7.1
Formal Organization of a Typical Modern Hutterian Colony

THE ASSEMBLY

All adult baptized males take part in the Assembly—the colony's group-decision body. Women do not participate or vote.

GOVERNING ROLES

ELDERS, AUFSEHERN, OR CHIEF EXECUTIVES OF THE COLONY

1. CHURCH ELDER OR FIRST MINISTER
(Spiritual leader; communications officer)
(Most colonies have a second minister)

2. HOUSEHOLDER OR COLONY BOSS
(Business manager; financial officer)

3. FARM BOSS
(Personnel director; crops manager)

4. GERMAN TEACHER
(Teacher; mediator; counselor; often a second minister. Not always an executive—must be voted in. Often the Gardener.)

(Authority principle: primus inter pares, but with slight gradation as represented by 1, 2, 3, 4.)
COUNCIL, OR VORSTEHEN DER GEMEINDE
Membership: 4 Chief Executives; Councillors; plus 2 or 3 Farm Enterprise Managers, as below:

ADDITIONAL ELDERS OR COUNCILLORS
(Semi-retired men not in executive jobs.)

AGRICULTURAL MANAGEMENT ROLES

FARM ENTERPRISE MANAGERS (elective) (Any number; varies with enterprise)

Cattle (Beef)	Swine	Sheep	Chickens, Eggs	Ducks, Geese	Crops	Garden

Technical
Blacksmith
Mechanic
Carpenter
Shoemaker
Etc.

(Authority: Over particular enterprises only—no gradation; no group organization.)

FEMALE HIERARCHY

HEAD COOK
(Only executive position for women—not elective.)

GARDEN WOMAN
SCHOOL WOMAN
KINDERGARTEN WOMAN
(Workers, usually spinsters, rotate in jobs.)

LABOR FORCE

A. LABORERS (All men 15 years or older not in executive or managerial positions. When baptized, in voting group.)

B. ALL MEN IN EXECUTIVE-MANAGERIAL ROLES (When available, or on call.)

WOMEN DO NOT VOTE OR PARTICIPATE IN ASSEMBLY

C. ALL WOMEN (Especially younger, unmarried.)

the Hutterites by friends on the outside, and so on—goes on continually, though always with restraint. Planting flowers in front of one's apartment, when allowed, is a way of saying "this place is ours." Such personal appropriations are highly symbolic, and their control likewise; but more serious is theft—when a member purloins a substantial amount of garden produce or a duck and sells it for cash to an outsider and pockets the proceeds.

However, the financial savings effected by communal property in the case of modern colonies are substantial. Imagine a colony in the 1970s consisting of about 120 people, divided into about seven nuclear families with about five children each. If each of these families owned and operated a fair-sized farm of their own, they would have been required to buy at least $200,000 worth of machinery, build an array of sheds and barns, buy at least one passenger vehicle, furnish a house, and buy clothing for the children. To maintain this agricultural investment and to meet the expenses of raising and educating five children the family would have needed a gross income of at least $100,000 per year. Turning to the colony, the collective of 120 persons would possess just one large passenger station wagon, about $350,000 worth of machinery, would house its families in row-apartment houses and furnish them austerely, mostly with hand-made articles. The typical mature male member of the colony would own one electric razor as his most coveted personal possession. The colony's gross income from diversified operations would have been about $75,000 per year. This means that the per-capita gross income for the family farm would be much greater than for the colony, but the comparison is meaningless because while the farm was probably just able to make its debt-service payments, the colony could quite likely have been operating in the black, with a regular surplus (see Bennett 1967, chapter 9, in I, for other financial data and comparisons). In other words, the Hutterian system of communal property plus austerity provides impressive savings, which can be plowed back into the enterprise.

But it is by no means invulnerable to economic difficulties. Much of the problem has to do with indebtedness. The North American colonies do not grow indefinitely, but divide when the population reaches between 100 and 150 persons. Hutterites have always fissioned, because they discovered early on that the maintenance of conformity is more easily achieved with smaller numbers—a principle of the "folk society": when the community is small enough so that everyone can see everyone else regularly, day after day, adherence to the rules tends to be more faithful and the consensus that the rules are worth obeying more pervasive (Redfield 1955, in IIC). However, the sixteenth-century Bruderhofen apparently allowed population to increase into the several hundreds in some cases before fissioning.

The colony as it exists in the twentieth century is smaller than most in the sixteenth and seventeenth due to a high-cost agricultural economy and the abandonment of craft manufactures in an industrial economy. Since the rate of natural increase is high (over 2 percent, but slowing, as Hutterites begin to make use of birth control and health programs), the new colonies must be able to count on an initial nest egg provided by the mother colony. This usually takes the form of cash for substantial payments on land. In addition, some of the farm equipment accumulated by the old colony is given to the "new farm." Thus there is a second major reason for austerity: to save money for the inevitable fission. But land in the large quantities needed for colonies is becoming increasingly scarce; the Hutterian system and population is being forced to change and to adapt to larger colonies and increased productivity.

We have emphasized the personal consumption side of the community of goods, but, as total communes, the colonies also own their land and water resources collectively. In most states and provinces the colony is registered as a cooperative company for official purposes, although in any given year this classification is sure to be challenged by some governing or taxing body. From one point of view, the operations of the agricultural enterprise automatically make the colony into a cooperative, with some resemblance to the agricultural cooperative that farms the land of the seven Amana villages in Iowa. The Amana villages are former communes of the later, seventeenth-century Pietistic Movement which had to dissolve their community of goods during the Depression of the 1930s (see Carman 1987, in IIC); the villages are now independent municipalities, but the agricultural resources of all the villages were assembled into a single cooperative, with shares held by residents of the villages. However, individual Hutterites do not own shares in the colony farm, since the principle of the community of goods applies to the land and farm equipment as much as to personal possessions, the dwellings, kitchen equipment, etc. No Hutterite can hold individual equity in the farm, since it belongs to the colony as a homogeneous institution, founded on the doctrine of the *Gütergemeinschaft*. And no Hutterite family is allowed to have its own kitchen garden (save for a flower bed), since the colony has its own large garden in which women and children do most of the work.

Resource Conservation and the Market

We have implied in the foregoing that the Hutterite socioeconomic system is based on particular ideas about property combined with a particular style of settlement. The value system, featuring communal property of a drastic and universal form, can be implemented only in a relatively small, face-to-face community; and the community can be sustained only by reducing the demand on its resources by its members, using the savings to finance the enterprise and fissioned colonies. This means also that the world view of Hutterites includes the idea that a colony is a permanent and universal phenomenon: it must not disappear, but continue to produce agricultural products and people, with daughter colonies springing off at regular intervals. Land and other agricultural resources owned by the colony are thus regarded as permanent invest-ments: the wherewithal to implement the continuity of social and demo-graphic existence. Unlike individual farmers and ranchers, who always have a part of their minds focused on the sale value of the establishment, Hutterites do not anticipate sale of the property and are interested in its accumulated equity only because they may have to be when they need a bank loan or because tax officials may require an estimate.

But, as noted earlier, Hutterites are not invulnerable to the economic fluctuations of contemporary society—just as they were vulnerable to political and social harassment in the sixteenth century at the end of the Moravian era, when the nobles were induced by the state and the church to expel them from their estates. A contemporary colony that decides to engage in highly specialized production may sell much of its land in order to raise the cash for the investment in new equipment, in which case the land may pass into the hands of neighboring farmers or ranchers, who may exploit it for quick gain. New colonies regularly over-use their land because they need big crops for the first few years to liquidate the debt. And since the soils and topography of the Northern Plains are extremely variable, it may take a decade for a colony to discover just how to treat different parts of its acreage in order to minimize soil erosion or salinization.

Thus, if one visits colonies at random he will discover that resource use and conservation vary considerably depending on the age of the colony, the nature of its land and water, the bank balance, and the skills of its managers. In one district of twelve colonies only three could be said to have done everything possible or technically necessary to fulfill standard resource-sustaining criteria. Hutterites take care of their resources for obvious reasons associated with their religious beliefs, their desire for continuous self-sufficiency, their concept of the colony as eternal, and the joint responsibility of maintaining communal property. But circumstances sometimes prevent complete fulfillment of the mission, and realizing the ideals is an evolutionary process in any colony. Moreover, Hutterites, like any other group of humans, vary considerably in ability and motivation; some are far more inclined or able to establish conservationist practices than others, and every group of colonies in the Northern Plains will have one or more which are known locally—and to other colonies as well—as a "rough bunch when it comes to farming." But Hutterites have also developed an intercolony assistance and information system, and such colonies can improve with age, if the better ones in the region give them advice and help.

The Rise and Fall (and Rise Again) of the Community of Goods

Recalling the abbreviated discussion of cooperative arrangements in an earlier section, we noted that co-ops avoid the practice of common property or restrict it to an equity-share basis. That is, the sanctions for what common property or the "common pool" of resources exists in cooperatives are practical: they confer an advantage to the shareholder, and he can save some of the costs of development and maintenance by spreading them across the membership. Cooperatives, in other words, avoid many of the problems of common property systems of the extreme type.

In the preceding description of the Hutterian experience we noted that the system requires an extraordinary degree of rational organization, internal or mutual surveillance, and collective socialization of the young. In other words, Hutterites realize that living in a state of total communalism is a difficult task and requires strict sanctions: Christ's way is the hard way. Therefore, it should come as no surprise to learn that all of the Brethren have fallen away completely from the community of goods at least twice in their long history—and this, of course, does not include the difficulties that individual colonies regularly have with communal property—difficulties that are often overcome by the countervailing sanctions that have evolved in Hutterian society along with the community of goods and the Bruderhof settlement system.

The first of these major episodes occurred in Hungary, where the Hutterites had fled after the Church and the rulers of Moravia forced the nobility to drive the Brethren from their estates. The "Golden Age"—as the Moravian period is called—thus ended in a hegira across Eastern Europe, plus a number of attempts by smaller groups to return to Moravia; the various comings and goings extended from about 1550 to the 1600s. However, since the Church quashed all these attempts, it became clear that the Brethren had to leave their promised land unless they consented to accept conversion to Catholicism (see Hostetler 1974, in IIA, for succinct accounts of the Moravian and post-Moravian eras).

The establishment of refugee Bruderhofen in Hungary occurred in the 1620s, during the Thirty Years' War. Armies of Turks, Hungarians, Germans, and the forces of the Emperor roamed the area, ruining farms, burning villages, and generally making life difficult. The Hutterites found it impossible to establish orderly communal life in the midst of social and economic chaos. By 1685 the remaining Brethren formally dissolved the commune and the *Gütergemeinschaft* and became individual peasant farmers, although they continued to adhere to basic Anabaptist religious beliefs. Numbers of the former Brethren were more or less forcibly converted to Catholicism by a Hapsburg cardinal, and persecution became a regular practice. The most important Bruderhof of the Hungarian period was Sabatisch, a large village that exists today, with many of the old Hutterian dwelling houses still standing. A Transylvanian prince invited some of the beleaguered Brethren to reestablish Bruderhofen in his domain, and these flourished until the last decade of the 1600s, when they, too, were subject to persecution and marauding military. So the community of goods was abandoned. It is clear from the history of the Eastern European period that the Hutterian system could not survive under considerable pressure from the outside.

The second major episode of abandonment of the community of goods occurred in Russia. After the failure of the Hungarian-Transylvanian communities (plus others in the general region), over a period of several years in the early 1700s the Brethren were invited to reassemble and move to the Ukraine by a Russian general acting partly under the direction of the Empress Catherine, who was interested in settling southern Russia with industrious German farmers. Most of the Brethren assembled in one large Bruderhof village, but, after initial rejoicing, began to fight over doctrinal issues. The problem arose from the fact that the many refugee communities from the Eastern Europe debacle had drifted away from some of the doctrines, and once they came back together it was difficult to resolve the issues. Perhaps the central one was the advocacy by vigorous dissidents to reform the Hutterian system along the lines of a Protestant sect or that of the Mennonites: establish a series of churches, a regular clergy, and start a missionary movement. These efforts were defeated by the "Old Brethren," as the conservatives were called, but the experience left a deep unease in the sect, and fissures were created that never healed.

The Russian count on whose estate the large Bruderhof was located made kindly but determined efforts to change the system, many of which were adopted. However, the lands given to the Brethren for their agricultural activities were insufficient to support the growing population, and unrest developed. Individual Hutterite managers began keeping funds for the use of their own families and groups, and the community of goods began to break up. The doctrinal divisions reopened, and dissent and conflict spread. By 1819 the community of goods was largely abandoned, and a division of function was established between the religious officials and the economic managers, effectively breaking apart the institutional homogeneity so characteristic of Hutterian life. This second major episode of abandonment of the *Gütergemeinschaft*, then, was principally caused by internal dissent and conflict, although induced at least in part by external forces.

We noted earlier that aside from these great historical episodes of the decline of communalism individual colonies in North America occasionally repeat some of these conditions. In the 1960s the writer studied two colonies in trouble, with individual members beginning to secrete property for their own use, distrust of the leadership, the fumbling of ineffective and confused officers, and the consequent rise of suspicion and internal division. One of these colonies solved its problems by simply fissioning, dividing the population in such a way as to defuse dissension.

The other colony had to be taken over by a nearby wealthy and well-or-ganized colony, which subsequently succeeded in reorganizing the fail-ing community. As this is being written, similar situations exist in a number of Montana and Manitoba colonies.

The North American phase was a case of revitalization, or, as Peter Stephenson (1991, in IIA) would call it—from the Hutterian viewpoint—a "rebirth." By the 1860s in Russia almost nothing was left of the original Hutterian system, and poverty among many of the former Brethren, now living as individual farmers, was severe. Several groups tried to recon-stitute the *Bruderhof-Gütergemeinschaft* system, and these became the pioneers who left Russia in the early 1870s as a result of pressure from authorities who wished to subject them to military service and other duties. These three groups, each called a *Leute* (the Lehrer, Darius, and Schmieden Leuten), came to North America and established colonies in Nebraska and later in South Dakota—although some of them left the sect and became Mennonites, not wishing to be subject to the discipline. Then in 1917 when the U.S. Government attempted to draft Hutterites, and when the anti-German hysteria of the period resulted in local harassment, all of the Brethren packed up and went to Canada, where the government promised to permit them to flourish without concession, since good colonists were needed in the Prairie Provinces. Eventually the South Dakota colony sites were reoccupied by fission from the Canadian colonies after the war, and the great expansion phase of the colonies began, aided by the extraordinary adaptive fit of the colony economic system to the conditions of grain-livestock production in the Northern Plains.

Bringing the story down to the 1990s, there might be signs that the Hutterian system is once again approaching a period of cyclical decline. Collectively the entire Hutterian population was wealthier than it was twenty-five years ago, when the writer began his research, but in the 1980s and 1990s there is a tendency for colonies to sort out on the basis of efficiency and wealth, with increasing numbers of poor colonies and a small number of very rich colonies, the middle ground consisting of colonies that could go either way, depending on their resources and market postures. The well-off and rich colonies by the 1980s were experiencing another crisis: the increasing disparity between personal consumption austerity and collective wealth. This situation creates se-vere strains in the social and ideological fabric; concretely, it means that young people become increasingly disenchanted with the demand for austerity when the colony itself is capitalized at millions. On the other hand, the poor colonies—many of them desperate—were either subject to mandatory stewardship by wealthy colonies or were contemplating dissolution.

Implications for Common Property Regimes

1. *Success or failure of common property institutions is strongly related to the extent of communal ownership as well as the kinds of property falling under communal control.* That is, the more pervasive the common property system, the stricter the sanctions and control mechanisms for governing behavior and productive activity. The Hutterian system is so bureaucratically complex and stringent not merely because of particular religious beliefs but also because the pervasiveness of the communal system places heavy demands on conformity and austerity. And the absence of any formal assignment of equity in the productive resources (land, water, tools, etc.) requires strict surveillance of individual behavior. On the other hand, a cooperative that consists wholly of a group of producers who pool their product expressly for the purpose of bargaining for a better market price can exist with minimal sanctions and surveillance.

Cultural variables will of course modify some of these generalizations. In the case of the kibbutz the sanctions and monitoring of individual behavior are less stringent than in the Hutterite case—even though the general scope of the common property system is comparable—because the kibbutzniks are members of a society that honors the kibbutz as one of its founding institutions. Hutterites, on the other hand, exist as isolated enclaves in a larger community that has never fully accepted them as participants in a common culture.

2. *Common property institutions run against the grain of socioeconomic organization in a majority of countries and communities;* consequently, they require special indoctrination and social reinforcement. The more communal the system, the more intensive the indoctrination system must become. This eventuates, in most communal groups, in degrees of separation of children from parents and a surrender of at least part of familial socialization to the larger community.

But it also means, for organizations, with a majority of adult members, that innovate along collective lines, a need for special training in the collective procedures: for example, the financial principles of "penny savings" in credit unions, the advantages of accepting a standard return on one's labor in production and marketing cooperatives, trading regularity and security for intermittent or unpredictable quick profits, or, in the more extreme communal cases, security and retirement guarantees in place of equity shares. Moreover, these procedures all require reinforcement, one of the most difficult problems of continuity in collectives. The Hutterites, as we have seen, do it by total and continuous immersion in a communal system: all institutions and experiences interlock to reinforce the survival of the *Gütergemeinschaft*. But even this all-embracing system of reinforcement is not enough to head off decay and disintegration in particular cases.

3. *Accumulating wealth tends to incite individual acquisitiveness in collectives, and, if it goes unchecked, can lead to cyclical disintegration.* Collectives must cope with recurrent instances of greed and action designed to reward the individual at the expense of the community. This process seems to be as common in cooperatives as in communes, although its manifestations will vary. In other words, the mechanism by which individuals seek to appropriate resources which are held in common is an instance of the "tragedy of the commons." And, in the terms of the principle, the more apppropriation, the more appropriation—the habit spreads like a behavioral disease.

4. *The forms of property and property ownership and/or control are numerous and complex, even in collectives which seek to maximize common property.* Hutterites, although they are about as communal as a human society can be, nevertheless manifest constant flux when it comes to the distinction between common and personal property, with the accumulation of personal property often used as a reward for respecting the communal existence and the withdrawal of it as a punishment in cases of infraction. Moreover, the various items of community property in a colony or kibbutz are viewed differently by the members, with some items considered capital goods, some personal entitlements, and others utilitarian facilities. To describe a particular regime as one of "common property" is therefore usually too simple.

5. *Equality of members of a collective is not guaranteed by a pervasive common property system, since other factors, like cultural patterns or*

religious beliefs, will influence status. Collectives, while possessing an aura of egalitarianism due to their usually rather small populations and face-to-face interaction systems, also contain the usual criteria of status differentiation based on age, sex, skills and abilities, and possession of ascribed or achieved criteria like baptism, certificate of competence in tasks, and so on. In Hutterian colonies women are not allowed to vote, although they exert considerable influence on the men, especially in issues affecting the domestic establishment. The kibbutz gives women the right to vote and to participate fully in kibbutz government, but in fact most kibbutz communities are governed by men. Important issues of status do not usually arise in cooperatives, since co-ops are not total communities but temporary assemblages of people with common economic interests and whose social life is absorbed into or determined by the larger external community.

6. *Cyclicality is a constant possibility for all collectives.* By this term we refer to cycles of decline and possible collapse, punctuated by rehabilitation or revitalization; that is, collectives behave like other human groupings: they are prone to change and dissolution of the social order and rule system. In the case of the more extreme collectives—communes—this is closely linked to the wealth-greed-equity cycle, as noted previously. Once established, a collective cannot be expected to endure indefinitely; inevitably, it will undergo changes that, from the point of view of those who regard the rules as ideal and stable, will be viewed as infractions or betrayal. Tension arises, these reactions feed on themselves, and the community organization undergoes a decline. But, as Hutterian history demonstrates, it can also undergo revival, and, in the case of the communes, this necessarily becomes a religious experience, a renewal of faith or belief.

7. *There is a link between collective organization and, especially, common productive property and physical resource conservation, but this link is by no means a simple causal relation.* Since all collective communities exist in a larger world, much of which is not devoted to the principles of common property, resource practices will vary. For example, market pressures will induce resource exploitation in a commune; however, the same commune may be concerned about the protection of its land and water for the sake of posterity.

Implications for Sustainability

The first is simply that, in the long run, sustainability means *social continuity*. That is, to produce goods and to conserve resources on a sustainable basis requires the persistent functioning of a social group. To visualize sustainability purely from an economic standpoint is to ignore its fundamental social identity. Hutterites and kibbutzniks know this, and they have devoted much attention to their social and managerial organizations. Hutterites lock the managerial function into the social, so that every person in the community plays at least two vital roles: a productive worker and a dutiful kinsman or community member. Hutterites also make sure that every colony has one or two dominant kin groups so that there will be connections between a majority of the nuclear families that make up the backbone of the population. The kibbutz, on the other hand, is much less reliant on kinship as the major bonding experience for communal life. Instead, kibbutz ideology and the practical, everyday experiences of decision making and task performance are used to guarantee the social continuity of the system. Although kibbutzniks are generally free to come and go, the system is sustainable because Israeli national society supports and subsidizes it and provides available roles on the outside for kibbutzniks on leave.

Time is of the essence: sustainability is, and must be, a temporal process. The planner must specify the expected duration of a sustainable production system or resource base given the existing or improved social arrangements. The temporal aspects of particular social arrangements are not well known: if labor is geared to a social organization which contains mutually antagonistic factions, then the planner should be aware of the cyclicality of all these systems, that cooperation and collaboration is always subject to decay and breakdown.

Another major implication concerns sequential relationships between production, resource conservation, social sustainability, and growth. Establishing a sustainable resource and production system is a temporal phenomenon: since population and demand are usually always growing in contemporary situations, so must production. Hutterites keep fissioning, but land for colonies is getting hard to find, so the colonies must either grow in size and productivity or population growth must be controlled. But as production increases, pressure on resources does likewise, so that techniques to confer resource conservation must be subject to constant revision and improvement. This dynamism of the system exerts considerable pressure on the social system, and inevitably—as it has in countless Third World cases—promotes stratification and growing inequality, as energetic and able individuals perceive opportunities in the change process. What all this means is that sustainability is not a simple achieved state, but a constant process of social and technological management and innovation.

Supplementary Information on Hutterian Life

This is supplied at the suggestion of a reader of the manuscript who felt that insufficient data on Hutterian institutions was provided in the specialized treatment given in the chapter. While readers interested in a more complete portrait of Hutterian (and kibbutz) culture can refer to the materials in sections I and II of the bibliography, the following notes may be helpful.

Health Care

Hutterian attitudes toward health and medicine were and are exceptional, given their sixteenth-century origins. In the Moravian period the Brethren had their own doctors among the converts and for a while operated simple medical training centers. Well in advance of professional medicine, they had doctrines of cleanliness as the way to avoid infection. In North America Hutterites use all available medical services, both private and public, including psychiatry. All Hutterite women give birth in hospitals, under the care of a physician.

Education

As noted above, all of the Anabaptist sects are especially concerned about education, since their beliefs and customs are quite different from those of North American majority society. Both Amish and Hutterites have been engaged in struggles with school boards and state and provincial governments over their need to control the educational experiences of their children. The Hutterites have worked out compromise arrangements with local school systems that usually include a school building constructed on the premises by the colony, with the teacher supplied by the local school board on a daily commuting basis. Some colonies in remote locations maintain a small cottage for the overnight use of a teacher in inclement weather or even for longer periods. These colony public schools usually have grades one through eight. All children also attend a colony religious school which is an extension of the nursery school where all young preschool children are given daily care while parents work on tasks. The colony nursery schools and religious continuation schools paralleling the public grades are essentially indoctrination facilities to ensure children's conformity to the faith and the colony routines. The system has proven to be quite effective: Hutterite elders, particularly the "Teacher," an elder who supervises the religious school and also the grades with the help of the public school teacher, make sure that the children study hard, do their homework, and generally become reasonably proficient in English-language literacy and basic knowledge. Hutterites could not function in The World without at least basic elementary school education.

Some colonies, particularly those of the Darius Leut (one of the three subsects), are inclined to encourage correspondence high school training for their brighter children, and some have experimented with junior college. In the South Dakota episode in the late nineteenth and early twentieth centuries a few Hutterites were sent to a teachers' college, but this proved to be an alienating experience and was terminated. Aside from regular schooling, Hutterites also practice self-education in literacy and technical training, reading dictionaries and encyclopedias. Hutterites, in dress and manner, may give an impression of retrogressive knowledge and sophistication, but on the whole these people are as aware of The World and its affairs as anyone in their larger communities and in many instances are more sophisticated than many rural residents of these relatively isolated areas of the Northern Great Plains.

Technical Proficiency

The acceptance by Hutterites of available agricultural science and technology regularly surprises people who expect these black-garbed people to replicate the horse-and-buggy posture of the Amish and some conservative Mennonite groups. The proficiency in construction, maintenance, and repair of sophisticated heating, refrigeration, electrical systems, computerized electronics, and the like is the more extraordinary considering that most of the knowledge is gained by careful self-study and practical experience on the colony premises. However, as colonies become more affluent more of this type of work is contracted out—but this also gives the Brethren a chance to see the procedures in action. Once acquired, these skills do not disappear but are communicated from person to person in the kinship networks which unite communities. Fathers will train sons, but the Hutterites also try to avoid father-to-son transmission of particular managerial positions, since this breeds monopolies or, in the terms of the *Gütergemeinschaft*, accumulations of property.

Sanctioned Occupations

Agriculture, and the profits gained from its practice, is the one officially and strongly sanctioned income-producing activity. However, individual colonies often engage in other pursuits: manufacturing simple farm machinery or implements for sale or trade to neighbors, the making of down comforters and similar needlework by women, sold to tourist visitors to the colony. Such activity is probably increasing, in response to a need for cash, or as young women and men find time on their hands during the long winters, when there is little farm work. Some of the colony technicians also fairly commonly do special jobs, like repairing supermarket refrigeration plants, and receive wages which are turned over to the colony. Hutterites are not allowed by their beliefs to invest in stocks and bonds, since this is equated with usury. But there is no doubt that colonies on the fringes of Hutterian society and its geographical range are beginning to loosen up on income-producing occupations. In the sixteenth and seventeenth centuries the Bruderhofen regularly engaged in a variety of crafts and manufactures for sale.

Literature Cited and Consulted

I. Author's Writings on Communes and Cooperatives

Bennett, John W. 1967. *Hutterian Brethren: The Agricultural Economy and Social Organization of a Communal People*. Stanford, CA: Stanford University Press.
_____.1975. "Communes and Communitarianism." *Theory and Society* 2: 63–94.
_____.1976. "Frames of Reference for the Study of Hutterian Society." *International Review of Modern Sociology* 6: 23–39.
_____.1977a. "The Hutterian Colony: A Traditional Voluntary Agrarian Commune with Large Economic Scale." In *Cooperative and Commune: Group Farming in the*

Economic Development of Agriculture, ed. Peter Dorner. Madison: University of
Wisconsin Press.

_____.1977b. "Social Theory and the Social Order of the Hutterian Community."
Mennonite Quarterly Review 51(4): 292–394.

_____.1983. "Agricultural Cooperatives in the Development Process: Perspectives
from Social Science." *Studies in Comparative International Development* 18(1–2):
3–68.

II. Some Classic and Current Sources on Collective Organizations.

*The literature dealing with communes and cooperatives stretches
across several disciplines: theology, religious history, rural sociology,
anthropology, specialized fields like the Cooperative Movement and
economic and rural development, and theoretical and philosophical
works.*

A. Hutterian Brethren

Baden, John A. n.d. "The Management of Social Stability: A Political Ethnography of
the Hutterites of North America." Doctoral dissertation, Indiana University, Bloomington.

Bax, E. Belfort. 1966. *The Rise and Fall of the Anabaptists*. New York: American
Scholarly Pub., Inc.

Canadian Mental Health Association. 1953. "The Hutterites and Saskatchewan: A Study
of Intergroup Relations." Duplicated report, Regina, Saskatchewan.

Evans, Simon M. 1973. "The Dispersal of Hutterite Colonies in Alberta, 1918–1971:
The Spatial Expression of Cultural Identity," M.A. thesis, University of Calgary,
Alberta.

Friedmann, Robert. 1960. "An Epistle Concerning Communal Life: A Hutterite Mani-
festo of 1650 and Its Modern Paraphrase." *Mennonite Quarterly Review* (October
1960): 249–74.

_____.1961. *Hutterite Studies*. Goshen, IN: Mennonite Historical Society.

Gross, Paul. 1965. *The Hutterite Way*. Saskatoon: Freeman.

_____.tr. n.d. "The Defense Against the Prozess at Worms on the Rhine in the Year
1557." (Orginally published in an early Hutterian document, the *Handbüchlein*.)
Privately printed, Lethbridge, Canada.

Hofer, Joshua. 1985. *Japanese Hutterites: A Visit to Owa Community*. Bilingual edition.
Privately published.

Horsch, John. 1931. *The Hutterian Brethren, 1528–1931: A Story of Martyrdom and
Loyalty*. Goshen, IN: Mennonite Historical Society.

Hostetler, John A. 1974. *Hutterite Society*. Baltimore: Johns Hopkins University Press.

Hutter, Jakob. 1964. "Jakob Hutter's Epistle Concerning the Schism in Moravia in 1533"
introd. by Robert Friedmann, tr. the Society of Brothers. *Mennonite Quarterly Review*
(October 1964).

Peter, Karl A. 1987. *The Dynamics of Hutterite Society: An Analytical Approach*.
Edmonton: University of Alberta Press.

Peters, Victor. 1965. *All Things Common: The Hutterian Way of Life*. Minneapolis: University of Minnesota Press.

Rideman, Peter. 1970. 1545. *Confession of Faith: Account of Religion, Doctrine and Faith, Given by Peter Rideman of the Brothers Whom Men Call Hutterites*. Rifton, NY: Plough Publishing House.

Riley, Marvin P. and Darryll Johnson. 1970. *South Dakota Hutterite Colonies: 1874–1969*. South Dakota State University, AES Bulletin No. 565, January 1970.

Serl, Vernon. n.d. "Stability and Change Among the Hutterites," in "Research in Progress in the Behavioral Sciences," Western Washington College of Education, Bellingham, WA.

Stephenson, Peter H. 1991. *The Hutterian People: Ritual and Rebirth in the Evolution of Communal Life*. New York: University Press of America.

Williams, George. 1962. *The Radical Reformation*. Philadelphia: University of Pennsylvania Press.

B. Israeli Kibbutzim and Moshavim

Bar-On, Dan and A. Niv. 1983. "The Regional Development of the Kibbutz in the 80s: Alternatives to the Deterministic Approach." *The Journal of Applied Behavioral Science* 19(3): 319-35.

Ben-Ner, Avner. 1987. "Preferences in a Communal Economic System." *Economica* 54: 207-21.

Bowes, Alison M. 1989. *Kibbutz Goshen: An Israeli Commune*. Prospects Heights, IL: Waveland Press.

_____. 1990. "The Experiment that Did Not Fail: Image and Reality in the Israeli Kibbutz." *International Journal of Middle East Studies* 22: 85-103.

Cohen, Erik. 1966. "Progress and Communality: Value Dilemmas in the Collective Movement." *International Review of Community Development* 15/16: 3-17.

Fishman, Aryei. 1983. "Judaism and Modernization: the Case of the Religious Kibbutzim." *Social Forces* 62: 9-31.

Klayman, Maxwell I. 1970. *The Moshav in Israel: A Case Study of Institution-Building for Agricultural Development*. New York: Praeger.

Mittelberg, David. 1988. *Strangers in Paradise: The Israeli Kibbutz Experience*. New Brunswick, NJ: Transaction Books.

Nadler, Arie. 1986. "Help Seeking as a Cultural Phenomenon: Differences Between City and Kibbutz Dwellers." *Journal of Personality and Social Psychology* 51: 976-82.

Rosner, Menachem and Arnold S. Tannenbaum. 1987. "Organizational Efficiency and Egalitarian Democracy in an Intentional Communal Society: the Kibbutz." *The British Journal of Sociology* 38: 521-45.

Rosner, Menachem. 1990. *The Second Generation: Continuity and Change in the Kibbutz*. Tr. Joseph R. Blasi and Lucy Jones. New York: Greenwood Press.

_____. 1992. "Organizations between Community and Market: The Case of the Kibbutz." *Israel Horizons* (Winter 1992): 10-27.

Shomaker, Dianna. 1984. "Economic Pressures Resulting from Aging of Kibbutz Society." *The Gerontologist* 24: 313-17.

Shur, Simon and Yochanan Peres. 1986. "Equality and Functional Imperatives: Another Examination of Distributive Justice in the Israeli Kibbutz." *The British Journal of Sociology* 37: 335-47.

Spiegel, Uriel and Joseph Templeman. 1985. "Interdependent Utility and Cooperative Behavior (Kibbutz)." *Journal of Comparative Economics* 9: 314–28.

Weintraub, D., M. Lissak, and Y. Azmon. 1969. *Moshava, Kibbutz, and Moshav: Patterns of Jewish Rural Settlement and Development in Palestine.* Ithaca: Cornell University Press.

Willner, Dorothy. 1969. *Nation-Building and Community in Israel.* Princeton, NJ: Princeton University Press.

C. Miscellaneous: Cooperatives, Comparative Studies, Theory

Barkin, David and John W. Bennett. 1972. "Kibbutz and Colony: Collective Economies and the Outside World." *Comparative Studies in Society and History* 14(4): 456–483. (Also published in *The Sociology of the Kibbutz*, ed. Ernest Krausz. New Brunswick, NJ: Transaction Books, 1983.)

Carman, D. Gary. 1987. "The Amana Colonies' Change from Communalism to Capitalism in 1932." *The Social Science Journal* 24(2): 157–67.

Christenson, James. 1984. "Gemeinschaft and Gesellschaft: Testing the Spatial and Communal Hypotheses." *Social Forces* 63(1): 160–168.

Cohn, Norman. 1961. *The Pursuit of the Millenium.* New York: Harper and Row.

Cooperstock, Henry. 1961. "Co-operative Farming as a Variant Social Pattern." In *Canadian Society: Sociological Perspectives*, ed. Bernard R. Blishen et al. Glencoe, IL: The Free Press.

Dorner, Peter. 1977. *Cooperative and Commune: Group Farming in the Economic Development of Agriculture.* Madison: University of Wisconsin Press.

Erasmus, Charles J. 1977. *In Search of the Common Good: Utopian Experiments Past and Future.* New York: Macmillan/Free Press.

Fishman, Aryei. 1989. "The Religious Kibbutz: A Note on the Theories of Marx, Sombert, and Weber on Judaism and Economic Success." *Sociological Analysis* 50: 281–90.

Goldberg, Albert I. and Chanoch Jacobsen. 1987. "Normative and Utilitarian Particularism: the Impact of Social Structure on Service Commitments." *Human Relations* 40: 75–95.

Hall, John R. 1988. "Social Organization and Pathways of Commitment: Types of Communal Groups, Rational Choice Theory, and the Kanter Thesis." *American Sociological Review* 53: 679–92.

Hillery, George A. 1968. *Community Organizations: A Study of Local Societies.* Chicago: University of Chicago Press.

Hobsbawm, E. J. 1965. *Primitive Rebels: Studies in Archaic Forms of Social Movement in the 19th and 20th Centuries.* New York: W. W. Norton and Co.

Little, Lester K. 1978. *Religious Poverty and the Profit Economy in Medieval Europe.* London: Paul Elek.

Preuss, Walter. 1960. *Co-operation in Israel and the World.* Jerusalem: Rubin Mass.

Redfield, Robert. 1955. *The Little Community: Viewpoints for the Study of a Human Whole.* Chicago: University of Chicago Press.

Smucker, Donovan, ed. 1977. *The Sociology of Canadian Mennonites, Hutterites, and Amish: A Bibliography with Annotations.* Waterloo, Ontario: Wilfrid Laurier University Press.

Tendler, Judith. 1983. *What to Think About Cooperatives: A Guide from Bolivia.* Rosslyn, VA: The Inter-American Foundation.

Van der Berghe, Pierre L. and Karl Peter. 1988. "Hutterites and Kibbutzniks: A Tale of Nepotistic Communism." *Man* 23:522–39.
Zablocki, Benjamin. 1971. *The Joyful Community: An Account of the Bruderhof, A Communal Movement Now in Its Third Generation*. Baltimore: Penguin Books.

III. Sustainability, Common Property, and Economic Development.

Nearly all of the literature on common property concepts and institutions appeared in the decade preceding publication of this book. "Common property" is a catchword invented by development specialists to refer to particular features of collective organization in relations to the economic development process.

Barbier, Edward B. and Anil Markandya. 1990. "The Conditions for Achieving Environmentally Sustaining Development," *European Economic Review* 34: 659–69.
Beller, W., ed. 1990. *Sustainable Development and Environmental Management of Small Islands*. Vol. 5 in the series Man and the Biosphere. Parkridge, NJ: Pantheon and UNESCO.
Berkes, Fikret. 1985. "The Common Property Resource Problem and the Creation of Limited Property Rights." *Human Ecology* 13: 187–208.
Brox, Ottar. 1990. "The Common Property Theory: Epistemological Status and Analytical Utility." *Human Organization* 49:227–35.
Brundtland, Gro Harlem, ed. 1987. *Our Common Future*. Oxford: Oxford University Press.
_____. 1989. "Sustainable Development: An Overview." *Development* 2/3.
Buck, Susan J. 1989. "Cultural Theory and Management of Common Property Resources (Western States)." *Human Ecology* 17: 101–16.
Chilcote, Ronald H. and Dale L. Johnson, eds. 1983. *Theories of Development: Mode of Production or Dependency?* Beverly Hills, CA: Sage Publications.
Clay, Daniel C. and Laurence A. Lewis. 1990. "Land Use, Soil Loss, and Sustainable Agriculture in Rwanda." *Human Ecology* 18: 147–61.
Cole, Sam. 1990. "Cultural Diversity and Sustainable Futures." *Futures* 22: 1044–058.
Conway, Gordon R. and Eward B. Barbier. 1988. "After the Green Revolution: Sustainable and Equitable Agricultural Development." *Futures* 20: 651–70.
Dahlberg, Kenneth A. 1990. "Towards a Theory of Regenerative Food Systems: An Overview." Paper presented at the Conference on Redefining Agricultural Sustainability, Agroecology Program, University of California, Santa Cruz, June 28–30, 1990.
Emel, Jacque L. and Elizabeth Brooks. 1988. "Changes in Form and Function of Property Rights Institutions Under Threatened Resource Scarcity (Groundwater om the High Plains)." *Annals of the Association of American Geographers* 78: 241–52.
Feeny, David et al. 1990. "The Tragedy of the Commons: Twenty-Two Years Later." *Human Ecology* 18(1): 1–19.
Flaaten, Ola. 1991. "Bioeconomics of Sustainable Harvest of Competing Species." *Journal of Environmental Economics and Managment* 20: 163–80.
Gamani, Corea. 1990. "Global Stakes Require a New Consensus." *Development* 3/4: 17–22.

Glaser, Bernhard. 1988. "A Holistic Human Ecology Approach to Sustainable Agricultural Development." *Futures* 20: 671-78.

Hardin, Garrett. 1968. "The Tragedy of the Commons." *Science* 162: 1243-48.

Hardin, Garrett and John Baden, eds. 1977. *Managing the Commons.* San Francisco, CA: W. H. Freeman and Co.

Hirschman, Albert O. 1984. *Getting Ahead Collectively: Grassroots Experiences in Latin America.* New York: Pergamon Press.

Jackson, Bruce, Wendell Berry, and Bruce Coleman. *Meeting the Expectations of the Land: Essays in Sustainable Agriculture and Stewardship.* San Francisco, CA: North Point Press.

Livingstone, Ian. 1986. "The Common Property Problem and Pastoralist Economic Behavior." *The Journal of Development Studies* 23: 5-19.

McKay, Bonnie M. and James M. Acheson, eds. 1987. *The Question of the Commons: The Culture and Ecology of Communal Resources.* Tucson: University of Arizona Press.

Miller, Morris. 1990. "Can Development Be Sustainable." *Development* 3/4: 28-37.

Moles, Jerry A. 1989. "Agricultural Sustainability and Traditional Agriculture: Learning from the Past and Its Relevance to Sri Lanka." *Human Organization* 48: 70-78.

Norgaard, Richard B. 1988. "Sustainable Development: A Co- Evolutionary View." *Futures* 20: 606-20.

Oakerson, Ronald J. 1986. "A Model for the Analysis of Common Property Problems." In *Proceedings of the Conference on Common Property Resource Management.* Washington, DC: National Academy Press.

Pearce, David W., Edward Barbier, and Anil Markandya. 1990. *Sustainable Development: Economics and Environment in the Third World.* Brookfield, VT: Gower Pub. Co.

Redclift, Michael R. 1986. "Sustainability and the Market: Survival Strategies on the Bolivian Frontier." *The Journal of Development Studies* 23: 93-105.

_____.1987. *Sustainable Development: Exploring the Contradictions.* London: Methuen.

_____.1991. "The Multiple Dimensions of Sustainable Development." *Geography* 76: 36-42.

Reilly, William K. 1990. "The Green Thumb of Capitalism: The Environmental Benefits of Sustainable Growth." *Policy Review* 54: 16-21.

Rodale, Robert. 1983. "Breaking New Ground: The Search for a Sustainable Agriculture." *The Futurist* 17: 15-20.

Runge, Carlisle Ford. 1986. "Common Property and Collective Action in Economic Development." *World Development* 14: 623-35.

Smith, James L. 1987. "The Common Pool, Bargaining, and the Rule of Capture." *Economic Inquiry* 25: 631-44.

Speth, James Gustav, ed. 1990. Special Issue of *Development*, "Human Centered Economics: Environment and Global Sustainability." v. 3/4.

Swaney, James A. 1990. "Common Property, Reciprocity, and Community." *Journal of Economic Issues* 24: 451-62.

Tisdell, Clem. 1988. "Sustainable Development: Differing Perspectives of Ecologists and Economists, and Relevance to LDCs." *World Development* 16: 373-84.

Tolba, Mostafa K. 1987. *Sustainable Development: Constraints and Opportunities.* Boston: Butterworths.

Wade, Robert. 1987. "The Management of Common Property Resources: Collective Action as an Alternative to Privatisation or State Regulation." *Cambridge Journal of Economics* 11: 95-106.

von Weizsacker, Ernst U. 1991. "Sustainability: A Task for the North." *Journal of International Affairs* 44: 523-26.

PART III

Literature Reviews and Field Surveys of Resource Management

8

Anthropological Contributions to the Cultural Ecology and Management of Water Resources: A Review of Literature to the 1970s

Introduction

On the whole, anthropologists have studied water resources as a by-product of their research on cultural history and human subsistence, rather than as a separate topic.[1] In surveying the literature I have tried to feature the most common types of information and to suggest some unifying themes from the field of cultural ecology. The subjects treated in this essay are as follows: (1) water resource development in prehistoric cultures, particularly the ancient civilizations of the Middle East and Middle America, (2) the theoretical concept of "hydraulic society" or "irrigation civilization," (3) the ecological and cultural consequences of modern, large-scale water development projects in the tropics, (4) eth-

This chapter, presented here in an edited version, was prepared for a conference on the social sciences and their contribution to the study of water resources sponsored by the U.S. Government-funded Water Research Institute at the University of Kentucky. The paper was published in the book edited by Douglas James, *Man and Water* (Lexington: University of Kentucky Press, 1974). The present version is without bibliographical updating, and I have also decided to preserve the bibliographic-footnote style of the original publication, which is appropriate for a literature review paper. The writer's experience in water-related research is based on two projects: field studies of community irrigation systems in western Canada and a survey of the social and political aspects of the Arkansas River Valley development program requested by the U.S. Corps of Engineers in the early 1970s. A cursory literature survey made in 1990 suggested that materials appearing since the 1970s are in large part elaborations of the main themes of this essay. In addition, much research dealing with "water" has been absorbed into applied anthropological studies of agricultural change and development. Perhaps the only significant new edition to the archaeological literature consists of work in the 1980s on irrigation and its contribution to the development and decline of Maya civilization in Central America.

nological and applied anthropological work on the use of water in modern tribal and peasant societies, (5) problems of water management, with special reference to economic maximization and competitive-cooperative interactions, and (6) some cultural implications of water resource development and conservation in North America.

The contributions of anthropology to water resource management are not limited to ethnological accounts. Some of the most useful studies have been produced by archaeologists, with their special historical and technical perspective. Much can be learned about the long-range implications of resources development schemes from the studies of ancient water systems by prehistorians working in arid and semiarid lands in Asia and North and South America. In addition, the level of *technical* analysis provided in these publications is often superior to that displayed by sociocultural and applied anthropologists, who are usually more concerned with features of contemporary human behavior than with the economic and technological feasibility of resource arrangements.

Contributions from Archaeology

River Basin Archaeology

Archaeological studies of areas inundated by large reservoirs have played an important role in the development of the discipline and have contributed historical perspective to the knowledge of human use of riverine resources and topography. The pioneer work in the field was directed by William S. Webb of the University of Kentucky in the 1930s and 1940s, in connection with the construction of the Tennessee Valley Authority dams. Webb's survey volumes of the Norris Basin and others on the Tennessee constitute the first publications in river basin salvage archaeology.[2]

This survey work was required because the inundation of portions of large river valleys by man-made lakes has destroyed countless archaeological sites—a fact that says something about the location of prehistoric settlements with respect to water. Incipient food producers and their successors, village agriculturalists, were usually attracted to rivers, lakes, and seashores, and their remains are characteristically stratified with respect to distance from the water source. For river basins, distinctive economies, often varying systematically by historical period, will be found occupying the upper terraces, the lower terraces, and the alluvial valley. Remains of purely hunting economies are usually dispersed across these loci without regard for riverine or lacustrine resources per se. Thus, prehistoric populations might emphasize the collection of fish and shellfish, water for irrigation, the river as a transportation artery, or all of these together.

Man-made reservoirs can flood up to and including tertiary terraces on large streams, thus covering successive cultural horizons and subsistence styles. When funds can be obtained—they were relatively abundant for this purpose in the United States—archaeological crews can salvage specimens before the lake fills. The most spectacular example was the work set in motion by the Aswan Dam, which endangered thousands of Nubian archaeological sites ranging from Paleolithic to early Christian. Sponsored by UNESCO, American and European archaeological teams surveyed and dug numbers of these sites, and the relocation and restoration of some thirty-two temples was begun.[3]

In the United States the most intensive work was done on the Tennessee River during the TVA construction period and later on the Missouri and Arkansas rivers, in connection with the Corps of Engineers dam-building programs.[4] As in Nubia, the sites explored in these American programs ranged from preagricultural through incipient urban settlement of later cultures.[5]

River basin salvage archaeology has contributed valuable ecological and geological data. In efforts to date sites, reconstruct primitive economies, and better understand cultural stratification with reference to basin topography, archaeological and natural science teams have made studies of the paleobotany and palynology of the valleys, the sequence of terraces and their dates, and human interventions with possible topographic significance.[6] The work of James Ford in the bayou region of Louisiana in the 1950s enabled geologists to date certain terraces and water levels of the Mississippi.[7] Photographic methods developed by archaeologists have been used to trace premodern systems of dams, fishing technology, and other riverine usages.[8]

Archaeological Studies of Prehistoric Waterworks

Of greater significance for water resources management are studies on the water utilization and development schemes of prehistoric and protohistoric peoples. Archaeological studies of water storage systems in Bronze and Iron Age times in the Negev and Sinai peninsula have been used as models for agrarian development schemes in Israel and elsewhere. In some instances, the old systems of terraces, check dams, and directed runoff have simply been restored.[9] Archaeologists can thus provide considerable information relating to the long-run practicality of alternative designs. Robert McCormick Adams, in describing studies in the Khuzistan region, stressed the lessons archaeological data on irrigation may provide for planners: "How do the current plans and promises compare, we may ask, with earlier achievements in the same area?"[10]

The sheer variety of structures created for obtaining and better utilizing water in prehistoric and early historic societies deserves more attention than it has received from contemporary hydraulic engineers. Such societies developed suitable water control systems for every precipitation pattern in climates ranging from desert aridity to variable humdity, and the technical functions of many of these structures were misunderstood for generations. In a well known case, Sir Aurel Stein misidentified the *gabarband* walled terraces in Baluchistan as dams; and since runoff in Baluchistan is not sufficient to fill the supposed pools, he concluded that the climate had undergone progressive dessication. The conclusion was modified by Robert Raikes,[11] who was also aware of the studies by Israeli archaeologists and engineers on ancient water conservation schemes in the Negev.[12] The Israeli work convincingly showed that Negev desert lands were fertile in ancient times because of well-engineered devices to extract maximum use from all available water and not because of a more humid climate.[13]

The waterworks constructed by low-energy agricultural societies fall into twelve classes: (1) diversions of running streams into nearby fields, (2) ponds to hold water for later use, (3) catchment basins for rainfall, (4) slope development to increase aquifer recharge by holding water in silted terraces behind ramparts, (5) dams for diverting streamflow into ditches for domestic and agricultural use, (6) large canal and distribution systems to carry river water to cultivated areas, (7) large reservoirs for long-term storage, (8) devices to tap groundwater at water-table levels, including the famous *qanats* of the Middle East and Africa, (9) artificial islands used for agriculture in permanent shallow lakes (the *chinampas* of Mexico), (10) aqueducts and tunnels transporting water for domestic supply, (11) a large variety of wheels, levers, and bucket systems to lift water to higher elevations, and (12) a variety of schemes for draining excessively moist soils.[14]

Some of these devices deserve special comment. The *qanats* were given considerable attention due to their long persistence and impressive simplicity and efficiency. They can be used wherever water-table elevations under a hillside are higher than the land surface of an adjacent valley. The *qanats* are constructed by digging a series of vertical "wells" on the hillside down to the water table and then tunneling horizontally from the bottom of the shafts out to the base of the slope, where the water is channeled fanwise onto fields. Iran is often viewed as the home of the *qanat* since the devices are numerous there,[15] but similar systems have been reported throughout the Middle East and western Sahara,[16] the coastal Peruvian civilizations,[17] and the Tehuacan Valley of Mexico.[18] The essential simplicity of the system as a means of increasing flows from natural seepages or springs often found at the base of scarps favored the independent development of *qanats* in many regions with water shortages and the requisite water-table and surface geology.

A considerable variety of prehistoric irrigation systems were found in Meso-American civilizations. The arid Pacific coast of South America has a particularly large assortment,[19] and Paul Kosok published a photographic album showing aerial views of many of these systems as well as a study of the Lambayeque multiple-valley stream.[20] Prehistoric peoples of the region also employed subirrigation by excavating fields to lower the zone of cultivation close to the water table. The sunken gardens of the Peruvian coast were traced through the Spanish colonial period, when they apparently were used more extensively than in prehistoric times.[21] The *chinampas* of Mexico were plots floated on permanent lakes. Elsewhere along the Peruvian coast the *mahama* consisted of walled fields situated along river terraces subject to flooding.[22] In Bolivia the ridged fields, called *camellones* by the Spanish, were essentially raised plots for elevating crop land above poorly drained areas.[23] The *riego a brazo*, or "pot irrigation," technique practiced by the Zapotec in the Oaxaca area of southern Mexico involves the digging of wells in the cornfield, down to the water table. Water is drawn up in ceramic jars and poured on the crop when needed.[24]

John Rowe informed me that in the Ica Valley of Peru dry slopes were watered for cultivation by moisture precipitated from dense fog impounded behind small terraces. In central Mexico dry valley slopes were terraced to receive flood waters and eventually built up deep deposits of arable silt.[25] In a detailed study of the *chinampas* Armillas made clear that the plots of saturated land as used by the Aztecs were the culminating product of several centuries of usage of the swamplands of the valley, including permanent towns erected on hummocks completely surrounded by water and connected by causeways.[26] These raised gardens (ridges of land protruding above the shallow water, not the floating gardens of legend) thus signify one of the most extensive and intensive uses of permanent wetlands in human history. As archaeological work uncovers a greater variety and intensity of water-control systems, few opportunities appear to have been missed by prehistoric peoples.

The variety of these schemes, relying on delicate, small-scale adjustments, contrasts with a modern philosophy which emphasizes large-scale projects of stereotypic design. The difference is a result of the maximization objective: to produce the largest possible amount of water in order to serve the largest number of people. The premodern systems were often ecosystemically related to low population levels and were substantively efficient in supporting the small population willing to devote much labor to the task. However, the more elaborate schemes produced by classical Oriental civilizations, involving extensive canals and reservoirs, like those of Ceylon, Southeast Asia, and Southwest Asia, were capable of supporting large and dense populations. On the other hand, the brittleness of the large, complex projects in the face of technical deterioration and marauding invaders resulted in periodic collapse and depopulation.

The existence of structural flood-control systems in early civilizations has been difficult to demonstrate. The case of the Mohenjodaro city ruin provides evidence that flood-proofing was used.[27] Works included ramparts, high platforms for houses, and drains in the settlement itself. However, at the time of writing I did not find evidence that this Bronze Age Indus River Valley civilization attempted to divert or control floodwaters upstream, and, in any case, repeated flooding of the city may have resulted in its eventual decline and abandonment. The Romans built several large dams in Italy and created diversion works to guard against flash floods in the Nabatean-Roman metropolis of Petra.[28] There are other instances of this kind, though they are insufficiently researched.[29] The use of lowlands along the Nile for annual agricultural irrigation became a means of flood-control by land use adjustment since over time settlements and monument sites were located above the highest flood levels. There is also evidence of careful channeling to direct floodwaters into the cultivated areas at the right time. Many of these systems also protected against erosion.[30]

The work by Robert McCormick Adams in Southwest Asia served as a model for a series of investigations seeking to describe the development of irrigation systems through time and evolving cultural horizons, with typical interruptions or stimuli furnished by invasions and conquest.[31] Particularly for Syria, Iraq, and Iran archaeologists have attempted reconstructions of technical and social history from earliest prehistoric times to the contemporary era.[32] The guiding approach of these studies has been cultural ecology, and the focus has been on the effects of particular technoeconomic adaptations on settlement patterns and social organization. As data on the last factor is hard to obtain, reconstructions of social structure probably will remain ambiguous.

From a purely technological standpoint, water usage systems can be classified on a simple-to-complex basis, beginning with complete reliance on rainfall through various local diversions for irrigation and culminating in the extensive canal systems of the city-states and urban-based civilizations. The actual chronological history of the various technical adaptations and the relationship of these schemes to the development of plant and animal domestication, settlement patterns, and sociopolitical structures, however, are less clear, and theories of the linkage of these factors have changed as data accumulates. An earlier and well-known position associated with the name of Robert Braidwood held that hunting-gathering peoples in the highlands, where the wild ancestors of seed grains and some domestic animals are particularly abundant, learned to cultivate these species and then moved down to the arid river valleys, developing irrigation in the process.[33] Eventually population pressure in the lowlands led to nucleated settlements, large-scale irrigation, and political centralization.

Binford and Flannery proposed an alternative to the Braidwood thesis.[34] They suggested that the upland areas were homes of hunting-gathering peoples who prospered on the abundant wild food supply, developing a "broad spectrum" subsistence base and thereby experiencing population increase. In the classic manner of such developed, "Mesolithic" food-collecting groups, daughter populations would move out of the optimal region towards the margins where water and natural foods would be less abundant or less easily available. Plant domestication and cultivation began as the food collectors brought the seeds of wild species with which they were familiar to the dryer lowlands. In arid climates this necessitated the development of irrigation and crop management in the marginal areas. Eventually farming moved back into the optimal zones.

Some prehistorians, like K. V. Flannery, as in the reference cited above, viewed the development of irrigation as the emergence of a new niche in natural ecology. The alteration of humidity had its impact on flora, with many new plants becoming established through weed growth and deliberate cultivation. The increase in human population on formerly resource-deficient habitats permanently transformed these regions, requiring continuous management and experimentation to the present day.

As food production permitted the growth of village populations in the dry lowlands and river valleys, irrigation would spread, linking villages by canals. The evolution of such an early village irrigation system, based on a lake and canal system and continuing through its subsequent decline due to ecological change, has been described by Hans Helbaek.[35] Increasingly extensive irrigation permitted the emergence of urban civilization. Truly large-scale irrigation would then be created by these emergent city-states, a thesis particularly emphasized by Robert M. Adams.[36] "Civilization" could thus be founded on essentially village-type irrigation works, and irrigation would not be the cause of the centralization necessary for the state-empire and its complex technology and military force.[37]

The essential element in this new approach is that environmental deficiencies, not abundances, explain the development of irrigation technology—a point of view reminiscent of Toynbee's "challenge and response" but on the whole possibly borne out by the accumulating evidence of village sites in oases on arid plains and in river valleys older than the earliest food-producing communities in well watered and grassy uplands.[38]

Later resource development is associated with the city-states in the large river valleys.[39] If Adams is correct, the urbanized state simply enlarged the older systems. Main trunk canals took water from major rivers, and a complex network of smaller canals distributed it throughout the entire valley. The acceleration in system development is noteworthy: whereas the development of rainfall-plus-small-scale-irrigation systems occupied three or more milennia in Southwest Asia, the development of the canal systems in the valleys seems to have taken an average of three to four centuries.

The major social implications of such development were articulated by Adams as follows: "In a way which had no parallel in earlier periods, vast efforts were devoted to comprehensive programs of irrigation extending over virtually the entire arable surface. This entailed bold and imaginative planning and administration, a whole series of technological innovations, and, above all, the investment of state funds on what must have been an unprecedented scale."[40] Thus a sociopolitical entity of a new type emerged: the *state*. This entity extended its rule and control of resources over many towns and villages under an administrative system with centrally controlled taxation to provide the funds for the waterworks. One remarkable aspect of this stage of development is the extension of canals into zones where under modern conditions agriculture is unprofitable even with a reasonable water supply. This evidence suggests an efficient irrigation system and also a driving need to use the system as a force for political unification and control—or the other side of the coin, the needs for political control generated by the system.

Another noteworthy aspect of these massive schemes, according to Adams, was the utilization of increased agricultural productivity for investment in new craft industries. The development of a luxury textile industry, use of irrigated areas as loci for settlement of war prisoners, and for fruit, sugarcane, rice, and other trade crops are all noted. Commercial activities began to replace subsistence agriculture. Trade to obtain exotic raw materials and seed and root stock became important.

A third major accompaniment of large-scale irrigation was the development of an advanced engineering technology for designing dams, weirs, pumping devices, canals, tunnels, conduits, siphons, and earthmoving equipment. The ingenuity, scope, and scale of the works produced are at least comparable to the modern water systems of western North America prior to the advent of huge, multipurpose projects beginning with the Hoover Dam. However, under ancient conditions wateworks were labor-intensive; thus water resource development represented a very large increase in "social capital." This situation proved dangerous when for some reason the labor could no longer be supplied.

While the system was capable of supporting true cities, villages remained the mainstay of the agrarian economy. The society thus displayed a complex pattern of settlement in which population was dispersed in nucleated centers of all sizes, the size of a community reflecting its position in a complex statewide division of economic function, rather than the subsistence value of its agricultural production. Gordon Childe saw the Southwest Asian rivers as inducing such growth as a result of human response to their distinctive ecological properties.[41]

There seems little doubt that the period of urban and agricultural expansion that came with the development of centralized irrigation systems in Southwest Asia represented the most complex indigenous culture the region ever supported. Much the same can be said for parts of Meso-America and perhaps Southeast Asia as well. These generalized assessments carry implications for contemporary development programs: the key to success is to be found in the sociopolitical organization that makes possible determined economic and engineering efforts. The remarkable fact about the origins of advanced agricultural economy and urban civilzation in the ancient world was its location in regions limited in water supply.

However, the later decline of these systems points to the fundamental precariousness of development in arid regions. These early urbanized civilizations, based on water resource development, were susceptible to determined military depredation, and their engineering capabilities, while remarkable, did not prevent inevitable silting and salinization. Social decline and depopulation were extraordinarily rapid once the network of canals and impoundments no longer functioned. There is no reason to assume that the situation is any different today. We are witnessing the potential fragility of comparable schemes in Arab-Israeli conflicts. Clearly, large-scale water resource development in moisture-deficient situations contains both the seeds of effective social and economic development—and also of its opposite: sociopolitical disintegration and depopulation.

The ever-present danger of overdevelopment has led a number of specialists to suggest greater reliance on local schemes less easily disrupted and producing at a lower level for a smaller and more stable population. In fact, the most enduring water development schemes in arid lands support small populations dispersed in town and village nuclei with a dominant subsistence basis. The *qanats* of Iran have endured through the extensive depredations of conquerors and destroyers of the larger canal and dam systems, and the regions served by them have retained a basic economic and demographic stability through the centuries, at the price of a static economy.[42]

Ancient irrigation systems can also be assumed to have suffered from the ills afflicting contemporary schemes: ponding due to poor land leveling and consequent waterlogging and salinization, inadequate drainage to export water with excessive mineral content, weed growth and leakage in canals and ditches, silting, soil exhaustion, and so on. It is possible that subsequent invasions were encouraged by the signs of agrarian decline in coveted regions.[43]

However, the ecological efficiency and duration of ancient water systems are extremely difficult to assess with archaeological methods since analysis of phase-outs of production requires very precise measurements over small intervals of time. A major paper on problems of silting and salinization of the great Sassanian-period schemes in the Diyala Valley of Iraq traces the ecological deterioration in contrast to the efficiency of the earlier and simpler systems.[44] Hans Helbaek utilized techniques that permit observations on ecological consequences of irrigation schemes based on the fact that changes in the remains of cultivated plants are indicative of water shortages or of the presence of minerals in damaging quantities.[45] There is a strong suggestion in Adams's work that the constant shifting of centers of power in Mesopotamian ancient history may have been associated with degradation of irrigation systems as well as with the unstable military and economic situation.

Investigations of the degradational effects on soils and crops might well be made in the Fayum, where in the twelfth dynasty an enormous impoundment of Nile waters was created by embankments, opening up about 27,000 acres for intensive cultivation. Reservoir operation required careful watch of the Nile flow in the south, at the Second Cataract, with information on the rise sent rapidly northward to the water masters. The arrangement also provides a good example of the sophisticated central organization and control required for large-scale irrigation.[46]

The problem of ecological decline suggests the need for a more complex theory of the rise and fall of irrigation-based civilizations. Let us assume that as irrigation systems increase in extent or gross production they also begin to decrease in efficiency or marginal productivity. As the irrigation system makes it possible for population to increase and political organization to expand, it also begins to develop serious ecological problems. The costs of repairing canals, plugging leaks in dikes, and proper leveling of land may increase until society is willing to bear them. An improperly maintained system may function well enough to sustain a considerable population but still be rapidly degrading. Even today a great many irrigation systems do not invest sufficient capital at the beginning to avoid these destructive cycles. Many systems, ancient and modern, are not able to sustain an adequate maintenance program because of ineffective organization or labor supply.[47]

Thus the ecological and technical problems of ambitious water resource developments relate to fundamental issues of civilization's decline and its growth. Both scholars studying the past and planners of modern large-scale projects have placed emphasis on growth, but it is perhaps time to study the causes of decline and collapse. Historically, these phenomena have been as apparent as their opposites. As this is written, the United States is entering a decisive phase of "infrastructure" deterioration, with few signs of the political will to invest the funds required for rehabilitation.

Hydraulic Societies

"Hydraulic societies" is a phrase referring to a version of the problem of irrigation and the development of civilization, and is, in addition, a major theoretical issue in anthropology and history. The issues involved received their first major public airing in a symposium edited by Julian Steward, where the concept of *irrigation civilizations* was offered as a case of cross-cultural regularity.[48] Karl Wittfogel, whose book *Oriental Despotism* was the next public statement, introduced the term *hydraulic society* in his contribution to Steward's volume.[49]

In keeping with other theses proposed by Marx and Engels, the type of society they called "Asiatic" features centralized bureaucratic controls and despotic power. While this concept was later revised by Marx and further modified in the twentieth century by Stalinists, Wittfogel adhered to the early Marx-Engels concept, that is, he called their "Asiatic type" of society *Oriental despotism*. As an historian of China, Wittfogel used China as the archetype of Asiatic society and stressed the importance of large-scale irrigation in consolidating centralized bureaucratic power. These bureaucratic elites could further entrench themselves through associations with religious hierarchies and through the development of centralized economies with redistributive features.[50] Wittfogel proceeded to identify true and quasi-Oriental despotisms or hydraulic societies around the world, developing a ramified typology. However, the notion of centralization stemming from the control of water and waterworks pervades the classification and thus translates it into a general theory of sociopolitical development. At the most minute level, this approach has produced some useful studies of cultural parallelisms in village peoples. An example is Richard Beardsley's field study of parallels in Japanese and Spanish rice-growing communities.[51]

At the most general level, Wittfogel's theory suggests a single sweeping explanation of complex historical events spanning considerable time. Such intellectual constructions often contain generalized truth set in a matrix of empirical error. In the Wittfogel case the truth lies in the plausible connection between large-scale water projects and the sociopolitical forms necessary to initiate or operate them. Even Robert M. Adams, probably Wittfogel's most Olympian critic, armed with detailed empirical knowledge of water systems in ancient Southwest Asia and Mexico, presented evidence to show the need for central political organization and nucleated population in societies with such systems.[52] It is reasonable that the larger and more geographically coherent the irrigation system, the more centralized the political control over the relevant territory is likely to become.

René Millon, on the basis of a comparative survey of seven societies of varying population magnitudes, concluded that "there is no simple tendency for centralization of authority over water allocation to increase with the size of the system or the numbers of people involved."[53] While the conclusion is reasonable, Millon's survey could not be taken as definitive, since its sample was limited and also because of the complexity of the issue; note the phrase "no simple tendency": the tendency does exist, but manifestations of specific relationships depend on other factors.

In one of the most revealing critiques of the Wittfogel thesis, Edmund Leach pointed out that Wittfogel, in his discussion of China, ignored a second major type of Asian hydraulic society, the Indian system.[54] This approach to large-scale development, as exemplified by Leach with data from ancient Sinhalese civilization (Anuradapura-Pollanarua), contains many village-scale irrigation works that are sustained by cooperative labor and, at the other extreme, grandiose waterworks constructed by the kings primarily used for irrigating ornamental gardens rather than agricultural fields. The king granted land with water rights to local magnates and religious bodies, and the huge waterworks were built slowly over centuries. They were not the instant creations of tyrants and did not require enormous levies of forced labor. Leach might have added that later the Sinhalese system declined and that one reason for this decline might have been the inadequacy of feudal systems in providing the labor needed for maintenance. However this may be, Leach acknowledges that because of the lack of good historical data on the sociopolitical structure of ancient societies his own reconstruction, like Wittfogel's, can be only tentative.

Other critics have noted that the use of the concept of hydraulic control to identify the cooperative discipline characteristic of such village peoples as the Hopi with the military statism of Mesopotamia is simply to ignore the diverse causes of social organization. The key to the social systems of rice-growing villagers is to be found in kinship and functional groupings of neighbors, not in political institutions associated with military and ritual elites. In such local societies cooperative interaction over water allocations is as likely to emerge as despotic control. Others have held that the approach ignores the interaction of many factors in social systems and attributes to a particular technological configuration a massive and uniform causal influence.[55]

Richard Beardsley's comparison of Spanish and Japanese rice-growing villages (cited earlier) observed that the cooperative tasks of water management introduced a "solidarity" or "vigor" in irrigation-oriented communities which other agricultural village peoples did not have.[56] While the strength of the social organization was manifest in a certain centralization of management and thus superficially resembled the Wittfogel concept (though Beardsley does not engage in a discussion of Wittfogel), solidarity and centralization of these rice-growing communities is not a case of despotism but of its alternative: voluntary allocation of authority among equals.

The Leach thesis may also relate to the situation in Egypt, where during the sixth dynasty central political authority collapsed as local magnates asserted their independence.[57] While this development cannot be clearly attributed to resource factors, it appears that irrigation facilities reached a peak of development during the sixth dynasty. With the localities becoming increasingly strong and independent, the increasing water resource development could have contributed to the breakdown of central power. While Wittfogel could argue that despotism was simply being transferred to local hands, a more subtle interpretation of his thesis would acknowledge the importance of the particular locus of despotism or the size of the units under examination. Peter Kunstadter found that in Thailand hill tribes the introduction of irrigation resulted in decreases in communal and centralized social and religious functions and *increases* in individualistic management and localization of governing functions.[58]

In another sense, the Wittfogel approach is part of a line of inquiry stemming from recognition of the persistent fact that in Egypt, Southwest Asia, and China urban civilization emerged in riverine environments, arid, or semiarid regions through which permanent streams flow. There is no question that the constellation of factors that influenced population to cluster in oasis-like centers serving a variety of social and economic needs lies at the basis of Southwest Asian and Oriental civilizations. These particular conditions placed an emphasis on strong political organization and its military-political controls.

In the New World the pattern was more diverse and water was more diffusely distributed.[59] Only on the dry Pacific coast of South America is there evidence for population nucleation and political centralization around extensive waterworks. The Lower Colorado River, in spite of its similarity to Southwest Asian conditions, did not become a focal point for the growth of a civilization and extensive irrigation. For example, the Hohokam, an indigenous tribal society practicing desert irrigation, in the fifteenth century emerged on the tributaries and not along the major rivers. High civilization in the Valley of Mexico was based on lakes, not rivers. Along European rivers the temperate-humid environment did not force population nucleation, and urban civilization appeared very late and then was largely derivative.[60] These variant patterns for the New World and Europe suggest that water deficiency or, more generally, the quantity available relative to need, may be paramount in determining the sociopolitical consequences of water resource development.[61] The important empirical relationship between water controls and sociopolitical organization definitely remains a significant arena for inquiry and comparative research. It is also an area having potential for planning modern water development schemes.

Modern Tropical River Development

Human Ecology of Dams and Man-Made Lakes

During the 1960s and 1970s a series of large river-control projects were initiated in Africa, Southeast Asia, and Latin America.[62] Since these projects were planned mainly by American and European developers, planning concepts were based on the large dams of the temperate regions of North America and Europe. These temperate-region dams customarily have been defended as multipurpose water-control schemes, but most of them were conceived in reponse to specific needs for power or flood control. In Africa as well the dams and lakes have been planned largely for major development purposes, although recreation, fisheries, and other secondary objectives have been widely advertised.

The basic issue in planning is the suitability for tropical regions of large reservoirs designed for a temperate ecology.[63] For none of these tropical reservoirs were the ecological impacts of creating large bodies of relatively still water in high-temperature climates intensively investigated. In fairness to the planners and engineers, the assessment of ecological and social impacts in such unprecedented circumstances and in an atmosphere of powerful nationalist advocacy was impractical and often beyond the capacity of the agencies. Each of the major dams has a history of complex political and financial negotiations that often prevented adequate or properly timed feasibility surveys. During the 1970s the writer was a member of a team of social scientists retained by the U.S. Corps of Engineers to study the social impacts and political economy of the Arkansas River Valley development program. Relevant to the present discussion was the finding that every cost-benfit analysis made for the project during the several decades of its political advocacy was unfavorable—except the last one, which was done expressly for the U.S. senator backing the bill in Congress for funding the project.

There is, of course, a more general issue here. Inherent in the nature of large-scale resource development and utilization schemes is the fact that certain elements of trial-and-error experience are hard to avoid. An example is the homesteading settlement on the United States and Canadian western frontiers in the nineteenth and twentieth centuries. While knowledge of ecological conditions in the West was sufficient to have avoided some of the subsequent depopulation and agricultural failure, the political situation required immediate settlement, and the approach was simply to fill the place with people and let Nature take its course. The authorities were aware that a human cost would be involved but guessed that the cost could be borne, given the economic potential of North America and the ready possibility of migration. While it is debatable as to whether the example is entirely applicable to modern dams, the pressures leading towards rapid development have been similar. Nevertheless, as technology and the capability for adedquate evaluation of consequences improve, the trial-and-error argument and the whole policy of "instant development" under political imperatives, become harder to defend. Despite the extent to which experience with error in the cases of the Kariba and Volta Dams demonstrated need for prefunding feasibility surveys in depth, the Koffu Dam in the Ivory Coast was constructed with no ecological studies, and a social impact survey was made *after* construction.

As of 1970 (and 1990) only one important series of monographs and papers was published on the human consequences of dam and lake building in the tropics. These included anthropological studies initiated by the Rhodes-Livingstone Institute, originally directed by Elizabeth Colson and carried on by her and Thayer Scudder. Less comprehensive studies by other anthropologists on the Mekong River development program were also at hand.[64] Studies of medical aspects of tropical water empoundments, agronomic studies, and animal and plant ecology research have contributed other materials with varying significance for the human context.

Scudder's cultural ecology research was focused on the Kariba Dam on the Zambezi River in a deeply entrenched reach between Zambia and Southern Rhodesia. Construction was undertaken for the purpose of providing power for industrial development in regions far from the dam site. The dam and lake area was the home of about 60,000 Gwembe Tonga who were not consulted and who had to be resettled in two major groups, one on the new lake, the other farther downstream. If the Volta River dam in Ghana, the Kainji Lake Basin scheme in Nigeria, and the Aswan project in Egypt are added to the record, a total of 275,000 Africans during the 1960s and 1970s had to be relocated to new environments.[65] In no case did planning for human impact, relocation, or rehabilitation equal the need.

A related need is for surveys that explore the possible consequences of a wide range of alternatives. For example, the preconstruction planning studies of agricultural rehabilitation after resettlement in the Volta Dam project in Ghana assumed simply that the existing regimes would be perpetuated and reconstituted. However, President Nkrumah decided to ignore these proposals in favor of a "big step": to develop a completely new irrigated and mechanized agriculture which would replace all existing systems, a policy which subsequently proven to be a failure.[66] If the assessments of disadvantages had been made, the decision might have been otherwise.

The Kariba Dam project is a complex and continuously evolving case, but several things appear to be clear: (1) the Tonga had a 90 percent subsistence economy that was destroyed by the relocation; (2) while the Tonga by the late 1960s had made considerable progress in developing a new agricultural regime, this progress occurred at the cost of greater dependence on government help and outside markets; (3) preplanning for the new agricultural program was nonexistent, and assistance in developing a new regime was minimal. The tentative conclusion was that the dam and lake did not result in an overall improvement in Gwembe agriculture or its productivity and returns, and readaptation has largely been a Tonga accomplishment.

Scudder described the Tonga pre-dam agricultural program as fluctuating with the rather erratic pattern of natural flow and flooding of the river. Crops were spaced between the annual flood and the rainy season, providing for two crop seasons each year. Erratic flooding and soil exhaustion had induced the Tonga to begin cultivation of dry, upland terrace soils by the 1950s, and some believe that resettlement of some of the Tonga would have been necessary even without the dam and lake due to increasing difficulties in the agricultural program. However, the dam forced the resettlement issue and virtually wiped out the two-crop seasonal system, requiring the Tonga to adopt a single rainy-season crop program. Cultivation along the shores of the lake has been difficult due to the extensive drawdown associated with the power uses of the dam water. The Tonga turned to livestock as a major supplement, but this had its difficulties due to the tsetse fly and capital shortages. Extensive irrigated agriculture could be developed downstream with the enhanced water flow, but this required much capital assistance from government.

(By the 1980s, however, considerable progress apparently has been made.)

Scudder noted that agriculture has been the least satisfactory aspect of these tropical water development programs, since the methods of production worked out by the indigenous population are usually the most productive and ecologically suitable for a region with difficult or specialized resources.[67] Movement to less suitable environments usually means the need for agricultural intensification requiring capital and technology beyond the capacity of the local people and/or their government's to provide or sustain.

The rise and fall of the Kariba reservoir level, a phenomenon always associated with large dams used for power production or downstream irrigation, has created further difficulties. The fluctuation of water surface levels in response to demands for power output made yields of crops dependent on marginal flooding unpredictable by the local farmers. While increased water supplies available for irrigation might confer greater predictability to downstream agriculture, this does not apply in situations such as the Kariba lake area, where natural flooding is the only socially feasible irrigation method. The effect on largely subsistence agriculture regimes is thus very serious, and development is forced into intensifying patterns with their increased capital requirements.

P.B.N. Jackson found that the cost of making fisheries economically viable in the African reservoirs always exceeded the original estimates.[68] The principal factor in the Kariba and Volta cases was that the clearing of the bush from the lake area, though extensive, was not adequate to avoid altered nutrient conditions mentioned previously, resulting in periodic "blooms" of algae. More recent observations suggested that the costs of bush clearing could be greatly reduced by simply clearing "bush lanes" to permit access channels and leaving the rest of the bush in place. The cycles of increase and decrease could then be endured, and eventually the bush areas will provide feeding and breeding grounds for fish populations. As the fish cross from one patch to another, men fishing in the cleared lanes could catch them.

The human health consequences of these dams and lakes were also studied. An unfortunate byproduct of the fisheries operation at Kariba Lake was the rapid spread of trypanosomiasis ("sleeping sickness") through the spread of the tsetse fly as fish traders moved from village to village in the resettlement area. The disease was more serious in its bovine than in the human form, but by 1966 the outbreak was reduced by about half, using standard control measures.[69] Malaria was often associated with the concentration of a large labor force at the dam site; Waddy notes that a special term, "the malaria of tropical aggregations of labor," is used for this syndrome.[70] One of the most publicized cases was the de Lesseps attempt at the Panama Canal, where over 52,000 men out of 87,000 employed were treated for malaria, with 6,000 deaths. Webster found that the medical expenditure for the de Lesseps venture was 0.5 percent of the total cost;[71] the percentage for the Kariba Dam project was the same.

Two debilitating diseases have been especially associated with the aquatic conditions created by large dam construction: schistosomiasis and onchocerciasis.[72] Schistosomiasis has been particularly prevalent in the Aswan High Dam project. "Egypt 10," a schistosomiasis research and control project sponsored by the World Health Organization, suggests that many of the irrigation advantages of the dam may be negated by the health debits.[73]

Schistosomiasis is a generic name for a series of illnesses caused by related organisms (liver flukes), which start their complex life cycle with man. The eggs deposited in human tissues hatch into larvae which leave the human body and enter water snails. In the final larval stage, the organism reenters the human body by burrowing into exposed skin in the water and causes a serious disease very difficult to treat. Propagation of the disease is enhanced as large numbers of people are exposed to a large body of sluggish water in which snails can breed—a condition created behind any large dam. Infection rates were high at Aswan in both the laboring population and the indigenous villages along the Nile. The disease, spread by villagers coming into contact with the infected snails in the newly irrigated land, has become a major cost factor in Nile irrigation. The practice of wearing of rubber boots, urged as protective device, was not carried out effectively due to Islamic rituals of ablution. Control could be effected by chemical eradication of the snail host, but this was extremely costly and beyond the financial capacity of most African countries.

Onchocerciasis is a less debilitating disease, although the occurrence of blindness in the terminal phase has made it a threat to local people. The filarial worm that causes the disease is spread by black flies, one of the world's worst insect pests. The Owen Falls damsite in East Africa was hit by a black fly invasion, leading to the flight of the entire worker population for several weeks. Actually, large reservoirs tend to control the disease because the worm breeds best in running, oxygenated water, and the slower stream velocities behind dams inhibit breeding. However, flow in irrigation canals and increased population density encourage the disease.

Scudder collected vital statistics on the relocated Tonga population.[74] After the dam began to fill in 1958, 7,600 Tonga were moved from the reservoir area and resettled, some at considerable distances from their villages. Of the 1,600 moved in 1958 forty-one children died during the first three months of 1959; and of of the 6,000 moved later 100 people, mostly children, died within four months after relocation. Fifty-three adults died the following year. These constitute high death rates, but Scudder was careful to point out that these mortality figures concern the transition period immediately after relocation and should not be taken as a permanent condition.

During the transition period before the Tonga reconstituted their agricultural regime, they subsisted largely on famine-relief food provided by the Zambian government on the condition that the food would be paid for by cash from the compensation funds allotted the Tonga. The idea was to stimulate adaptive behavior on the part of the Tonga. However, the cash was given to the household heads, who, in accordance with Tonga customs, found other ways to spend the money, withholding much of it from food purchase. Consequently, the Tonga fell back on the collecting of wild vegetable foods, as they had been accustomed to doing during drought periods, and since they were unfamiliar with the flora in their new home they collected and consumed a poisonous root that caused a number of deaths and much sickness.

Scudder also noted that the high death rate following resettlement was associated with a general homesickness and despair possibly leading to reduced vitality among the youngest and oldest segments of the population (a effect noted by students of urban renewal projects in the United States). This effect seems to have been particularly acute for the 6,000 who were moved 100 miles away from their original home to a sparsely populated area inhabited by tribesmen speaking a different language and practicing different customs. Homesickness was probably aggravated by the failure of the government to provide full information on the need for resettlement since the relocated groups lived at considerable distances from the dam and did not comprehend the full extent of the new lake. More extreme reactions were encountered in the Sudan from the Aswan relocation program, where riots and chronic civil disturbance accompanied the relocation.[75] Obviously, considerable time needs to be devoted to planing mass relocation programs.[76]

In the volume containing Scudder's paper on man-made lakes, R. Jackson, in his own paper, illustrated how the complex political and economic factors involved in these big schemes make it virtually impossible to achieve continuity in planning.[77] After the initial Preparatory Commission Report of 1956, a five-year interval ensued while funds were sought internationally for the Volta project. The *economic* justification used for the project was that the power generated by the dam would be used for the production of aluminum to be sold on the world market. The *public* justification of the project was to lessen the reliance of Ghana on a single crop, cocoa. Fluctuations and uncertainties in the aluminum market delayed financing and construction until 1961, and Jackson remarks, "during this hiatus the scientific problems got into the background."[78] He also noted that ten years of work went into planning resettlement, but a "crash program became inevitable" because of the hiatus and outmoding of the previous plans. The clearing of the lake for fishery development involved enormous costs which could not be financed from the expected returns from the aluminum sales. Such experiences illustrate the extent to which the people affected by these large-scale projects become pawns of international policy and processes. Better planning is desirable, but where consequences are unforeseeable, even with more research, it is doubtful if planning contains all the answers.[79] We need a sense of values which recognizes that a slower, experimental approach to resource development, with many preconstruction surveys, can avoid much of the ecological and social damage that is the product of the crash, big-solution approach. (By the 1980s such reforms in the planning process had been inaugurated.)

Even where reasonable preparation is made to receive the settlers in their new locality, mistakes were made in basic accommodations due to the failure to study the cultural habits of the people. Some examples from Scudder's work: The relocated Tonga had formerly lived in villages spaced across the landscape with minute attention to the distribution of shared resources. The annual agricultural procedures were controlled by a ritual leader who signalled the times for planting, cultivating, and harvesting and controlled the amounts of land used in various ways. Over time, these patterns had contributed to a homeostatic balance of the size of the local population, its spatial dispersion, and its use of resources. After relocation disrupted the entire cultural-ecological regime, the ritual leadership role ceased to acquire players. This was caused not only by the absence of detailed knowledge of the locality and resources, but also because the Tonga ceremonial specialists felt that their gods did not accompany them to the new location. This belief delayed the reestablishment of effective agricultural regimes and was a contributing cause to the need for food relief.

The Tonga funeral ceremony included lengthy drumming. The indigenous inhabitants of the areas to which the Tonga were brought lacked this custom. When the Tonga began to drum, the local people asked them to stop, lest their own spirits be offended. Hunting shrines, magical routines, and many other security-conferring rituals of Tonga culture associated with life crises and economic activities could not be established for similar reasons. For several years after resettlement, Tonga culture was disorganized.

The Tonga required up to four years to innovate new strategic patterns of decision and task performance.[80] One of the first adaptations was to use their institution of "instrumental friendships" to establish a better relationship with the Goba people with whom they now had to live and share land. The incentive was to obtain the right to use additional agricultural land, badly needed by the Tonga, from the half-utilized Goba fields. Cattle and money were given in exchange. A number of other symbiotic arrangements between Tonga and Goba gradually emerged.

Another adaptation concerned the emergence of spirit mediums (*mangelo*) who claimed they could cure a number of anxiety-produced or accentuated illnesses. While these functionaries had always existed in Tonga society, the need for their services increased because of the desire of the poeple to contact the new spririts of Goba territory and reassure them that the Tonga would not harm or offend them. As the *mangelo* went into action, the death rate dropped, the Tonga farmers came to have more confidence, funeral drumming resumed, and the society became more stable.

Papers on the Mekong River development program provide a comparative perspective on tropical river development, although most of the studies concerned future possibilities since the program was in its early stages as of 1970. The Mekong project involved the Lao, Thai, Khmer, and Vietnamese peoples since the basin is in all four countries; its very inception constituted an historic change in mainland Southeast Asian politics because all four were hereditary enemies.[81]

Sewell and White voiced the familiar criticism of the lack of social evaluation in contrast to the excellent technical feasibility work.[82] The magnitude of the investments required to insure efficient operation of the big dams without excessive social and ecological costs can be gathered by reading some of the duplicated or semipublished documents prepared by various advisory groups. For example, Jasper Ingersoll, in a duplicated report on the social feasibility of the huge Pa Mong dam and reservoir in Laos, noted that irrigation relates to physical, economic, and social systems and that feasibility studies are meed for all three if economic "profitability" and social "usability" are to be attained.[83] His list of requirements and conditions that should be present "if the Pa Mong project is actually undertaken" included adequate and predictable water supply, control of diseases, accessible markets for new products, no land speculation, fair and just land compensation, small services areas for irrigation districts, prevention of "corruption" that affects irrigation efficiency, a "vast increase in credit facilities for farmers," effective education to utilize irrigation properly, fully technologized preparation of irrigated lands, provision for domestic water systems, promotion of participation by local people in all Mekong irrigation schemes, and coordinated environmental and social research.[84] The report did not examine the probability of such measures being carried out. They would have been equally relevant, perhaps even utopian, for a project in North America.

Another series of papers by ecologists, resource analysts, and anthropologists offered a more critical picture of the Mekong program.[85] In these, the potential ecological consequences of the Pa Mong mainstream dam in Laos were considered to be as serious as the African cases, with dangers from the usual tropical diseases, fertilizer pollution, fishery troubles, changes in human nutrition, and needs for resettlement of several hundred thousand persons. Some of the specialists advocated a series of small dams on the Mekong tributaries in place of the big mainstream impoundments. A number of such dams were built by the 1970s; the big dams, however, because of their electric power potential, were not cancelled and may still be built. Thailand needs power for industry, and poor Laos would be happy to export it from the mainstream dams. Even the Pathet Lao in the 1960s acceded to the big-dam approach, simply by not harassing the Japanese team in charge of the construction of the Nam Ngum dam (although an American technician on the site was attacked). But the papers also questioned the inevitability of economic gains to Laos. The increased urbanization and difficulties of financing social services, the disruption of an adapted agriculture, migration from rural to urban areas—all usual consequences of this type of development—would increase the potential for social conflict many times and also the amount of dependence on outside resources.

Ethnological and Applied Anthropological Studies

Water and Culture

The descriptive ethnological literature dealing with water usage among tribal and peasant peoples is considerable and deserves treatment in its own right. The resources utilization patterns of tribal peoples often reflect a generalized pattern of evolutionary development associated with their general subsistence base. A convenient guide is C. Daryll Forde's classic text, *Habitat, Economy, and Society*.[86] Forde reported on tribal groups arranged in three grand classes: Food Gatherers, Cultivators, and Pastoral Nomads. From Gatherers to Cultivators one moves from nomadic to sedentary life. The change presumably increases the amount of human energy available for more complex activities. Pastoralism was viewed as an offshoot from Gathering, its practitioners often attaining the cultural complexity of Cultivators but with nomadism often imposing limitations on cultural development.

The assumption of increasing cultural complexity as one moves towards cultivation applies best to long spans of time and to many societies. For smaller or shorter units of observation one finds more exceptions. Forde designed his text to show this combination of general tendency and local variation, and the groups he describes ethnographically were chosen with this idea in view. For example, one of his Gatherer groups is the Paiute of the Great Basin, who roamed the desert in search of vegetable foods and small animals but who also occasionally used snowmelt water to grow patches of desirable wild plants on mountain slopes, a form of irrigation one might expect in more settled peoples.

The use of water resources by tribal people is basically dependent upon the nature of the supply. Thus, Forde's Cultivator groups ranged from oceanic-rainfall yam growers and sea fishermen through intensive-irrigation rice growers of South Asia to the Hopi of the American desert, who water their corn by hand from natural springs in their arid land. As Forde made clear in his theory chapters, the key to the pattern in a particular society lay in the constellation of resources in its particular locality—rather than in evolutionary laws. If generalizations can be made across the many variable adaptations rooted in usable resources, they would issue from factors such as food supply, energy, time, and population base, which confer greater or lesser stability and exploitative capability depending upon their frequencies and combinations.

Another facet of the ethnological literature concerns attitudes and values associated with water, including its use in rituals from simple bathing to elaborate purification ceremonies. The frequent use of water for these purposes, and the elaborate attitudes often associated with them, is a symbolic recognition of the transcendent importance of water to life. Often, however, the elaboration in ritual use does not correlate with the amount of water available. In both India and Japan water is an important ingredient in religious symbolization, but in India potable water is often scarce and in Japan it has always been abundant. Clearly, the role of water in myth and ritual can develop out of nonutility factors.

The cultural position of water has an ecological and physiological underpinning one does not find, for example, for air or soil. Air is *too* pervasive, and soil is of indirect utility. Water, on the other hand, exerts a constant pressure in the form of thirst, one of the basic biological drives underlying human behavior.[87] Obviously, no human activity that persistently thwarts satisfaction of the drive for water can endure very long. This truism, however, does not explain the many persisting human activities that interrupt the thirst-satisfaction drive for relatively long periods, such as the search for visions and the feeling of mastery of bodily pangs. At the same time, prolonged water shortages caused by natural conditions generate anxiety and fear, and thirst will condition acceptance of new water systems opposed on ritual or social grounds.[88] Since water resource project planners often assume universality for certain attitudes in their own cultures, it is useful to comment on some variations found by ethnologists. Taste or flavor is a factor in water preferences in many village cultures, where water from a particular source of supply has been used for generations: Lebanese Arabs came to like stagnant pool water, offensive to the development team, and rejected a new fresh water supply on the grounds that the iron pipe would ruin the flavor;[89] Indian villagers preferred mud-tasting river water to water from a new well, which was perceived as hot and saline.[90]

While taste preference varies, most people prefer *clear* water. Applied anthropologists have noted the influence of the preference for clear water in conditioning acceptance of new wells. This preference, however, can work both ways. The writer recalls an incident in an archaeological field camp when the crew persisted in drinking sparkling clear water from a well known to be contaminated with microorganisms and rejected brown, gritty, iron-tasting water from a clean well. Persistent cases of the "trots" eventually forced a change.

The use of water for cleanliness and its gradual merging into ritual has similar contradictory dimensions. Indians bathe in contaminated water supplies. The Japanese proclivity for hot baths has been analyzed as part of the Japanese emotional surrogate for sexual pleasure, but medical researchers have known that the hot public bath is a source of various parasitic diseases.[91] In a Peruvian village the residents scrupulously boil their drinking water, not because they know about germs but because since their illness is culturally defined as a "hot" entity they believe it can be countered with another "hot" substance, boiled water.

Applied Anthropological Studies

The anthropologist is often the person most informed concerning microenvironments and microcultural features affecting natural resource usage. He is in an excellent position to advise planners on the geographic, technological, and sociocultural feasibility of their proposed changes— from putting wells in villages to building big dams. The mistakes already noted as stemming from inadequate ecological and social feasibility studies for large projects also apply to many small water development schemes introduced by development planners around the world over the past generation. Much applied anthropological literature was devoted to analyses of these mistakes.[92]

Several important factors contribute to the frequent omission of an anthropologist from project planning teams. These include the ethnocentric assumption that behavioral response patterns are alike the world over, the length of time required for detailed cultural feasibility studies, a willingness to sacrifice microsocial entities for large schemes or to accept a certain percentage of error and failure, and the scarcity of well-trained anthropologists. Moreover, the anthropology profession often awards greater prestige to research topics remote from these practical concerns, and some of the more able people in the field cannot be induced to participate in resource management decision making.

Another difficulty with applying richly detailed but highly localized research findings concerns the inevitability of trial-and-error experimentation in development work as suggested by many of the technological failures of water systems in tribal enclaves. Tom Sasaki studied a reservoir on the Navajo reservation constructed in the early 1940s.[93] By the late 1950s the reservoir no longer held significant amounts of water and had become the site of agricultural fields. The scheme failed because the lack of rainfall in dry years led to drawdowns so severe as to eliminate irrigation, and winds filled the ditches and plots with sand. Navajo technology was insufficiently capitalized to permit a massive attack to overcome these difficulties. Since this reservoir was planned with inadequate knowledge of local weather conditions, the project could be reckoned as one of the trial-and-error experiments in arid-land water development forced by political pressures before sufficient research could be done. The lag in communication between the project planners and the anthropologists who do the post-hoc evaluation studies is a major unsolved problem.

Another factor evident in the Navajo reservoir example is the need to take into account *extreme* as well as average climatic conditions in planning. Studies of resource and climatic fluctuations and the consequent cultural adaptation have received less attention than they deserve because it is difficult to keep records in precise localities over long periods of time. For over four generations on the semiarid northern Great Plains farmers tried a variety of measures designed to cope with marginal and fluctuating moisture, experienced repeated failure, and only recently have developed techniques of diversification that permit changes in crop to anticipate or conform to moisture fluctuation. Various governmental measures designed to cushion income fluctuation due to climatic variability also have helped.

Many anthropological studies pertain to cultural factors not usually in the sphere of awareness of the planners and engineers. To typify the situation, we shall assume that a government development team is sent to a village to install a new water system, consisting of wells, pumps, and facilities for washing clothes as well as water for irrigation and consumption. The team talks to one or two people in the community who indicate that the facilities should be located as near to the village as possible, for the sake of convenience. Often this plan works; if it works twice for the same team, they are reinforced in their conviction that they have discovered a generally applicable rule: locate water where it is most convenient to the greatest number.

However, unanticipated factors often invalidate conclusions of this type. A particular ritual taboo in another community may make water facilities located too close to the center of the village a source of considerable tension. In still another community, a daily journey by the women from several villages to a common point to exchange necessary social information may be required to maintain the smooth functioning of the social system. Wells located outside of the community may provide this place of exchange. Convenience has to be defined more broadly than by sheer physical distance or location. It depends on cultural factors and social arrangements.[94]

New water facilities often receive too little use because of the failure of planners to budget funds for training in the operation of the equipment involved. Old habits and preferences may inhibit learning, a problem endemic in new irrigation systems in North America as well as in the emerging countries. In a study in the state of Bihar, India, D. P. Sinha (personal correspondence) found two tribal communities in which new wells for stock watering had been installed by Block Development teams. In one village the wells doubled livestock production; in the other the wells fell into disuse. The successful case was due entirely to the presence in the village of a veteran of the Indian Army who had received training in the skills required to operate the facilities correctly. A trained person introduced into the other community for a period of only a month or two could have trained the villagers. Allen describes how a resident technician in Iranian villages was able to train the villagers to operate a rather complex irrigation system based on cistern storage of water. Without this training the systems would have deteriorated.[95]

Much if not most human action is motivated by the need to accomplish particular tasks that must be performed in particular ways in order to permit goals to be accomplished with available resources and also to deal with circumstances created by previous adaptive responses. Much behavior is therefore responsive to particular situations. However, in the absence of adequate cues of obvious rewards, behavior is often guided by past precedents, equivalent to what have been called cultural patterns or traditions. Thus anthropologists, though not always clearly distinguishing among the relevant sectors of behavior, have contributed a great deal to our knowledge of the pragmatic motives for problem solution and to repetitive, stylized behavior that emerges as unanticipated response to resource development projects.

Dobyns showed in his studies of the Papago irrigation project that a critical factor in the failure of the Indians to accept the system offered them by the Indian Service to enhance subsistence agriculture was their desire to realize a higher standard of living through wage labor.[96] During a previous historical period the Papago had made a significant adaptation to the consumption standards provided by a cash wage economy. The Indian service built a reservoir in the belief that the Indians really wanted to return to subsistence agriculture. The critical mistake was the assumption by a bureaucracy that it knew what the people wanted. Because people themselves often don't know what they want, there is no simple solution to the ambiguity.

A more elaborately analyzed case of this type was supplied by Allen Holmberg for the Viru Valley in Peru.[97] The introduction of tube well irrigation into the valley, at the request of the farmers, triggered a series of difficulties. The government team carried out a model survey and requested the help of local people in drilling wells. However, resistance quickly mounted. The project was stopped after sinking only one well because the team consistently ignored local people with knowledge of the local water supply, including one with experience with tube wells. In addition, the wells were drilled on private instead of public land, an act that accentuated a series of hostilities as well as a clash between rich and poor.

Another common problem in government-planned water schemes for tribal people arises over the prevalence of extended kinship networks in societies with subsistence agriculture. In such cases, individual ownership of natural resources is a rare thing. Ownership is usually vested in kinship networks and often emphasizes usufruct patterns rather than simple title. In spite of this, development teams have persistently constructed systems as if private property concepts governed the use of water.

Competition and Cooperation in Water Development

Certain ecological problems associated with water recur in all societies at all levels of technology. Water as a resource moves; it is a transient substance. This means that whenever people wish to utilize water in one place they must capture and store the water when and where it is available. Since water that *flows past* is not captured and may be used by another person downstream, water use for agriculture or human consumption automatically imposes problems of sharing and, generally, of water as a form of property.

Because of its unique fluid characteristics, it is not particularly surprising to find parallels in the social organization of rice irrigators in Japan or Spain or to note that the technical adaptations made by the Nabataeans in the Negev are comprehensible to Israeli hydraulic engineers.[98] Moreover, the technical uniformity of particular types of waterworks sometimes makes it possible to deduce the generalized patterns of social organization required to maintain them, although this may be more difficult than some scholars have believed.

Therefore, while it is correct to emphasize social and technical parallels due to water's transient nature, one must also be aware of possible differences. Local communities vary considerably in the forms of land tenure, social organization, and decision-making mechanisms useful in solving problems of transiency and limited supply. These differences exemplify one of the more difficult issues in the anthropological study of local societies and one that poses problems as to the applicability of the anthropological approach to evaluation of large-scale water development programs. For a large-scale program to be studied scientifically a number of variables need to be known exactly. If anthropologists were to insist on managing *all* the variables to be sure of their recommendations, many questions could never be answered.

Sharing of a fluid resource requires cooperative relationships. However, in most cases, the specific forms of sharing will depend on preexisting legal rules, social relations, and cultural styles. Thus the cooperation displayed by water users in Thailand may be intervillage and kinship-based while the cooperative mechanisms of ranchers in the

American West involve ordered competition for water through an individual water-right system administered by courts. Functionally the two patterns may be identical; organizationally they are disparate since they are based on differing conceptions of property rights. This example shows that attempts to encourage cooperation over the use and management of water must take into account existing social, economic, and legal institutions and not proceed on the basis of hazy notions of the innate cooperativeness or inherent competitiveness of human nature,[99] or the assumption that all people conceive of water as individually owned.

The argument may be illustrated by additional data from a region of western Canada introduced in chapter 6 of the present volume.[100] In this region water projects included (1) small, private schemes developing government-assigned, appropriative water rights by means of ditches dug from creeks to fields that are used to produce forage crops; (2) "small water" partially financed by government and consisting of stock watering dams, dugouts, and other small reservoirs; (3) large-scale community irrigation programs involving dams and large reservoirs with impounded water used to irrigate plots of land and supervised by the government and rented out to farmers and ranchers, with small charges for the water as well as land rentals.

This system encouraged cooperation in the use of water on the following bases. (1) The water-right system gave people a right to a fixed number of acre-feet during the designated spring-flood period. The amounts were adjusted so everyone would obtain his share, and therefore cooperation was based on a guarantee inherent in the legal regulations governing water rights. (2) The "small waters" system was controlled by the government so that a man applying for a dam would have his permit studied with reference to his neighbor's need for the same water. The review often suggested the desirability of cooperative schemes to users. Here, again, cooperation was encouraged by third-party (government) adjudication. (3) Informal neighborly assistance and labor exchange existed among plot-renters on the community irrigation tracts. (4) A Water Users' Association emerged to manage and partly finance community watershed schemes. Here cooperation was partly voluntary and emergent within the social system and partly fostered by a government anxious to get out of the business.

Competitive mechanisms were encouraged by this system in the following ways. (1) Individual water-right holders could violate the law and take more than their share, indirectly encouraging others to do likewise. A "water fight" might result as water ran short. More commonly, however, excess use would be stopped after clandestine reports of stealing were made by one neighbor about another to the government water bureau. (2) Competition in the "small waters" program could emerge as enterprising operators endeavored to influence the government bureau to build the installation for their convenience. (3) Competitive relations also existed among the plot-renters in the form of stealing water from each other by digging illegal diversion ditches. (4) Competition also emerged in the form of illegal sprinkler irrigation devices installed clandestinely on the creeks and operated late at night.

All these patterns of cooperation and competition were possible in the mixed system of agriculture found in the semiarid North American West. Private agrarian entrepreneurs compete for resources which they desire to "own" since they must operate their enterprises individually. However, government-regulated irrigation schemes that require various forms of agreement and sharing in order to receive financial benefits induce cooperative relations. The water-users take advantage of the government regulations to enjoy the benefits of cooperation, to secure water, and to allay destructive competition by government regulation. One set of institutions—private entrepreneurial ownership and exploitation of resources—interacts with another—government-regulated sharing—to produce a mixed system of cooperative-competitive relations. Most modern—and probably most ancient—systems of water use have this mixed character.[101]

The key factor in this process concerns the issue of tenure or ownership rights. Water cannot easily be "owned" in watercourses running through separately owned tracts. The issue is apparently of no great moment in the Orient, where a tradition of individual resource ownership has been much less consistent. However, the issue is extremely important in North America, especially in water-deficient regions. Water-right holders in the West have been notoriously reluctant to acknowledge that they do not "own" the water, and one of the commonest abuses is for a man to take his water *after* the time period alotted in the firm belief that he had a right to it.

The issue of title was also paramount in the community irrigation plot system in the case reviewed previously. Although the users did not "own" either the plot or the water, the fee required for use of the water encouraged the same competitive abuses noted in the case of the private water-right system. More important, the lack of true title to the plot made the users extremely reluctant to form associations and regulate the schemes themselves. They were content to permit the government to finance and regulate the system. Repeatedly, government has had to force water users to take responsibility by terminating public support. This process can be contrasted with the effective cooperation interaction over irrigation by the Mormons and some other groups with traditions emphasizing collective organization.

While the value systems of North American agriculturalists clearly emphasize individualistic and competitive patterns, they also include neighborly cooperation and exchange. Values alone do not promote cooperation or competition; one must look at values as they are encouraged or inhibited by property institutions and government regulations operating in particular cases. The same men who could fight bitterly over water could also manifest intimate cooperation over stockraising if the government assigned them a joint grazing lease! In other words, the same institutions and cultural values can work toward cooperation and/or competition, depending upon the mix of institutions and objectives in particular cases.[102]

Cooperation and competition become alternative ways of exploiting the hydraulic commons. The nature of water as a transient resource argues for cooperative sharing because if each user maximizes his use, the finite supply diminishes and other users are deprived. If this point is reached, either cooperative measures to distribute the goods or a third party empowered to penalize those who violate the rules of sharing will emerge.

Sasaki and Adair provided an example from the Navajo. The federal government furnished irrigation for the Indians along the San Juan River near Fruitlands in 1933.[103] Operating on the asumption that the Navajo would respond in terms of democratic images of interfamilial cooperation on the use of water, the Indian Service invited Navajo to settle in the area. The Indians crowded onto the irrigated tract and opened ditches and irrigated whenever they wished. At one point they responded to urgings to cooperate by simply opening all the ditches at once. The project was reported in the 1970s to be in a continual state of ecological degradation and social confusion because the government failed to follow through with a detailed training program. Individual Navajo families, used to cooperating only with their kin, ignored the need to work together. The settlement was planned without reference to these kin groups by government officials who had too little knowledge of the structure of Navajo society. In the single case where more than one family unit from a kin group was present, cooperative rotational rules were worked out and observed.

Weingrod's study of a *moshav* farming cooperative in Israel showed how collective sanctions may impose the discipline of the commons.[104] The village was comprised of Moroccan immigrants who had considerable difficulty in working out cooperative measures on irrigation. In the first stage the *moshav* as a cooperative unit paid for the water, which meant that the more intensive cultivators were penalized by having to bear the share of the less efficient. The created considerable dissension, and many of the better farmers began to sell their produce on the black market, leading to a decline in *moshav* revenue. The second stage involved the creation of individual payment responsibility, including metering of each farmer's water and locked valves permitting cutoff if monthly payments were not made. This procedure worked, and it provides still another example of how mixed systems will evolve in adaptation to the resource supply and the social institutions.

Anthropological Implications for Water Development in American Society

Anthropological studies of attitudes toward resource development in American culture are an important but neglected need. The urgency of such an inquiry is indicated by the current concern over environmental quality and conservation—one of the major problems of contemporary civilization. The basic isssue, as Clarence Glacken indicated, is "anthropocentrism": the value, especially pronounced in North America, placed on man as the measure of all things.[105] This value, as apparent in humanistic positions and in anthropological theory as in engineering technology, is seen as an underlying cause of environmental exploitation. There is a need for a more humble position, viewing man as one element in a global ecosystem subject to the limited resources of spaceship earth.[106]

The American attitude toward water has contradictory aspects. We deplore the abuse of water commons but refuse to cooperate with neighbors to control the amount of use or with government intervention, as Walter Firey observed in his Texas research (see Firey 1957, cited in chapter 3). Increasing population pressure in California has led to hydrologic disruption and severe soil erosion. We drain wetlands in order to "reclaim" land that becomes too friable and dry for agriculture.[107] The attitude toward rivers and floods is equally paradoxical: the public demands adequate flood protection while new buildings on floodplains invite recurrent disaster. Engineers often reassure the population that everything possible has been done to protect them. They build more dams, induce a feeling of greater security, and leave settlements exposed to a flood too large to control. Our search for outdoor leisure creates more lakes, with untold ecological consequences.[108] Raymond Dasmann has cogently characterized the cultural pattern as follows: "Americans are impatient with the slow processes of nature, with the normal events of biotic succession and change. They prefer the simplicity of a machines to the intricacies of a biota. The day-to-day problems of watershed management seem tiresome, whereas a large dam built to stop floods 'for all time' has popular appeal. Even when we preserve nature we like to get the job over with, and by some spectacular act of Congress decree preservation forever."[109]

Can societies learn to control their use of the "commons"? In a culture with dominant emphasis on individual rights, the first stage is probably always the imposition of controls by an external agency. In the Canadian region I studied several thousand acres were salinized because farmers were ignorant of the proper irrigation methods and engineers failed to level the tracts properly. Effective control required a complete rebuilding of the works and fields and imposition by a government agency of strict controls over water use. The second stage is the creation of a local Water Users' Association that will take over maintenance of the system and impose its own penalties and rules. This will be difficult, but it will come, as it has in other regions of North America.[110]

In the nearly twenty years since the original version of this chapter was written, the situation with regard to water in North America has developed as predicted: increasing unregulated usage with increasingly acrimonious competition for water—competition between urban and rural populations, between recreational and industrial uses, and between advocates of unrestricted growth and those speaking for conservation and restraint. Point impacts of excessive use of water have become all too visible: the writer recalls the Tucson, Arizona region in the late 1940s as possessing several active streams, with bordering lush vegetation, ponds, marshes, and the like. By the 1980s most of the streams were gone or reduced to intermittent trickles; the galley vegetation copses and marshes were nearly gone, with the desert winds blowing hot and dry—except in select spots on the mountain slopes where the elite had constructed watered gardens and swimming pools—and suffered hot, humid nights as payment for the water they had extracted.

The West became a major locus of water fights in the 1980s, and to some extent the issue of water and water rights emerged as an academic specialty. Perhaps the two best studies are Donald Worster's *Rivers of Empire* (1985) and Marc Reisner's *Cadillac Desert* (1986); both books make the point that the American spirit, and especially the Western spirit, brooks no restraint on gratification and that the process of using and abusing the increasingly scarce water resources of the West shall continue until panic and emigration reduces demand.

Bibliographic Notes

The writer acknowledges the assistance of Miss Nancy Edwards and Dr. Henry Dobyns in assembling the materials examined in this paper. The paper was read and criticized by a number of professional colleagues, notably Thayer Scudder, John Rowe, Robert McCormick Adams, and Patty Jo Watson. The first complete draft of the paper was submitted in 1970; subsequent revisions kept the literature citations up to date as of March 1973.

1. *Anthropologists* are defined to include persons identifying themselves as members of this academic discipline and, in some instances, researchers in geography, economics, and the medical-biological sciences. *Anthropology* is viewed as a multidisciplinary field, engaged in studies of cultural contexts of resource development in the past and present. A few professional anthropologists have participated in field studies initiated by water resources institutes at land-grant universities, but we decided to omit mention of this particular body of literature since it is closer to a sociological approach and since the abundant materials from non-North American contexts deserved detailed consideration.
2. For a history of Kentucky archaeology and Webb's role in it, see Douglas W. Schwartz, *Conceptions of Kentucky Prehistory* (Lexington: University of Kentucky Press, 1967).
3. William Y. Adams, "Organizational Problems in International Salvage Archaeology," *Anthropological Quarterly* 41 (1968): 110-21; George J. Armelagos, H. G.

Ewing, and D. L. Greeme, "Physical Anthropology and Man-Made Lakes," *Anthropological Quarterly* 41 (1968): 122–46.

4. John M. Corbett, "River Basin Salvage in the United States," *Archaeology* 14 (1961): 236–40; Fred Johnson, "Archaeology in an Emergency," *Science* 152 (1966): 1592–97.

5. For theory and methods of salvage archaeology see Corbett, "River Basin Salvage"; James J. Hester, "Pioneer Methods in Salvage Anthropology," *Anthropological Quarterly* 41 (1968): 132–46; Johnson, "Archaeology in an Emergency"; A. J. Lindsay, "Saving Prehistoric Sites in the Southwest," *Archaeology* 14 (1961): 245–49; W. W. Wasley, "Techniques and Tools of Salvage," *Archaeology* 14 (1961): 283–86. For salvage archaeology on the Volta River in Africa see O. Davies, "Archaeological Salvage in Man-Made Lakes," in *Man-Made Lakes*, ed. R. H. Lowe-McConnell, Institute of Biology Symposia no. 15 (New York: Academic Press, 1966).

6. James Schoenwetter and F. W. Eddy, *Alluvial and Palynological Reconstruction of Environments: Navajo Reservoir District*, Papers in Anthropology no. 13 (Albuquerque: Museum of New Mexico, 1964).

7. James A. Ford and G. I. Quimby, *The Tchefuncte Culture: An Early Occupation of the Lower Mississippi Valley*, Memoirs no. 2 (Menasha, WI: Society for American Archaeology, 1945).

8. Carl H. Strandberg and R. Tomlinson, "Photoarchaeological Analysis of Potomac River Fishtraps," *American Antiquity* 34 (1969): 312–19.

9. Michael Evenari et al., "Ancient Agriculture in the Negev," *Science* 133 (1961): 979–96; Michael Evenari et al., *The Negev: The Challenge of a Desert* (Cambridge, MA: Harvard University Press, 1971).

10. Robert McCormick Adams, "Agriculture and Urban Life in Early Southwestern Iran," *Science* 136 (1962): 109; Robert McCormick Adams, "A Synopsis of the Historical Demography and Ecology of the Diyala River Basin, Central Iraq," in *Civilizations in Desert Lands*, ed. Richard B. Woodbury, Anthropological Papers no. 62 (Salt Lake City: University of Utah Press, 1962). See also Robert A. Fernea, "Land Reform and Ecology in Post Revolutionary Iraq," *Economic Development and Cultural Change* 17 (1969): 356–81.

11. Robert Raikes, *Water, Weather and Prehistory* (London: John Baker, 1967), chapter 11.

12. Nelson Glueck, *Rivers in the Desert* (New York: Farrar, Strauss and Cudahay, 1959). On the Stein identification see George F. Dales, Jr., "The Role of Natural Forces in the Ancient Indus Valley and Baluchistan," in *Civilizations in Desert Lands*, ed. Richard B. Woodbury, Anthropological Papers no. 62 (Salt Lake City: University of Utah Press, 1962).

13. See, especially, the photographs and maps of climatic patterns in Evenari, "Ancient Agriculture in the Negev."

14. I was unable to find many detailed studies of the sociocultural aspects of drainage of swamps and wetlands. (For a brief note on Hohokam drainage practices see Richard B. Woodbury and John Q. Ressler, "Effects of Environmental and Cultural Limitations upon Hohokam Agriculture, Southern Arizona," in *Civilizations in Desert Lands*.) In any case, such drainage would present unusually difficult problems of archaeological recovery, and apparently the practice was not extensive in native states or tribal societies, who more often than not found wetlands economically useful, as in the *chinampa* case: P. Armillas, "Gardens on Swamps," *Science* 174 (1971): 653–61. The extensive use of swampy forestland by Mesolithic peoples

in the Baltic area is another instance, according to J. G. D. Clark, *Excavations at Star Carr* (Cambridge: Cambridge University Press, 1954). In recent historical periods, the capital inputs for drainage have often exceeded those for water supply; the Netherlands is a case in point. The organization of water and land resources for wet rice production in the swampy Mekong delta also represents a major feat of drainage plus control of a useful supply, but the anthropological studies of wet rice growers have emphasized the existing irrigation facilities and their social implications, as we noted later in the paper. Throughout the anthropological literature the emphasis has been placed on water *supply* measures, particularly in water-deficient environments, due to the importance this problem has assumed in certain questions related to the origins of agriculture and complex sociopolitical life.

15. The *qanat* is called, among other things, *foggara* in Algeria, *rethara* in Morocco, and *kariz* in Baluchistan-Turkestan. For a detailed description of *qanats* and their influence on human settlement patterns in Iran see Anthony Smith, *Blind White Fish in Persia* (London: Goerge Allen and Unwin, 1953), Chap. 3. Other descriptions of *qanats* may be found in George B. Cressey, "Qanats, Karez, and Foggaras," *Geographical Review* 48 (1958): 27–44; Paul W. English, *City and Village in Iran* (Madison: University of Wisconsin Press, 1966); H. E. Wulff, "The Qanats of Iran," *Scientific American*, April 1968: 94–105.

16. Lloyd C. Bridges, *Tribes of the Sahara* (Cambridge: Harvard University Press, 1960), 8–12.

17. Isaiah Bowman, *Desert Trails of Atacama*, Special Publication no. 5 (Concord and New York: Geographical Society, 1924); Iwao Kobori, *Human Geography of Methods of Irrigation in the Central Andes: The Report of the University of Tokyo Scientific Expedition to the Andes in 1958* (Tokyo: Bijitsu Shuppan Sha, 1960).

18. Donald D. Brand, "Review of E. C. Smith, *Agriculture: Tehuacan Valley*," *American Anthropologist* 70 (1968): 417; Earle C. Smith, "Something Old, Something New: Farm Practices Near Tehuacan, Mexico," *Economic Botany* 17 (1963): 210–11; Earle C. Smith, "Archaeological Evidence for Selection of Chupandilla and Cosahuico under Cultivation in Mexico," *Economic Botany* 22 (1968): 140–48.

19. Hans Horkheimer, "Nahrung und Nahrungsgervinnung im vorspanischen Peru," *Veroffentlichungen der Ibero-Amerikanischen Bibliothek zu Berlin*, Band 11 (Berlin: Colloquim Verlag, 1960).

20. Paul Kosok, *Life and Water in Ancient Peru* (New York: Long Island University Press, 1965); Paul Kosok, *El valle de Lambayeque*, Actos y trabajos del 11 Congreso Nacional de Historia del Perú (época pre-hispánica), 1958, vol. 1 (Lima: Congreso Nacional de Historia del Perú, 1959).

21. John H. Rowe, "The Sunken Gardens of the Peruvian Coast," *American Antiquity* 34 (1939): 320–25.

22. M. Edward Moseley, "Assessing the Archaeological Significance of Mahamaes," *American Antiquity* 34 (1970): 485–587; Jeffrey R. Parsons, "The Significance of Mahamaes Cultivation on the Coast of Peru," *American Antiquity* 33 (1968): 80–85.

23. William M. Denevan, "The Aboriginal Cultural Geography of the Llanos de Mojos of Bolivia," *Ibero-American* 48 (University of California Press, 1966); J. J. Parsons and William M. Denevan, "Pre-Columbian Ridged Fields," *Scientific American*, July 1976: 92–101. An indispensable paper on various forms of drainage of agricultural fields in pre-Columbian America with reference to comparable phenomena elsewhere is William M. Denevan, "Aboriginal Drained-Field Cultivation in the Americas," *Science* 169 (1970): 647–54. The paper is important not only because it clears up some of the confusion in the older literature over *chinampas*,

ridged fields, garden beds, *camellones*, and other forms, but also because it calls attention to the very much neglected topic of aboriginal drainage systems. Denevan distinguishes between (1) soil platforms built up in permanent water bodies; (2) ridged or mounded fields on seasonally flooded or waterlogged land, (3) ditched fields for subsoil drainage, (4) fields on naturally drained lands, such as river margins, (5) diked and banked fields, (6) aquatic cultivation. Denevan's accounts of these various systems indicate that such "land reclamation" is associated with increasing populations and the corresponding need for greater agricultural production. Most of these works were given up after European conquest because of the large amounts of labor required to maintain them—a point made later with reference to large-scale irrigation and water impoundment systems.

24. José L. Lorenzo, "Aspectos físicos del Valle de Oaxaca," *Revista Mexicana se Estudios Antropológicos* 16: 49-64; K. V. Flannery et al., "Farming Systems and Political Growth in Ancient Oaxaca," *Science* 158 (1967): 445-53.

25. The *lama-bordo* system: Ronald Spores, "Settlement, Farming Technology, and Environment in the Nochixtlan Valley," *Science* 166 (1969): 557-69.

26. Armillas, "Gardens on Swamps."

27. Dales, "Natural Forces in the Ancient Indus Valley"; Raikes, *Water, Weather and Prehistory*, 182.

28. Norman A. F. Smith, "The Roman Dams of Subiaco," *Technology and Culture* 2 (1970): 58-68.

29. John Rowe, personal correspondence, reports check dams for flood diversionin the Ica Valley, Peru. I am indebted to Douglas James for pointing out that, in general, adequate flood control requires more extensively engineered and costly works than irrigation and other supply devices, which would help explain why floodproofing was more common than true flood control in labor-intensive socities.

30. Raikes, *Water, Weather and Prehistory*, 172.

31. R. McCormick Adams, "Agriculture and Urban Life"; Adams, "Diyala River Basin"; Adams, *Land Behind Bagdad*; Kent V. Flannery, "Ecology of Early Flood Production in Mesopotamia," *Science* 161 (1968); 334-38; Frank Hole, Kent V. Flannery, and J. A. Nealy, *Prehistory and Human Ecology of the Deh Luran Plain*, Memoirs of the Museum of Anthropology, no. 1 (Ann Arbor: University of Michigan Press, 1969). For a brief description of the transition to irrigation argiculture in arid lands see Homer Aschmann, "Evaluations of Dry Land Environments by Societies at Various Levels of Technical Competence," in *Civilizations in Desert Lands*, Woodbury. Some anthropological work on land and water resources in the aridity context is summarized by Richard B. Woodbury, "Role of Social Science in Land and Water Utilization," in *Arid Lands in Transition*, ed. Harold E. Dregne, publication no. 90 (Washington, DC: American Association for the Advancement of Science, 1970).

33. Robert C. Braidwood and C. Reed, "The Achievement and Early Consequences of Food Production," *Cold Spring Harbor Symposia on Quantitative Biology* 22 (1957): 19-31.

34. L. R. Binford, "Post Pleistocene Adaptations," in *New Perspectives in Archaeology*, eds. L. R. and S. R. Binford (Chicago: Aldine Publishing Co., 1968); Kent V. Flannery, "Origins and Ecological Effects of Early Domestication in Iran and the Near East," in *The Domestication and Exploitation of Plants and Animals*, ed. P. J. Ucko and G. W. Dimbleby (Chicago: Aldine Pub. Co., 1969).

35. Hans Helbaeck, "Appendix I," in *Prehistory and Human Ecology of the Deh Luran Plain*, Hole, Flannery, and Nealy. For a New World example (Hohokam) see Woodbury and Ressler, "Effects of Environmental and Cultural Limitations."

36. R. McCormick Adams, *The Evolution of Urban Society*.

37. Suggestive evidence for comparable preclassic irrigation in Mexico is provided by Melvin L. Fowler, *Un sistema preclásico de distribución de agua en la zona arqueológica de Amaluacan, Pueblo* (Pueblo, Mexico: Instituto Poblano de Antropología y Historia, 1968).

38. The oasis is a particularly significant element in this picture since it is an island of relatively abundant resources in the midst of desolation. For a revealing picture of contemporary development of these concentrated resources see the classic account of the Siwa oasis by G. E. Simpson, *The Heart of Libya: The Siwa Oasis* (London: Harper and Brothers, 1929).

39. For some appreciations of the rate and circumstances of the onset of urban civilization see R. McCormick Adams, *The Evolution of Urban Society*; Robert J. Braidwood and G. Willey, *Courses Toward Urban Life*, Viking Fund Publications in Anthropology, no. 32 (New York: Wenner Gren Foundation, 1962); Frank Hole, "Investigating the Origins of Mesopotamian Civilization," *Science* 153 (1966), reprinted in *Man in Adaptation*, I, ed. Yehudi Cohen (Chicago: Aldine Pub. Co., 1968); John A. Wilson, *The Burden of Egypt* (Chicago: University of Chicago Press, 1951); Woodbury, *Civilizations in Desert Lands*.

40. R. McCormick Adams, "Agriculture in Urban Life," 116.

41. V. Gordon Childe, *Man Makes Himself* (London: Watts and Co., 1941); *What Happened in History* (London: Harmondsworth, 1942).

42. English, *City and Village in Iran*, 38.

43. The generalized theory sketched here is based in part on the discussion of the collapse of civilization in the dry zone of Ceylon in Rhoads Murphey, "The Ruin of Ancient Ceylon," *Journal of Asian Studies* 16 (1957): 181-200. Murphey cites the ever-present dangers of weeds, flash floods, and other disasters associated with the large-scale water impoundments and canal systems, although he does not appear to believe that soil exhaustion, siltation, or salinization were significant factors in this case. He throws the weight of the argument on malaria epidemics and social disorder that destroyed the capacity of the regime to muster sufficient labor to maintain the works and the subsequent advantage taken of the situation by invading Tamils.

44. Thorkild Jacobsen and Robert McCormick Adams, "Salt and Silt in Ancient Mesopotamian Agriculture," *Science* 128 (1958): 1251-58. Also, see especially the references in R. McCormick Adams, "Diyala River Basin."

45. Helbaeck, "Appendix I," *Prehistory and Human Ecology*.

46. Wilson, *The Burden of Egypt*, 133-34.

47. On the question of capital costs of irrigation and water development generally see Bert F. Hoselitz, "Capital Formation, Saving and Credit in Indian Agricultural Society," in *Capital Savings and Credit in Peasant Societies*, eds. Ramond Firth and B. S. Yamey (Chicago: Aldine Pub. Co., 1964); Colin Clark, *The Economics of Irrigation* (New York: Pergamon Press, 1967). The extent of social investments can be gathered in Clifford Geertz, *Peddlers and Princes: Social Development and Economic Exchange in Two Indonesian Towns* (Chicago: University of Chiacgo Press, 1963); his chapter, "Economic Development in Tabanan," describes the social forms emergent with wet-rice culture.

48. Julian H. Steward, ed., *Irrigation Civilizations: A Comparative Study: A Symposium on Method and Result in Cross-Cultural Regularities,* Social Science Monographs, no. 1 (Washington, D.C.: Pan American Union, 1955).

49. Karl Wittfogel, *Oriental Despotism: A Comparative Study of Total Power* (New Haven: Yale University Press, 1957).

50. For discussions of redistributive economy—essentially a form in which production is husbanded by the state and doled out to consumers, eliminating true market on any significant scale, see Karl Polanyi, Conrad M. Arensberg, and Harry W. Pearson, eds., *Trade and Market in the Early Empires: Economics in History and Theory* (Glencoe, IL: Free Press, 1957).

51. Richard K. Beardsley, "Ecological and Social Parallels Between Rice-Growing Communities of Japan and Spain," in *Symposium on Community Studies in Anthropology,* ed. V. E. Garfield (Seattle: University of Washington; American Ethnological Society, 1964). See also Peter Kunstadter, "Irrigation and Social Structure: Narrow Valleys and Individual Enterprise," (Tokyo: 11th Pacific Science Congress, 1966); Rene Millon, "Variations in Social Responses to the Practice of Irrigation Agriculture," in *Civilizations in Desert Lands,* Woodbury.

52. R. McCormick Adams, *Land Behind Bagdad.* See also Marvin Harris's defense of Wittfogel against Adam's critique in Marvin Harris, *The Rise of Anthropological Theory* (New York: Cromwell, 1968). For criticism of Wittfogel see Clifford Geertz, "Two Types of Ecosystems," in *Environment and Cultural Behavior,* ed. Andrew P. Vayda, American Museum Sourcebooks in Anthropology (Garden City, NY: The Natural History Press, 1969); S. M. Eisenstadt, "The Study of Oriental Despotisms as Systems of Total Power," *Journal of Asian Studies* 17 (1958): 435–46. For a look at some of the Meso-American data with a bearing on the thesis see Robert F. Heizer, "Agriculture and the Theocratic State in Lowland Southeastern Mexico," *American Antiquity* 26 (1960): 215–22 (reprinted in *Man and Adaptation,* I, Cohen); William T. Sanders, "Hydraulic Agriculture, Economic Symbiosis, and the Evolution of States in Central Mexico," in *Anthropological Archaeology in the Americas,* ed. B. J. Meggers (Washington, DC: Anthropological Society of Washington, 1968); William T. Sanders, "Cultural Ecology of Nuclear Mesoamerica," *American Anthropologist* 64 (1962): 34–44 (reprinted in *Man in Adaptation,* I, Cohen). In a larger context the Wittfogel concept in another in the family of explanations of culture growth based on energy accumulation: William F. Cottrell, *Energy and Society: The Relations of Energy, Social Change, and Economic Development* (New York: McGraw-Hill, 1955).

53. Millon, "Variations in Social Response," 80.

54. E. R. Leach, "Hydraulic Society in Ceylon," *Past and Present* 15 (1959): 2–26.

55. Murphey, "The Ruin in Ancient Ceylon."

56. Beardsley, "Rice-Growing Communities of Japan and Spain."

57. Wilson, *The Burden of Egypt,* chapter 4.

58. Kunstadter, "Irrigation and Social Structure."

59. Sanders, "Hydraulic Agriculture"; Sanders, "Cultural Ecology of Nuclear Mesoamerica"; Woodbury and Ressler, "Hohokam Agriculture."

60. H. T. Waterbolk, "The Lower Rhine Basin," in *Courses Toward Urban Life,* Braidwood and Willey.

61. Grahame Clark, "Ecological Zones and Economic Stages," in *Prehistoric Europe: The Economic Basis* (London: Methuen and Co., 1952; Stanford: Stanford University Press, 1952), reprinted in *Man and Adaptation,* I, Cohen.

62. For some general surveys see Aloys A. Michel, *The Indus Rivers: A Study of the Effects of Partition* (New Haven, CT: Yale University Press, 1967); A. K. Snelgrove, ed., *Indus River Symposium*, Transactions of the Society of Mining Engineers, vol. 244 (American Institute of Mining Engineers, 1969); C. Hart Schaaf and R. H. Fifield, *The Lower Mekong: Challenge to Cooperation in Southeast Asia* (New York: D. Van Nostrand Co., 1963); Edward H. Spicer, "Developmental Change and Cultural Integration," in *Perspectives in Developmental Change*, ed. Art Gallagher, Jr. (Lexington: University of Kentucky Press, 1968); N. Rubin and W. Warren, eds., *Dams in Africa* (London: Frank Cass, 1968); Karuna Moy Mukerji and K. John Mammen, *Economics of River Basin Development in India* (Bombay: Vora and Co. Pub., Pvt., Ltd., 1959).

63. It should be noted that comparable problems have arisen in other climates. A detailed study of the ecological hazards associated with the attempts to settle the Bedouin of Arabia in irrigated areas is provided by Harold F. Heady, "Ecological Consequences of Bedouin Settlement in Saudi Arabia," in *The Careless Technology: Ecology and International Development*, eds. M. T. Farvar and J. P. Milton (New York: Natural History Press, 1971). The result was overuse of water for irrigation by these untrained people and consequent salization, siltation, reduction of the water table, and extinction of many wild species.

64. For the African cases see David Brokensha, "Volta Resettlement and Anthropological Research," *Human Organization* 22 (1963): 286-90; David Brokensha and Thayer Scudder, "Resettlement," in *Dams in Africa*, Rubin and Warren; Robert A. Fernea, ed., *Contemporary Egyptian Nubia*, HRAFLEX Book no., MR8-001, vol. 1 (New Haven, CT: Human Relations Area Files, 1966); Thayer Scudder, *The Ecology of the Gwembe Tonga*, Rhodes-Livingstone Institute, Kariba Studies, vol. 2 (Manchester: Manchester University Press, 1962); Thayer Scudder, "Man-Made Lakes and Social Change" *Engineering and Science* 24 (1966): 19-22; Thayer Scudder, "Man-Made Lakes and Population Resettlement in Africa," in *Man-Made Lakes*, Lowe-McConnell; Thayer Scudder, "Social Anthropology, Man-Made Lakes and Population Relocation in Africa" *Anthropological Quarterly* 41 (1968): 168-76; Thayer Scudder, "Relocation, Agricultural Intensification, and Anthropological Research," in *The Anthropology of Development in Sub-Saharan Africa*, ed. D. Drokensha and M. Pearsall, Society for Applied Anthropology, monograph no. 10 (1969); Thayer Scudder, "Ecology and Development: The Kariba Lake Basin," in *The Careless Technology*, Farvar and Milton; Thayer Scudder and Elizabeth Colson, "The Kariba Dam Project: Resettlement and Local Initiative," in *Technological Innovation and Culture Change*, Bernard and Pelto. For the Mekong see John E. Bardach, "Some Ecological Implications of Mekong River Development Plans," in *The Careless Technology*, Farvar and Milton; Jasper Ingersoll, *The Social Feasbility of Pa Mong Irrigation*, a report to the U.S. Bureau of Reclaimation and the U.S. Agency for International Development (duplicated) (Washington, DC, 1969); W. R. Derrick Sewell and Gilbert F. White, "The Lower Mekong: An Experiment in International River Development," *International Conciliation* 558 (May 1966); Wilhelm Solheim and Robert Hackenberg, "The Importance of Anthropological Research to the Mekong Valley Project," *France-Asie* (September-October 1961); Joel Halpern and James Hafner, "Preliminary Bibliography of Miscellaneous Research Materials on Laos, with Special Reference to the Mekong Development Scheme," *Centre d'Etude de Sud-Est Asiatique et de l'Extreme Orient*, Brussels, 1971. For brief summaries of various cases see Julian McCaull, "Conferences on the Ecological Aspects of International Development," (UN-

ESCO) *Nature and Resources* 5 (1969): 5–12. Papers on various phenomena associated with man-made lakes can be found in McConnell, *Man-Made Lakes*; Rubin and Warren, *Dams in Africa*.

65. Scudder, "Social Anthropology, Man-Made Lakes and Population Relocation in Africa," 168.
66. For a summary see McCaull, "Conference on the Ecological Aspects of International Development." For details see Scudder, "Ecology and Development"; Scudder and Colson, "The Kariba Dam Project."
67. Thayer Scudder, personal correspondence.
68. P. B. N. Jackson, "The Establishment of Fisheries in Man-Made Lakes in the Tropics," in *Man-Made Lakes*, Lowe-McConnell.
69. For a study of trypanosomiasis and its ecological and human-settlement effects see Frank L. Lambrecht, "Aspects of Evolution and Ecology of Tsetse Fliues and Trypanosomiasis in Prehistoric African Environment," *Journal of African History* 5 (1964): 1–24.
70. B. B. Waddy, "Medical Problems Arising from the Making of Lakes in the Tropics," in *Man-Made Lakes*, Lowe-McConnell.
71. Ibid.
72. An informative account of schistosomiasis is found in John M. Weir, "The Unconquered Plague," *Rockefeller Foundation Quarterly* 2 (1969): 4–23. For a study of the effects of onchocerciasis (river blindness) on human settlement and ecology see John M. Hunter, "River Blindness in Nangodi, Northern Ghana," *Geographical Review* 56 (1966): 391–416.
73. McCaull, "Ecological Aspects of International Development"; Henry Van der Schalie, "WHO Project 10: A Case History of a Schistosomiasis Control Project," in *The Careless Technology*, Farvar and Milton.
74. Brokensha and Scudder, "Resettlement"; Scudder, "Man-Made Lakes and Population Resettlement in Africa."
75. Fernea, *Contemporary Egyptian Nubia*.
76.
Scudder, "Man-Made Lakes and Population Resettlement in Africa," 102.
77. Ibid.
78. Jackson, "The Establishment of Fisheries in Man-Made Lakes in the Tropics," 113.
79. For a classic study of "unanticipated consequences," in the TVA program, see Philip Selznick, *TVA and the Grass Roots: A Study in the Sociology of Formal Organization*, University of California Publications in Culture and Society, vol. 3 (Berkeley: University of California Press, 1949).
80. Scudder, "Social Anthropology, Man-Made Lakes and Population Relocation in Africa," 172.
81. Jasper Ingersoll, "Mekong River Basin Development: Anthropology in a New Setting," *Anthropological Quarterly* 41 (1968): 147–67.
82. Sewell and White, "The Lower Mekong."
83. Ingersoll, *The Social Feasibility of Pa Mong Irrigation*.
84. Ibid, 219.
85. For example: Bardach, "Some Ecological Implications of Mekong River Development Plans"; John Milton, "Pollution, Public Health, and Nutritional Effects of Mekong Basin Hydro-Development," mimeographed (Washington, DC: Smithsonian Institute, 1969); Joel Halpern, "Mekong River Development Schemes for Laos and Thailand," *Internationales Asien Forum* (Munich), Heft 1, Jahrgang 3, Jan. 1972; Joel Halpern, "Some Reflections on the War in Laos, Anthropological or

Peter A. Russell, Ph.D.
History/Economics

Box 189
2552 Trans Canada Hwy. N.E.
Salmon Arm, B.C. V1E 4N3

OKANAGAN
UNIVERSITY
COLLEGE

Tel. (604) 832-2126 Loc. 217
Res. (604) 832-0544
Fax (604) 832-4368
E-mail:parussell@okuc02.okanagan.bc.ca

Otherwise," *Centre d'Etude du Sud-Est Asiatique et de l'Extreme Orient*, Brussels, Public. mensuelle, 4e année, no. 44, 1972.

86. C. Daryll Forde, *Habitat, Economy and Society* (London: Methuen and Co., 1934). For similar typological treatments of tribal societies and their economic adaptations see Elman R. Service, *A Profile of Primitive Culture* (New York: Harper and Brothers, 1958); Richard A. Watson and Patty Jo Watson, *Man and Nature: An Anthropological Essay in Human Ecology* (New York: Harcourt Brace and World, 1969). Some of the best studies of the emergence of various forms of water resource development in tribal societies are being contributed by archaeologists, who can trace the evolution of various uses and their relationships to settlement patterns and population size and movements, through a series of related groups in a given habitat. For an example see Thomas C. Patterson, "The Emergence of Food Production in Central Peru," in S. Struever, ed., *Prehistoric Agriculture* (New York: Natural History Press, 1971). For some typical ethnological monographs with considerable information about water use see Harold C. Conklin, *Hanunoo Agriculture: A Report on an Integral System of Shifting Cultivation in the Philippines*, FAO Series on Shifting Cultivation, vol. 2, FAO Forestry Development Paper no. 12 (Rome: Food and Agriculture Organization of the United Nations, 1957); John Fee Embree, *Suye Mura: A Japanese Village* (Chicago: University of Chicago Press, 1939); Raymond William Firth, *Primitive Polynesian Economy* (London: Routledge, 1939); Raymond William Firth, *Malay Fishermen: Their Peasant Economy* (London: Kegan, Paul, Trench, Trubner, 1946); Thomas M. Fraser, Jr., *Fishermen of South Thailand, the Malay Villagers* (New York: Holt, Rinehart and Winston, 1966); J. D. Freeman, *Iban Agriculture: A Report on the Shifting Cultivation of Hill Rice by the Iban or Sariwak*, Great Britain Colonial Office, Colonial Research Studies, no. 18 (London: H. M. Stationary Office, 1955); P. H. Gulliver, *The Family Herds: A Study of Two Pastoral Tribes in East Africa, the Jie and Turkana*, International Library of Sociology and Social Reconstruction (London: Routledge and Kegan Paul, 1955); Bronislaw Malinowski, *Argonauts of the Western Pacific* (London: George Routledge, 1932); Bronislaw Malinowski, *Coral Gardens and their Magic* (London: George Allen and Unwin, 1935); Audrey Isabel Richards, *Land, Labour and Diet in Northern Rhodesia: An Economic Study of the Bemba Tribe*, the International Institute of African Languages and Cultures (New York: Oxford University Press, 1939); Ruth M. Underhill, *Social Organization of the Papago Indians* (New York: Columbia University Press, 1939). It should be noted that the emphasis in this paper has been on direct uses of water as providing energy in some form. We have not been concerned with water uses in the sense of fishing or transportation. However, there is a very large ethnological literature on these uses that would deserve a separate review. A recent study of one of the least known technological adaptations to watery coasts and marshland areas, the "mud sled," is provided in Asahitaro Nishimura, "The Most Primitive Means of Transportation in Southeast and East Asia," *Asian Folklore Studies* 28 (1969): 1–93; also, Nishimura, *A Preliminary Report on Current Trends in Marine Anthropology*, Occasional Papers of the Center of Marine Ethnology No. 1, Tokyo, Waseda University, 1973.

87. Bronislaw Malinowski, "Man's Culture and Man's Behavior," *Sigma Xi Quarterly* 29 (1942): 182–96.

88. A case from India is cited by Thomas M. Fraser, Jr., "Sociocultural Parameters in Directed Change," *Human Organization* 22 (1963): 95–104. Another case from the Papago is cited by Henry F. Dobyns, "Thirsty Indians: Introduction of Wells among People of an Arid Region," *Human Organization* 11 (1952): 33–36.

89. Afif Tannous, "Extension Work among the Arab Fellahin," *Human Organization* 3 (1944): 1–12.
90. Sunil K. Basu, "Water Could not Flow: Case Study into Failure of Technological Aid," Government of West Bengal, *Bulletin of the Cultural Research Institute, Scheduled Castes and Tribes Welfare Department* 6 (1967): 43–48.
91. William Caudill, "Patterns of Emotion in Modern Japan," in *Japanese Culture: Its Development and Characteristics*, ed. R. J. Smith and R. K. Beardsley (Chicago: Aldine, 1962).
92. For collections of cases of this type see Charles Erasmus, *Man Takes Control: Cultural Development and American Aid* (Minneapolis: University of Minnesota Press, 1961); Arthur H. Niehoff, *A Casebook of Social Change* (Chicago: Aldine, 1966); Edward H. Spicer, ed., *Human Problems in Technological Change* (New York: Russell Sage Foundation, 1952).
93. Tom T. Sasaki, "Changes in Land Use among the Navajo Indians in the Many Farms Area of the Navajo Reservation," in *Indian and Spanish American Adjustments to Arid and Semi-Arid Environments*, ed. C. S. Knowlton, Committee on Desert and Arid Zone Research, Texas Technological College, contribution no. 7 (1964).
94. Applied anthropological studies that demonstrate this: (Orissa, India) Fraser, "Sociocultural Parameters in Directed Change"; Nityananda Patnaik, "Digging Wells in Barpali, Orissa: An Experience in Rural Reconstruction," *Man in India* 31 (1961): 83–99; (Papago Indians) Dobyns, "Thirsty Indians"; (Iran) Harold B. Allen, *Rural Reconstruction in Action: Experiences in the Near and Middle East* (Ithaca, NY: Cornell University Press, 1953). For a classic study of rejection of wells due to identification with landlords see Allan R. Holmberg, "The Wells that Failed: Attempt to Establish a Stable Water Supply in Viru Valley, Peru," in *Human Problems in Technological Change*, Spicer. A useful survey of varying responses to irrigation in different societies is provided by Millon, "Variations in Social Responses."
95. Allen, *Rural Reconstruction in Action*.
96. Henry F. Dobyns, "Blunders with Bolsas: A Case Study of Diffusion of Closed-Basin Agriculture," *Human Organization* 10 (1951): 25–32; Henry F. Dobyns, "Experiment in Conservation: Erosion Control and Forage Production on the Papago Indian Reservation in Arizona," in *Human Problems in Technological Change*, Spicer; Dobyns, "Thirsty Indians."
97. Holmberg, "The Wells that Failed."
98. Beardsley, "Rice-Growing Communities of Japan and Spain"; Evenari, "Ancient Agriculture in the Negev."
99. See, for example, the rather simplistic formulations in Henry Orenstein, "Notes on the Ecology of Irrigation Agriculture in Contemporary Peasant Societies," *American Anthropologist* 67 (1965): 1531.
100. John W. Bennett, *Northern Plainsmen: Adaptive Strategy and Agrarian Life* (Chicago: Aldine, 1969), chapter 9.
101. That the amount of irrigation practiced by farmers varies with the cost, below a certain level of rainfall, is shown in a paper on well irrigation in Texas by Jack P. Gibbs, "Human Ecology and Rational Economic Behavior: Agricultural Practices as a Case in Point," *Rural Sociology* 29 (1964): 138–51. This example of "economic rationality" suggests the need for consideration of rationalizing models in sociological analysis in other instances where they apply. The study is a good one, but Gibbs does not consider the effects of such rationality on water supply, which in this part of Texas is diminishing due to reduction of ground water supplies by the wells.

"Community economic rationality" must consider the effect of individual maximization on the hydraulic commons.

102. Some anthropologists also tend to generalize about the social effects of technology, in a search for what is called "techno-environmental determinism" by Harris in *The Rise of Anthropological Theory*. There is nothing wrong with this search, providing one is aware of the level of generality on which he is examining the problem. Where the generalizations are based on microsocial levels, they are subject to continual refutation on the basis of differing constellations of institutional reinforcements and modifiers. An example of misplaced generalization is found in the literature on the relationships of cooperation, competition, and conflict over water irrigation management. The generalization that canal irrigation leads to conflict between farmers and a diminishing of cooperation is proposed by Orenstein, "Notes on the Ecology of Irrigation in Contemporary Peasant Societies"; and that conflict over water provided the most important cause of interfamily and intercommunity quarrels in traditional China is concluded by Hsiao Kung-Chan, *Rural China: Imperial Control in the Nineteenth Century* (Seattle: University of Washington Press, 1960). A review of these positions is found in Burton Pasternak, "Social Consequences of Equalizing Irrigation Access," *Human Organization* 27 (1968): 332–43. He properly notes that irrigation will be the source of *both* competition and cooperation, but then presents his own data in order to show that "equalization of access to irrigation water is associated with a reduction of conflict over water" (342) in a Taiwan village—another broad generalization. He fails to give sufficient attention to the increasing dedication to commercialization in Taiwan agriculture, which might be the key factor in this case.

103. Tom T. Sasaki and J. Adair, "New Land to Farm: Agricultural Practices among the Navajo Indians of New Mexico," in *Human Problems in Technological Change*, Spicer.

104. Alex Weingrod, *Reluctant Pioneers: Village Development in Israel* (Ithaca, NY: Cornell University Press, 1966).

105. Clarence J. Glacken, "Reflections on the Man-Nature Theme as an Object for Study," in *Future Environments of North America*, ed. F. F. Darling and J. P. Milton (New York: Natural History Press, 1966).

106. For a discussion of the issues see Kenneth E. Boulding, "Economics and Ecology," in *Future Environments of North America*, Darling and Milton.

107. The California case is also a monumental example of how water development in an expanding, high-technology society becomes a political and economic institutional saga. The capture of the Ownes Valley water supply in the early years of the century for the benefit of Los Angeles destroyed the agricultural potential of the valley, and subsequent attempts to capture additional supplies from northern California have become a major source of political tension in the state. Similar patterns have emerged throughout the arid-semiarid West (for some discussions see Donald Worster, *Rivers of Empire* (New York: Pantheon, 1985) and Marc Reisner, *Cadillac Desert* (New York: Viking, 1986).

108. For information on the increase in popularity of water-based recreation, see Marion Clawson, "Economics and Environmental Impacts of Increasing Leisure Activities," in *Future Environments of North America*, Darling and Milton.

109. Raymond F. Dasmann, "Man in North America," in *Future Environments of North America*, Darling and Milton, 330–31.

110. For a study of American water management techniques see Gilbert F. White, *Strategies of American Water Management* (Ann Arbor: University of Michigan Press, 1969).

9

Adaptations by Tribal and Modern Populations to the North American Great Plains and Other Arid and Semiarid Lands: A Survey of Issues and Problems

Introduction

John Wesley Powell's famous "Report on the Arid Lands of the United States" classified as arid lands the entire Great Plains west of the 100th meridian—not merely the drier western half. Powell, writing in the 1870s as the Native American populations of the West were meeting defeat, had relatively modest expectations for American civilization on the Plains and accordingly emphasized the limiting effects of shortages of water and other basic resources. He acknowledged that human expansion would occur and that an economy could emerge, but only with great effort (Powell 1962). A Canadian analogue to Powell's report, written by John Palliser (1859), drew even more pessimistic conclusions with respect to the Canadian section of the Plains.

But these qualified judgments were only one chapter in a long story. Throughout the history of exploration and colonization of the Plains by Euro-Americans the image of environmental potential fluctuated from desert to garden and back again. The concept of the Great American Desert preceded Powell and Palliser, but both of their reports were followed by more optimistic assessments by others, as settlement proceeded through political necessity and entrepreneurial drive. By 1900 the

This is an edited and reorganized version of a paper published as chapter 1 of the book *Struggle for the Land* (ed. Paul Olson; Lincoln: University of Nebraska Press, 1989). This paper was delivered at a conference at the University of Nebraska in 1988, and its style reflects oral delivery. Its main purpose was to contrast aboriginal and modern styles of adaptation to moisture-deficient physical environments.

Great Plains and the "desert" were believed to be a potential garden, with water and rich soils available in abundance, providing they could be properly developed. Then came the Dust Bowl, and the pendulum swung back to pessimism, leading Henry Nash Smith to observe that the "West should submit to a rational and scientific revision of its central myth"— that is, of potential abundance (Smith 1950; Blouet and Luebke 1979)— that is, back to Powell and Palliser.

But the myth of abundance never died, and with intensive exploitation of Plains soils and ground water resources the promises would, at least at intervals, seem to be fulfilled—albeit with external subsidies as a helping hand.[1] In larger terms, these attitudes have formed the intellectual basis of Western settlement—*the illusion that constraints were illusory*—in the sense that North American aspirations simply could not tolerate a sense of limits. Even Walter Webb (1932), who certainly had a sense of the way Eastern adaptive styles had to change to meet western resource realities, was not pessimistic or especially prudent—all the easterners had to do was "adapt" and things would work out.[2] Adapt, yes, but at what level of exploitation and at what environmental and social costs?

The adaptations used in arid and semiarid regions by indigenous preindustrial societies are radically different from contemporary industrial strategies. The constrained strategies and institutional arrangements such environments require if the cost of living in them is not to be prohibitive are not those generally pursued by contemporary societies, which demand much greater yield from dryland resources. In analyzing this difference I will first examine the demands that semiarid environments place on human beings, the differing adaptive assumptions of their cultures, and the implications of modern concepts of economic progress and entrepreneurial exploitation. I will then turn to accounts of American Indian and Euro-American occupations of arid and semiarid North America. The basic view is that whereas in preindustrial cultures adaptations are made primarily to a local physical environment and to a self-regulating social environment, in industrial regimes adaptation requires coping with external institutional factors outside the control of local resource users. They respond not so much to Nature as to Culture. However, a sustainable way of life created by indigenous peoples in arid lands characteristically required a lower level of expectations than those in industrial, consumer-centered cultures. Indigenous peoples displayed a willingness to live with uncertainty and modest consumption levels, and they were determined to protect their locality from outside exploitation.

Environment and Adaptation

All scientific and scholarly fields concerned with living things use the term "adaptation," each defining it in accordance with its special interests. Whereas the biological sciences interest themselves in both the genetic changes associated with natural selection and other processes in evolution and also in the physiological changes occurring in the lifetime of individuals in response to particular environmental pressures, the social sciences use "adaptation" in the sense of behavioral changes and adjustments. In general, when we use "adaptation" in the social-behavioral sense we refer to the changes in the posture and activities of human beings vis-à-vis the physical and cultural environments that enable them to cope with daily life or to improve their life chances.[3] The root meaning therefore refers to defensive strategies and life-enhancing accomplishment.

Biological Adaptations to Aridity

Genetic or inheritable somatic and physiological adaptations to any aspect of the physical environment are extremely hard to find in *Homo sapiens sapiens* for two main reasons. First, human beings extensively use their cultural apparatus—technology, purposive movement, strategic manipulation—to adapt rather than change genetically. Second (and this is really a corollary), human populations migrate, and therefore few are really long-term indigenous inhabitants of particular and specialized environments (I will mention some exceptions later). Most substantial populations of the North American Great Plains —both the Plains Indians and the later Euro-American and Euro-Canadian settlers —were relative latecomers, living in the region (or moving in and out of it) for about two centuries for Indians and less for the European-derived settlers.

Concerning physiological adaptation, we are dealing principally with three processes: (1) adjustments made by an individual's body processes over the course of his growth and maturation in a particular environment, generally called "acclimatization"; and (2) learning or devising technical, social, or ideational modes of coping; and (3) genetic change, which can be ruled out as a significant source of physical adaptation, especially for peoples who have only recently entered specialized habitats. Both processes require two or three human generations—one needs to grow up in a particular specialized environment to become fully acclimated physiologically and fully educated culturally and behaviorally.

Although the geographic focus in this chapter is the semiarid grassland section of the North American continent, we will also look at human adaptation to environments that have moisture deficiencies wherever they may be found.[4] Since the literature on acclimatization distinguishes between hot, dry, and cold, dry conditions, let us begin with the former: animals other than human beings have found ways, through evolutionary change, to cope with physical stress resulting from dry heat. Some promote evaporation through perspiration, which cools the organism—in which case a fairly reliable external water supply is needed; some insulate themselves with coats of hair or hide in the cool shade during the day; some acquire their water from eating plants, and others are never far from surface water. The problem of handling excessive heat and dryness is common to all, but there is no single method of coping. One conclusion, generally agreed upon, is that environments featuring dry heat impose considerable stress on animals—more so than the tropical forest (Newman 1970).[5] The heat is transferred from the environment to the organism in the presence of open skies, drying winds, and glaring sun; the organism has to avoid or get rid of it, and water is crucial in doing so.

Where does the human animal stand in relation to other animals? At first sight *Homo sapiens sapiens* appears to be one of the creatures least likely to accommodate to hot, dry climates since we are rather large organisms and so absorb a lot of heat. Human beings also have little body hair, so they cannot use it as insulation; they perspire freely—more freely than any other mammal, so far as we know—and while this helps them cool off through evaporation it also requires a good water supply to replenish the loss.[6] Their skin is susceptible to ultraviolet radiation; yet the search for water and food in the sparse environments so often associated with aridity requires movement in the open country. There are a series of trade-offs here: dangerous exposure to the sun combined with movement assists in evaporative cooling; large body size means much heat, but it also promotes cooling, since the surface area per unit of body volume is minimized and therefore distributes the heat throughout a greater body mass, protecting particularly vulnerable organs.

But the biggest trade-offs concern the behavioral capacity of human beings to devise ingenious ways to cope with heat and drought that have little or nothing to do with basic physiological attributes: the technological and behavioral modifications mentioned previously. If water holes are far apart, you carry water in containers; if the sun is too hot, you invent cloth or skin coverings; if food is scarce you make use of the hot, dry air or salt deposits to preserve it; and if things get too difficult, you pack up and go to the cool, moist woods or mountains. The very incompleteness or unevenness of the human physical adaptation to aridity promotes innovation and movement. Nevertheless, the human presence in arid and semiarid lands has always had problems: although humankind can exist biologically in these lands, it is at the cost of a specialized adaptive behavioral and institutional profile. The constraints are severe, the possibilities for transcending them limited; thus the ultimate expansion of human potential has been historically less for arid lands than for the temperate and humid lands. To expand this potential beyond the level that an indigenous population can supply from its own resources usually requires subsidies. In indigenous cultures nature is the primary source of adaptive pressure, but in industrial, arid-land, subsidy-based cultures the primary pressures are likely to come from the donors of the subsidies.

To return to nonindustrial adaptation for a moment, I should say a word about possible physical changes in indigenous populations coping with heat and aridity. There are several classic cases of very long-term residence: the Australian Aborigines of the central desert and the Bushmen of South Africa are probably the best known. Some recent researchers of the Australian tribal groups have suggested that these populations—present in Australia for at least 20,000 years—have a few physiological specializations regarding metabolic rate, blood flow, and perspiration (Kirk 1981, chap. 8). For example, research seems to show that Aborigines can drink large volumes of water without distress; they excrete water more rapidly through the kidneys; they perspire more freely but can also suppress this high rate of sweating in humid environments. Hence, as a rule, they can travel long distances with less water than can people of European or Asian background. There are other differences, but it is not known whether these specializations result from maturational acclimatization or are actual heritable traits due to selective adaptation.

People reared in temperate, humid environments can readily adapt to hot, dry environments, given time and sense enough to take advice on how to beat the heat.

Concerning cold stress, anthropologists have done some research on special adaptations to cold in tribal populations like the Eskimos and the "original peoples" of Tierra del Fuego, but the results, as with adjustment to heat, are not conclusive about genetic transmission. In any case, for modern Plains inhabitants clothing, shelter, and heat from fire, stoves, and such were the main protective devices. Both summer heat and winter cold caused suffering for Euro-American-Canadians in the first year or two of settlement, according to the reminiscence literature we have examined,[7] and deaths from exposure, particularly among infants and the aged, were significant. But even here the reactions were as much due to economic privation and the inability to build adequate shelters or find enough food as to the weather itself.

A study of such firsthand accounts of European farmer immigrants to the Great Plains suggests that though some never accepted the discomforts and departed after a few months or years, acclimatization in the *behavioral* sense—learning protective techniques as well as accepting the situation—took at least one full year in the best of cases and as long as a generation in others. The basic physiological requirements for water, heat retention and loss, and so on were hard enough to meet, but the sweating, blowing dust, frequent failure of garden crops, uncertain diet, and winter cold and blizzards were simply too much for many emigrants. The impact on human survival and health in these populations was severe: infant and old-age mortality was very high; in some districts families anticipated the death of at least one out of every three infants born there or brought into the area. The first two winters and summers were the hardest to bear, since not only was the physical stress high, but the failure of economic adaptation caused severe privation.

The difficulty of agrarian adjustment to such lands is not new, particularly when agriculture and nuclear settlement are involved. Although arid lands with rivers running through them (e.g., Mesopotamia, Egypt, the Punjab) were the sites of earliest urban trading-based civilizations, most of these cultures eventually had severe difficulties with aridity. Irrigation was essential to support large populations in such lands, and most of the ancient irrigation systems eventually succumbed to siltation, salinization, or crumbling banks, sometimes encouraged by invading armies. Trade was therefore essential, and the superstructure was vulnerable to collapse when the farmers suffered prolonged drought or the deterioration of water supply or soil fertility (see chapter 8). These civilizations accumulated and concentrated wealth by extracting fertility from the soil (and whatever minerals the area might possess) by manufacture and trade, by subsidies from other cultured populations (often booty acquired by military conquest), and by regular episodic out-migration of surplus population that spread the limited "take" among fewer people. The economic-ecologic picture was also marked by extreme or at least recurrent fluctuation—much of which was due to natural cycles like drought or failures in the social or material apparatus needed to maintain a constant flow of wealth or at least survival needs for a given number of people. If this pattern sounds familiar, one need only call attention to the physical, economic, and demographic fluctuations of modern populations of the North American Great Plains. The external subsidies are larger, but vulnerability remains great in the face of physical constraints and variability.

Contrasting Adaptations in Low- and High-Energy Societies

If agricultural societies have often run into trouble in dry regions, what of tribal societies that practiced limited agriculture or none? Although civilizations residing in arid/semiarid lands had difficulty sustaining a high level of economic output or wealth accumulation, the tribal societies, particularly the transient or nomadic ones relying more on animal husbandry than on plant crops, or those that subsisted, where it was possible, on hunting and gathering, were probably the most enduring and stable human cultures in these constrained environments. All of these were small, fertility-limiting populations, existing at low levels of economic output and consumption. The migratory life-style and communal land tenure and use fitted the specialized and sparse resources, and their habit of movement and dispersal allowed easily damaged resources to regenerate.

Such societies can be considered "low-energy" adaptations. "Energy" here refers to the amount of effort required to extract a product, whether nutritional, material, or social.[8] The word can also refer to the secondary energy-producing potential of the product itself, after extraction and processing. Low-energy societies use human and animal muscle power, and with this limited technology they can extract just enough energy from the habitat to provide sustenance and shelter for the resident population with little left over for luxuries. Such societies were relatively self-sufficient, although a certain amount of trade and barter always occurred between groups. They were generally "in balance" with the environment, which means that their technology permitted a regeneration of resources. However, there was always a degree of cyclical use, overuse, and recovery, and, in some instances, as with the Plains Indians' habit of driving bison herds by firing grass and thereby further reducing tree cover, there was significant long-lasting impact. On the whole, low-energy societies were ideally suited to the highly variable and constrained physical environments of arid/semiarid lands.

In a "high-energy society" the product obtained from resources is produced with technology supplying a larger quotient of energy than that available from human or animal muscles. Moreover, the machinery, generated power, or chemical transformations permit a riskier use of resources, particularly in situations where regeneration is difficult or impossible. Characteristically, such technologies of production supply larger populations than those immediately engaged in production. Markets are the main objective, and typically the local population loses control of its resource base, or at any rate the people no longer produce for their own subsistence.

Thus high-energy uses of arid/semiarid lands have a proclivity toward resource abuse, primarily because their extractive processes are extensive and exhaustive and the external demands for such resources are so high. The local population must survive on the cash benefits their resources can bring from outside buyers, who seek a supply with little or no concern for sustaining the yield of the resource. In agriculture, this tendency to push such specialized and often marginal resources beyond regenerative capacity is encountered in grasslands in the form of overgrazing; in cropping areas, in the tendency to pump groundwater excessively in order to irrigate, in the local impoundment of streams that formerly watered extensive dry areas, and in the disturbance of friable soils in agriculture and urban fringes, causing wind and water erosion. When multiple causes and effects result in extensive loss of vegetation, surface water, and groundwater, the term "desertification" has been applied. Although the term lacks scientific precision, the best-known case is the Sahel, the band of scrub vegetation constituting the transition between the true Sahara desert on the north and the forest on the south that has undeniably undergone increasing dessication, much of it due to overgrazing, the opening of marginal lands to cultivation, and drought cycles. The "advance" of desert conditions southward into the Sahel was variously estimated in the 1970s, depending on the year and district, but there seems little doubt that resource degradation has accelerated.

Variability of Arid/Semiarid Resources and the Problem of Adaptation for Indigenous and Industrial Cultures

Perhaps the most crucial aspect of arid/semiarid environments is their highly variable climate, water, and soil (although the nature of this variability differs by location). Thus, semiarid grasslands in the Northern Hemisphere are subject to a great seasonal temperature range and highly variable rainfall, both characteristics responsible for human physical stress and also high-risk agriculture. Desert regions in the tropical latitudes have considerable night/day temperature extremes; indeed, tribal nomads in these environments require not only acclimatization to dry heat, but also tolerance of very cold nighttime temperatures (the voluminous robes of the Bedawi protect against both heat and cold). People in arid/semiarid lands experience "drought" as a permanent condition, but really severe droughts appear at intervals not subject to reliable forecast: they may last a year or two, or they may endure for a decade or more, as they did in the Great Plains in the 1930s. This variability creates special problems for high-energy adaptations to these lands, since production for markets demands responsive flexibility in changing the nature and the volume of crops to suit prices and costs— changes that are always subject to environmental constraints. Variability simply makes the response less confident.

Since variability is as much a characteristic of these environments as drought, we need the special acronym: arid-semiarid-variable, or ASAV. For the Great Plains of North America this implies that humans must cope with heat, cold, drought, torrential rains, blizzards, and the highly variable rhythms of all of these. In addition, the soils of these regions are extremely varied owing to the savage action of glaciation and glacial melting, which created vast lakes and rivers, moving the particles of soil according to current speed and topography and segregating them into sand, gravel, silt, and other forms with differing agricultural potential.

This was of no great significance for pastoral nomads like the Plains Indians or the early range cattlemen, but the homesteading farmers found it hard to cope with.

Culture is always part of the adaptive process, if the concept of culture is defined as the proclivity of humans to create new and changing ways of dealing with nature and each other. Even more important, it is the human ability to remember these ways and store them up for future use. This accumulation of precedents and their changes permits human beings to anticipate future needs and to call forth both innovations and traditions to suit particular demands or to handle emergent constraints. Thus humans are not in any simple way "determined" by physical phenomena but cope with or adapt to them. However, this dynamic quality of human adaptive behavior does not obviate the need to restrain ambition or cultural interests when environments create difficulties or when culture does not permit adequate management. So in a qualified sense the environment does set limits, but it also provides opportunities—and it is often difficult to know which is which, since limiting factors often can stimulate innovation that transforms them into opportunities. This is as true for low-energy as for high-energy societies.

For example, Amerind populations across the North American continent were markedly different in cultural style, and ethnologists have long recognized a role for the environment in helping bring about such differences in low-energy tribal cultures (Kroeber 1953).[9] The Plains Indians, in adapting to open spaces and to horse and bison pastoralism, evolved a vigorous, mobile, aggressive style, a common type for ASAV lands in Asia and Africa as well. This style can be compared with its virtual opposite: that developed by Indians in the lush environments of New England. William Cronon attributed the rather leisurely lifeways of these tribes to the ecological abundance and diversity of the environment, both within and between the markedly different four seasons (Cronon 1983). The Plains Indians, on the other hand, had to cope with less diverse and more specialized resources and with an essentially two-season annual round: short, hot, dry summers and long, cold winters.

In the Great Plains, where physical resources were widely dispersed and one, the bison, was mobile, the Indians were required to move long distances to obtain the raw materials and climates they needed for survival or for different types of encampments suited to different seasons (open-country sites during the hunt, sheltered permanent camps during the winter, etc.). The New England agricultural tribes, able to obtain locally most of what they needed at all times of the year, could build permanent villages and remain in them indefinitely, although some groups moved their villages at long intervals to permit soil regeneration or simply to find new opportunities.

This "eastern leisurely style," as Cronon calls it, also extended in some degree to the European immigrants. When the Europeans arrived, resources in the lush eastern lands permitted the settlers to reproduce the institutions and settlement patterns familiar to them from European homelands, since the environments were so similar. However, the Euro-American settlers who came into the Great Plains of Canada and the United States were confronted with an unfamiliar milieu and had to innovate—a theme classically explored by Walter Webb (1932) and Frederick J. Turner (1958)—and also oversimplified by both.[10] Nevertheless, in the early days of western North American settlement attempts were made to reproduce eastern institutions, such as the rectilinear land survey system that ignores the complex drainage patterns and sparse water supplies of the West.

The Euro-American-Canadian settlers in the Northeast could establish permanent communities immediately, since relatively little energy had to be expended in order to locate water, good soils, game, and fuel. On the other hand, in the Plains the search for these basic necessities of settled life dragged on through two or three generations of settlers. In our work on migration to and within the Northern Plains we have found that fewer than 20 percent of all settlers in the more northerly portions stayed put—that is, found a homestead on the first try and stayed there. Most kept wandering, looking for more salubrious climate, soil, water, and neighbors. For many the final settlement locus was a last resort—weary of the constant movement, they came to realize that there was really nothing better. Resources in many areas never seemed to come all together; if the well was good, the soil might be bad or the topography too rough.

But such a constrained environment is not likely to be accompanied by limited expectations by people from modern industrial cultures. In an entrepreneurial economy, fueled by high aspirations and the notion of continual progress, adaptation comes to be viewed as a directional change process; by "adapting" things are expected to improve; by solving problems life becomes easier, and thus progress is served as well as validated. However, if resources are only marginally sufficient to realize these goals, subsidies need to be found, and if subsidies are not forthcoming then the resources must be *made* to yield, at whatever cost.

Once this course of action is set in motion, the process may appear to change from a directional one, with ever-rising vectors, to a cyclical one, with ups and downs, booms and busts. And the question of whether these cyclical movements are simply squiggles on the generally ascending curve of prosperity is difficult to answer, particularly when some of the changes, like resource degradation, appear to be accelerating downward and creating costs. As prairie soils lose fertility in continuous cropping expensive fertilizer must replace it, and the cost of replacement may be met by rising economic values elsewhere, such as increased federal subsidies or higher food prices. But all of these factors are hard to define and difficult to sustain. Consequently, cyclical movement and uncertainty as to the precise phasing of the cycles becomes the pattern.

Moods of optimism and pessimism, caution and daring, innovation and resignation accompany these movements. If one uses the modern North American Great Plains population as a model, one finds that these fluctuations are geared not only to climate and economic conditions but also to the human generations. The first generation of settlers was basically optimistic, but many turned pessimistic and disillusioned when the weather and the economy turned against them. The second generation—those who stayed in the West despite the difficulties—worked hard to adapt to the fluctuations and uncertainties, and many of them made it; but an equal number did not, and defeatism and despair, optimism or cautious satisfaction were the fluctuating attitudes. The third generation, benefitting from government subsidies and supports, tends to feel that the difficulties of Western existence have been met successfully: confidence, tempered with preparatory caution, is the dominant attitude. And by the third and fourth generations of Western settlers the difficult and even disastrous past may be romanticized, the suffering and failures offered as proof of the strong human fiber that made the effort. Whatever the attitude or mood, the social costs have been massive: for every family that survived dozens more departed or failed, and the out-migration rate continues to be high; at most, one member of every set of siblings finds it possible to stay in country districts.

In the Great Plains cyclical dangers persist and environmental downgrading continues because resources are uncertain and the pattern of human use is marginally conservationist at best. Droughts will recur. Income fluctuations will continue because of our system of speculative commodity markets. The extraction of minerals for use by the outside world continues to drain the region of its substance. Whether the Plains Indians would have evolved to a point of similar difficulties and threats to the environment will never be known, but it is important to remember that they belonged to our species, a being who sees the future in terms of gratification and does not usually treat the earth as an investment to be sustained. All things come to an end, but prudence, modesty, and a sense of history can often delay their demise.

The History of Behavioral Adaptations to Semiarid Lands

How, then, are we to decide how to use such areas as the Great Plains with all their variability?[11] Given the distinctive and specialized resources of the ASAV lands of North America (and elsewhere), what capacities of human behavior were, and may still be, required to deal with them?

Diversity of Low-Energy ASAV Adaptations

In considering adaptations to ASAV environments created by human beings before industry and nationhood, we note that these regions and their cultures were and are by no means uniform. Indeed, the strategies for exploiting the many variations and microhabitats of ASAV environments, especially deserts, are almost as numerous as those for more humid lands, although certain common themes run through them all, based on resource variability. Coping with economic uncertainty, establishing networks of mutual aid, coping with physiological effects of aridity and temperature extremes and many other devices on the whole characterize ASAV adaptations to a greater extent than life in humid environments. However, we must be careful with such generalizations, because humans define their resources partly on precedents, and it is possible that a society in a relatively well endowed region might neglect or ignore certain valuable resources and thus create problems comparable to those commonly found in drier environments.

Our knowledge of preindustrial adaptations to ASAV environments comes mainly from ethnological studies of biological and social-behavioral adjustments (see, for example, Moran 1979, chaps. 7 and 8). These studies present a picture of the remarkable intelligence and skill of *Homo sapiens sapiens* at any level of technical development. This brief chapter cannot hope to convey the complexity of these tribal adaptations, but several key points stand out:

1. There is no ASAV region or microhabitat that has not been exploited by humans at even the lowest social and technological energy levels, and all the available evidence indicates that these adaptations were capable of sustaining human existence indefinitely. That is, to live a continuous and reproductive social and biological existence in these presumably difficult environments does not require advanced technology (although it does require specialized techniques).

2. The anthropological literature focuses on self-subsistent societies or reconstructs the precontact modes of adaptation in order to separate out the influences from exogenous high-energy cultures. This means that the subsistence cultural ecology of these tribal adaptations constitutes a story of self-help—of indigenous "possibilism," to use a favorite term of geographers. Using mainly local resources, these societies are independent and hence all the more admirable from the standpoint of modern adaptations to ASAV lands, which depend heavily on external energy inputs.

3. Doing it on your own also means exercising choice over which resource to specialize in, even though the resource base is limited compared with other habitats.

4. Nearly all of the tribal adaptations to these environments involve more than a single microhabitat. These people have worked out complex transhumant adjustments to a variety of differing seasonal, topographic, vegetational, and environmental features in the general region; the human "possibilist" adaptations are analogous to the ecological principle of diversity.

We can illustrate this with a brief summary of the available habitats in North American ASAV environments: desert oases, mountain meadows, shortgrass plains traversed by intermittent sparse streams, midgrass prairie with frequent streams with gallery forest and shrublands, major river valleys with associated forests, bottomlands, and tributaries, drylands covered with shrub growth, drylands with sparse and xerophytic vegetation ("deserts"), and upland regions with parkland vegetation (see Shelford 1963). The list is considerable, and each habitat harbored distinctive forms of human existence: foot hunters of wild game, horse-raising bison hunters, agricultural pueblos on mesas, streamside agricultural villagers, hunters and horticulturalists in forests, and combinations of these types. Some groups, like the Cree, lived in the prairie areas but returned to the forests for hunting seasons. Bison-hunting horse tribes like the Crow had agricultural relatives along the river valleys and frequently visited and interacted with them. Many tribes had dual or even triple adaptations and were accustomed to a variety of subsistence undertakings and to using a large variety of animal and plant substances from several habitats.

Cultural changes occurred regularly. The relatively open topography and sparse vegetation of many regions permitted a great deal of movement and contact: war, raiding, trading, political negotiation, constant travel, and exploration of new foraging grounds were typical of plains and prairie and mountain foothill people.[12] Learning new ways took place regularly, and cultural traits and concepts were diffused across large geographical areas, with constant change and permutation. The bison hunters with horses derived from Spanish herds—the so-called typical Plains Indians—were of recent origin and derived from bands and villages of tribes of varied subsistence types on the borders of the plains. There was no real shortage of food anywhere in the prairies, plains, and deserts for those who knew how to find it. The Shoshone Indians of the Great Basin, roaming in one of the North America's most "barren" lands, were able to supply themselves with adequate vegetable and animal food and raw materials.[13]

Hunting-and-Gathering Adaptations

Thus the earliest indigenous adaptations to ASAV lands are called food collecting or hunting and gathering (HG) by ethnologists, and there is no doubt that they represent the earliest forms of hominid adaptations to all physical environments. HG peoples varied in ideational culture and social organization, but the mobility associated with HG adaptations and the total reliance on foods collected from the natural world appears to have conferred certain broad similarities. The sexual division of labor, with men hunting animals and women gathering vegetable foods, was nearly universal. Most HG bands had base camps and wide-ranging foraging territories, the areas divided among the various bands by customary arrangement. Tools were all of the hand variety, but the types of projectile weapons, snares, traps, storage facilities, and even in some cases knowledge of simple irrigation to encourage the growth of wild plants constituted a sophisticated armament adequate to the tasks and appropriate for the support of a small population.

These peoples were, above all, oriented to large geographical spaces. Lacking nucleated permanent settlements other than the base camps, and lacking a concept of fixed land tenure, they came to know the signs and markers of special boundaries and places with great precision. Territories were traversed by many trails and tracks; the foraging individual or band was never "lost." The tracking capability of HG peoples was impressive and has been featured in modern novels and stories. The kinship social organization of HG populations was not simple but, as in the case of the Australian Aborigines, enormously complex and included hundreds of persons dispersed over very large territories. Ethnological accounts of these peoples have emphasized the ability to locate exact positions in social networks, even when the individuals or groups had never previously met or interacted.

The mode of HG adaptation was risky in that severe drought and other interruptions of normal physical resource cycles could induce starvation or severe privation. However, the technology and modes of resource use were adequate to support optimal populations—perhaps larger numbers, in some instances, than could be supported with the undeveloped agricultural or ranching modes of production used by the earliest European settlers in ASAV lands. In some regions, like central Australia, this latter situation would be true even today. However, the intervention of modern settlers' high-technology economies has greatly modified HG adaptations, and they are becoming extremely rare everywhere, perhaps effectively extinct. Settlers' occupancy of the land destroys the "food habitat" of HG peoples just as it destroys the natural habitats of animals and plants. HG humans are an endangered cultural species.

At the same time, the environmental movement as a worldwide ideology and action program has produced new threats to the continued existence, however qualified, of HG and other traditional adaptations. Friction between environmental campaigners and indigenous tribal peoples exists in many places (noteworthy cases are the Columbia River, with regard to fishery rights, and central Australia, with regard to hunted animals). To pursue an indigenous HG strategy in a greatly restricted territory accentuates the problem of species destruction, and such techniques as brush firing reduce plant cover, both things alarming to enviromentalists. But this problem is just one among many; the solution to the existence of remnant populations of indigenous HG people, as well as herds and agriculturalists, is nowhere in sight. It was and always will be a *political* issue, since it involves rights, property-productive resources, and ideology, and such considerations will tend to dominate biologically rational adaptive formulas.

Pastoralism

Through portions of Africa, the Middle East, and Central Asia there remain substantial indigenous populations of people who lack permanent nucleated settlements and who follow or drive their herding animals from pasture to pasture. This is a fundamental and long-lasting mode of low-energy adaptation to ASAV lands, derived from borderland agricultural civilizations, or, in the more ancient instances, an autonomous mode of adaptation dating to prehistoric times. Many such populations, particularly those in Central and Southwest Asia, retained contact with settled civilizations, and consequently they enjoyed cultural standards of considerable sophistication.[14] The ingenuity with which (especially) Asian pastoralists, especially, managed to translate these standards into portable forms has been a favorite theme of ethnologists; the large substantial, insulated, yet easily collapsible tents, horse trappings, leather trunks, metal jewelry, and intricate, well-tailored clothing attest to the ability of these people to live a comfortable life and accumulate wealth and possessions, all in the absence of long-term permanent settlement or, what is most significant, a concept of wholly owned land or space. This transiency was shared, of course, with the pastoralists of most of Africa, but in other respects the African tribal herders had a simpler material culture, perhaps because they had weaker connections with the older urban-based civilizations.

In North America pastoralism was represented by the Plains Indians after the seventeeth century, when they acquired horses. Ethnologists once debated whether to consider these people "true pastoralists," since, in contrast to the Asian and African pastoralists, they did not breed cattle. However, this was really a quibble, since the issue is the extent to which the pattern of human existence is shaped by movement with or because of herding animals. The bison had their own movements but were frequently driven or guided by the Indians for slaughter. Moreover, the Indians were active horse breeders, breakers, and riders. The Plains horse culture was relatively recent, with the animals descended from strays from Spanish herds in the Southwest. It was characterized by a strong set of distinctive technological, military, social, ritual, and aesthetic patterns that overlay the differing cultural elements of the component tribes, derived from different stocks and subsistence adaptations on the margins of the Plains. Thus nearly all tribes had an annual collective ritual like the Sun Dance; all of them used transportable dwellings, furniture, and clothing; they all established societies of young males for war training, the hunt, or fraternal ritual; and of course there was the technical dependence on the products of the bison.

As the Indians gave way to the Euro-American and Hispanic movements into the Plains, cattle displaced bison, but horse-dominated pastoralism continued under new auspices. The initial range livestock phase consisted of driving herds from Spanish settlements northward to supply mounts, meat, and hides for miners and other settlers; this soon evolved into open-range horse and cattle raising but was equally rapidly replaced by fenced ranching—the latter an adaptation to the land survey and the openings of various sections of the Plains to freehold agricultural settlement. The open-range version resembled Asian pastoralism in many details (although of course the cultural base was very different). The range horse breeders and cattlemen were members of settled borderland societies who elected to take up a pastoral existence and yet retained the basic outlines of urban culture. While they always had a home base, most of their life was spent on the range, supervising and driving the animals. Like the great Khans of Central Asia, the horse/cattle barons might frequently entertain visiting and exploring members of financial and social elites from distant entrepôts or foreign countries. And both scorned the farmers and villagers yet were more than willing to take title to land and invest in urban pursuits when civilization moved their way. The range cattlemen practiced rudimentary conservation by not concentrating the herds of different owners in the same grazing areas, through conservative or even quasi-military (armed cowboys, vigilantes) action. In addition, the adaptation was similar to Old World pastoralism and its intermittent, *surficial* use and exploitation of grasslands.[15]

In contrast, *fenced ranching* required management of both water and forage, since the herds had to be confined to designated areas and hay raised as a crop for winter feed. *This transformed open-range pastoralism into livestock agriculture.* That is, where there was an absolute necessity to take control of the finite resource base and create a new rhthym of use and regeneration under the control of human beings (i.e., the "ecological transition"; Bennett 1976). Irrigation, tame-seeded forage plants, fenced grazing areas, appropriately located salt licks, shelter for brood cows and calves in the winter—and so on; all these are now universal but were things the old range cattlemen would have regarded as silly or at least unnecessary, given the open availability of enormous areas of grassland or scrub.

The movement to fencing changed everything. *Mobile* resource utilization differs ecologically, fundamentally, in its use of Nature from uses based on a fixed tract of land that must be made to produce year after year. ASAV lands have always been naturally suited to mobile resource utilization regimes, and attempts to make them conform to fixed and repeated production strategies have always experienced difficulties, and always will. The constraints are severe, and the ability of these environments to respond to production pressure is limited. The modern world exploits ASAV lands by requiring them to produce larger volumes of a relatively small number of products for the maintenance of indigenous populations and for trade with populations at indefinite remove from the ASAV environment. When such external demands were weak, the pattern of adaptation was locally diverse, conservationist on the whole, and geared to subsistence. It is true, of course, that there were exceptions in the area of conservation, like the burnoff of grasslands and local overgrazing or the hunting to extinction of certain mammals, but on the whole the human populations remained modest and the pressure on resources was sufficiently benign to permit regeneration.

The attempt to force or persuade pastoralists to settle down and become ranchers has fostered considerable research on the way physical resource use was geared to social organization and symbolic ritual. The hunt, the raising of livestock, observation of the seasons, food preparation, and other things constitute a style of "cultural ecology" much less evident in contemporary adaptations. The intricate interrelations between human activities and beliefs and the physical environment became more than an academic subject when Third World countries attempted to convert their inhabitants to commercial agrarian regimes. The failure and confusion attendant upon this effort have been particularly evident in Africa, where the attempts to convert pastoralists into limited-pasturage tenured ranchers had poor results despite the investment of several million dollars in development funds and loans. (The details are considered in the next chapter.)

No better example than these attempts to "develop" pastoralism could be found to illustrate the consequences of upsetting the careful balance between social institutions and resource ecology among the traditional users of ASAV environments. It also underlines the precarious and exploitative nature of attempts to use these lands with the same set of profit-making, high-production institutions devised, over the centuries, for humid environments.

Agricultural Settlement in the Great Plains

Industrialized agricultural settlement of North American ASAV lands began in most areas in the second half of the nineteenth century. It, too, required special techniques. Viewed from the comparative perspective of the humid East and Europe, the problems of the ASAV West center on the *uncertainty* derived from the variable resources. Since nothing can be counted on—streams dry up part of the year, rain falls on your neighbor's fields but not on yours, your field may be loamy and your neighbor's pure sand, and so on—it is necessary to devise special techniques for farming; for example, financial hedging, innovation, experimentation, the courage to convert a constraint into an opportunity, these were and remain essential in trying to make a living off the country. One risk was overreliance on a particular physical feature such as the soil that was converted into a resource and that in turn was eventually degraded. Such overreliance and specialized production made settlers financially vulnerable and ultimately culminated in a boom-and-bust economy for many localities. The attempt to convert an inherently variable resource base into a monocultural production system also resulted in a loss of biological diversity—the extinction of many useful plants and animals.

Uncertainty, from a behavioral standpoint, means that the expectation of *particular* desired outcomes is low; that they are a matter of low or ambiguous probability. When the probability of occurrence—for example, the annual rainfall needed to produce a crop of given potential—is not known with precision, the uncertainty quotient is high. The extent to which the probability can be calculated measures the amount of risk; if the probability of good rainfall is 50 percent, one may know one's chances of obtaining a good crop are 50-50. Thus the settlers in the Plains—or the Indians, chasing bison herds that fluctuated in numbers and location—had to learn to calculate risk subjectively. And when scientific knowledge of the processes involved was low, experience and the calculations derived from that had to substitute and gambling strategies were necessary ("seat-of-the-pants" farming).

A second important concept is *flexibility*. Settlers in the East might be able to make a good living by doing the same things every year, since they could depend on resource potential, but in the Plains one had to be prepared to shift different crops or use entirely different strategies. If cropping became too expensive because of the need for fertilizer and such, one had to shift to livestock or look for oil on the property. Experience counts: the longer the producer copes with the situation, the more *alternatives* he may learn about and experiment with. Indian grassland hunters had to be able to shift from large to small game during heavy winters or severe drought; grain farmers have to disperse their holdings across a wider region to maximize the chance of obtaining good rainfall or better soils.

Flexibility in the face of high uncertainty also means the need to accept *trade-offs* between alternatives, when the possibilities of realizing one goal may be compromised by the need to fulfill another. In an environment of chronic marginality and shortage, people learn to do what they can with what they have and to juggle competing needs. This also means that opportunity costs are generally high: the cost of shifting from one alternative to another may be higher than one can or wants to bear. However, the necessity is there—one changes or one does not survive. Thus the risk factor again: beg, borrow, or steal to change to the new alternative and find some way to pay the costs. In some circumstances, however, it may be wiser to "sit it out" rather than attempt the shift to a new course of action, particularly when the alternative is especially costly in either financial or social terms. Constant movement from one homestead to another—so common among the early settlers—required weighing the cost of staying or leaving and the probability of finding an even worse site in the next country or state. Still, the chance might have to be taken if the current site was not productive and the family's welfare was at stake. Essentially only three alternatives were available: stay, try a new place, or go back to the original homeland (or some intermediate location).

Accumulation was another important strategy. Cash was essential for settlers—in the early days its only source might be wage labor, and, pressing as most needs were, full satisfaction often had to be deferred in order to acquire a small reserve for future needs, including the expenses of a possible move, the purchase of more land, or a necessary machine or horse. Similarly, Indians had to exercise these prudent strategies—not only on the Plains but almost everywhere. The preparation of dried, portable high-protein and vegetable foods and the digging of storage pits in encampments are familiar to ethnologists and archaeologists. The heavy reliance on "futures"—that is, the annual return of the bison herds, the flowing of spring floods, or the flowering and fruiting of plants— meant that some preservation, storage, and transport of surpluses was essential in the case of a cyclical failure.

None of these behavioral survival strategies were or are unique to ASAV lands; they are the stuff of everyday practical life and subsistence adaptations everywhere and in all climates. However, the ASAV situation enforced them with a vengeance; the marginality and unpredictability of many resources meant that the modern residents of such lands have tended to be prudent and daring in turn, depending on the fluctuating resources. When market economic fluctuation was added to the picture, the result was "boom-and-bust" strategies, which exert severe pressure on the physical environment.

Is this "adaptation"? Of course it is, but adaptation of the producers to the institutions, not to Nature; or rather, not to the limits of safe exploitation but only to some partly illusory ultimate potential. To include environmental values in the activity pattern it is necessary to make them economically profitable so as to encourage choice of alternative, less abusive uses of the land. This will take some doing—something more than a well-meant conservation program. The problems will remain; only a fundamental change in the institutions can solve them.

Farming in the boom-and-bust manner is designed to permit the farmer to survive, but it has no particular relationship to resource conservation or abuse—unless these strategies are combined with some specialized techniques, like the avoidance of over-cultivation of the soil, preserving "trash" (plant debris) on the surface, contour plowing, and so on, all devices to minimize the destructive effects of wind on light soils typical of former grasslands. The only foolproof device, of course, is to return the land to grasses and use it as forage for animals, and in many failed grain-growing areas this is what has happened.

The consequences of several generations of cultivation of Plains-Prairie soils, combined with the destructive disturbances around cities in the Plains and the Southwestern desert areas, has been described as a form of "desertification."[16] However, there are no persuasive cases of actual "spreading of deserts" in North America, but certainly some of the associated effects are visible throughout the West and elsewhere: soil blowing, drying up some landscapes owing to stream impoundment for domestic agricultural water use, loss of plant cover, and so on. While some of these things are to be found throughout North America, there seems little doubt that the consequences are accentuated in moisture-short regions, especially those with considerable solar radiation. The critical margin appears to be the less than twenty-inch zone of rainfall. West of the line defining this zone (approximately the 100th meridian), one encounters increasing degradation of resources.

There is, for example, no way of farming shortgrass plains so as to eliminate completely soil erosion and loss of fertility and tilth. The effects can be moderated by careful methods: preserving trash cover on plowed fields, contour plowing to control water erosion, plowing plant refuse back into topsoil to rebuild tilth, and avoiding cultivation to the extent possible, especially during windy periods. New methods emerge almost yearly, as North Americans begin to understand ASAV environments. This is good, but the course of change still seems downhill: overgrazing and consequent destruction of forage cover continue; drastic disturbance of friable soils around the spreading urban centers of the Southwest is unrestricted; and chemical fertilizers continue to be used in large quantities in the Plains regardless of their destructive effects on tilth, including the deposition of harmful nitrates. Irrigation continues to salinize acreage and diminish water tables. Conservation and "alternative agriculture" groups insist on controls and changes: regrassing of high-risk cultivated areas, cessation of "soil mining" tactics of big grain farmers, control of all-terrain vehicles, and so on. Drought accentuates the consequences of such uses, and the system of market agriculture does not allow for release of pressure during periods of drought. The new round of intensive grain production and cultivation that began in the 1950s may be setting up the region for another socioeconomic disaster, given another long drought period—for which the region is probably overdue.

Concerning the Amerind occupation, I noted that this had its dynamic qualities as well: it began with simple hunting bands and concluded with a major exploitative pastoral phase, with varying implications for physical resources. Although moisture levels in much of the Plains are certainly marginal at best for the growth of permanent tree cover, recent research suggests that deliberate firing of grass cover by Plains Indians to facilitate the bison hunt accentuated the treelessness.[17] Certainly trees always existed along watercourses; these "gallery forests" were crucial for both animal and human adaptation to the Plains for millenia, and the islanded forests in higher elevations like the Black Hills and the Cypress Hills were important refuges for both humans and animals. Grass cover has been "managed" by humans at least since the onset of effective horse/bison pastoralism, and one might conclude that the contemporary emphasis on cattle in the drier portions is technically a continuation of the indigenous adaptations centered on bison. However, agriculture also was not foreign to the Plains in aboriginal times and was particularly prominent in the eastern half, along the major rivers and streams. But there is no doubt that Indian adaptations of all types, due to low-energy technology and small populations, exerted much less pressure on resources than the contemporary commercial regimes.[18]

Let me illustrate the consequences of the contemporary scale of pressure on resources with a vignette: the events in Kiowa and Crowley counties in eastern Colorado—in the less than twenty-inch rainfall area of the Great Plains.[19] In February of 1977 high-velocity warm winds—a massive chinook—swept down from the Rockies and in seven hours caused a major dust storm that moved eastward from Colorado, eventually becoming visible over the mid-Atlantic. The fallout from the storm shadowed 248,000 square miles of the south-central United States, and in some districts as much as eleven inches of topsoil was removed from plowed fields.

Nearly the entire land surface of these two Colorado counties consists of friable soil that should be returned to grass and used as rangeland, but since the late 1960s precisely the opposite has taken place: the soil had been used for grain production because the economics of livestock production and the costs of converting plowed land to range prevent individual farmers, however large in scale, from doing otherwise. One of the important economic factors is the federal disaster relief payment system, in which farmers simply turn over the checks to their local banker to finance the loan payments for annual operations. This is part of what we might call the "Worster effect" (from Donald Worster's 1979 book on the dust bowl, where he suggests that federal programs for welfare relief and soil conservation since the 1930s, however well meant, have often created an unearned financial cushion, encouraging exploitation of fragile, high-risk lands). *The crucial element here is institutional, not ecological*; that is, in a market and profit-making economy, agriculture is subject to forces outside the control of local resource users, who have to do what the general economic system requires of them, regardless of economic costs.

Community Patterns and Problems in Arid/Semiarid Regions

Whatever the settlement pattern, some community problems persist across changes in methods of adaptation. For example, we noted previously that the fate of communities is bound up with the problem of small and dispersed settlement. In recent years this has been summed up in the concept of *sparselands*, the term referring mainly to regions settled by emigrants from the more densely populated areas of western North America, Asiatic Russia, Australia, New Zealand, Argentina, Brazil, and northern Scandinavia.[20] Though this list contains a wide variety of habitats—temperate or tropical lands, rainforest tropics, and the subarctic—the essential factor in the availability and convertibility of resources; energy levels are not sufficient to permit dense settlement and the financial cushion that uncertainty requires.

But social phenomena, not resources, are the topic of this section. How do people get along with few and distant neighbors? What substitutes for the more intimate social contacts and networks or high-density population? How do people adjust to the social deficits? If they do not find ways of compensating locally they seek help, and hence the practical problem of sparselands for national governments is how local systems demanding more substantial benefits can be financed: Are jobs to be provided by government investment in productive business, or are people to be encouraged to migrate to better endowed regions? How are the indigenous relict populations, like Indian reservation communities, to be handled? Do they deserve the same benefits as the settlers?

To begin with the Indians, the nomadic aboriginal life had its own problems of association. The long periods of the hunt, when the tribes broke up into bands, created a need for wider contact—especially to seek marital partners, since bands were for the most part exogamous and composed of single kin groups. The Sun Dance was the principal adaptive response, a vast group ceremony or festival when all the bands came together for days to enjoy one intense period of socializing when friendships were resumed, mates found, and the kin networks reaffirmed.[21] Some of the patterns were based on the social organization and cultural interests of the pre-Plains period for many groups, who had forged their culture in more settled life in the richer environments on the fringes of the Plains. As with the Euro-American and Euro-Canadian settlers, accustomed to the intimate associations of small towns and more densely populated rural neighborhoods, ways had to be found to resume this earlier social existence in the wide open spaces. Adaptation to ASAV lands does not necessarily means one starts from scratch—it is a matter of reproducing earlier forms of social life but modifying them to cope with the changed environment.

Thus, whether we are dealing with nucleated Euro-American settlers or tribal revitalists, we find that people who came into ASAV environments with their own customs forged in different climates had to recreate new versions of these traditional forms in a resource context that tends to work against human association. The women who wrote reminiscences of homestead life almost universally complained of loneliness, but they also described their joy and contentment at the occasional opportunities for socializing—the monthly dance in the schoolhouse, the sodalities and clubs, the long drives through inclement weather in democrat wagons or the Model T, the chances at regaining human contact that made it possible to endure the solitude and hardships. Some simply gave up—the isolation was too much for them—and population fluctuation in the Plains was not entirely a matter of economic difficulty. Many of the settlers left because it was impossible to reproduce the social life they desired.

Settlement and sedentarization also had a profound effect on the Indians. The shift from mobile horse/bison pastoralism and transient use of resources to settled reservation life was a traumatic episode to which the indigenous people of the Plains never fully accommodated. As early as 1932, in her classic study of a Plains Indian reservation, Margaret Mead observed that although the Omaha reservation she studied required agriculture and other sedentary economic pursuits to provide an income, the ideas and habits of the male members of the tribe remained firmly rooted in the nomadic hunting and warring past. Village life was not for them; cultivating fields was seen as an insult to a real man, essentially women's work. The kind of associational life represented by permanent settlement seemed dull and vapid compared with the comradeship of hunting and war parties, the fraternal societies, and the annual ceremonies. The social organization and ideology of pastoralism have died hard; the adaptive shift is still not complete in many reservations. The delay of course is also partly attributable to bad policies on the part of the federal government: dishonesty and prevarication, failure to fund education and agricultural training programs in the early days, confused land allocation and tenure rules, and misguided welfare procedures. The difficulties underline the vast cultural gap between nomadic and settled life as well as the trials of nucleated settlement and existence for all peoples who must establish themselves in ASAV lands.

The villages and towns established by Euro-American-Canadians have not been exempt from "sparseland" problems. The expectations of settlers familiar with viable nucleated communities are not easily met in these lands. In central Australia, the U.S. and Canadian West, and northeastern Brazil villages and towns were founded immediately after colonization; in all countries, maintaining these communities has been a constant struggle. In North America villages were constructed overnight along the railroads, as division points, service centers, settler ports of entry, and pickup spots for farm produce. In western Canada villages were established about every eight miles along the Canadian Pacific Railway main line; today fewer than half these communities remain populated. Yet about half *do* remain, many of them clinging to existence with miniscule populations of aged retirees or the managers of a handful of service facilities. One can deplore the losses, but the other side of the coin is the amazing persistence of villages even when most of their economic rationale for being has withered. Nucleated settlement is hard to kill, even in ASAV environments.

The basic issue appears to be the existence of linkages—social and economic—between the nucleated settlements themselves and between the settlements and more densely settled and prosperous regions on the margins. I have underlined the importance of relying on the external inputs if human adaptations in ASAV environments are to provide for their inhabitants at a level exceeding the productivity of the local resources; this can be done for nucleated settlements *only if they depend on and exchange with each other*. In the capitalist environment of North America many such communities tend to reach a level of equilibrium that does not change for a very long time, even though the national economy undergoes many changes. The communities achieve a relative stability provided by connections with external economic resources. The resulting geographic pattern is analyzable with locational theory, as developed originally by Wilhelm Christaller and elaborated subsequently by many researchers.[22] A hierarchy of communities of varying but rather precisely calibrated sizes form a grid on the land surface, and the grid takes predicted shape best in a relatively level semiarid environment with an established agricultural economy, such as the northern plains of North America.[23]

Such a stable community is the town of Maple Creek in southwestern Saskatchewan, a tertiary service center community in the Palliser Triangle, the driest portion of the Canadian section of the northern plains (cf. Bennett 1969). Maple Creek has had a population of about 3,000 permanent residents for the past eighty-five years, varying up and down only by a few hundred souls. The number of locally owned businesses has averaged about twenty-five for this same period. In periods of prosperity this number can increase by fifteen to twenty, with the excess disappearing within a decade or so because of dwindling financial resources. With the help of the federal and provincial governments, the town of Maple Creek has gradually accumulated adequate medical services and facilities for the aged and retired. The basic businesses serve the country agricultural community: grain elevators, farm machinery dealers, automotive repair, hardware, and so on. In recent years several chain stores have moved in and currently are doing well. In 1969 we calculated that the annual value of all external government financial inputs into the town totaled about $5 million. By the 1980s this had doubled.

The town persists despite the presence, sixty or seventy miles to the west and east, of small, secondary service-center cities with abundant wholesale and retail services. The only type of businesses in Maple Creek to have become extinct in the past twenty-five years were two or three locally owned groceries, now replaced by the co-op store and the IGA, both chain operations in a sense but locally managed and operated. Maple Creek's persistence is at the expense of several primary village centers located on a periphery of ten to twenty miles in all directions; these communities—those still on the map—have declined to little more than places to pick up mail or fill a gas tank. Thus the survival of small service towns like Maple Creek is evidence of the workings of the locational settlement patterning and processes in the age of the automobile.

But these declining or even defunct communities still display cyclical movement from time to time. The existence of a framework—an infra-structure of buildings, streets, business locations, and so on—becomes a magnet, even in conditions of low-level needs. Small entrepreneurs or service agencies may be inclined to risk a start in such a frame even though the risks are high and the expectations minimal. Or the regional school authority may decide to invest in a new central high school, and this in turn attracts residents and small businesses. So the community begins a modest revival. But these revivals go just so far; their duration is based on the specific needs served, not on automatic growth dynamics. Since wealth is hard to accumulate in ASAV environments, people must learn to live with specialized resources and a more modest scale of consumption. Boosterism persists—it is inherent in North American culture—but one feels increasingly that people in these utilitarian and circumscribed settlements have come to understand it as mostly a sym-bol, and underneath is a growing realism and comprehension of the constraints governing existence in Plains settlements and the "social deficits" these create (Kraenzel 1967).[24]

Fort Benton, Montana, is another example. Founded on Missouri River transportation, Fort Benton today is no longer the *entrepôt* it was in 1870, and in the 1950s it nearly died. But it remains a service center, thanks to its function as a magnet for agricultural settlers in the 1880s and the early twentieth century. Its great trading companies are long gone, but in their heyday they serviced not only river and overland trade and traffic but the mercantile needs of the farm and ranch settlers. For some communities like Fort Benton tourism continues to supply a small but reliable income. Fort Benton, like Maple Creek, is helped by its interme-diate location between larger towns—Great Falls to the south and Havre to the north.

We may conclude that in a modern economy the settlement of ASAV lands will be closely guided by functions and services and less so by human desires. That is, will and intention must take their cue from the specialized possibilities and opportunity structure, not from visionary or ambitious energy. The successful community builder in this situation is the person who perceives a "niche" opening up, however small, and manages to obtain enough energy in the form of social action and money capital and the interest of outside suppliers to start the ball rolling. Thus the entrepreneur in the ASAV settlement process is by no means dead; he or she is as necessary as in the early days of pioneer and frontier settlement, but the task now is continuity, maintenance, and controlled revival.

Given this survival context, it is not surprising that in the belles lettres produced on Great Plains topics one persistent theme has been material-ism: devotion to humdrum affairs and hard work and distrust or neglect of the arts and things of the mind. Intellectuals flee these communities, then in later years write wistful or nostalgic but critical appraisals of the deadening effect of life in the little towns. Even Wallace Stegner, willing to invest a major portion of his career in writing novels and memoirs based on his boyhood in such a community, with its colorful characters and adventurers, nevertheless was unable to say anything positive about cultural matters (Stegner 1962, 306). We must find other values in these communities: the steadfastness of people who have lived with less and yet nourished hopes of better things; people who are willing to work hard for little return by other standards; a culture that, while emphasizing individual accomplishments, does not stint in providing help and coop-eration. The values are social, not intellectual.

In some ways we now have a more positive appreciation of the old cultures of the indigenes. Fear of the terrifying Plains Indians has gradually given way to admiration of their fortitude and determination in defending their world. Belles lettres has glorified the works stimulated by Black Elk or written by Louise Erdrich, N. Scott Momaday, James Welsch, Harold Cardinal, and others, and the very nomadism of the Indians can be romantically appreciated precisely because it is so differ-ent from our own abiding attachment to sedentary nucleated settlements. And now, of course, the Plains Indians are economically, if not wholly psychologically, committed to the system. The grand paradox of our culture is that while we are so attached to nucleation we find difficulty appreciating the values and meaning of small- settlement existence. We tend to make fun of it, deplore it, and perennially decide it is on the way out. I think it will be here for a long time to come and will continue its pattern of rise and fall, of decline and revival. We also, of course, deplore this fluctuation as debilitating and destructive of human aspiration; yet there is another side: the courage and persistence of people who stick to something even in times of despair and make the best of it.

Notes

1. Data on the effects of recent agricultural activities in the Great Plains are analyzed in McGinnies and Laycock 1988.
2. Webb's pioneer social-ecological analysis of the adaptation problem was done before the environmental movement had sharpened our perception of human irresponsibility and greed. Adaptation for Webb meant largely the fulfillment of human needs by overcoming the constraints of the environment.
3. Or, stated another way, "adaptation," as we have already defined it in the preceding chapters, refers to the behavior of people confronted with changes in their milieu that require corresponding changes in established routine. The popular meanings of the term are specific: "getting along," "making do," "doing what you have to in order to survive," "putting up with the situation as best one can," or "making the necessary changes." Studies of the use and management of physical resources, when accompanied by concepts from the adaptational lexicon, are likely to focus on specific empirical circumstances, such as the time of planting as related to weather cycles. Two anthropological case studies of agrarian situations utilizing the concept of adaptation effectively but differently are Bennett 1982 and Hanks 1972. In my own work adaptation refers mainly to decision making in the uncertain physical and economic resource environment of market agriculture in the northern Great Plains. For the farmers in a Thai village in the completely different environment described by Hanks adaptation refers to different and changing modes of raising rice and the effect these modes have on culture and social organization. However, both approaches refer to people adjusting to changing or fluctuating conditions. A collection of papers on Indian and Spanish American adaptations to the ASAV regions of North America is Knowlton 1964.
   International conferences pertaining to arid lands have produced several volumes of proceedings, and the following are probably the best: UNESCO 1962, Hodge and Duisberg 1963, Dregne 1970, Whitehead et al. 1988. Perusing these works in order of publication can provide an idea of the expanding knowledge of aridity and human adaptation and, at the same time, the persistence of inappropriate methods of use. The symposia contain few papers on cultural and institutional aspects of arid lands adaptation, mainly because the study of aridity has been principally a specialty of natural scientists and some applied fields like irrigation agriculture.
4. There are a number of ways of classifying the differing environments or "biomes" in moisture-marginal portions of temperate lands. Shelford (1963) uses the following for North America: northern and southern temperate grasslands, the hot desert, a number of semidesert biomes, and a number of ecotones and "marginal contact" regions associated with deserts and grasslands and adjoining areas. The classifica-

tion is complex; there are few hard boundaries. Data on human population and resources for arid lands are also difficult to interpret because of the ambiguous definition of the concept of aridity. Alan Eyre, of the College of the West Indies, in a paper presented at the International Arid Lands Conference in Tucson, Arizona in 1985 (Eyre 1988), calculated the total number of inhabitants of "arid lands" of Asia, Europe, Africa, Australia, and the Americas in 1980 as 412 million persons, the figure representing an 81% increase since 1960. About 62 percent of the 412 million were supported by "seasonal and irrigated agriculture," and 27 percent by "light industry, commerce, services"; the remainder, 11 percent, lived by various activities, including pastoral nomadism, tourism, and mineral extraction. The figures should not be taken literally, but the trends are probably representative.

5. Newman's paper also contains a good general review of human physiological adaptations to both humid and dry high-heat climates. See also the relevant chapters in Moran 1979.

6. This also leads some anthropologists to propose that hominids first evolved in the dry tropics. This idea is supported by the fact that the best prehominid fossil species are found in such an environment: southern and southeastern Africa. As Newman 1970 suggests, we are hairless, sweaty, thirsty mammals.

7. I refer here and elsewhere in this chapter to a current research program: the Northern Plains Cultural History Project, supported by the National Endowment for the Humanities (the associated book is in preparation).

8. The study of energy as a factor in social organization and change has attracted some attention among social scientists but has not become a major topic. The sociologist Leonard Cottrell (1955) and more recently Howard Odum (1970, 1983) have developed the issue in research on social and natural systems. In general, the current approach in the institutional social sciences is to fuse the energy concept with systems analysis. In anthropological studies of the culture-nature interchange in tribal societies the analysis of energy has been identified with ecological research in which the main issue is how far tribal culture becomes part of the natural ecosystems in the search for and production of food (Ellen 1982). Important concepts related to energetics theory are found in Lotka (1922: 147–51). Lotka was a biological ecologist, and his theories apply most cogently to aspects of food and energy among animals and plants. Applications to human affairs are largely analogic and should be handled with care.

9. Kroeber 1953 endeavored to correlate specific cultural types and patterns with various climatic and physiographic factors in an effort to put to rest a long-standing controversy over the nature of "cultural areas" and their relation to the physical environment. He found some relationships, but no simple one-to-one concordances. The Plains Indian/grasslands concordance was one of the best.

10. Webb 1932 was primarily concerned with the environmental differences between the West and the more humid East and how eastern institutions would have to change in order to adapt. Turner 1958 was concerned with the "role of the frontier"—the bold individualistic spirit of the pioneer encountering a new world and how this pattern left its imprint on American culture. Webb underestimated the capacity of established institutions, such as land tenure, to handle new circumstances, for better or for worse; Turner neglected other forces in American society that were as influential as the "frontier" in shaping American character. James C. Malin, writing a generation later, updated both writers, adding new insights (Malin 1984 is a recent collection of his essays).

11. The concepts discussed in this section are derived from "decision theory," a blend of economic behavior analysis and rational choice theory in social psychology. A standard treatment is Collingridge 1982. For an application of some of the concepts to farming strategies in the Great Plains see Bennett 1982.

12. For an illuminating discussion of the variability and dynamism of western tribal economic and political culture, both before and after European contact, see Friesen 1984.

13. Classic ethnographic descriptions of such peoples are found in Forde 1937. Forde's analysis of Shoshone adaptations was a pioneer ethnological statement of tribal peoples' ability to extract a living from even the most refractory environments. More recent ethnological studies of human groups at the hunting-gathering level in dry environments provide a more dynamic analysis of coping behavior; see, for example, Turton 1977.

14. Considerable literature has accumulated on pastoralism owing to the efforts made by developing countries in Africa and the Middle East to sedentarize these peoples. For ethnographic description one of the best works is Gulliver 1955. For analyses of the pastoralism development problem in various parts of Africa see Bennett, Lawry, and Riddell 1986.

15. Similarities and differences between Plains Indians and the rancher/cowboy population and its culture were noted by Webb 1932 and by Franz and Choate 1966. For a comparison of rancher culture with that of pastoral nomads in the Old World see Gilles 1987. Biographical accounts of the early range cattlemen are found in Atherton 1961.

16. The following works provide an overview, with emphasis on social aspects, of the "desertification" literature and issues: Spooner and Mann 1982, Council on Environmental Quality 1981, Dregne 1977. The map in Dregne's paper, which aims at showing the lands at risk, was originally drawn for the 1979 United Nations Conference on Desertification. Version of the map have appeared in many other publications. The map is really only a cartography of ASAV lands and not an index of desertification causes and effects.

17. A more recent study is Hildebrand and Scott 1987. For a recent archeological analysis of aboriginal Plains inhabitants see Caldwell, Schultz, and Stout 1983.

18. See the maps in chapter 1 of Petulla 1977 for distribution of rainfall, vegetation, and other physical features of the United States in the context of early settlement history. A recent general source of data on moisture regimes is Geraghty et al. 1973; cf. McGinnies and Laycock 1988.

19. This descriptive material is taken from Council on Environmental Quality 1981 (75-87).

20. See Lonsdale and Holmes 1981; cf. Parker, Burnley, and Walker 1985. These studies feature the urban/rural dialogue; nucleated urban settlement is costly and reduces certain rural amenities but is necessary to provide desired facilities like higher education.

21. A modern study of the Sun Dance is Jorgensen 1972.

22. An introduction to locational theory is Haggett 1965.

23. See, for example, Royal Commission on Agriculture and Rural Life 1956. This report diagrams the location of towns and villages of various sizes in western Saskatchewan, showing patterning characteristic of Plains landscapes as predicted by locational theory. However, this pattern is the result of some eighty years of economic development that eliminated many early communities and permitted others to become larger.

24. There is, of course, an issue concerning Kraenzel's concept of "deficits" similar to
     that noted for Walter Webb: Kraenzel's idea that the inhabitants of the Plains deserve
     better is based on the assumption that, granted resources are refractory, correct
     adaptation will permit both human gratification and resource conservation. The
     possibility that people in regions like this, under our present economic system, must
     learn to live with less if they choose to remain in the region or if resources must be
     conserved, is difficult to acknowledge. The "out" is, of course, extensive govern-
     ment subsidy, which transfers the costs of the economic deficit onto more fortunate
     populations and regions. The problem is identical for the Third World ASAV
     countries. In other words, "social deficits" are inescapably rooted in resource
     deficits. Further difficulties in evaluating the social and economic position of
     populations in the drier parts of the United States arise when social indicators that
     define some measure of social well-being are compared with "hard" data on income,
     cultural facilities, and other signs of "progress" and urban amenities. David Smith
     1973 used data on "social pathology" and "socioeconomic well-being" to create a
     series of scores for all forty-eight contiguous states expressing social well-being.
     The Great Plains and southwestern states split into two large groups: the north and
     central states had consistently high scores, some among the highest in the nation;
     the southern Plains states had much lower scores, with some of the high scores being
     negative, like Texas with -536. That is, the index shows the effect of minority-group
     poverty populations in depressing "well-being" in the South; conversely, the more
     egalitarian rural society of thee northern and central states raises the index (Idaho
     has +606). Thus the "social deficits" of Kraenzel 1967 here to be reversed in the
     sense that, while sparse populations may limit access to certain facilities, it also may
     produce social harmony. Big cities are another factor: the low scores of Texas and
     Arizona are similar to those for certain eastern states with large cities, where crime,
     poverty, and so on depress the figures. Americans have always had two images of
     rurality: limited and sullen, or free of conflict and replete with bucolic enjoyment.
     (For other dicussions of cultural differences see Gastil 1975.)
     Little research has taken place on the problems of urban environments in ASAV
     lands. Perhaps architects, occupied with the problems of hot, dry, climate and
     energy-saving cooling methods, have done more than anyone else. For a review of
     current research on various urban aspects see Whitehead et al. 1988. Issues of
     domiciliary adaptation are in the long run less important ecologically than the
     demands that growing adaptations in ASAV lands place on the surrounding hinter-
     land and its friable resources.

Literature Cited and Consulted

Atherton, Lewis. 1961. *The Cattle Kings*. Bloomington: University of Indiana Press.
Bennett, John W. 1969. *Northern Plainsmen: Adaptive Strategy and Agrarian Life*.
     Chicago: Aldine.
_____.1976. *The Ecological Transition: Cultural Anthropology and Human Adap-
     tation*. New York: Pergamon Press.
_____.1982. *Of Time and the Enterprise: North American Family Farm Manage-
     ment in a Context of Resource Marginality*. Minneapolis: University of Minnesota
     Press.

Bennett, John W., Steven W. Lawry, and James C. Riddell. 1986. *Land Tenure and Livestock Development in Sub-Saharan Africa*. AID Special Evaluation Study 39. Washington, DC: U.S. Agency for International Development.

Blouet, Brian W. and Frederick C. Luebke. 1979. *The Great Plains: Environment and Culture*. Lincoln: University of Nebraska Press.

Caldwell, Warren W., C. Bertrand Schultz, and T. Mylan Stout. 1983. *Man and the Changing Environments in the Great Plains: A Symposium*. Lincoln: Nebraska Academy of Sciences.

Collingridge, David. 1982. *Critical Decision Making: A New Theory of Social Choice*. New York: St. Martin's Press.

Cottrell, Leonard. 1955. *Energy and Society: Relations of Energy, Social Change and Economic Development*. New York: McGraw-Hill.

Council on Environmental Quality. 1981. *Desertification of the United States*. Washington, DC: Council on Environmental Quality.

Cronon, William. 1983. *Changes in the Land: Indians, Colonists and the Ecology of New England*. New York: Hill and Wang.

Dregne, Harold E. 1970. *Arid Lands in Transition*. Washington, D.C.: American Association for the Advancement of Science.

_____. 1977. "Desertification of Arid Lands." *Economic Geography* 53: 325.

Ellen, Roy. 1982. *Environment, Subsistence and System: The Ecology of Small-Scale Social Formations*. New York: Cambridge University Press.

Eyre, L. Alan. 1988. "Population Pressure on Arid Lands: Is it Manageable?" In *Arid Lands: Today and Tomorrow*, ed. Emily C. Whitehead et al., 989–96. Boulder, CO: Westview Press.

Forde, C. Daryl. 1937. *Habitat, Economy and Society: A Geographical Introduction to Ethnology*. New York: Harcourt Brace.

Frantz, Joe B. and Julian Ernest Choate, Jr. 1966. *The American Cowboy: The Myth and the Reality*. Norman: University of Oklahoma Press.

Friesen, Gerald. 1984. *The Canadian Prairies: A History*. Lincoln: University of Nebraska Press.

Gastil, Raymond D. 1975. *Cultural Regions of the United States*. Seattle: University of Washington Press.

Geraghty, James J. et al. 1973. *Water Atlas of the United States*. Port Washington, NY: Water Information Center.

Gilles, Jere L. 1987. *Nomads, Ranchers, and Townsmen: Socio-Cultural Dimensions of Pastoralism Today*. American Association for the Advancement of Science Symposium. Boulder, CO: Westview Press.

Gulliver, P. H. 1955. *The Family Herds: A Study of Two Pastoral Tribes in East Africa, the Jie and Turkana*. London: Routledge and Kegan Paul.

Haggett, Peter. 1965. *Locational Analysis in Human Geography*. London: Arnold.

Hanks, Lucien. 1972. *Rice and Man: Agricultural Ecology in Southeast Asia*. Chicago: Aldine Atherton.

Hildebrand, David V. amd Geoffrey A.J. Scott. 1987. "Relation-ships between Moisture Deficiency and the Amount of Tree Cover on the Pre-agricultural Canadian Plains." *Prairie Forum* 12: 203–16.

Hodge, Carle and Peter C. Duisberg, eds. 1963. *Aridity and Man: The Challenge of Arid Lands in the United States*. Washington, DC: American Association for the Advancement of Science.

Jorgensen, Joseph P. 1972. *The Sun Dance Religion*. Chicago: University of Chicago Press.

Kirk, R. L. 1981. *Aboriginal Man Adapting: The Human Biology of Australian Aborigines*. New York: Oxford University Press.

Knowlton, Clark S., ed. 1964. *Indian and Spanish American Adjustments to Arid and Semiarid Environments*. Contribution 7, Committee on Desert and Arid Zone Research. Lubbock: Texas Technical College.

Kraenzel, Carl. 1967. "Deficit Creating Influences for Role Performance and Status Acquisition in Sparsely Populated Regions of the United States." In *Symposium on the Great Plains of North America*, ed. C. C. Zimmerman and S. Russell. Fargo: North Dakota Institute for Regional Studies.

Kroeber, Alfred L. 1953. *Cultural and Natural Areas of Native North America*. University of California Publications in American Archaeology and Ethnology 38. Berkeley: University of California Press.

Lonsdale, Richard E. and John H. Holmes. 1981. *Settlement Systems in Sparsely Populated Regions: The United States and Australia*. London: Pergamon Press.

Lotka, Alfred J. 1922. "Contributions to the Energetics of Evolution." *Proceedings of the National Academy of Sciences* 8: 147–51.

Malin, James C. 1984. *History and Ecology: Studies of the Grassland*. Ed. R. P. Swierenga. Lincoln: University of Nebraska Press.

McGinnies, William G. and William A. Laycock. 1988. "The Great American Desert— Perceptions of Pioneers, the Dustbowl, and the New Sodbusters." In *Arid Lands: Today and Tomorrow*, ed. Emily Whitehead et al. Boulder, CO: Westview Press.

Mead, Margaret. 1932. *Changing Culture of an Indian Tribe*. New York: Columbia University Press.

Moran, Emilio F. 1979. *Human Adaptibility: An Introduction to Ecological Anthropology*. North Scituate, MA: Duxbury Press.

Newman, Russell W. 1970. "Why is Man Such a Sweaty and Thirsty Animal: A Speculative Review." *Human Biology* 42: 12–27.

Odum, Howard T. 1970. *Environment, Power, and Society*. New York: Wiley-Interscience.

_____ .1983. *Systems Ecology: An Introduction*. New York: Wiley-Interscience.

Palliser, John. 1859. *Papers relative to the exploration by Captain Palliser of that portion of British North America which lies between the northern branch of the river Saskatchewan; and the frontier of the U.S.; and between the Red River and the Rocky Mountains*. Presented to both Houses of Parliament by Command of Her Majesty. London, June, 1859. Facsimile reprinting by Greenwood Press, NY, 1969.

Parkes, D.N., I.H. Burnley, and S.R. Walker. 1985. *Arid Zone Settlement in Australia: A Focus on Alice Springs*. Tokyo: United Nations University.

Petulla, Joseph M. 1977. *American Environmental History: The Exploitation and Conservation of Natural Resources*. San Francisco: Boyd and Fraser.

Powell, John W. 1962. *Report on the Lands of the Arid Regions of the United States*. Ed. Wallace Stegner. Cambridge, MA: Belknap Press.

Royal Commission on Agriculture and Rural Life. 1956. *Service Centers*. Rural Life Report 12. Regina: Government of Saskatchewan.

Shelford, Victor W. 1963. *The Ecology of North America*. Urbana: University of Illinois Press.

Smith, Henry Nash. 1950. *Virgin Land: The American West as Symbol and Myth*. Cambridge, MA: Harvard University Press.

Spooner, Brian and H.S. Mann, eds. 1982. *Desertification and Development: Dryland Ecology in Social Perspective*. New York: Academic Press.

Stegner, Wallace. 1962. *Wolf Willow: A History, a Story and a Memory of the Last Plains Frontier*. New York: Viking.

Turner, Frederick Jackson. 1958. *The Frontier in American History*. New York: Henry Holt.

Turton, D. 1977. "Response to Drought: The Mursi of Southwestern Ethiopia." In *Human Ecology in the Tropics*, ed. J. P. Garlick and R. W. J. Keay. New York: Halstead.

UNESCO. 1962. *The Problems of the Arid Zone*. Proceedings of the Paris Symposium. Paris: Arid Zone Research.

Webb, Walter Prescott. 1932. *The Great Plains*. New York: Ginn.

Whitehead, Emily C., Charles E. Hutchinson, Barbara N. Timmerman, and Robert F. Varady. 1988. *Arid Lands: Today and Tomorrow*. Boulder: Westview Press.

Worster, Donald. 1979. *Dust Bowl: The Southern Plains in the 1930s*. New York: Oxford University Press.

10

The Changing Socionatural System of Migratory Pastoralism in Eastern Africa: A Review of Literature to the 1980s

Introduction

Eastern Africa includes the following countries: Sudan, Ethiopia, Somalia, Kenya, and Tanzania, while the term *East* Africa refers mainly to Kenya and Tanzania. Significant numbers of migratory pastoralist people live in all five countries, and attempts at inducing these populations to relinquish their migratory way of life and to shift their distinctive mode of livestock production to one approximating sedentary ranching have been made repeatedly from the late nineteenth century to the present. Efforts to intensify livestock production, and the associated requirement of nucleated settlement, are not unique to eastern Africa, but have taken place elsewhere in Africa and in the Middle East and Central Asia, wherever substantial numbers of people raise livestock on transient pasturage. Such people represent the last large body of Old World human beings following a pattern of social and economic life differing from the now ubiquitous sedentarism. The fact that the pastoralist style of life has proved to be remarkably resistant to change is mainly due to the relative

This chapter is based on two monographs reporting on research done as an associate of the Land Tenure Center of the University of Wisconsin: "Political Ecology and Development Projects Affecting Pastoral People in East Africa" (Bennett 1984) and "Land Tenure and Livestock Development in Sub-Saharan Africa" (Bennett, Lawry, and Riddell 1986). Some material is also taken from my chapter in the book *Power and Poverty: Development and Development Projects in the Third World* (Bennett 1988). The research was underlain by two field trips to easternAfrican countries, the first sponsored by the American Association for the Advancement of Science and the second by the Land Tenure Center and USAID. Since the topic is dynamic, I have chosen to date the materials and conclusions.

geographic isolation of people exploiting marginal lands not easily or profitably used for crop production.

By the 1880s, the migratory utilization of pasturage was viewed as politically incompatible with the expectations of African colonial governments interested in preventing tribal disputes over land occupancy. After independence was achieved, the institutions of the new African nations required citizens to reside in one place, receive social services and intensively utilize resources in order to contribute maximally to the productivity of the country. Thus the fate of migratory pastoralists became tied to the political systems of the new nations in which they are now enclaved.

This process of change and adaptation is ecological insofar as a new relationship between humans, animals and the arid-semiarid grass and range lands must be worked out if the social disruption and environmental degradation so frequently associated with the economic development of pastoralism is to be minimized. Drastic disturbance of balanced socionatural systems has not ceased in the contemporary era of independent nations. From this perspective, "development" might be best viewed as a matter of achieving a new set of relationships between pastoralism and physical resources and between pastoralists, their agriculturalist neighbors, and government agencies. This cannot be achieved overnight, nor exclusively by means of development projects, but will emerge as part of the adaptive evolution of populations and social institutions.

Pastoralism and Nomadism

We shall attempt to avoid the use of the terms "nomadism" and "nomads" since there is no one-to-one association between the migratory way of life and livestock raised in the pastoralist manner. Table 10.1 illustrates the relationships between the relevant terms and concepts as developed by ethnologists.

In popular usage, the term "pastoralism" refers to the relatively mobile adaptations concerning pasture use in cell 6. Technically speaking, the term should apply as well to the modes in cell 5. "Nomadism" refers to a mode of production that requires a population to move regularly and often in search of food or resources and to permit their livestock to breed while moving, so to speak. Thus, 'nomadic pastoralism' would refer to those groups in cell 6 who move often or continually. Livestock raised by people in cells 2 and 3 are usually of different breeds or varieties that those produced by people in cells 5 and 6. In this chapter the people in cells 5 and 6 are called *migratory pastoralists*, but obviously they need not be continuously nomadic. 'Transhumant' is the term most often applied to people who live in more or less permanent villages but go out on grazing expeditions in the local dry season (cell 5) and who operate livestock regimes based on permanent agricultural settlements.

Table 10.1
Pastoral and Nomadic Economies

Settlement Types	Food-Collecting Bands and Tribes	Crop Farming Village Dwellers	Livestock Raising Peoples
	(1)	(2)	(3)
Sedentary, nucleated settlement	Rare or extinct tribes (e.g., Northwest Pacific Coast Indians)	Crop raising often combined with livestock	Ranching, dairying, etc.
	(4)	(5)	(6)
Mobile, transient settlement	Hunter-gatherer bands (e.g., Bushmen of the Kalahari)	Combinations of seasonal cropping plus livestock, with wet-dry seasonal movement	Regular, frequent movement for pasture use: nomadic pastoralists

In the earlier literature on migratory pastoralism, the problem of settlement versus nomadism was generally handled via the concept of sedentarization. This implies that to become sedentary, that is, to accept fixed settlement of some kind, usually a village, is a major evolutionary change from one mode of life to another. This concept was based on nineteenth-century theories of evolution of subsistence modes of tribal peoples. In fact, most pastoralist peoples have had both sedentary and migratory sections or groups, and changing from one mode to another is relatively common. The migratory habits of pastoralists are matters of economic necessity, but the "nomads" are fully aware of settled life and have repeatedly demonstrated their capacity to adapt to this form of settlement when the occasion or necessity arises (see Ole Saibull 1974 and Ndagala 1982 for a discussion of Masai "sedentarization").

Still, if a group which has been moving frequently begins to accept a degree of settled life, there will be consequences for the social organization and daily routines, or, as P.T.W. Baxter observed for the Ethiopian Boran people, "sedentarization tends to narrow the range and alter the texture of social relationships" (1975, 224). This occurs with acceptance of crop agriculture, in which close relationships tend to develop among a small number of neighboring farmers. On the other hand, in the migratory mode, kinship relationships and other social patterns become geographically wide ranging. However, it should be remembered that such changes are reversible: pastoralists, as cosmopolites, are remarkably flexible and can modify social relations as they alter their mode of production.

The main institutional differences between a transient adaptation and a settled one pertain to land tenure, inheritance and other customs concerning property ownership and transmittal. Such institutions are intimately adapted to the transient mode of life and production, although they are not completely resistive to change. Of the set, land tenure is perhaps the most crucial, since the communal use of range means that the notion of freehold ownership of defined tracts cannot function. In its place, the herding group will have rights to use particular tracts at certain times; others will have rights to use the same pasture land at other times of the year. There is no simple way to combine this system of overlapping customary usufruct tenure with the Western institution of legal freehold tenure. In any event, once the nation-state comes into existence, land tenure becomes a matter of constitutional control and guarantee. The customary usufruct systems, regularly altered as herding groups interact, become impossible to maintain or tolerate. Similar difficulties pertain to the taxation of land or animals (since, for example, animals can be detached from herds, and, in severe droughts, "lent" to associates in more fortunate areas).

Since pastoralists generally inhabit marginal lands, they are familiar with fluctuating climate and variable soil and pasturage and with the uncertainties these bring to the production process. A variety of defensive social and economic strategies have evolved through the years to cope with these conditions. Migratory life itself permits adjustment through moving to a more fortunate locale. Other adaptations are technical, including traditional ways to minimize the effects of bovine diseases and cope with drought (see D.L. Johnson 1973 for a description of how Sahelian pastoralists coped with drought prior to government intervention). Significant strategies also exist in the social system and involve exchange relationships with friends and relatives. In special circumstances, the "nomads" can raise crops and engage in trading and other sources of income.

A Model of Change in Migratory Pastoralism

The model is historical: Figure 10.1 presents the chief events and processes in, mainly, East African pastoralism on a generalized time scale beginning with the precolonial era in the early nineteenth century, passing through the colonial era, and culminating in the era of independence in the early 1980s. The objective is to show how the basic institutions of production were influenced by government intervention and how this in turn affected the ecological aspects of pastoral socioeconomy.

Beneath the time scale are listed two basic strategic systems or institutions used by most migratory pastoralists to manage livestock that appear to represent the key to the problem of change. These are, first, a form of "communal" land tenure of pasture utilization combined with, second, ownership and management of the herds by individuals (that is, not by collectivities like tribes or clans). Producers move with the herds at intervals, in varying patterns of combinations of semipermanent residence and encampments, in order to maximize the availabilities of pasture in a droughty or seasonably variable environment. If herds are going to move at intervals, then it is impossible to assign permanent "ownership" of land; in its place will arise a complex system of customary usufruct rights to use land (and wells, etc.) at certain times and under certain conditions—the whole subject to renegotiation. The individual cattle owner's right to graze his stock over broad areas was derived from his membership in a herding group—or possibly a tribal subsection—that held customary rights in those areas; hence the term "communal."

The combination of communal tenure and individual herd ownership has an inherent potential for abuse of the range; that is, the conditions envisaged by the "tragedy of the commons" model can emerge given appropriate conditions. That such conditions appeared at times in the precolonial era can be assumed—there is no intention here of glorifying

Figure 10.1
CHANGE AND TRANSITION IN AFRICAN PASTORALIST PRODUCTION
TIME SCALE

1910	1910–present
Basic Institutions	

This combination has a potential for resource abuse if controls are absent.	"Communal" resource tenure ←————————→	Toward mixed systems of resource tenure, requiring restriction of grazing freedom
	Private herd ownership ←————————→	no change

Preintervention Systems of Resource Management and Production	**Postintervention Systems of Resource Management and Production**
1. *Range management* tended to be conservationist because herders agreed to respect mutual needs for resources necessary to maintain a style and volume of production over a given period of time (facilitated by low population density, "natural systems" constraints, reciprocity and redistribution, and other factors).	1. *Range management* tends to be abusive because herders no longer maintain or initiate agreements pertaining to resource and production allocation and control and have restricted choice of pasture (facilitated by population growth, income diversification, technological change, markets, development projects, and alternative land uses.
2. *Production* was maintained by the herd-owning household and other primary social organizations and regulated by collective agreement and mutual constraints, within and between herding units (facilitated by authority systems, styles of negotiation, economic interdependency, participation in pursuits other than livestock production, and others).	2. *Entrepreneurship* emerges. Herd ownership, when unrestrained by collective controls, becomes entrepreneurial, i.e., private rather than collective benefits are "maximized" (facilitated by breakdown of local and/or hierarchical authority systems, increased reliance on external economic forces and inputs, and others).
3. *Human and animal populations* were relatively static and not affected by factors extraneous to the physical and social constraints.	3. *Human and animal populations* fluctuate and change in response to factors extraneous to physical and social constraints.

the ecology of precolonial pastoralists. Nevertheless, the herd owners worked out mutual arrangements to handle various "commons" management problems. Both by negotiation and pushing and shoving, understandings were reached among tribes or herding groups as to mutual needs for pasture and water—understandings flexible enough to compensate for variability of climate and range conditions in arid-semiarid regions. Armed resistance or raiding was often resorted to. Depending on pressure on pasture resources, the rights-holding groups had greater or lesser control over their members' grazing practices. Among individual herders "herd-friend" relationships—often kinship-based—could develop that operated so that if one of the pair was affected by serious drought, the other, at some distance, and in a less droughty location, would take a portion of the other man's herd temporarily until conditions changed. "Payment" would be taken as a portion of the cash crop.

These and other techniques, functioning in a low-fertility and low-density population, were reasonably effective in maintaining an ecological balance among humans, animals, and land and water resources. The balance was probably helped along by recurrent natural crises: animal disease, water shortages, extreme droughts. The pastoralists were never in complete control of the situation; it was simply that, over time, a reasonable continuity of production was sustained.

Changes introduced in this socionatural system by colonialism, and their prolongation into the era of independence, had the effect of disturbing the balance among the human, animal, and physical components. Tribal warfare was banned. Communal-usufruct land and water rights were modified in a variety of ways. Each country developed its own particular mix of tenures and uses for land—some traditional, others European, and others innovated to meet particular needs. Such changes had the effect of restricting pasturage for migratory pastoral production, introducing competition for range and relative overproduction of animals and overgrazing when animal management strategies did not change to cope with altered resource conditions. The system of customary agreements among herd owners and groups broke down in many areas, since the physical basis of these arrangements changed or disappeared. Pressures for more off-sale of animals has driven many herders out of business and encouraged others to shift toward a ranching form of production, creating a new entrepreneurial class, and this means a kind of kin-group ranching in which a vigorous herd owner mobilizes his relatives as a labor force, thus driving out many of the smaller herd owners, who, if lucky, become workers for the new rancher boss. The collective benefits sought under the traditional system are replaced by an attempt to maximize individual gain, further disrupting customary arrangements. This process affects the distribution of the human population changes without relationship to the former ecological balances. "Excess" population—people displaced by the changes—leave the range areas and move into towns, seeking employment. Finally, herd size is no longer governed by collective controls operating in accordance with climate and range conditions but by the search for individual gain and commercial opportunities.

The predictable results for the resource base—visible everywhere in eastern Africa by 1980—were chronic shortages of water and severe overgrazing. These conditions generated a demand in the local governments for better conservation, but, at the same time, these objectives were subverted by the escalating demands for more production. Parastatal companies that concentrated commercial cattle production in intensively managed locations were another response, but these companies have not been markedly efficient or profitable. It is possible that some degree of control can be reintroduced into the system, and, as this is being edited in the 1990s, some experiments in more intensive management of herds, range, and water have appeared—but these usually introduce higher costs of production, costs which African countries find difficult to meet with their growing populations and increasing demands for products of all kinds.

A Note on Pastoralist Demography

Table 10.2 gives data assembled by Stephen Sandford (1976a, 1976b) on the populations of various pastoralist groups in Africa south of the Sahara for the period covered. These figures contain some implications for policy. Pastoralists constitute an unevenly distributed population and mode of production in the countries of eastern Africa, ranging from 70 percent of the Somalian population to 1 percent or less for Tanzania. This suggests that there can be no single solution to the pastoralist issue; it must be handled by the respective countries in their own ways, with concern for demographic significance or the lack of same.

Table 10.2
Eastern Africa Pastoralist Populations, ca. 1970

Country	Pastoralist Populations	Percent of Total Country Population
Angola	500,000	8%
Ethiopia	1,600,000	4%
Kenya	1,500,000	12%
Somalia	1,700,000	70%
Sudan	3,900,000	22%
Tanzanian	100,000	1% or less

Sources: Angola: Sandford's estimate based on Carvalho 1974; Ethiopia: Sandford's estimate based on unpublished Ethiopian data; Kenya: FAO Expert Consultation 1972; Somalia: FAO Group Fellowship Study 1972; Sudan: FAO Group Fellowship Study n.d.; Tanzania: FAO Expert Consultation 1972.

However, the number of pastoralists in any country will not necessarily correlate with the degree of concern or attention paid them. Botswana, in southern Africa, with only about 2 percent of the national population classifiable as migratory pastoralists, has apparently had more success with its cooperative ranching schemes than other countries; this is due in large part to the fact that important members of the national government come from the pastoralist minority, and to the fact that the majority of farmers are also cattle raisers. This has encouraged more intensive planning and experimentation with circumscribed grazing regimes, with careful attention to the needs and interests of the tribal groups themselves. Since the majority of peasant agriculturalists in Botswana also raise livestock, pastoralist traditions and interests pervade the general culture even though only a small minority are continually transient. (For a study of a typical Botswana mixed farming-pastoralist development scheme, see Gulbrandsen 1980).

Kenya, with 12 percent of its population classifiable as migratory pastoralists (mainly Masai, Samburu, Turkana, Somali, Rendille, Borana, and Gabbra tribal entities), has experimented with a variety of livestock, grazing and cooperative production schemes, but most of its national development investment has gone into intensive cultivation, commercial and private ranching, and export crop production. Pastoralists in Kenya account for a small proportion of national income, whereas in an agrarian society like Botswana, the livestock output of the minority nomads, plus the majority farmer-pastoralists, account for as much as 30–35 percent.

In Sudan pastoralists constitute 22 percent of the national total, but this fraction represents nearly 100 percent of the population of the western half of the country. The government has done relatively little with its pastoralists from the standpoint of sedentarization or ranching schemes. Most agrarian development programs in Sudan have concentrated upon large districts in the central and southern portions of the country, where crop-livestock farmers can benefit from irrigation, improved roads, and marketing schemes. Many of these projects involve pastoralists since the affected tracts cut into traditional dry-wet season grazing migration routes. Projects like those in the vicinity of El Obeid have attempted to organize symbiotic relationships among pastoralists and farmers, with limited success.

Tanzania's development work with its Masai groups in the northern part of the country has attracted more attention than the relatively small numbers of pastoralists might warrant, as compared with other countries. This is because the region west of Arusha in the Tanzanian Masai heartland has been the site of many technical livestock projects, villagization experiments and regional development programs. These projects have received careful scrutiny by a large number of livestock, anthropological and rural development specialists over a period of fifteen years and have influenced the literature on pastoralist development.

Aspects of Research

Knowledge of pastoralism as a way of life has a foundation in studies made by ethnologists during the past forty years. Migratory pastoralists were viewed originally as a detached segment of mankind: an autonomous society with prehistoric origins and representing the type of the isolated, culturally integral tribe (for a discussion, see Galaty 1981b). The focus of interest in these earlier studies was on spatial movement and the way this movement affected social organization and subsistence patterns (for typical tribal monographs, see Evans-Pritchard 1940, Gulliver 1955, Lewis 1972). Research in the 1950s and 1960s shifted to a more specialized ecological inquiry into how balance was maintained, under presumably undisturbed conditions, between the human population, animals, and pasture resources.[1]

Following independence, the new governments of East Africa endeavored to convert pastoralists to sedentary livestock producers. Such projects were in the main continuations of colonial experiments. The schemes rarely fulfilled expectations and disrupted the relationships between pastoralists and their cultivator neighbors and associates.

These experiences led country governments and the international development assistance agencies in the 1970s to promote research designed to determine the reasons for failure of the schemes. In addition to research, the development agencies sponsored a series of conferences to permit an exchange of data and views. These efforts by anthropologists and livestock and range specialists contributed to the literature on pastoralism as an econo-ecological type. They also supplied a realistic view of pastoralists as people required to cope with greatly altered geographic, economic, and political conditions (for a symposium volume illustrating this broadened perspective, see Galaty, Aronson and Salzman 1981).

The relative failure of development schemes and projects was important for two reasons: first, in many African countries, pastoralists were an important source of animal products and nutrition; hence, their activities deserved encouragement, not inhibition. Second, the persistent failure of development schemes was a matter of concern to ministries and technical assistance agencies because of their cost, and because the schemes represented "failures" of planning. Success in agricultural development never comes easily; however, it was harder to achieve in the livestock programs involving pastoralists than for other modes of production. Clearly, reasons had to be sought.

In many respects, development schemes attempted in eastern Africa became a testing ground for pastoralist development everywhere; likewise, much of the innovative research took place in this region,[2] although valuable work has also been done in West Africa, North Africa and the Middle East.

Much of the research of the 1970s focused on the difficulty of encouraging pastoralists to increase the offtake of animals for commercial sales, and the way this problem has led to excessive size of herds and consequent overgrazing: seemingly a classic case of "tragedy of the commons" (e.g., Hardin 1968; Brokenshaw, Horowitz, and Scudder 1977). That is, development schemes that were supposed to reduce herd size and increase offtake, thereby permitting a more adaptive response to grazing restrictions, appeared to have the opposite effect: larger herds and a static or reduced offtake. Another factor related to this was the tendency for pastoralists to fail to increase production when prices rise: the so-called "negative price response" (Low 1980). Research on this behavioral pattern showed that pastoralists distrusted development initiatives that promised financial rewards or enchanced resources but failed to deliver. Moreover, intermittent droughts led pastoralists to maintain large herds in order to retain some animals as breeders in case of losses. These and other factors have persuaded pastoralists to "rationally preserve a measure of traditional production strategies, geared to subsistence rather than markets" (Livingstone 1977).

A second major theme in the research of the 1970s and 1980s was an attempt to view migratory pastoralism as a system larger in scope than a single tribe or a group of herd owners speaking a common language. This came about as a result of the growing realization that one major reason for the disappointing results of so many development projects was their concentration on a few segments of an interconnected whole. By intervening in one segment, key processes of linkage and dependence were interrupted, leading to system breakdown. The most obvious evidence was the abuse of pasturelands and the failure of programs for reducing the number of livestock to correct this abuse. Much of the later development-inspired research and the conferences were devoted to defining the dimensions of pastoralism and its relationships to other economic and social sectors.

Eastern Africa has a transitional economy in the sense that the indigenous population is required to use cash as the major medium of exchange, even though an important fraction of production continues to be used for subsistence. The pastoralist population (like all agriculturalists in the developing countries) thus finds itself in the middle: its successful subsistence economy, plus its long-term barter exchange with townsmen and cultivators, has been greatly modified by commercial relations. While pastoralists have always sold a proportion of their stock, recent economic change, plus insistent development programs of the country governments, requires them to sell more in order to obtain the money they need to live and to retain a place in the regional and national networks. This means that governments need to find a niche for pastoralists to permit them to obtain substitutes for food obtained from animals. Equally important is some means for them to invest their cash income from animals in productive enterprise. Investments in real estate, gold and houses are typical of some groups, such as Baggara pastoralists in Sudan, but not of others, particularly the Masai of Kenya and Tanzania, who have clung to conservative tribal economics. Unfortunately, invest-ments in herds alone do not yield the leverage needed in a modernizing economy.

On the other hand, involvement of pastoralists in commercial systems has been found to increase income disparity among the herd owners. The larger owners find it easier to enter the modern economy and many are amassing wealth and exerting control over property, land, and labor. Smaller herd owners lose ground and turn to wage labor in the towns and cities. Many of these part-time pastoralists receive the backing of rela-tives who continue to raise livestock; thus, as Anders Hjort concluded, pastoralism in some regions supports the modern economic sector by providing partial subsistence for the families of wage laborers (1981, 141).

Others turn to farming as a way into the new economic system. Crop raising was never foreign to pastoralist tribes, nearly all of whom have had cultivator sections or have resorted to farming during periods of drought or other disturbance of the livestock regime (for a study, see Haaland 1972). Again, the wealthy herd-owning kin groups invest in farmland and even subsidize village cultivators in other tribes to produce forage for their herds. Poorer herd owners, on the other hand, tend to become transformed into small-holder peasants who exist as marginal producers or who are caught up in agrarian development programs or agribusiness schemes. There were no reliable statistics in the early 1980s to tell us how common this was or what its effect on livestock production over time might be. Since pastoralism is in a transitional era in Eastern African economic development, it is difficult to predict final outcomes. However, increasing wealth for the few and the creation of extensive patron-client systems among the wealthy and the poor seem to be the order of the day.

Some development programs were designed to integrate pastoralists into dryland crop farming communities as livestock producers, users of farm-raised forage and as mixed farmers. The best known of these schemes was the ASAL (arid-semiarid land) approach in Kenya (Ngutter 1979). Where pastoralists like some Masai are moving into crop raising as an important adjunct to livestock, the ASAL programs would permit the Kenya groups to receive seed for drought-resistant crops, loans for development of difficult soils and facilities for developing exchange relationships with local marginal farmer-settlers in the region. (In the 1970s in both Kenya and Tanzania there were hostilities between the Masai and such newcomers). Aside from the ASAL program in Kenya, the Sudanese experimented with integrated pastoralist-farmer programs in western Sudan and the El Obeid and Abyei regions for a number of years, and a similar project was inaugurated in the upper Blue Nile, where pastoralist refugees from Ethiopia are interacting with local farmers. These integrated programs have their difficulties, but they offer the first approach to pastoralist development that appears to take account of the changing realities of resource distribution and modes of production in eastern Africa.

As pastoralists become part of more complex modern systems of exchange, the research topics extend beyond the classic ones of social organization, herds, ecological ratios or range and water management. Pastoralist peoples must find a place in the emerging national social systems; hence, they need to be considered in the contexts of employment, income levels, standard of living, socioeconomic class and power positions, job training and skills, and education. As I. Nkinyangi (1981) showed for Kenya, education became a major factor in social and occupational advancement, and pastoralists were increasingly disadvantaged since their mobility made it difficult for them to send children to school. The government tried a number of experiments to assist them: waiving tuition in the boarding schools; providing mobile schools in automotive trailers; and special fellowships. None of these worked very well, partly because the government was unwilling or unable to provide funds for the extra costs associated with special or unusual facilities. The Kenya Masai did not use the facilities, Nkinyangi felt, mainly because of the inadequate instruction, relatively high fees, poor food and unreliable transportation. Conflicts between cultivator and pastoralist children were also serious. However, these may be transitional phenomena; there are signs of the Masai moving toward education and other participative involvements.

In conclusion, note should be made of the "cattle complex" worked out by Melville Herskovits (1926) and other anthropologists in the 1920s and 1930s. The concept was based on the anthropological approach known as the "ethnographic present," which refers to the reconstruction of patterns of native life previous to substantial European or American contact and to the presentation of the resulting depiction as contemporary. This appears to be what Herskovits did in his 1920s writings on Africa. Obviously, in his day, aspects of the traditional system were indeed operative. However, vital elements of pastoralism were ignored—in particular, the agronomic sophistication of the native regimes: their intricate cultural ecology of livestock and pasture use and management, their familiarity with markets and the commercial value of their animals (aside from or in addition to their insistence on the wealth factor of herds), and their skill with trading and symbiotic relations with cultivators and townsmen.

East Africa as a Socionatural System

Academic historians of East Africa have customarily interpreted the principal movements and events in political and social terms. Among these, the slave trade, colonial repression and colonization are viewed as the major forces affecting indigenous populations and shaping their reactions. A focus on the distinctive problems of indigenous production systems, especially pastoralism, calls attention to a different set of factors that, while brought into being by political and social conditions, may have been of more direct influence. Helge Kjekshus (1977) referred to these as the collapse of a "man-controlled ecological system." Whether cause or effect, there is no doubt that the European investiture of East Africa was followed by a series of changes in the physical environment and animal and human populations. Disease, population fluctuation, disordered grazing patterns and famine were all frequent events in the late nineteenth and early twentieth centuries. The recurrent human famines were viewed by colonialists as cyclical or normal in the indigenous socionatural system, since they were unwilling or unable to acknowledge the extent to which European intervention contributed to the problems. Modern development programs could be redefined as a continuation of the attempt to recover a reasonable balance in human-natural relationships, instead of ways to increase production or income.

There seems little doubt that the interpretations of East African ecological history contributed by Kjekshus, Ford and others contain elements of truth. However, it is a matter of various levels of causation: for example, while Europeans may or may not have directly caused all animal and human diseases, their activities in disrupting delicate balances of human and animal populations and resources were responsible for a general reorientation of ecological relations. The slave trade, thought by many historians to be a primary factor in socionatural breakdown, probably had less significance: population reduction or disruption of production do not appear, in the analysis of available accounts, to have been of sufficient magnitude to account for the disasters beginning in 1890. Also significant is the fact that the slave trade had diminished to a trickle by 1890 and was stopped shortly after. The major changes were subsequent to this.

The ecological history of East Africa provides one background theme for the interpretation of pastoralist development: attempts at changing livestock regimes among indigenous populations must contend with a heritage of fear and distrust based on the feeling that European intervention produces disasters. Since the country governments have, on the whole, continued to follow development policies with roots in the past, the reluctance of pastoralists and cultivators to accept such methods with enthusiasm is understandable—even when they value and desire improvements such as animal health measures, tractors, marketing facilities, and the like.

Thus, it would appear that foreign attempts at understanding these complex socionatural systems have distorted their meaning and complexity, for good as well as questionable intentions. These distortions have accompanied, and in many instances created, havoc in these systems; this appears to have been a continuous process, not a recent episode.

Perceptions of Pastoralism

Some observers of the eastern African scene attribute the difficulties encountered by developers to attitudes forged in the elites of the sedentary indigenous societies, combined with Western concepts of the culture and evolutionary status of nomadic societies. One source of Western concepts has already been mentioned: the 1920s idea of the "East African cattle complex." This conception held that migratory pastoralists lived in a world apart from other producers of agricultural commodities, insofar as they raised livestock for wealth, prestige and subsistence, rather than for monetary gain. In the course of research associated with development programs, this conception has been greatly modified and largely replaced by a more sophisticated concept of pastoralism as a complex system involving many economic activities and involved in markets and commercial relationships in varying ways and degrees.

Peter Rigby noted that up to the 1960s the principal conception of pastoralism held by many scholars, government officials, and Western livestock specialists was related to "conservatism," meaning the stiff resistance by pastoralists to efforts to commercialize their livestock regimes (for an example, see Shorter 1974). In reviewing accounts of pastoralism dating from the 1960s, Rigby noted that these accounts attributed the conservatism to sociocultural phenomena: "it could be generalized that the conservatism attributed to predominantly pastoral societies is thought to derive from intrinsic features of their social systems: their economic and social organization and their cultural values. External factors are recognized as contributing to conservatism, but are assigned a secondary place" (1969, 43-44). He continues, "These generalizations compete with an equally popular but contradictory one. Lurking behind all but the most sophisticated theories of social change at the macro-historical level is the idea that there is some kind of natural evolution from one kind of economy to another."

Thus resistance to innovation among pastoralists was attributed to distinctive patterns of culture or social organization, and that this idea in turn was probably based on the nineteenth century theory which held that pastoralism was a residue from an earlier stage, or that it was possibly an offshoot of indigenous development, representing an end product of one line of evolution and therefore not amenable to modification. This theory was elaborated by anthropologists in different ways, with considerable disagreement; for example, C.D. Forde in 1934 argued that pastoralism was inherently unstable since pastoralists concentrated on only one mode of production, which could, therefore, easily make its transition to combined farming-livestock modes (1934, 403). Others reversed the sequence, holding that pastoralism was a late, specialized offshoot of crop agriculture (see Johnson 1973, for a summary of this view).

Randall Baker observed in the 1970s that evolutionary ideas continued to influence planners and administrators in the country governments and development agencies: "Initially, early administrators and travellers framed their account of the pastoral peoples in terms of noble-savage imagery, thus establishing a trail of false mysticism which bedevils interpretations of pastoral behaviour to the present day" (1974, 3). He continued by noting that the idea is akin to the concept of the gypsy who lives a romantic, free life, refusing to put down roots in settled civilization. We should add that such romantic images always have a counter-image: people who refuse to accept the norms of civilized life can be seen as untrustworthy, thieving, petty criminals. Such attitudes prevented an understanding of the complex land tenure and ecological systems of pastoralists. By the post-World War II period, Baker noted, this romantic mystique had changed to the conceptions of irrational production and resource management and resistance to innovation.

Monod developed the criminality theme in his 1975 symposium volume, noting that Europeans were particularly concerned with this, due to their awareness of frequent cattle raiding and tribal feuding by pastoralists. He suggests that these attitudes may have psychological origins in European peasant fears of predatory nomads, as well as more specific and recent experiences by settlers in East Africa. (Perhaps the attitudes might even go back to the Middle Ages and the Mongol invasions!)

C. Widstrand (1973) in a paper on the Kenya Special Rural Development Program and its involvement with pastoralists described still another facet of the interpretations of pastoralism made by sedentary peoples: paternalism. A paternalistic attitude, like the earlier romantic images, is double-edged: a feeling that pastoral peoples are a special charge, a burden, and that one must do his best for them, coupled with a fear of their unpredictable or childish behavior. This is translated into action in the form of apparently benevolent development programs which limit the mobility of pastoralists but fail to compensate for the resource deprivation such schemes have usually caused. "Native reserves," "block grazing schemes," and "group ranches" are seen by Widstrand as implementations of a subjectively determined policy to contain pastoralists, remove their dangers, avoid open repression and help them accommodate to modernity-but without really doing so.

Clare Oxby provided additional details. She described the main arguments used by governments—colonial and postcolonial—to justify interventions with pastoralists (1975, 4) as including just about everything: paternalism, economic assistance, fears and need for containment and pacification, needs for settlement of boundary problems, facilitation of relations with government, giving them a more responsible role in the national economy, etc. Such grandiose objectives were based on historical experiences, and, like all such judgments, were colored by values and prejudices as well as rationalizations and guilt from the colonial era, or resentments of barbarous tribals on the part of villagers and city elites. The economic-assistance theme received substantial reinforcement from World Bank and USAID sources in the mid-1970s, with their emphases on alleviation of poverty and guarantees of "basic needs." Pastoralists were viewed as "poor" because they lacked possessions; however, from the point of view of peasant smallholders, pastoralists were the rich, since they possessed a store of capital: animals. If they were indigent in some localities, it was because of drought or development programs, not some intrinsic defect in their mode of production. If they had been dangerous and unruly, it was because they needed land to permit expansion of herds—itself a source of misunderstandings, since with communal land tenure no one was supposed to "own" or "appropriate" land. The attitudinal dynamics of the situation closely resemble those of American settlers and military on the American Western frontier in the latter half of the nineteenth century, and these are inevitable formations in imperialist frontier situations.

The ease-of-administration argument for pastoralist development is an especially common one and lies beneath, in particular, the elaborate programs followed by Tanzania with regard to the Masai. Generally this argument is spelled out as a matter of providing social services and agricultural inputs to pastoralists, who must undergo sedentarization. Such arguments are based in part on evolutionary dicta: that by sedentarizing pastoralists, one turns them into agriculturalists, from which they pass to the third stage: townsmen or industrial workers. The "villagization" attempts (as they were known in northern Tanzania) were thus viewed as historically inevitable by the socialist reformers of the Nyerere regime. Such conceptions ignore the fact that pastoralists in the Middle East and Africa have become familiar with manual labor, taxi driving, oil-well rigging, factory work, and so on without the transitional stages of settlement mandated by the evolutionary theorists.

The responsibility and obligation theme must be taken seriously; however, the anthropological commentators and the pro-pastoralist spokesmen have not always shown an awareness of the basic imperatives of the nation-state framework. A note of ethnic preservationism has been present in some of the anthropological defenses of migratory pastoralism as a way of life, and this perspective has generated considerable controversy, within anthropology and between anthropologists and development specialists. Modern nations do require their citizens to be incorporated into productive activities which have some relationship to the needs of the whole population: such demands will be made and must be met in some degree. The alternative would seem to be a tribal reserve system in which the ethnic group is kept in a kind of living museum status, which creates persistent social and political difficulties for everyone.

A History of Development Initiatives in East Africa to 1980

England, Germany, and France competed for domination of eastern Africa during the latter half of the nineteenth century, the issue reaching a stage of resolution in the late 1880s and 1890s with the assignment of Tanganyika to Germany; Kenya and Sudan to Britain; and Madagascar to France. World War I saw a shift of control in Tanganyika from Germany to England; France remained in control of the island until World War II, and its subsequent independence. The countries of the Horn had a brief Italian period.

British policies dealing with Kenya can be summarized. J. Lamphear (1976) examined the relations of the Turkana to the British in the period around 1900, when the various bovine diseases became epidemic and the tribes resorted to raiding in order to replace depleted herds. The British responded with punitive expeditions which stopped much of the raiding, but also disrupted Turkana movements for pasturage, aggravating their difficulties. British policies with respect to the Masai in the same period were detailed by, among others, R. Waller (1976). As a result of the rinderpest epidemics, many Masai turned to agriculture, both in the southern semiarid range areas and also in more suitable lands farmed by Kikuyu and Kamba. The latter movements were based on familiarity with the region due to the Masai custom of permitting their young men to seek farm labor employment among these tribes in the past. However, the farming episode had some aspects of an invasion and was occasionally resisted by the agricultural tribes. As herds increased, the mutual hostilities did likewise, requiring British intervention. The upshot was a curious alliance between the British and the Masai, in which the latter served as a kind of mercenary army, raiding other tribal groups with a history of depredation. These activities served to create an enmity for the Masai that persists today.

E.R. Turton (1972) detailed the history of groups of Somali tribesmen in Kenya in the period 1893 to the 1960s. By 1919, British punitive expeditions had succeeded in pacifying these people and pushing them into the far northeast region where they would presumably constitute less danger to Turkana and other indigenous Kenya peoples. However, Somali never accepted pacification and continued to follow their historical pasturage routes down to and into the period of independence. British attempts at corralling Somali into block grazing schemes were also resisted, and the persistent hostility of the Somali to the British culminated in 1960 in a serious secession movement of these people, echoes of which continue to be heard in northern Kenya.

The evolution of British policies in Kenya (see Mighot-Adholla and Little 1981) featured attempts to develop superior grazing facilities and water resources, but most of the measures emphasized conservation and less intensive use of pasturelands, which they perceived as undergoing progressive deterioration. Occasionally, the British admitted that this deterioration was largely caused by colonial disruption of land-use patterns. However, on the whole, the traditional system was faulted as the cause of the environmental problems. Pastoralist livestock was ignored as unsuitable for commercial production, and due to bovine diseases, was rigorously quarantined so as to shield European cattle from infestation (a policy that had little effect). This also meant that no attempt was made to develop markets for pastoralist livestock; indeed, in many districts, efforts were made to prevent them from entering sales programs favoring livestock farmers or British ranchers. The period of World War II marked a change in policy to the extent that the British embarked on a campaign to encourage African agriculturalists, including pastoralists, to intensify commercial food production for war preparation; this effort, however, had little effect on the migratory pastoralists due to restrictions on pasture availability and to lack of interest on the part of pastoralists in increased commercial sales, since they had less need for cash to buy cultivator-oriented tools and urban consumer goods.

Continued deterioration of rangeland led the British to inaugurate their first coordinated development program aimed at pastoralism, and the lineal ancestor of all subsequent development plans down into the contemporary period: the "Ten- Year Plan: 1946–55," which was based on a resettlement scheme for the semiarid regions of Kenya and Tanganyika. The activities included nearly all of the specific targets of later plans: rinderpest control, locust control, tsetse eradication, borehole development, irrigation, erosion control, reforestation, rural road construction, and some marketing boards and programs. Pastoralist and semicultivator groups were moved into new areas to control overuse. The plan conceived of the problems of pastoralism and range areas as essentially those of conservation of physical resources, caused by overstocking. The pastoralist population was considered a vehicle of deterioration and abuse, and secondarily as a body of people deserving education or assistance in overcoming the disruption of their livelihood induced by colonial intervention.

By the mid-1950s, the Ten-Year Plan evolved into a somewhat different approach, based on concepts of resource management and land tenure. It was considered that the pastoralist style of management of communal grazing was inherently defective or nonrational. In 1954, the Ten-Year Plan was supplemented by the Swynnerton Plan which aimed at the introduction of private land ownership among pastoralists coupled with encouragement for a shift to cultivation of export crops. Excess pastoralist population was urged to migrate to cities and enter the labor force. Field projects included the earlier types, but also included more emphasis on marketing of livestock, and also the first intensive attempts to reduce herd size and control grazing movements by introducing block territories for particular sets of herd owners and tribal sections. Such attempts to limit migratory pasturage were not entirely new, since the British had tried them in northern Kenya earlier in the century, and were more in line with pacification or corralling policies, rather than as attempts to improve grazing resources or adjust herd size to carrying capacity. Most of these schemes had dwindled to inconspicuous efforts by 1960, but the period also saw the beginning of the second major facet of the contemporary development program: the attempt to tackle the central issue of overstocking and pasture and range management.

While this represented a gain in the sense that attention was finally being directed toward the key components of the pastoral system, there was no coherent theory or model of migratory pastoralism as a system, nor of pastoralists in conjunction with other modes of production and occupation. Basically, the problem was viewed narrowly as one of "proper" land use, not as a matter of transforming a socionatural system out of adjustment with its physical and socioeconomic environments. Thus, 1960 can be taken as the beginning of the era of frustration among the developers: while they were aware that the direct or obvious sources of trouble were being addressed, the efforts at change were consistently defeated by resistance from pastoralists, or by their seeming inability to learn the correct routines.

East Africa suffered a serious drought in the early 1960s that resulted in a predictable response: a return to conservation themes in assistance and development programs. In 1963, Kenya established a Range Management Division in its Ministry of Agriculture, and this new agency was put in charge of pasture development and range conservation. A few years later a Livestock Marketing Division was created to facilitate the sales programs for surplus animals, particularly in pastoralist groups. This agency was responsible for a continuing program involving the sale of pastoralist animals from the northern ranges to farmers in the south who finish them. This program had some advantages insofar as it assisted pastoralists in participating in stratified production systems, but according to some critics (e.g., Mighot-Adholla and Little 1981, 147), the policy hampered more potentially productive programs to integrate pastoralist and farmer economies in particular regions built on traditional barter systems.

In 1965, the International Livestock Research Centre inaugurated its East African Livestock Survey with the cooperation of the country governments. This provided the first substantial body of comparative information on production, marketing, and other facets. It resulted in new initiatives and agencies, and an awareness of the importance of animal husbandry, which up to that time had taken a back seat to crop production. Among other things, the survey underlined the need for positive measures to establish pastoralist production on a commercial basis, and its possible significance as a source of national income in the export livestock markets. For Kenya, the major effect was the Group Representatives Act of 1968 which created the grazing-block system, or at least put the institution of pastoralist grazing reserves—an old idea—on a formal legal tenure basis. Pastoralists were enabled to register for tracts of land which would be assigned to them as their "group ranch"—the term by which the institution came to be known. The system was implemented mainly in Masai districts, and comparable developments in Tanzania, although based on somewhat different principles, were established about the same time.

The history of the group ranches is complex, and in the earlier literature (i.e., Hess 1976) is viewed as a failure. Restricted pasturage required stock reduction, and quotas were set in order for the herding group to qualify for assistance in the form of veterinary services, borehole drilling and the like. This led to conflict within the herding groups, with the large herd owners seeking quotas proportionate to their holdings and urging enforcement of the quota system in order to keep small owners from building up their herds. The big owners simply kept increasing their herds regardless of quotas in accordance with the natural momentum of pastoralist livestock production under climatic uncertainty. The restricted pasturage combined with individual herd ownership resulted in social tension and overgrazing, and no device emerged or was created to ensure responsibility for controlling herd sizes or pasture use.

However, the "failure" of the group ranch is strictly relative to the objectives one expects it to achieve. The more recent literature strikes a different note: Clare Oxby pointed out (1981), that while group ranches in Kenya were not capable of serving the goal of commercializing beef production (the commercial ranches being more suitable for this purpose), the group ranch does confer tenure rights to land on pastoralists, and pastoralists have shown some ability to adapt to the more intensive modes of production that such restricted grazing requires, although this process has been slow. Moreover, in some districts the group ranch has gradually become a focus of settlement: Masai in Kenya and Tanzania were, in the early 1980s, using the government-created centers of social services as places to house aging relatives and as places of temporary residence for mothers and children of families who take advantage of educational facilities. Whether these movements could be considered as first steps toward "sedentarization" is a matter of debate. Finally, the Masai, at least, developed a sharp sense of property ownership concerning land, and have defended their titles to group ranch territories with tenacity (Galaty 1980).

"Supervised Grazing Blocks" were simply a continuation of the old grazing blocks in the northeast introduced by the British many years previously, but now with greater government intervention and control. Grazing fees were charged, a device expected to provide a negative incentive to pastoralists to control stock population. However, as in the case of the group ranches, pastoralists did not stay within the boundaries of the blocks, and they ignored grazing fees or failed to provide accurate reports on herd sizes. In addition, the pastoralist herds of the northeast are multispecies, and it proved impossible to pasture cattle, camels, sheep and goats in the same restricted areas. Pasture rotation schemes were worked out for cattle by government supervisors who had inadequate knowledge for the task.

The problems created by restrictions on grazing are many, but are all underlain by drought. None of the schemes—early or late—considered the effect of greatly reduced forage production due to moisture deficiencies on grazing and herd health and survival. Nor were marketing facilities created to deal with emergencies of this kind. The onus was thrust on the pastoralists themselves, who were expected to make quick adjustments. While they were and are capable of handling drought, their ability to do so was hampered by the changes in grazing introduced by development projects. The "conservatism" of pastoralists, as seen by developers, is often little more than the reduced capacity for strategic choice. The ecological consequences have been severe: range development projects have often worsened the conditions they were designed to correct (Talbot 1972).

Pastoralists perceive land as a place to practice grazing and raise as many livestock as possible for domestic use and for markets when that is feasible or profitable. They use land for foraging for useful plants, charcoal, honey, occasional wide game. Governments, on the other hand, view land as a multiple-use resource, of significance to the entire nation. Game parks, plantations, farming, commercial livestock production, urban settlement are all potential uses for rangeland, particularly the better range in semiarid and subhumid regions. When rangeland formerly used by pastoralists passes into new uses, pastoralists experience increasing difficulty in doing what is necessary to raise the animals they wish to raise, and to cope with recurrent conditions, such as drought, that require flexible responses. The history of development in pastoralist districts shows a consistent failure to consult the pastoralists themselves, arbitrary modifications of land tenure and use patterns, and assistance programs that are neglected or withdrawn at the first sign of trouble. Pastoralists have been low-priority populations; until some means is found to enhance their contribution to the political economy of East

African countries, they will continue to lose ground, both figuratively and in reality.[3]

Some 1970s Development Projects

Beginning in the 1960s, development initiatives in eastern Africa were dominated by U.S. funds, administered primarily through the World Bank and USAID, although many projects enjoyed participation from CIDA and European agencies.[4] USAID in 1980 estimated that the agency had spent approximately $618 million on livestock projects over the 1970–1979 period in all countries of Africa with an AID mission. A strictly unofficial estimate made by the writer for World Bank livestock-related projects in East Africa alone was about $100 million (mostly in the form of loan credits). These figures omit, of course, direct expenditures by country governments and supplemental funds provided for projects not directly related to livestock, or to their human raisers, but which would serve the industry; for example, range conservation, rural roads that might help move animals to market, or village development schemes. Obviously many millions of dollars were spent in the fifteen to twenty years of postindependence livestock-related projects in eastern Africa alone.

However, most projects benefitted farm-cattle producers or groups transitional between migratory and village life, not true migratory herders. A rough calculation by the writer aimed at determining just what proportion of foreign aid funds were directed toward migratory pastoralists in eastern Africa (Ethiopia, Somalia, Kenya, Tanzania), suggests that not more than one-third and not less than one-fifth of all development funding was supposed to benefit these people. However, since many of the projects were poorly conceived and were not designed in a way that could benefit pastoralists, the amount of money that actually assisted pastoralists in their transition to a new and viable ecosystem was probably small.

One reason for this was to be found in the tendency to conceive of the development task as centered on the construction and improvement of government bureaus or parastatal organizations charged with the responsibility of developing commercial livestock systems. Such organizations may concern range management, land tenure, commercial ranch operation, marketing, road construction, water resource development, abattoirs, hide processing, milk processing, and any other relevant aspect of animal industry. While all international development agencies participated in such activity, the World Bank projects were especially characteristic. The reason for this lay in the structure of Bank funding operations: funds are not direct grants, but loans, and a responsible agency must exist for guaranteeing repayment. By establishing a company with government patronage, this responsibility element was presumably secured.

However, on the whole and in the views of the evaluation teams hired by the agencies, none of the USAID or World Bank projects funded between 1960 and 1975 were considered to be a "success." Nearly every organization created by the projects was judged to be in or close to bankruptcy, organizational disintegration, or operating in a state of gross inefficiency within a few years after inception. A second funding project usually would follow, designed to revive the organization or to render its services more effective. Most of the second-stage livestock projects in eastern African countries were, in whole or part, attempts at recouping losses. However, whatever else they may have accomplished, such projects simply increased the indebtedness of the country governments, especially in the Bank projects.

The reasons for the failure of these government and parastatal organizations charged with the task of commercializing production among pastoralists and farmers were to be found in their ignorance or neglect of ecological and economic reasons for herd movement; marketing and pricing policies that discouraged, rather than facilitated, offtake; the failure to deliver promised improvements such as water supplies; the tendency for the project to operate over a short time period, on the assumption that production regimes with generations of indigenous success could be transformed quickly; and others. Underlying the design of most livestock projects was a view derived from Western economic theory: that to induce changes in production strategies among agriculturalists all one has to do is provide market incentives; or more generally, appropriate economic-technological inputs automatically yield expected economic outputs.

For example, most projects designed to encourage pastoralist offtake were based on the assumption (rarely stated) that national livestock prices would provide the necessary incentive for a flow of animals toward the companies, and hence, the revenue which would permit the organization to function at a profit, returning funds to the government which could then repay the loan. However, frequently governments would fix live-stock prices artificially low in order to keep meat and other animal product prices low for the consumer, thus sabotaging producer incentives to sell animals.

Attempts at introducing modern marketing systems were often con-ceived in a vacuum—as if the traditional social reciprocities and market-ing systems of the villages and rangelands did not exist. An occasional project paper might mention the inefficiency of these systems of middle-men and moneylenders, usually in a derogatory sense as impeding adequate pricing or as manipulating the producers so as to maintain small monopolies, but the activities of the marketing companies established by the projects were defined simply as offering "better" services. Since in nearly all cases these had only modest success, the traditional systems persisted. In addition, local livestock buyers in African countries play roles in the general social well-being and financing of small producers, however inefficient or even exploitative they might be considered from the technical-aid standpoint. However, in some cases, as in Somalia, the development projects had the effect of increasing the activities of the traditional middlemen, to the disbenefit of the producers (Aronson 1982).

While the later projects were conceived under the aegis of "basic needs" philosophy of the mid-1970s development milieu, most of the project designs appeared to give only lip service to the goal. The "bene-ficiaries" in these later projects could be formally designated as pasto-ralists (and/ or farmers), but a careful analysis of the project objectives and budgets turned up little that could be considered beneficial to the producers. Most of the financial emphasis was, as already noted, on organizations—and on various construction projects such as holding pens, range improvements, road building, the purchase of bulldozers, trucks and so on. While in the later projects funds were allocated to "training," in most cases these were minuscule compared to the expen-ditures for organization and construction, and almost always concerned with the training of technical experts from the companies, ministries, or research institutes, not the producers themselves. In addition, in Kenya and Tanzania, larger proportions of project money often went to the commercial ranching sector or parastatal companies than to the pastoral-ist and farmer producers, suggesting that the underlying government motive was really to develop export beef production.

Summing up, it can be said that the internationally sponsored livestock development projects aimed at pastoralists in the 1960s and 1970s were concerned mainly with commercial beef production, the creation of government and company organizations and with financial arrangements to repay loans, rather than with the general welfare or even the increase of livestock production among smaller indigenous producers. These objectives reflected familiar constraints in the international development agencies, but there is little doubt that they also mirrored objectives of the country governments as well—objectives that have many causes, including the general financial consequences of previous projects. As for migratory pastoralists, there is no doubt they have responded to the pressures on them to settle down and raise wanted products, but the precise direction of change, and its rate, is still unclear. That it will vary for different populations and countries goes without saying.

In an emerging national system, political power is needed to guarantee the expensive programs needed to promote transition, and this requires leadership. Although the Kenya government has appointed a number of Masai to ministerial positions, these people have not exerted leadership and political mobilization skills among their own people. In the long run, political organization and representation for pastoralists, along with forms of entrepreneurship, will be the essential instruments for economic development, if this remains a significant objective.

Notes

1. For a monograph, see Dahl 1979; early attempts at synthesis or discursive modelling of the main lines of the two stages of ethnological research may be found in Spooner 1971 and Dyson-Hudson 1972. For symposia illustrating the thrust of the earlier work, see Monod 1975; and Irons and Dyson-Hudson 1972.
2. Salzman 1980; Galaty, Aronson, and Salzman 1981; but for an earlier conference, stimulated mainly by West African work, see Lefebvre 1979. For some attempts to construct systemic models of pastoral ecology and production, see the following: Carr 1977; Dahl and Hjort 1976; Picardi 1974.
3. This historical summary of early development policies was based mainly on the following: Hess 1976; Jahnke 1978; Livingstone 1979; Mighot-Adholla and Little 1981; Nkinyangi 1981. Some detailed accounts of the "group ranch" are: Ayuko 1981; Baker 1976; Galaty 1980, 1981; Hopcraft 1981; Jacobs 1975. Although Kenya was selected as the principal example, more attention is given Tanzania in the monographs. However, for Tanzania the following items are useful: Hyden 1980; Ole Saibull 1974; Ole Parkipuny 1975; Kigby 1980. The main issue in the Tanzanian Masai situation is the attempt of the government to promote sedentariza-

tion in line with its Ujamaa policy to develop a cooperative-collective village form—an initiative largely abandoned by the mid-1980s.
4. This section is a very brief summary of a study of most of the key project documents for World Bank and USAID livestock projects in the following countries: Kenya, Tanzania, Somalia, Ethiopia. These projects were operative in the period 1970–1981, although aspects of some of them are still in effect. The detailed analysis of the materials is found in Bennett 1984.

Literature Cited and Consulted

Agency for International Development. 1980. AID Program Evaluation Report No. 4. The Workshop on Pastoralism and American Livestock Development. Washington, DC: USAID.

Aronson, Dan R. 1980. "Must Nomads Settle: Some Notes Toward Policy on the Future of Pastoralism." In *When Nomads Settle: Processes of Sedentarization as Adaptation and Response*, ed. P. Salzman. New York: Praeger.

_____ .1982. "Pastoralists: Losing Ground in Somalia." *Anthropology Resource Center Newsletter*, March.

Ayuko, Lucas J. 1981. "Organization, Structures, and Ranches in Kenya." *Pastoral Network Paper* 11b. London: Overseas Development Institute, Agricultural Administration University.

Baker, Randall. 1974. *Perceptions of Pastoralism*. Edinburgh: Center for Tropical Veterinary Medicine.

_____ .1976. "Innovation Technology Transfer and Nomadic Pastoral Societies." In *The Politics of Natural Disaster*, ed. M. Glanz. New York: Praeger.

Baxter, P.T.W. 1975. "Some Consequences of Sedentarization for Social Relationships." In *Pastoralism in Tropical Africa*, ed. T. Monod. London: International African Institute and Oxford University Press.

Bennett, John W. 1984. "Political Ecology and Development Projects Affecting Pastoralist Peoples in East Africa." Land Tenure Center, research paper no. 80. Madison, WI.

_____ .1988. "The Political Ecology and Economic Development of Migratory Pastoralist Societies in Eastern Africa." In *Power and Poverty: Development and Development Projects in the Third World*, ed. Donald W. Attwood et al. Boulder, CO: Westview Press.

Bennett, John W., Steven W. Lawry, and James C. Riddell. 1986. "Land Tenure and Livestock Development in Sub-Saharan Africa." Land Tenure Center, research paper no. 39. Madison, WI.

Boserup, Ester. 1965. *The Conditions of Agricultural Growth: The Economics of Agrarian Change Under Population Pressure*. Chicago: Aldine Publishing Co.

Brokenshaw, David, Michael M. Horowitz and Thayer Scudder. 1977. *The Anthropology of Rural Development in the Sahel*. Binghamton, NY: Institute for Development Anthropology and USAID.

Campbell, David J. and George H. Axinn. 1980. "Pastoralism in Kenya," *Report No. 30; Africa*. Hanover, NH: American Universities Field Staff.

Carr, Claudia I. 1977. "Pastoralism in Crisis: The Dasanetch and their Ethiopian Lands," research paper no. 180. Department of Geography, University of Chicago.

Carvalho, Cruz de. E. 1974. "'Traditional' and 'Modern' Patterns of Cattle-Raising in SW Angola." *Journal of Developing Areas* 8(2): 199–225.

Dahl, Gudrun. 1979. "Ecology and Society: The Boran Case" In *Pastoral Production and Society*, ed. C. Lefebvre. L'Equipe Ecologie et Anthrolpologie des Societies Pastorales; Cambridge: Cambridge University Press.

Dahl, G. and A. Hjort. 1976. "Having Herds: Pastoral Herd Growth and Household Economy," *Studies in Social Anthropology* 2. Department of Social Anthropology, University of Stockholm.

Dalby, David and R.J.H. Church. 1973. *Drought in Africa: Report of the 1973 Symposium*. London: University of London Center for African Studies.

Dyson-Hudson, Neville. 1972. "The Study of Nomads." In *Perspectives on Nomadism*, ed. W. Irons and N. Dyson-Hudson. Leiden: Brill & Co.

Evans-Pritchard, E. 1940. *The Nuer*. Oxford: Oxford University Press.

FAO Group Fellowship Study Tour Reports. n.d. "Settlement in Agriculture of Nomadic, Semi-nomadic, and Other Pastoral People." FAO-TA 2810. FAO Near East Regional Study.

_____ .1972. "Animal Husbandry, Production and Range Management in the Near East."

FAO Expert Consultation. 1972. "The Settlement of Nomads in Africa and the Near East." FAO-RP20.

Ferguson, Donald T. 1980. *A Conceptual Framework for the Evaluation of Livestock Production Development Projects and Programs in Sub-Saharan West Africa*. Ann Arbor: Center for Research on Economic Development, University of Michigan.

Ford, J. 1960. "The Influence of Tsetse Flies on the Distribution of African Cattle." In Proceedings of the First Federal Science Congress, Salisbury, Rhodesia.

_____ .1971. *The Role of Trypanosomiases in African Ecology*. Oxford: The Clarendon Press.

Forde, C. Daryll. 1934. *Habitat, Economy and Society*. New York: Harcourt Brace.

Fumagalli, Carl T. 1978. "An Evaluation of Development Projects among East African Pastoralists." *African Studies Review: The Social Sciences and African Development Planning*, vol. 29 (special issue), 49–63.

Galaty, John G. 1980. "The Massai Group-Ranch: Politics and Development in an African Pastoral Society." In *When Nomads Settle: Processes of Sedentarization as Adaptation and Response*, ed. P. Salzman. New York: Praeger.

_____ .1981a. "Organizations for Pastoral Development: Contexts of Causality, Change, and Assessment." In *The Future of Pastoral Peoples*, ed. J. Galaty, D. Aronson, and P. Salzman. Ottawa: International Development Research Centre.

_____ .1981b. "Introduction: Nomadic Pastoralists and Social Change." In *Change and Development in Nomadic and Pastoral Societies*, ed. J. Galaty and P. Salzman. Leiden: Brill & Co.

Galaty, John, D. Aronson, and P. Salzman. 1981. *The Future of Pastoral Peoples*. Ottawa: International Development Research Center.

Gulbrandsen, Ornulf. 1980. "Agro-Pastoral Production and Communal Land Use: A Socio-economic Study of the Bangwaketse." Rural Sociology Unit, University of Bergen. Issued by the Ministry of Agriculture, Botswana.

Gulliver, P.H. 1955. *The Family Herds: A Study of Two Pastoral Tribes in East Africa: Jie and Turkana*. London: Routledge and Kegan Paul.

Haaland, Gunnar. 1972. "Nomadism as an Economic Career among the Sedentaries of the Sudan Savannah Belt." In *Essays in Sudan Ethnography*, ed. I. Cunnison. London: C. Hurst.

Hardin, Garrett. 1968. "The Tragedy of the Commons." *Science* 162: 1243–48.

Herskovits, Melville. 1926. "The Cattle Complex in East Africa." *American Anthropologist* 28: 230-72; 361-88; 494-528; 633-44.

Hess, Olean. 1976. "The Establishment of Cattle Ranching Associations Among the Masai in Tanzania." Occasional Paper No. 7. Ghana: USAID (Cornell University).

Hjort, Anders. 1981. "Herds, Trade and Grain: Pastorlism in a Regional Perspective." In *The Future of Pastoral Peoples*, ed. J. Galaty, D. Aronson and P. Salzman. Ottawa: International Development Research Centre.

_____. 1982. "A Critique of 'Ecological' Models of Pastoral Land Use." *Nomadic Peoples* 10: 11-27.

Hopcraft, Peter N. 1981. "Economic Institutions and Pastoral Resources Management: Considerations for a Development Strategy." In *The Future of Pastoral Peoples*, ed. J. Galaty, D. Aronson and P. Salzman. Ottawa: International Development Research Centre.

Hyden, Goran. 1980. *Beyond Ujamaa in Tanzania*. Berkeley: Universiry of California Press.

Irons, William and N. Dyson Hudson, eds. 1972. *Perspectives on Nomadism*. Leiden: Brill & Co.

Jacobs, Alan H. 1975. "Masai Pastoralism in Historical Pespective." In *Pastoralism in Tropical Africa*, ed. T. Monod. London: International African Institute and Oxford University Press.

Jahnke, H.E. 1978. "A Historical View of Range Development in Kenya." Nairobi: International Livestock Centre for Africa, Livestock Development Course, Note 23, 1.

Johnson, Douglas L. 1973. *The Response of Pastoral Nomads to Drought in the Absence of Outside Intervention*. New York: United Nations Special Sahelian Office.

Khazanov, A. M. 1978. "Characteristic Features of Nomadic Communities in the Eurasian Steppes." In *The Nomadic Alternative*. The Hague: Mouton.

_____. 1981. "Myths and Paradoxes of Nomadism." *Archives Européenes de Sociologie* 22: 141-53.

Kjekshus, Helge. 1977. *Ecology Control and Economic Development in East African History*. London and Nairobi: Heinemann.

Konczacki, Z.A. 1978. *The Economics of Pastoralism: A Case Study of Sub-Saharan Africa*. London: Frank Cass.

Lamphear, John. 1976. "Aspects of Turkana Leadership During the Era of Primary Resistance." *Journal of African History* 17: 225-243.

Lefebvre, Claude. 1979. "Introduction." In *Pastoral Production and Strategies: Proceedings of the International Meeting on Nomadic Pastoralism*. Paris/New York: Cambridge University Press.

Lewis, B.A. 1972. *The Murle*. Oxford: Clarendon Press (British Social Anthropological Study of Southern Sudan Group).

Little, Peter D. 1980. "Pastoralism and Strategies: Socio-economic Change in the Pastoral Sector of Baringo District, Kenya," Working Paper No. 368, Institute of Development Studies, University of Nairobi.

Livingstone, Ian. 1977. "Economic Irrationality Among Pastoral Peoples: Myth or Reality?" *Development and Change* 8: 209-30.

_____. 1979. "Socio-Economics of Ranching in Kenya." In *Research in Economic Anthropology*, ed. G. Dalton (vol. 2). Greenwich, CT: JAI Press.

Low, Allan. 1980. "The Estimation and Interpretation of Pastoralists' Price Responsiveness," Pastoral Network Paper 10c. London: Overseas Development Institute, Agricultural Administration Unit.

Lundgren, Bjorn. 1975. *Land Use in Kenya and Tanzania*. Stockholm: Royal College of Forestry, International Rural Development Division.

Mighot-Adholla, S.E. and Peter D. Little. 1981. "Evolution of Policy Toward the Development of Pastoral Areas in Kenya." In *The Future of Pastoral Peoples*, ed. J. Galaty, D. Aronson and P. Salzman. Ottawa: International Development Research Centre.

Monod, Theodore, ed. 1975. *Pastoralism in Tropical Africa*. London: Oxford University Press.

Ndagala, D. 1982. "'Operation Imparnati': The Sedentarization of the Pastoral Masai in Tanzania." *Nomadic Peoples* 10: 28–39.

Ngutter, L.G.K. 1979. "Kenya Government Policy in Semi-Arid Areas: Its Evolution." Paper presented at the Workshop on the Development of Kenya's Semi-Arid Areas. Institute of Development Studies, University of Nairobi.

Nkinyangi, John A. 1981. "Education for Nomadic Pastoralists." In *The Future of Pastoral Peoples*, ed. J. Galaty, D. Aronson and P. Salzman. Ottawa: International Development Research Centre.

Ole Saibull, S.A. 1974. "Social Change Among the Pastoral Masai of Tanzania in Response to the Ujamaa Vijijini Policy." Dar es Salaam, Tanzania: University of Dar es Salaam, Faculty of Arts and Social Sciences.

Ole Parkipuny, M.L. 1975. "Masai Predicament Beyond Pastoralism: A Case Study in the Socio-Economic Transformation of Pastoralism." Dar es Salaam, Tanzania: University of Dar es Salaam, Institute of Development Studies (duplicated report).

Oxby, Clare. 1975. *Pastoral Nomads and Development*. London: International African Institute.

_____ .1982. "Group Ranches in Africa," Pastoral Network Paper No. 13D. London: Overseas Development Institute.

Picardi, A.C. 1974. "A Systems Analysis of Pastoralism in the West African Sahel: Evaluating Long-term Strategies for the Development of the Sahel-Sudan Region," Annex 5, Centre for Policy Alternatives, Massachusetts Institute of Technology.

Rigby, Peter. 1969. "Pastoralism and Prejudice: Ideology and Rural Development in East Africa." In *Society and Social Change in Eastern Africa*, ed. P. Rigby. Kampala: Makerere Institute of Social Research, Nkanga Editions, 4: 42–52.

_____ .1980. "Pastoralist Production and Socialist Transformation in Tanzania." In *Jipemoyo 2/1980*, ed. A.D. Anacleti. Dar es Salaam and Helsinki: University of Helsinki for Ministry of National Culture and Youth, Dar es Salaam, and Finnish Academy.

Salzman, Philip C. 1972. "Multi-Resource Nomadism in Iranian Baluchistan." In *Perspectives on Nomadism*, ed. W. Irons and N. Dyson-Hudson. Leiden: Brill and Co.

_____ .ed. 1980. *When Nomads Settle: Processes of Sedentarization as Adaptation and Response*. New York: Praeger.

Sandford, Stephen. 1976a. "Size and Importance of Pastoral Populations." Design and Management of Pastoral Development, Pastoral Network Paper 1c.London: Overseas Development Institute, Agricultural Administration Unit.

_____ .1976b. "Human Pastoral Populations." Design and Management of Pastoral Development, Pastoral Network Paper 2e. London: Overseas Development Institute, Agricultural Administration Unit.

Shorter, Aylward. 1974. "Conservative Pastoral Societies." In *African Societies*, ed. A. Shorter. London: Routledge and Kegan Paul.

Spooner, Brian. 1971. "Towards a Generative Model of Nomadism." *Anthropological Quarterly* 44: 198–210.

Swidler, Nina. 1980. "Sedentarization and Modes of Economic Integration in the Middle East." In *When Nomads Settle: Processes of Sédentarization as Adaptation and Response*, ed. P. Salzman. New York: Praeger.

Talbot, L. 1972. "Ecological Consequences of Rangeland Development in Masailand, East Africa." In *The Careless Technology: Ecology and International Development*, ed. M.T. Farvar and J.P. Milton. Garden City, NY: Natural History Press.

Turton, D. 1976. "Response to Drought: The Mursi of Southwestern Ethiopia." In *Human Ecology in the Tropics* ed. J.G Garlick and R.W. Keay. New York and Toronto: Halsted Press (Symposia for the Study of Human Biology, vol. 16).

Turton, E.R. 1972. "Somali Resistance to Colonial Rule and the Development of Somali Political Activity in Kenya, 1893-1960." *Journal of African History* 13: 117-143.

Waller, Richard. 1976. "The Masai and the British 1895-1905: The Origin of an Alliance," *Journal of African History* 17: 529-553.

Widstrand, Carl G. 1973. "Pastoral Peoples and Rural Development: A Study." Vetenskapssamhallet I; Uppsala. *Annales* 17: 35-51.

11

Epilogue: The Rise of Ecophilosophy

*But there is one vocation—philosophy—which
knows that all men, by what they think about and
wish for, in effect wield all tools. It knows that
men thus determine, by their manner of thinking
and wishing, whether it is worthwhile to wield
any.*

—Aldo Leopold, *A Sand County Almanac*

Introductory Note

Since the philosophical ideas presented in *The Ecological Transition*
lie in the background of the essays in this volume, I will begin this final
chapter with a resume.

Human beings create values out of their needs and desires, while the
other animals have only needs. It is the human proclivity to create values
transcending need that results in the ever-growing ("exponential") pressure on the earthly environment. Desire extends beyond need; desire is
transformed into culturally sanctioned "necessities"; and institutions and
production are configured around such demands. Thus the pressure on
resources is a projection of the sociopsychological basis of human
behavior. Until this process can be brought under a more reliable means
of control and some independent check on the validity, desirability, and
derivation of values is created, *Homo sapiens sapiens* will continue to
consume and abuse the earth's substance. This means as well that
ecological inquiry, in any scientific discipline, cannot be neutral in this
process. Impact on the environment, or the consequences of human

During the heyday of the environmental movement in the 1970s I taught environmental and
ecological subjects, and I therefore found it necessary to maintain contact with the more influential
works in environmental philosophy. While I never committed any of the lectures and classroom
discussions to print, the notes remained, and this chapter is based on those materials.

action (including research itself and the production of knowledge), must always be a part of ecological inquiry. To leave it out is, in effect, to sanction the abuse, or at least the process that begets the abuse. No existing institution provides for this; control must be exercised from outside the system, in the form of exhortation or regulation.

The preceding summary, however, is just one version of ecophilosophy, and in this final chapter I shall review some of the major varieties emerging since the 1960s and the rise of the ecological and environmental movements.

One difficulty, of course, with the term "ecophilosophy" is that it implies the old shibboleth of homeostatic equilibrium, but I have chosen it as a compromise among several possible terms. "Environmental philosophy" is perhaps more accurate but too long, and "environmental ethics," Nash's (1989) term, is too specific. By "ecophilosophy" I mean any frame of reference or set of beliefs that places the value of the physical surround as a phenomenon at least as important as humanity itself, thus implying that humans must be prepared to accept constraints on their freedom of will.

The principal accomplishment of contemporary ecophilsophy is its interjection of doubt about the human role in the universe and Man's relationship to Earth and Nature. Although fear of human destructiveness toward the physical environment appeared as soon as Europeans began colonizing and exploiting the southern hemisphere in the 17th and 18th centuries—the protests by scientists and scholars reached a crescendo in the mid-nineteenth century (Grove 1990)—there was never any doubt about the main current of thought about this matter: humans were conceived as basically superordinate over Nature and thereby could be trusted to do right by it. "It's not nice to fool Mother Nature" was a familiar joke (and in the 1980s was actually used in a humorous television advertisement for margarine). But the ecological movement that began in the 1960s took the message seriously: it certainly was *not* nice to offend Mother Nature; in fact, it was a scandal, an ethical wrong, a moral sin. This reversal of the paradigm of the preceding two thousand years and the rediscovery of earlier dissenting voices suggest the beginnings of a basic cultural change.

Thus contemporary ecophilosophy took its place alongside a number of other changes occurring in the 1960s and 1970s: sexual freedom, active self-fulfillment, intense grass-roots democracy, indulgence in mind-expanding behavior such as the taking of hallucinatory drugs, radical experimentation with clothes and personal appearance, fascination with Oriental religions—many things that have now become themes in the larger culture. Among these, environmentalism stood out because it was largely selfless: rather than advocating the rights of the individual, it proposed the assignment of general rights to Nature which all humans must respect. It was, in a phrase of the 1970s, "white communism."

Ecophilosophy is, of course, an extension of human philosophy. Humans struggle to interpret the human-environmental relationship in familiar terms, or, as noted in other chapters, human beings treat the environment of Earth in much the same way they treat other human beings. One should therefore expect to find most of the frames of reference in the field of environmental philosophy that one finds in general humanistic scholarship, along with ethical dilemmas and double binds: feeding human beings at the expense of habitat and other species, balancing social goals against environmental goals, or preserving animals out of kindly motives to the point where their population increases and threatens the food supply. And the question of *rights*, a dominant preoccupation of the 1960s and 1970s, has inevitably come to the forefront of the discussion. Whose rights, for example, should prevail in a fight over animal experimentation, the animals' or the sick humans'? All of these and countless other problems that arise within human society also implicate the environment in the process of its incorporation into human culture in the "ecological transition."

Because the term is ambiguous, ecophilosophy is really up for grabs, susceptible to a variety of interpretations. If 'limiting ethic' is taken as the key concept then practically every document produced during the two decades of environmentalism fits the bill. But some of the most persuasive or eloquent arguments for constraints on the human use of the Earth do not really qualify as "philosophy" in the accepted sense of the term and in fact were generated by the behavioral-economics and behavioral-sociology approaches that arose in the 1960s: for example, Herbert Simon's theories of rational behavior (1957), Mancur Olson's theories of collective action (1965), Fred Hirsch's exposition of the social limits to economic growth (1976), the Club of Rome's doomsday forecasts that pioneered global environmental-social modelling (Meadows, ed. 1972), and, much later, the "ecological economics" approaches to sustainability (e.g., Costanza 1990). Garrett Hardin's "tragedy of the commons" idea was another influential source (Hardin 1968; Hardin and Baden 1977), and it generated a considerable literature with implications for the nature of human behavior and character, some of which Hardin explored in subsequent collections of essays: triage, control of human fertility, competition, responsibility, cultural taboos and the need to break them (Hardin 1972, 1973, 1980). While all of these approaches and themes acquired philosophical or at least speculative dimensions, they are based on empirical phenomena; that is, they were predictions of things to come, events that might transpire if humans behaved in certain ways.

In the interest of presenting material with more properly philosophical content, I have chosen to discuss three areas of ecophilosophy: global ontologies, the critique of humanistic anthropocentrism, and the advocacy of the rights of natural species. Roderick Nash (1989) provides a convenient summary of environmental philosophy into the 1980s, but it is focused on ethical issues and ignores more generalizing approaches, like the Gaia hypothesis. Nash also was not concerned with the literary and spiritual branches of the field, the so-called "deep ecology." And even in the few years that elapsed between Nash's writing (about 1988) and the time of this composition (1991) new ecophilosophical ventures have become prominent. An example comes from deep ecology: the "New Age" melange of metaphysical and supernaturalistic paraphernalia, sold mainly through catalogues, defining a mystical attitude toward Nature fueled by a media-oriented reading of tribal culture and religion. This is easy to dismiss as fringe phenomena, but it is an important demonstration of the fact that environmentalist philosophy is beginning to penetrate the cultural underbrush, where it contributes to the formation of cults and feeds the fanaticism of radical environmental groups.

Global Ontologies

Ecology cannot be known as a totality since no effective scientific method has been found to make complex wholes easily comprehensible as wholes (Thompson 1987). Ecology is multiorganismic: its identity, and the generalizations one seeks when doing ecology, are not statements about a single phenomenon but about relationships among an indefinite number. The ecological process is not a single process, but the intersections and resultant feedbacks of many processes. The only way to grasp a multiorganismic concept is symbolically: to create an image or idea of a holistic entity and then treat that image as a real entity: the "environment," "human ecology," Gaia or the organismic Earth, the universe, God. By asserting the unity of such phenomena one does not, of course, prove that they are in fact singular. However, even though the idea, the "model," is not necessarily demonstrable empirically does not make it less interesting or valuable. It can be the beginning of new ways of thinking.

If ecology or the environment are abstract concepts, one might be on the track of an explanation of the difficulties of mounting a more coherent scientific and philosophical approach to their problems. That is, the problem is not merely the way relevant branches of knowledge are parcelled out as "disciplines" but also the way these branches are parts of a larger and more complex mental construction that defies easy synthesis. This suggests that we never can fully solve the environmental problem, that we shall continue to worry about our inability to do so without fully understanding that the reasons are parts of a complex whole. The argument that holds disciplinary fragmentation responsible for our obtuseness or ignorance has in its favor the fact that the scholarly branches of knowledge are to a considerable extent the creations of humans in a historical process of academic and scholarly formation and therefore subject to human error as well as to intellectual revision. The ontological argument has in its favor the fact that everything is indeed connected to everything else and divisions between phenomena are matters of convenience and therefore not "real." Thus with the environmental problem the limits of positive knowledge are reached. What we do about the environment is, in the final analysis, a matter of attitude and concept.

The dilemma is one of choosing an approach that synthesizes natural phenomena with the human but that is largely purely conceptual or even imaginary, as over against an approach that must be partial and incomplete because one rejects false synthesis. Ecophilosophy must be an example of the former; the narrower, empirical inquiries into technical problems of human-environmental relations constitute the latter. The first gives us visions of where *Homo sapiens sapiens*, other species, and the Earth may be going; the latter solves technical problems created by previous problems—that is, "adaptation." How does one best solve the problem of loss of species diversity? By imagining a world without this diversity and then pulling out all the stops in order to persuade people to conserve Nature, or by setting up special breeding zoos for one or two species at a time? or both?

Traditional zoology was based on the proposition of discrete species: each species was believed to have evolved or adapted as a personal trajectory, and the identity, the essence of the species, was conceived of as singular. This was a late Renaissance idea, unmodified through the nineteenth century, and was, of course, influenced by the concept of creation. Zoology texts on the whole still describe a species as singular, even though biologists know that no species could exist as a discrete entity without other species, that its structure and functions are the results of interactions with other species. In fact, all species are in some way refracted expressions of each other.

It would be nonsense to assert that the traditional notion of discrete species has not produced valuable knowledge about Nature. This knowledge is by now a depiction of the visible elements of biology and geology, with the processes of earthly dynamics (e.g., plate tectonics) and ecological interactions fairly well worked out. But the long-term interactions and their possible teleological implications and feedbacks are unknown. The linkages are only suspected, for example, in the way the evolution of the human mind was shaped by the evolution of other mammals or by geological processes like glaciation. Some of the dangers of human interventions, like the fluoride attacks on the ozone layer, are just coming into awareness, and the way the ominous new epidemics, like the immune-suppressing virus diseases, have been shaped by man's own environmental presence and interventions is only guessed at or reluctantly acknowledged.

And this brings us to *Gaia*. Of all the imaginative ecophilosophies spawned in the past quarter century this is the most sweeping, controversial, and quixotic, especially from an environmentalist point of view. Gaia—the Greek word for the Earth—was used by biologist James Lovelock (1979) as the term for the functioning cybernetic system that is Earth. That is, Earth in this view is not simply a large rock with disparate biological and geological systems, but a single large system of feedbacks and interrelationships of which life is the most significant. The latter statement was proposed as the only way to explain the peculiar chemistry of Earth, which differs from all other planets because it contains an abundance of *both* reducing gases: methane, like the big gas giant Jupiter, and oxidizing gases, like the lifeless planets Venus and

Mars. Only life could create this chemical anomaly, since the quantities of both oxygen (oxidizing gas) and methane (reducing gas) in the Earth's atmosphere are too great to be produced by the available raw materials: water, carbon dioxide, and sunlight. If this is true, then the environment of Earth has been created by life, and the implication follows that Gaia is a kind of giant organism. And since this giant has managed to survive and flourish in spite of the impacts of asteroids or whatever it was that destroyed all or much of life at least once, it may well be resistant to anything that humans can do to it. It is this deterministic element in the Gaia hypothesis that disturbs environmentalists.

However, Lovelock points out that human interventions can easily produce new "adaptations" (in Thompson 1987, 96), some of which might be unfriendly or lethal for humans, so that the environmentalist arguments are still relevant. If we view the Earth as some kind of dynamic—if not as a fully "living" phenomenon—then the concept of "environment" must include the sentient species, *Homo sapiens sapiens*, along with all other species and the physical surround. That is, humans are part of the system, not apart from it. Does this make Culture also a part of the system? Logically, yes—or in the term used in this book, part of socionatural systems. *But* humans are currently attacking the Earth, not husbanding it.

There is no doubt that the Earth is some kind of giant material interaction process, but more important is the issue of how this holistic process or entity is to be understood and studied. Lovelock based his argument mainly on the composition of the atmosphere and certain biochemical processes, but this approach neglects other phenomena whose role in the larger system is unknown or not relevant. What of parasitism? Since parasitic organisms and processes exist throughout the living world there is no reason why they should be absent in Gaia. The order of incompleteness of the Gaia macrosystem thus should be the first order of business: what subsystems exist because they depend on Gaia but contribute little or nothing to Gaia's functioning? Organisms like the *Homo sapiens* varieties might well have contributed to Gaia's functioning at an earlier, lower level of population and technology, but as both of these factors increase exponentially *Homo sapiens sapiens* and all his works might become a genuine threat to the functioning of the system. This proposition has at least to be examined. Big technology is something new on earth.

René Dubos (1981, 187–192) was concerned with some other ambiguities in the Gaia hypothesis; in particular, the temporal aspects involved in the intersection and interinfluence of the many subprocesses. Lovelock seemed to view these as existing in an eternal homeostasis, but Dubos points to the constant "creative evolution" taking place on Earth: a more dynamic process, with random activity, independent movement, confrontation, and subsequent changes in the system. And this is where *Chaos* comes in. James Gleick's book with that title (1987) caused a considerable stir in the late 1980s, much like the excitement created by the Gaia literature in the early 1980s. And the significance of Chaos science—it is not, like Gaia, a hypothesis but a series of mathematically demonstrable processes—is that regularity may lurk in the most apparently chaotic or random situations and, conversely, that a minor change in a single variable in a such a complex system can have massive consequences for the entire system. So far as Gaia is concerned, Chaos science cuts both ways: on the one hand, it might be understood as an explanation of the nature of the Gaia macrosystem in that many apparently disparate subsystems, over a sufficient period of time, intersect and permutate to create a larger entity; on the other hand, it can be understood to imply that the chaotic cycling of phenomena on Earth gives the impression of a living organism, whereas in fact it is really the consequence of mathematical functions (i.e., any complex array of more or less related phenomena will display complex cyclical regularity).

An example of the type of inquiry generated by Chaos science is the question asked by Edward Lorenz: is there any such thing as a climate for Earth? (cited in Gleick 1987, 168). A "climate" means a moving average of some kind; that is, certain phenomena repeat themselves in a pattern that can be found to have central tendencies, and this tendency is the "climate." Lorenz was interested in climate as a case study of the difficulties or impossibilities of using linear equations to describe complex phenomena, the technical issue that would much later form one basis of the science of Chaos. From an anthropological standpoint, the problem is whether human perceptions are an adequate basis for analyzing or interpreting natural phenomena unaltered by the human presence.

Now, our understanding of climate is based on our cultural need to predict it, and in order to predict something one needs a central tendency from which deviations can be calculated or observed. We therefore attempt to configurate the daily chaotic movements of weather into a long-term pattern of climate; but since the Chaos effect—emerging patterns distorted by small changes in a few variables—continually recurs, the task is difficult. Meterological mathematicians are still working on the problem, although Chaos reasoning and mathematics have shed more light on it. Daily weather reports have benefitted from this growing understanding by playing down prediction and instead giving presentations of *possible* weather for the general public and more specific mathematical probability estimates for the professionals who need to know the weather in more exact terms. In general, we have adjusted to tentative day-by-day forecasts and have geared many of our activities that depend on weather to this incremental approach. For the longer term we put up with approximations, rough averages that may be wrong but are good enough. Our imperfect and sketchy knowledge of the permutations is matched by adaptive flexibility. But Chaos theory also holds out the possibility that climate—long-term regularities—exists and that one day it will be discovered.

Gaia is, from a literary standpoint, an example of a utopia. Utopias, where authors have imagined and described alternative civilizations and ways of life, are nothing new and date from the Renaissance. In the twentieth century the mode shifted to science fiction and science fantasy writing to satisfy the interests of a mass readership market. And with it utopias lost some of their depth; earlier utopian writing, like that of More and Swift, was serious stuff: political and philosophical commentary on the present world seen through refracting lenses.

But the environmental movement has spawned a return to serious utopian writing. One of the most widely read was Ernest Callenbach's *Ecotopia* (1975), an attempt to design a new country (which consists of northern California, Oregon, and Washington, seceded from the old United States) founded on ecological principles. The book was written in the form of travel notes by a journalist assigned to write a book about the new country. Ecotopia turns out to be a mixture of good and bad. Settlements consist of small, socially beneficent towns, forest cutting is rigorously controlled, employees own all businesses, all chemical pollutants are controlled, the government is dominated by nurturant females, and so on—all the liberal-libertarian-ecological shibboleths of the Berkeley pundits of the 1960s and 1970s. Among the less congenial elements are blood sports and games as a substitute for war and militarism in recognition of the innate aggressiveness of human beings. But the thrust is utopian, the conviction simple: humans *can* create a benign, steady-state balance between Man and Nature if they work at it. There is quite a list of such books, most of them portraying benevolent utopias, and a few films, like *Blade Runner*, describing their exact opposite: the crime-ridden, filthy, overpopulated, polluted human hells of future cities (although the descriptions are often not so futuristic, echoing newspaper accounts of the rotten inner cities of the present).

The ontological theme should not be dropped without some mention of the works of Kenneth Boulding, a major figure in the environmental and social analysis movements of the 1960s and 1970s. Boulding, trained originally as an economist, wound up as a theoretical social scientist and behavioral sociologist, president of six major scholarly societies, and plenary session speaker for countless international congresses. His environmentalism was tangential; he made no sharp distinction betweeen society and environment, since he took the position of a global ontologist: Man and Nature were one interacting whole, and human evolution was part of the evolution of the cosmos. These olympian ideas were expressed in a series of books and shorter pieces, of which *Ecodynamics* (1978) is perhaps the most representative.

Ecology for Boulding was "the dynamics of interacting populations" (1978, 77), and the "populations" can be human, animal, vegetable, or mineral (the book has, for example, a graph of "Automobile Population Dynamics"). He held that human social systems and cultural artifacts can be analyzed with the same basic interactive mathematics as the systems of other species. Boulding never went so far as Lovelock in his global views and nowhere characterizes the Earth as a unitary system, but the intellectual vector is similar, and, in the final analyis, "ecodynamics" is an attempt to bridge the gap between the concepts of Nature and Culture. And, like other such attempts, the ideas are often overgeneralized and the analogies intriguing but forced. From another intellectual perspective, *Ecodynamics* is a contribution to the classical tradition of philosophical anthropology, prevalent in the late seventeenth and eighteenth centuries (for example, Immanuel Kant and Alexander Pope).

Anthropocentrism

Otherwise known as *humanism*: the various doctrines in Western civilization which place Man above all other aspects of Nature. Humanism embraces dogmas in Judeo-Christian thought, the glorification of human achievements in the Renaissance, and secular ideas of man as the measure of all things and as the steward of Nature, in control of his destiny (God becomes a benign fiction). The moral vector is benignity, kindliness, but the doctrines contain very little humility, especially with respect to Man vis-à-vis other species. David Ehrenfeld called it "the arrogance of humanism" in the book of that title (1978).

Above all, humanism holds to the nature-culture dichotomy, and in this context anthropology might be considered the principal humanistic science. The field is focused on the works of Man, and its major concept, Culture, is a profoundly humanistic, phenomenological idea. Despite denials and qualifications, anthropology will have considerable difficulty finding a way around this dichotomy and its implications for environmentalism. From this standpoint, anthropology is part of the problem of environmental degradation and not the solution. Perhaps this is the reason why anthropologists have difficulty in facing up to the destructive potential of human beings, an attitude which helps account for their belated participation in environmental action. Sociology has, on the whole, similar hang-ups.

But humanism is much more than a philosophical bent arising in the Renaissance or the Enlightenment; it has been the guiding ideology of modern society since the Industrial Revolution. The doctrines of humanism—the faith in the goodness of human intentions and reason and the optimistic assumption that all problems can be solved and all resources can be renewed or improved upon and the conviction that humans will survive no matter what happens to the world—are also basic to the concept of progress and faith in industry and science. These ideas are shared by all political and ideological factions: totalitarian and democratic, liberal and conservative, secular and religious. Humanism, in this sense, is simply the underlying ideal of Western—and now World Industrial—Civilization. In a literal sense, humanism has become a philosophical rationale for human power and human dominance of the planet.

But there is a contradiction between the exclusive anthropological focus on human phenomena at the expense of Nature and the use of nonindustrial ethnological data as examples of a benign attitude toward Nature. The tribalists' concern for landscape, their tendency to view humans as part of the natural world, the tribal reverence for game species and careful management of game and food resources, and the subtle natural symbolism in art and ritual have been used by environmentalists during the past thirty years to exemplify a "better" way of dealing with Nature. The approach, developed initially in the late 1960s, subsided and then in the late 1980s and early 1990s underwent a revival with the "deep ecology" and "New Age" fads with their commercialization of shamanism and mysticism. Many anthropologists are confused and embarrassed by this since they know that tribalists were not as benign toward Nature as advocates would like to believe; and they are also aware that the underlying themes of anthropological effort are humanistic and therefore contain environmental contradictions.

To overemphasize traditional notions about the tribal relationship to Nature is to confuse necessity and idealism. The tribal attitudes are cited by some environmentalists as profound philosophical positions when they are really pragmatic symbolizations of a low population, low-energy life-style. Life on the tribal edge was usually precarious and confining, and it bred rituals and symbols of anxiety over the chance that Nature and the supernatural might fight back. These ceremonials and attitudes were produced by populations that were small relative to resources, and this meant relatively little competition for resources between various aggregates or societies. It is this systemic package—few people, low technology, and rationalizations of the necessity to exploit Nature—that explains the apparently benign attitudes. But there was no doctrine of conservation in the modern sense: Nature was being managed at a modest de facto level of intervention, not consciously conserved or preserved. Ideologically based conservationism arises in societies who have contributed to environmental degradation and are trying to make up for it.

Classical humanistic benignity toward Nature is a mask for control and dominance; and with that attitude goes an inability to face up to the extent and possible irreversibility of many of the changes resulting from human intervention. At the same time, the ambiguity of the ecological process makes it difficult to be certain of the extent of damage and its ultimate consequences. No process in Nature is completely reversible, and, even without substantial human intervention, natural species constantly reshape the milieu in a series of fluctuating alterations. It is a question of emphasis and magnitude; there seems no doubt that the changes wrought by humans are much larger in scope and irreversibility: desertification, extensive deforestation, poisoning of oceans and the atmosphere, and loss of biological diversity are all examples. And there is the question of time: perhaps everything is recoverable to some degree or kind if you give it enough time, but the critical issue is that slow recoverability means damage to human endeavors or health in the short run. Thus, even the benign attitudes of environmentalists inevitably contain human standards of significance.

As David Ehrenfeld pointed out (1978, 174), imbedded in some humanistic approaches to Nature is a rationalist tendency to devalue the unreasoning or purely symbolic aspects of human thought and behavior, for example, the contemporary resumption of mystical attitudes toward Nature and tribalism. These movements are in a subtle sense an attempt to denigrate Reason, to assert the nonrational side of human behavior and to link this with environmentalism. In this sense, these movements are not trivial and must be given a modicum of respect. Anthropologists do so at their meetings and conferences where papers are given on the topics. But anthropologists are of two minds on this: on the one hand, as students of the symbolic and subjective side of behavior, they must accept inquiry into it; but, on the other hand, as scientists they must be suspicious and even intolerant of approaches which imply knowledge or certainty not based on empirically demonstrable fact.

Anthropocentrism leads to a preoccupation with mastery and growth, and in the age of industry and capital this has meant what Kirkpatrick Sale calls "gigantism." Sale's *Human Scale* (1980) was one of the three or four most influential popular environmentalist books of the 1980s— although it preceded by an equally popular book, E.F. Schumacher's *Small is Beautiful* (1973), which pioneered the idea of the evils of gigantism but from the special viewpoint of economics. Sale's book was not really about ecology and the physical environment, but he presented his ideas as ecological: humans should take a cue from the modest homeostatic "harmony" of Nature and cease overbuilding. Environmentalists, in the same period, were pushing ecosystemic harmony and speaking of the "built environment" as a part of the larger environment that humans have created or managed. The issue (as discussed in *The Ecological Transition*, chapter 4) concerns whether or not the *social* environment—humans interacting with humans and their creations—is really a legitimate part of an ecological approach. Whether the "environment" of human society has anything in common with the "environment" of Nature is the problem, and one suspects an element of word magic: because we have invented a general term, *environment*, which refers to anything surrounding the individual human being, it is possible that Society and Nature are interrelated only in the human mind, that is, *analogically* (in any case, ecophilosophy has much analogic thinking). Sale defines ecology, for his purposes, as "the grand system of the interaction of all elements of the natural world: plant, mineral, animal, human" (1980, 146). But who can possibly study this "grand system" as a whole?

Sale's book is in essence a social polemic. He is concerned with what he sees as the basic or underlying cause of some 106 (by my count) major social evils or what he calls "crises," ranging from the first on the list—"imperilled ecology"—to the last—"the end of the American imperial arrangement." The full range of moral, social, cultural, ideological, economic, chemical, and biological ills are attributed to "exponential growth," which not only generates crises but also Gregory Bateson's famous double binds: growth means linkage and mutually dependent resources, so to alleviate one problem one must accept or create another (e.g., to alleviate traffic congestion one builds more roads, but more roads mean that more cars can be accommodated, so the congestion increases rather than diminishes). Such double binds lead Sale to use the ecological analogy: until we recognize that everything is interdependent and getting more so, we will continue to experience "crises." And this requires the scaling down of just about everything: fertility, use of minerals, building, levels of gratification, money.

The argument for scaling down is thus initially based on crisis-avoidance—the return to a more modest style of living and doing—but there are other factors in the argument: Sale praises earlier and simpler lifeways: the agrarian, the medieval, and the tribal, where society had smaller, more localized units in which face-to-face interaction was possible among a majority of residents (Robert Redfield's folk society). Much of the discussion is based on population data for "successful commune movements" (184), which were and are relatively small. As we noted in chapter 7 with reference to the Hutterites, these small community populations result from economic as well as sociopsychological forces, not all of them benign (e.g., mutual suspicion and surveillance). But at least among the Hutterites these are not only a function of the forces in human behavior leading toward growth but also the result of external economic pressures. Since sixteenth-century Hutterian colonies had as many as a thousand people, community size would seem to be variable. I am not sure that the small populations of communes prove anything other that when people can isolate themselves they can more easily support a modest scale of living—but the problem is to maintain that isolation.

Sale's human-scale societies should also, he believes, develop reasonably self-sufficient economies with small manufactories and a recycling or conservationist policy toward physical resources. Similar arguments are featured in the common property movement, but *Human Scale* is a popular production and not an attempt to forge a serious strategy for change and development. Sale's writing also belongs to an old tradition of nostalgia for the simple, the medieval, the rural—social environments in which peace and harmony are expected to prevail since they lack the haste, crime, corruption, and overwhelming technology of cities. But human behavior is the same everywhere, and evils—deception, cruelty, chicanery, and so on—are as likely to appear in small communities as in large ones. The basic problem with Sale's argument is his assumption that size alone can be the sole or major cause of all these social crises.

Human Scale also contains a basic humanistic fault—or at least an attitude typical of the more liberal brand of humanist thought: that humans are basically good but are corrupted by external forces and circumstances. Sale does not entertain the possibility that the behaviorally based growth dynamic that produces gigantism is unstoppable—or that it will and must continue until it collapses under its own weight. And at that point we encounter the arguments of the economics pundits who, in the 1970s, were concerned with limiting or even stopping economic growth. Fred Hirsch's *Social Limits to Growth* (1976) was the most eloquent and possibly most sociologically sound contribution, and its arguments can be taken as a kind of sequel to Sale's: gigantism would proceed until it generated so much social disorder and deprivation that there would be a pastoral reaction. Sale enunciates the "Beanstalk Principle": "for every animal, object, institution, or system, there is an optimal limit beyond which it ought not to grow" (59)—and that if it does grow beyond this limit it "will be affected adversely." Aside from the difficulties of defining limits, sizes, and adverse consequences, there is the problem of adaptive innovation: that even if under present conditions a size limit can be found for an object or institution, modifications of the conditions can compensate for the problems that arise. What can be said from an anthropological standpoint is that magnitude affects people through their culturally trained perceptions, which in turn suggests that absolute magnitudes of size probably have no invariable and universal effects.

One problem that ecophilosophy needs to tackle concerns the extreme diversity of environmental disturbance and the need to trade one kind for another. The question is whether it is possible to find a philosophical position that covers all possible cases. If so, it would have to be very general—basically admonitions to respect Nature, to scale down human wants and eliminate greed—and to sanction these and similar ideas with some binding moral or spirital command. However, the "environmental crisis" is itself created by the progressive relaxation of such commands taking place since the onset of the Industrial Revolution. Thus, to return to preindustrial standards would require a fundamental change in the institutions fostering this relaxation—not to mention control over human fertility. Such changes seem utterly utopian; the political forces benefitting from relaxed standards are extremely potent, and only unmistakable present danger to the health and survival of large numbers of people would effect major changes.

On the whole, the most successful instances of control of resource use or withdrawal of damaging practices have taken place in small, intensely defended localities. A factory that discharges waste into a river, timber companies determined to cut the last remaining virgin forest, a seacoast of exceptional beauty that should be put in a conservancy district, a recreational developer who wants to strip a scenic mountainside of its trees to put in a ski resort thus creating damaging water runoffs for the residents on the downslope, an old and inefficient dam that should be opened up to permit the recovery of needed wetlands—each of these and others like them require active participation on the part of the local people, often working with national organizations, politicians, companies, or conflict mediation specialists before some degree of success can be achieved. "Environmental philosophy" was manifest in the determination and dedication of local residents and their associates to solve the problem or redress the perceived environmental wrong rather than in scholarly punditry. Still, the latter provides the source and the inspiration needed, in a highly literate civilization, to foster the dedication.

The question of the relationship of Judeo-Christian philosophy to the treatment of the physical environment was raised initially in an essay by the historian of technology Lynn White, Jr. (1967) but prefigured in some of his earlier historical writings on medieval technology (e.g., White 1962). The issue was also indirectly raised in the debate over the responsibility of Christianity, and particularly Protestantism, for the rise of aggressive capitalism (e.g., Weber 1930, Tawney 1926). Obviously the technological transformation of physical substances and the growth of capitalist enterprise are closely linked, and the rise of the first is probably dependent on the second. And certainly this exploitative and expansionistic mode of human existence developed faster and more decisively in the West than anywhere else—and the West was shaped by the Judeo-Christian ethic.

The problem is that some form of capitalist enterprise is as old as *Homo sapiens sapiens*—or at least resource exploitation, financial manipulation, manufacturing, organized trade and banking are as old as the Bronze Age, so that one cannot lay the accumulated environmental consequences entirely at the door of Judeo-Christianity. Thus, the influence of Protestantism on the liberation of the individual capitalists and engineers simply reinforced institutions that had been in place for centuries, although often held in check by moral or religious values. John Black (1970) and others have shown how the medieval world stressed communal ownership and partnerships between Man and Nature in the production of food and other physical substances—activities held in check by the Catholic Church's rules against usury, excessive profits, and limits on the magnitude of property ownership—institutions and practices echoed in the eighteenth and nineteenth centuries in Japan during the Tokugawa regime. Once the power of the European church and the Japanese feudal aristocracy to restrain capitalist activity was broken or modified, the brakes against economic development were off. And in Euro-America, as in Japan, they have been off ever since.

While anthropocentrism implies a kind of worship of the human species and a confidence in its ultimate integrity and success, more pessimistic assessments of *Homo sapiens sapiens* have appeared from time to time in all civilizations. The environmental movement of the twentieth century has produced another, expressed in the famous remark by the cartoon character Pogo: "we have met the enemy, and he is us." But such distrust of Man, this terror over what humans can do when they are heedless, enraged, or uncontrollably greedy, has a basic futility: hatred or distrust of Man does not contribute to a constructive philosophy of the human relationship with the environment. *Homo sapiens sapiens* may be the Great Destroyer, but at the same time his gifts of Reason and Compassion are available to modify his behavior and to generate hope for a more constructive and modest posture vis-à-vis the environment of Earth.

The Rights of Nature

The idea that natural—that is, noncultural, non-man-made—phenomena have "rights" is mainly a creation of the ecology movement of the 1960s. The concept proposes that Nature has rights that are inherent and "natural" and therefore subject to the same moral, ethical, and legal protection afforded humans. However, Nature lacks a legislature and a constitution, and all doctrines and legal systems based on the concept of rights since the Enlightenment are inextricably bound up with these institutions, so if Nature has rights who demands them, who can can guarantee them? Certainly not Nature—although if humans are part of Nature then it could be argued, casuistically, that they have a "right" to demand rights for other domains of Nature. And so on, through other medieval-type arguments. In fact, as Roderick Nash implies in his book on the history of the concept of natural rights, it has many characteristics of medieval scholasticism.

But this is by no means bad, since debate on such issues is precisely what the shift toward a more environmentally conscious position will require. The reason is found in the odd twist that Western thought put on the Biblical abduration to hold dominion over Nature—the word coming from the Hebrew *radah*, which unfortunately can be given the meaning of assault, dominate, rule, although in more benign translations it simply means to have dominion over without necessarily implying to consume or destroy. So expansionistic Christianity came to interpret the passages to mean that humans had the "right," the destiny, to dominate and use Nature for their own ends, thus precluding any allowance for the rights of Nature. If, on the other hand, it is believed that humans are simply part of Nature, then while they use Nature, as do all other natural species, they also must respect it and not abuse it; or even apologize to Nature (or to the species) when it is necessary to use or kill a member (a common tribal hunting ritual). So in order to reestablish some aspect of this preindustrial view of Nature and the human position within it, it is necessary to engage in theological or at least philosophical debate; and that has been happening since the 1960s.

The general doctrine of rights is a peculiarly Western idea, originating in the political sphere with the concept of *natural rights*: people have rights because they are inherent in the natural order; that is, the ecology of society is an extension of Nature, and therefore civil or status elements of the sociological process are somehow linked to the lawful processes of the natural world. Although rights were supposedly "natural," they did not apply to living species other than humans—a paradox which a number of philosophers became aware of and attempted to resolve. There were some precedents: Roman law, for example, contained the notion of *jus animalum*, the social ordering of other animal species. But the main line of thought denied the inclusion of natural species: only humans, endowed with Reason, were privileged to enjoy ethics, morality, rights.

The emerging biological and medical sciences of the seventeenth, eighteenth, and nineteenth centuries required animals as experimental objects, and in the science of "natural history" living things became objects of study, not partners with Man in the universe. So any movement toward incorporating the animal world in rights policy had to come from a different source: the emotions, as expressed in concepts of humane treatment or from the Golden Rule which teaches that one should treat others as one wishes to be treated. This stream still flows in the Humane Societies of most Western nations—organizations that avoid linkage or ties with the radical, politicized animal rights groups. In the background, of course, lay scholarly controversies about the nature of species, the uniqueness or commonality of the human species in relation to the others, the study of comparative anatomy, and the truth or falsity of Biblical dogma relating to the natural world. Doubts about human superiority emerged as zoologists found that animal senses were often far better than human capacities. Prominent among the Americans in this group was John Moore, whose book, *The Universal Kinship* (1906), was really the first American publication formally to advocate animal rights (England had such organizations and literature by the 1870s).

Nash's chapter 5, "The Greening of Philosophy," describes the emergence in the U.S. of the natural rights philosophy in the 1960s and 1970s. The emergence was extremely rapid: Nash lists five periodicals devoted to the topic and related to issues in "deep ecology" and a 1981 bibliography of 3,200 entries on animal rights. The issues were also discussed in textbooks designed to serve courses in environmentalism, natural rights, and ecology. The rapidity was due, of course, to the intense interest in ecology that arose during the 1960s and 1970s but also to a backlog of writings on the rights of nature in Western punditry, philosophy, and scholarship: Nash mentions A.N. Whitehead, Spinoza, Bentham, Darwin, Henry Salt, Albert Schweitzer, Thoreau, and John Muir, among others. This "extension" of ethics and morality to the natural world—a form of what I have called exceptionalism—was a component of the late nineteenth- and early twentieth-century conservationist movement and was used by Theodore Roosevelt to argue the necessity of reserving large tracts of wild land as national parks. So while the period of "greening" in the rebellious 1960s and 1970s seemed a decisive episode, the ideas were by no means new.

While "animal rights" had been the historic basis of the movements toward ethical extension, the rise of the environmental movement in the 1970s included a further extension of the rights doctrine toward inanimate natural phenomena. One eloquent statement was Christopher Stone's *Should Trees Have Standing?* (1974). Stone began by observing that any extension of rights is initially "unthinkable" because up to that point the object or organism was viewed as a "thing," a utilitarian phenomenon, and things lack any claim to special status. Can a tree have status, rights, "standing" in the law? The answer, of course, as noted in the beginning of the chapter, is "yes," *if we say so.* But it is not as easy to say so for a plant or a rock as it is for an animal. Since the rights in question are legal, the question is one for lawyers not philosophers, although the latter have set the stage by insisting that the environment *must* have rights because this is the only way, given our system of justice and decision making, it can be reliably protected against depredation by humans.

What are these rights to be assigned the physical environment and living species other than the human (it would seem that no one has seriously proposed that humans be included in the pan-Nature concept of rights)? From a strict legal standpoint, there is just one right: the right to be considered a "person" by courts of law, that is, to be defended by counsel or to have suits against other persons mounted on its behalf—"it" being any object of Nature animate or inanimate. Examples are the redwoods of California, the fish of the Columbia river, the spotted owl of the Sierra forests. In these and other cases coming before the courts in the 1980s and 1990s objects of nature were given "standing," though often indirectly. The process was well advanced at the time this chapter was written—and attracting vigorous opposition.

But this is the legal side—what of the moral and ideological? Some notion of the moral and ethical rights of Nature is very old, as we have observed, and its antecedents in the U.S. are part of the history of conservation, from John Muir's advocacy of Yosemite's preservation to Aldo Leopold's philosophical essays on Nature as irreplaceable heritage and Rachel Carson's poetic indictment of pesticide hazards (Carson 1962). And there were a few early novels, like Romain Gary's *Roots of Heaven* (1958), a defense of elephants. By the 1980s the radicals had appeared; prominent among them was the Earth First organization, whose members chained themselves to bulldozers and drove spikes into trees to stop loggers (Davis 1991). That is, the issue of natural rights among the radical preservationists becomes something akin to the activities of the left revolutionaries of the nineteenth century, only now Nature, not the oppressed proletariat, is the beneficiary.

The spectacle of people engaged in violent action to protect Nature is stunning, especially in an era of diminishing expectations, starvation wages, literal starvation for thousands of refugees, and the slaughter of thousands because of ethnic origins. In a human population that is almost everywhere pressing against resources and the political and economic capacity to supply them, human life has become cheaper. And Nature, being irreplaceable and threatened by this encroaching human population and its need and greed, becomes the more defensible victim.

While emotions may fuel the protest movements, there is a need for more sophisticated views of the growing competition between human culture and the natural world. In one sense, the artifacts—machines, furniture, houses, art works, synthetic foods—made by humans are material "species" that compete with living species, while the latter are herded into zoos and breeding pools as relict forms. From this point of view, every new cultural artifact has the potential of displacing a living creature of some kind, and this suggests a view of technology and material culture that puts it into the context of evolutionary theory. Philosophers of science have their work cut out for them in such novel realms of thought.

Spiritual Ecology

By the late 1980s viewers of educational television had become familiar with "talking heads" of attractive indigene men and women describing the way their tribe views Nature, emphasizing mystical and spiritual unity with land and animals. Such appearances are often included in nature programs dealing with species and landscapes under attack by the oil companies, road-builders, lumbermen, tourists and sports entrepreneurs, industrialists, and politicians. The message is simple and clear: urban industrial humans have lost their unity with Nature but we—the tribe—are still trying to maintain it, although under difficult circumstances.

The field might also be described as "literary ecology," since its beginnings are with the poets of the conservationist movements like Henry David Thoreau, John Muir, Aldo Leopold, and Rachel Carson, all of whom celebrated unity and oneness, trying to bring the order and beauty of natural things into the human psyche. But the latter-day spokesmen are likely to be activists like Jim Nollman, whose book *Spiritual Ecology* (1990) may be taken as an approximation of current aims. Nollman was one of the chief figures in the attempted rescue of the three whales trapped in an ice dam near Point Barrow in 1988. He was, and still is at the time of writing, the founder of Interspecies Communication, Inc., a consulting firm attempting to find ways to communicate with animals, which is also a kind of ecological tourist service, escorting parties to spots where herding species gather in an attempt to find some common ground or communication between human beings and the animals. Publicity is essential for much of these activities, and the whale rescue exercise was a virtual orgy of same, involving journalists and television crews from several countries.

Nollman also writes about his experience with a deer who insisted on invading his garden. Nollman describes his own responses: initially hostile, they gradually turned interactive when he realized that the situation was not so much a matter of the deer becoming sneaky, secretive, etc. (the deer had come to anticipate when Nollman might be waiting for him)—"but that the relationship had evolved to include *neighborliness*" (166); that is, Nollman and the deer had become partners in growing, enjoying, and eating a garden. And finally Nollman revised his plantings to include only native plants that could continue to grow under grazing or produce edible portions the year round. Thus, "inter-species communication" means both humans and animals—and in the example plants as well—watching each other, learning to cooperate, and then modifying behavior as a consequence. Tribal hunters and gatherers did it for millennia, but it is hard to see how communicating with deer will solve the increasingly awkward problem in the northeastern United States of protected wildlife invading suburban gardens. And, from the scholarly perspective, what can be learned from this kind of communication that animal psychologists or dedicated pet owners don't already know? These are, of course, unfair questions from the viewpoint of the deep ecologists, since the knowledge is gained and publicized for the purpose of promoting new philosophies of Man-Nature relations.

The basic message of the deep or spiritual ecology is articulated in Thomas Berry's *Dream of the Earth* (1988). As he remarks in his concluding chapter,

> In this late twentieth century we are somewhat confused about our human situation. . . . Our immediate tendency is to seek guidance from our cultural traditions, [but] . . . [o]ur cultural traditions, it seems, are themselves a major source of our difficulty. . . . we need to go to the earth . . . to ask for its guidance, for the earth carries the psychic structure as well as the physical form of every living being on this planet. Our confusion is not only within ourselves; it concerns also our role in the planetary community. . . . we need to go to the universe, and inquire concerning the basic issues of reality and value, for, even more than the earth, the universe carries the deep mysteries of our existence within itself. (Berry 1988, 194–95)

Berry's book is a contribution of the Sierra Club's Nature and Natural Philosophy Library, an outlet for calmer ecophilosophical writings. But, as the quoted passage indicates, the outlook is no less metaphysical than that of the fringe groups and their perpetuation of fanciful hippy-style ideas and mysticism of the 1960s. Precisely *how* we shall inquire of the Earth and the Universe as to our proper role is not, of course, specified, and it cannot be in any empirical sense, because it is a matter of faith, of looking into oneself to discover the kinship with Nature. And so ecophilosophy begins to make its transition to religion, a possibility prefigured in all of the early conservationist and preservationist writings and in a minor but persistent theme in all of the great universal religions, from the Buddha to St. Francis.

We noted earlier that ecophilosophy is really human philosophy: the projection or extension of human ideas about responsibility and behavior into the physical environment, with some clues derived from observations of interaction among the species. If this is so, then it would seem that the master theme should be *guilt*: guilt over the fact that it is Man who destroys Nature, but guilt as well over the inevitability of this destruction, since one cannot reject Humanity simply because Nature is being abused. The philosophy, in other words, of the trade-off, the double bind to end all double binds. And this leads straight toward triage. And triage, of course, means hard decisions about who lives and who dies in the populations of all species, including the human. Who shall make these decisions, decisions that are just down the pike?

As suggested, when philosophy begins to tackle the big questions of meaning and survival, there is an inevitable transition to religion. Only religion deals with such questions as Man's inhumanity to Man—and now, also, to Nature. Scientifically we need to abolish the division between Nature and Culture, but morally we need to preserve the distinction in order to act responsibly toward both. Can we compartmentalize the two approaches: the ecological synthesis of humans and the natural world, so necessary to creating defenses against thoughtless destruction, and the humanistic distinction between human and natural, in order rationally to construct a shared balance for the future?

No satisfying answers emerge either from disciplines like anthropology or from public discussions at the time of writing, and the absence of answers encourages the distrust of Reason, the disenchantment with Humanity, the disgust with the behavior of *Homo sapiens sapiens*. In its place appears preoccupation with outmoded ideologies like ethnicity, patriotism, and nationalism: substitutes for serious thought and decisions about where we are going and what we are doing to Earth. The problem of control of human fertility is not being faced seriously by any nation, and yet the disorders attributable to "politics" or "religion" are mostly created by surplus population: too many people to share the same resources and their intrusion into the cultural spaces of established groups. So ecophilosophy is needed, but it also needs to transcend environmentalism and conservationism in order to deal with the larger questions of the future of mankind, the appropriate forms of behavior for the coming culture of constraint, and the duties and rights of humans in the crowded spaceship Earth. It also must be a *social* philosophy, not only a "dream of the earth."

Literature Cited or Consulted

Ashby, Eric. 1978. *Reconciling Man with the Environment.* Stanford, CA: Stanford University Press.

Bennett, John W. 1976. *The Ecological Transition: Cultural Anthropology and Human Adaptation.* London: Pergamon.

Berry, Thomas. 1988. *The Dream of the Earth.* San Francisco: Sierra Club Books.

Black, John. 1970. *The Dominion of Man: The Search for Ecological Responsibility.* Edinburgh: Edinburgh University Press.

Boulding, Kenneth E. 1978. *Ecodynamics: A New Theory of Societal Evolution.* Beverly Hills, CA: Sage Publications.

_____. 1981. *Evolutionary Economics.* Beverly Hills: Sage Publications.

Breuer, Reinhard. 1991. *The Anthropic Principle: Man as the Focal Point of Nature*, tr. Harry Newman and Mark Lowery. Boston: Birkhäuser.

Brown, Lester et al., eds. 1992. *State of the World 1992: A Worldwatch Institute Report on Progress Toward a Sustainable Society.* New York: W. W. Norton & Co.

Callenbach, Ernest. 1975. *Ecotopia.* New York: Bantam.

Carson, Rachel. 1962. *Silent Spring.* Boston: Houghton Mifflin.

Costanza, R., ed. 1990. *Ecological Economies: The Science and Management of Sustainability.* New York: Columbia University Press.

Cronon, William. 1983. *Changes in the Land: Indians, Colonists, and the Ecology of New England.* New York: Hill and Wang/ Farrar Straus Giroux.

Davis, John, ed. 1991. *The Earth First! Reader.* New York: Gibbs Smith.

Dubos, René. 1981. *Celebrations of Life.* New York: McGraw-Hill.

Ehrenfeld, David. 1978. *The Arrogance of Humanism.* New York: Oxford University Press.

Gary, Romain. 1958. *The Roots of Heaven.* Tr. Jonathan Griffin. New York: Simon and Schuster.

Gleick, James. 1987. *Chaos: Making a New Science.* New York: Penguin Books.

Goldfarb, Theodore D. 1989. *Taking Sides: Clashing Views on Controversial Environmental Issues.* Guilford, CT: Dushkin Pub. Group.

Grove, Richard H. 1990. "Colonial Conservation, Ecological Hegemony, and Popular Resistance Towards a Global Synthesis." In *Imperialism and the Natural World*, ed. J.M. MacKenzie. Manchester: University of Manchester Press.

Hardin, Garret. 1968. "The Tragedy of the Commons." *Science* 162: 1243–48.

_____. 1972. *Exploring New Ethics for Survival: The Voyage of the Spaceship Beagle.* New York: Viking Press.

_____. 1973. *Stalking the Wild Taboo.* Los Altos, CA: William Kauffman, Inc.

_____. 1980. *Promethean Ethics: Living with Death, Competition, and Triage.* Seattle: University of Washington Press.

Hardin, Garrett and John Baden. 1977. *Managing the Commons.* San Francisco: WH Freeman and Co.

Hirsch, Fred. 1976. *Social Limits to Growth.* Cambridge, MA: Harvard University Press.

Leopold, Aldo. 1949. *A Sand County Almanac.* New York: Oxford University Press.

Lovelock, James. 1979. *Gaia: A New Look at Life on Earth.* New York: Oxford University Press.

McPhee, John. 1989. *The Control of Nature.* New York: Farrar Straus Giroux.

Meadows, Donella et al. 1972. *The Limits to Growth: A Report for the Club of Rome's Project on the Predicament of Mankind.* New York: Universe Books.

Moore, John H. 1906. *The Universal Kinship*. London.

Nash, Roderick Frazier. 1989. *The Rights of Nature: A History of Environmental Ethics*. Madison: University of Wisconsin Press.

Nollman, Jim. 1990. *Spiritual Ecology: A Guide to Reconnecting with Nature*. New York: Bantam.

Olson, Mancur. 1965. *The Logic of Collective Action: Public Goods and the Theory of Groups*. Cambridge, MA: Harvard University Press.

Olson, Mancur and Hans H. Landsberg, eds. 1973. *The No-Growth Society*. New York: W. W. Norton & Co.

Petulla, Joseph M. 1980. *American Environmentalism: Values, Tactics, Priorities*. College Station: Texas A&M University Press.

Sale, Kirkpatrick. 1980. *Human Scale*. New York: Coward, McCann & Geoghegan.

Schumacher, E.F. 1973. *Small is Beautiful: Economics as if People Mattered*. London: Blond and Briggs, Ltd.

Seidenberg, Roderick. 1974. *Posthistoric Man: An Inquiry*. 1950. New York: Viking Press.

Simon, Herbert A. 1957. *Models of Man: Social and Rational*. New York: Wiley.

Stone, Christopher D. 1974. *Should Trees Have Standing? Toward Legal Rights for Natural Objects*. Los Altos, CA: William Kauffman, Inc.

Tawney, R. H. 1926. *Religion and the Rise of Capitalism*. New York: Harcourt Brace.

Thompson, William I., ed. 1987. *Gaia: A Way of Knowing*. Great Barrington, MA: Lindisfarne Press.

Wagner, Philip. 1960. *The Human Use of the Earth*. Glencoe, IL: The Free Press.

Weber, Max. 1930. *The Protestant Ethic and the Spirit of Capitalism*. Tr. Talcott Parsons. London: Allen and Unwin.

White, Jr., Lynn. 1967. "The Historical Roots of Our Ecologic Crisis" *Science* 155: 1203-7.

_____ .1962. *Medieval Technology and Social Change*. New York: Oxford University Press.

Index

(Names occurring in this index are those in text sentences. Names of authors in paren-thetical bibliographic references, footnotes, or bibliographies are not included.)